ENDURING
IDENTITIES

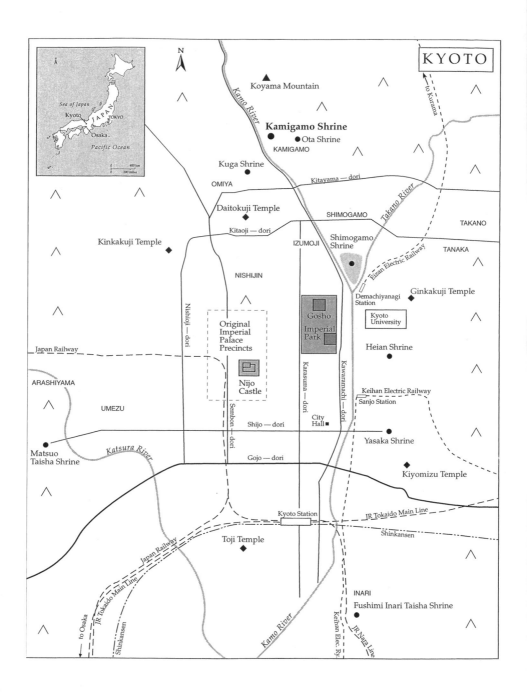

ENDURING
IDENTITIES

*The Guise of Shinto in
Contemporary Japan*

JOHN K. NELSON

UNIVERSITY OF HAWAI'I PRESS
HONOLULU

00   01   02   03   04   05   5   4   3   2   1

LIBRARY OF CONGRESS CATALOGING-IN-PUBLICATION DATA

Nelson, John K.
Enduring identities : the guise of Shinto in contemporary Japan /
John K. Nelson.
p.   cm.
Includes bibliographical references and index.
ISBN 0−8248−2120−3 (cloth) — ISBN 0−8248−2259−5 (paper)
1. Shinto.   2. Shinto shrines.   I. Title.
BL2220.N45   2000
299'.561—dc21   99−044520

University of Hawai'i Press books are printed on acid-free paper and meet the
guidelines for permanence and durability of the Council on Library Resources.

Designed by Ellen McKie

Printed by Versa Press, Inc.

CONTENTS

CONTENTS

ACKNOWLEDGMENTS

This work would not have been possible without the assistance of others. My heartfelt gratitude goes to Mr. Makoto Abe, the former head priest of Kamigamo Shrine, whose permission and tolerance permitted this study. I would also like to thank the current head priest, Mr. Mitsuyoshi Takeuchi, as well as senior priest Mr. Yasumasa Fujiki for their time and valuable assistance. The other priests at the shrine also helped me in ways small and large that are too numerous to mention. I also enjoyed my conversations with Mr. Masanao Fujiki of the Kamo Parishioners' Group and am sincerely grateful for his understanding of the wider scope of this project. The study was funded by the Fulbright Commission, whose administrators were most helpful and responsive in providing me with long-distance support in Tokyo, especially when I needed to return to the United States for family matters. Professor Toshinao Yoneyama of Kyoto University provided institutional support, and I am grateful to Professor Minoru Sonoda (also of Kyoto University) for much encouragement and guidance. Additional funding from the Yanagawa Foundation is gratefully acknowledged.

Closer to home, Professor Delmer Brown, Professor George De Vos, and Professor Nelson Graburn, all of the University of California at Berkeley, provided me with the kind of intellectual environment as well as support and encouragement that nurtured the growth of this study. I am very grateful to all of them for their friendship, knowledge, and wide-ranging experience. Many colleagues have also helped shape my thinking and approach, in particular Jennifer Beer, Pedro Lewin, David Boggett, Shigeru Hayashi, Bill Kats, and Shigeru Handa, all of whom provided input in important ways in the early stages, with Karen Smyers, Patrick Olivelle, Norman Havens, and Gregory Schopen assisting me in various ways down the home stretch.

Thanks also to Miko Omura for her faithfully accurate illustrations of the *aoi* flower and to Victoria Zaldua for the maps. My deep thanks to Susan Stone for her copyediting professionalism when faced with an unruly manuscript and to Patricia Crosby and Masako Ikeda at the University of Hawai'i Press for their encouragement and support.

Finally, I want to acknowledge and thank my parents for having raised me to appreciate the joys of discovering new places and people, and for instilling in me an optimism that seems resilient enough to weather vast extremes of situation and circumstance. Though I lost both of them during the course of this study, I think of the final book as a tribute to their intellectual curiosity and open-mindedness, not always easy in a small town in the center of Kansas. Saving the most important for last, I owe a tremendous amount of thanks to my constant partners and assistants Miko Omura and Junet Nelson, whose good humor, patience, research support, and sympathetic understanding accompanied this project at every stage.

CONVENTIONS

As is the custom in books employing Japanese terms and names, I will indicate Japanese terms by italicizing them except when they are used as proper nouns or have become common in English contexts. Japanese names appear with the family name followed by the given name. "Shinto" appears without the macron over the final "o" when used by itself in the text, as is the practice for other words that are familiar to Western readers (Tokyo, Kyoto, sumo). I use Wade-Giles romanization for Chinese.

OPENING ORIENTATIONS

What seems to Be, Is, To those to
whom it seems to Be. . . .
WILLIAM BLAKE,
THE BOOK OF MILTON

In 1970 scientists and administrators of Japan's Space Development Agency were ready to launch the country's first satellite. Under great pressure to succeed and thus further demonstrate to the world Japan's continuing postwar recovery, they carried out their plans meticulously. Then they took one final precaution. Shortly before the launch, senior representatives of the agency visited Chichibu Shinto shrine located near Tokyo. Their goal: to petition its deity Myōken (the North Star) that their endeavor might succeed. When the rocket blasted off and placed a satellite in its intended orbit, these same individuals made a return trip to express their gratitude before moving on to other projects (Sakurai, Nishikawa, and Sonoda, 1990:14).

By the end of the tumultuous 1960s, the Japanese people had much to be proud of in addition to their new space program. They had successfully staged the 1964 Olympic games in a rebuilt capital city, and they had the most advanced high-speed train system on the planet. Their economy was growing at a double digit rate as corporations like Sony, Datsun/Nissan, and Toyota became household words around the globe. Significantly, they had managed these accomplishments while dealing with labor protests at leading manufacturers and disruptive student demonstrations at most major universities. As other developed countries took notice of these achievements and with Japanese-produced consumer goods reaching markets worldwide, people wanted to know just how the Japanese had managed to do it only thirty years after one of the world's most devastating wars had left their major cities in ruins. What made Japan's society and culture so "unique" that the nation and its people could rise from the rubble in phoenixlike fashion?

It is now apparent that many of the domestic explanations offered little save a diverse range of theories together called *"nihonron"* or *"nihonjin-ron"*—theorizing about contemporary "Japaneseness." Beginning in the early 1970s, publishing houses fed what seemed an insatiable public appetite for information on how the Japanese people (or their culture, language, or history) had turned out as they did (see Yoshino 1992). What appeared to Western (and, to be fair, many Japanese) observers as contradictions in the drive toward a rational industrialized society on a par with those in the West—the fact of rocket scientists petitioning a Shinto deity or a democracy that still retained an emperor—worked as a kind of reverse orientalism. Part analysis and part homily, explanations about success as well as contradictions were attributed to Japan's fabled groupism, homogeneity, community-as-family bonds, the prevalence of spirits in material objects, and so on. The more totalizing the theory, the better it sold.

While targeting domestic audiences, the content of *nihonjinron* publications not only shaped popular discourse but also had an impact on governmental policymakers and trade negotiators. Seeking to deflect critical analysis of key power relations within state and corporate bureaucracies, spokesmen deftly combined ahistorical and cultural reifications with Western misconceptions and stereotypes about Asia and Japan. Aided also by a number of U.S. and European academics, called "the Chrysanthemum Club" (Patrick Smith 1997) for their emphasis on innate Japanese virtues that stress harmony, peaceful coexistence with nature, and mystical religious sensibilities, Japan's success appeared to be the "sanitary consequence of altogether agreeable [social] arrangements" (ibid.:18). As for those rocket scientists visiting the Shinto shrine, *nihonjinron* writers might have answered that, unlike their Western counterparts, Japanese rocket scientists see no opposition between their physics and computations, and the spirits of powerful deities *(kami)* that animate life, influence physical phenomenon, and enhance creativity. After all, this perspective is part of Japan's cultural heritage, and besides, what does it hurt?

The trend of quick-and-profitable theorizing about what constitutes Japaneseness has abated, as has the Japanese economic "miracle" that engendered and sustained it, but the concern with cultural identity remains an integral part of social discourse. If anything, the Japanese today are searching for answers and directions like never before. The passing of an emperor, the prolonged economic recession, the Gulf War, delinquency and violence in Japan's lauded educational system, a series of corruption scandals among politicians, terrorism within Japan, rising unemployment—the list could go on. In each case, fundamental assumptions about the order and stability of social life in Japan have been shaken and dislodged. And if socially related turmoil wasn't enough, the Kobe earthquake in 1995 (in which over five thousand people died in an area thought safe) added a harsh, physical dimension to the rush of paradigm-shifting events. After two decades of economic growth and relative political stability, citizens were now forced to confront what it means to be Japanese in a land where change and uncertainty are as much a part of social realities as they are of geological instabilities.

In times like these, precedent has shown that people frequently turn to religion. One might suppose that Buddhism would enter the picture, with its existentially soothing philosophies of impermanence and transience. But as these situations and incidents played out in the early 1990s, the Japanese were less enamored with Buddhist philosophy than with their other, and older, tradition of reassurance: Shinto. While cultural and religious trends come and go, shrine Shinto remains one of the most long lived of all Japan's institutions, largely because (after nearly fourteen centuries) it continues to help form, orient, and empower a sense of local and ethnic identity. Still relevant in the shaping of contemporary cultural identity as well, Shinto's social presence—amplified by seasonal festivals, the influences they have on communal dynamics, as well as the rituals provided by local shrines to mark life transitions and manage anxieties—is an institution that is "culturally loud" (Parkin 1992 : 15). Shrines large and small are found everywhere one goes. Both urban and rural shrines stage numerous festivals, requiring significant resources and many participants, that delineate certain kinds of activities as falling within the realm of deities. And yet the "volume"of these events might never reach the level of conscious awareness among their participants about exactly why they are carried out. In fact, an event that a scholar might interpret as representative of cultural values and religious sensibilities—such as a local festival—might be so taken for granted among its participants that it is not even considered to be a "religious" activity.

Consider the following further examples: one of the world's most powerful electron microscopes (at Osaka University) until recently had a Shinto amulet attached to it (Sakurai et al. 1990 : 11); Japan's first and highly controversial nuclear waste repository was dedicated by a Shinto priest waving a purificatory wand over the site in 1992; after a small shrine was relocated for a runway expansion project at Narita International Airport, one of its torii gateways remained for years because local people feared reprisals from the shrine's agitated deities (*Asahi shinbun* 1998). Many companies and corporations continue to venerate in-house shrines whose deities include the company's founder, are specific to the geographical place of business, or are related to the product in some way (Uno 1987; Lewis 1993).[1] Ise Grand Shrines spent over two billion yen (U.S. $16 million) between 1990 and 1993 to rebuild their imperial sanctuaries, which were in no actual need of physical repair but which, following a custom at least 1,200 years old, are thought to require spiritual rejuvenation every twenty years in order to keep the imperial institution (and, by extension, the nation) strong. Additionally, millions of average Japanese continue to visit shrines and petition an array of deities for everything from purifying a new car, to asking for a marriage partner (or a baby, or success in school), to prayers in gratitude for *goriyaku,* those benefits received thanks to the intercession of *kami,* Buddhas, bodhisattvas, and, very possibly, certain demons as well.

In addressing what appears to Western eyes as an exotic and incongruous blending of reason and superstition, often displayed in photogenic juxtapositions of present and past, this study will look in depth at one important Shinto shrine *(jinja)* in the city of Kyoto: Kamo Wake Ikazuchi Jinja, more commonly called Kamigamo Jinja. What began as a project to document and interpret this important shrine's yearly cycle of rituals and festivals became an exploration into the connection between overt activities that, depending on the interpreter, may or may not be religious but that seem to be of continuing relevance for the cultural identities of contemporary men and women.

A number of English-language works provide research and commentary on particular rituals and festivals (Casal 1967; Ellwood 1973; Sadler 1976; Yanagawa 1988; Ashkenazi 1993) or historical and cultural overviews of Shinto traditions (Hardacre 1989; Brown and Araki 1964; Earhart 1989). This study, rather, encompasses fifteen months of firsthand observation of a variety of shrine rituals, exploring the often problematic manner in which such rituals are staged, the day-to-day functioning of the shrine as an institution and the people who work there, and how a repertoire of traditions becomes involved in the economic, political, and social discourses of modernity. Although some of these topics can be found in my exploration of Suwa Shrine in Nagasaki (Nelson 1996b), here I take a more sustained anthropological tack in assessing these themes.

At the time of my fieldwork, a particular juncture of politics, culture, and economics was once again reshaping the institution of shrine Shinto, not to mention the way in which Japanese regarded the social significance of these institutions and their ritual activities. An example of this book's ethnographic focus, identification as a member of the shrine's founding clan, the Kamo, is based on lineage and genealogy but also on control of certain ritual activities and historiographic representations validating this control. But because of demographic change and occupational mobility that has affected northern Kyoto and displaced a number of key Kamo households, there are growing challenges to this privileged position. Pressure from non-Kamo individuals, many more than willing to make substantial financial contributions to both clan and shrine, aims to gain them participation in ritual affairs as a way of validating their own identity (or enhancing their status) as Japanese or as residents of Kyoto. For a young man to ride a horse at full speed in Kamigamo's *kurabe-uma* ritual of early May (discussed in Chapter 7), if traced to its historical origins, is akin to traveling a path that lands back the early sixth century, predating the city of Kyoto itself.

Such maneuverings of agency reference themes including the symbolic construction of communities and the role of social memory, what constitutes the nature of locality, how both of those themes may (or may not) be sacralized, and the way they intersect with the politics of historical representation and cultural nationalism. Taken as a whole, these "cultural productions of public identity" (Fox 1990:4) actively shape conceptions of what it means to be Japanese in the modern world. As such, they may be seen as part of worldwide movements to reclaim, refashion, and otherwise realign one's identity in societies that have, until recently, afforded little latitude for doing so. To paraphrase Clifford Geertz, people today want to hold beliefs about religion, locality, and the value of work rather than be held by them (1968:17).

As might be expected, these efforts are all too often appropriated into nationalistic agendas where ready associations concerning history, values, and consensual meanings serve as blueprints for imagination and social action. But some caution is advised before jumping to the conclusion that contemporary Shinto rituals and shrines contribute directly to nationalism as they did so dramatically from the 1930s to the end of the war. Rather than thinking of Shinto rituals as representing ideologies operating through single ideas addressed to specific social classes, Kenneth Thompson believes that ideologies are better understood as operating through discursive chains, symbolic clusters, and semantic fields that find their expression in social and cultural practices as well as intellectual doctrines (1986:33). For example, Western scholars long assumed that, from the 1870s onward, emperor worship was pervasive throughout Japan and central in people's lives. However, the meticulous scholarship and new perspective offered by Carol Gluck (1985) and others reveals this ideology less as domestic imperialism and an inescapable center of gravity than as a contested system of imposed silences, conflicting discourses, and decades-long center-periphery tensions. Nationalism may still be present, but how people see and respond to it takes on variability and affords a personal negotiation of its intended messages.

My thinking on culture and its use throughout this book in assessing the organizational structures and strategies of Shinto is strongly influenced by this kind of dynamic. Instead of holding culture to be a "heavy weight of traditions, a set of social configurations, or a basic personality constellation" that coerces and compels individuals (Fox 1990:10), it can be thought of as an ever-changing set of understandings within a consciousness under active (but not always self-aware!) construction (Fox 1990; Dirks et al. 1994). Based on a combination of class, gender, racial, or religious factors (to name only a few of the possibilities), people inherit scenarios within which they must act. How individuals interpret their roles and the degree of success they have in carrying them out or subverting these roles into new applications are very much dependent on their intentionality and creativity within specific social settings. From this perspective, change and innovation (whether for individuals or society) can never be anything but constant and ongoing.

In attempting to posit a society's innermost meanings and values, scholars have long looked to ritual performances as "windows" or "texts" that open into understanding. But ritual cannot be isolated as a text any more than a war, political campaign, or parade. There may indeed be significant correspondences and associations expressed through ritual events, but we must nuance our interpretations with a kind of checks-and-balances approach that avoids essentializing or reducing complex social phenomena to one particular reading. I will have much more to say about these issues in Chapter 6, after introducing specific examples in the next several chapters. Though more demanding for the analyst, we need to consider rituals as "context-markers" (Hastrup 1996:20) that propel us into more complicated webs of significance, which must reference if not fully engage the entire range of social scientific approaches to reality.

Just as early attempts to classify the animal world met with specimens like the warm-blooded yet egg-laying duck-billed platypus, so have similar taxonomic endeavors in the fields of religion and anthropology been faced with "curiosities" like Shinto. Most writers dealing with the subject, and I should probably include myself, feel compelled at some point to offer their versions of its inner characteristics. Shinto (usually referred to in a reified, monolithic sense) is all about sincerity (*makoto;* Ross 1965), or about festivals and *matsuri* (Mayumi 1989), or about a fusion of religion and politics (*matsurigoto;* Murakami 1970), or comprises an amalgamation of "-isms" such as imperialism, realism, and purity-ism (Muraoka 1964). These attempts usually reveal more about the predilections and agendas of the writers than the complexity of multifaceted, historically complex, and conceptually shifting traditions grouped together under the rubric "Shinto."

To Western missionaries, businessmen, and governmental officials in Japan in the mid—nineteenth century, Buddhism fit any number of categories thought to constitute a religion. It had a charismatic founder, lineages of schools and teachers, sacred texts, transcultural appeal, and established moral and ethical codes that, if followed, could help an individual attain salvation. But Shinto? Where were the worship services or the leader preaching to a congregation? Where were the texts promoting an organized eschatology? And, in the midst of a frenzied rush to build an industrial, economic, and educational infrastructure to modernize and compete with the West, surely the Japanese were not serious about venerating the emperor as a living deity? How could a person who called himself or herself a "Shintoist" be said to believe in anything? "To say a man is a Shintoist [because he is] an ardent believer in the *kami*," summarizes Creemers, "would be almost as much of an exaggeration [as] to say that he is a fervent Christian because he went to a Christmas party" (1968:xvi).

A number of Buddhist sects have maintained intellectual and aesthetic appeal to those interested in Japanese culture and the application of some key ideas to Western contexts. Neo-Confucianism as well, with its philosophy of correct conduct for the individual and the interpenetration of society's civil and political elements, has been proposed as having a more timely relevance to contemporary life than the often confusing, semi-mystical wanderings of Shinto (see Dore 1987; De Vos 1984). Even W. G. Aston, one of the early transmitters of Japanese mythology and beliefs, delivered in 1921 the following elegy on the relevance of Shinto to modern society: "Without a code of morals, or an efficient ecclesiastical organization, with little aid from the arts of painting, sculpture and architecture, and with a sacred literature scanty and feeble compared with those of its foreign rivals, Shinto is doomed to extinction. Whatever the religious future of Japan may be, Shinto will assuredly have little place in it. Such meat for babes is quite inadequate as the spiritual food of a nation which in these latter days has reached a full and vigorous manhood" (1921:81).

And yet, wherever one goes in contemporary Japan, there are refutations of Aston's prediction; it is almost impossible to avoid bumping into little or large shrines at the heart of neighborhoods or overlooking entire communities. It is thus surprising that after more than fifty years of postwar scholarship on Japan, one of the most prevalent institutions in Japanese cultural, religious, and social life remains so understudied and enigmatic. There is certainly no shortage of available research sites, with at least six hundred shrines employing full-time staff and with 81,400 offering periodic priestly services.[2] One of the few areas in the world with a comparable richness is India's Punjab. There, more than twenty thousand local Sikh shrines (called *gurudwara*s) form a well-established network to disseminate information, mobilize social and political action, and function as local points of access to the spiritual benefits of venerated saints and gurus (see Fox 1985). The parallel to shrine Shinto is more than institutional, since many of the ethnic and nation-building characteristics of Sikh shrines are familiar in the histories of local Shinto shrines, especially from the 1930s on to the end of the war in 1945. Shrines were designated as government institutions responsible for fostering national consensus and patriotism under the themes of prosperity, purity, and the promotion of Japaneseness, all to counter threats perceived as issuing from Western imperialist powers.

Societies where present-day political power is fashioned to appear as an extension of mythical and spiritual worlds (the very situation transpiring in prewar Japan) exist in a number of examples (Bloch 1974:79; see also Gluckman 1962). Since 1990 the government of Kyrgyzstan in the former Soviet Union has been promoting the cult of Manas—through postage stamps, empty tombs, and official rites—as a way to recall a past unfettered by economic and political difficulties (LeVine 1996). Although scholars say Manas never existed, he has come to stand as a founding grandfather of the nation and worthy of ancestral veneration. In Nicaragua, recasting Jesus as a guerilla and the Bible as a revolutionary text in the 1980s helped to infuse meaning among the poor that their actions were not only expressing faith but furthering the revolution against the U.S.-backed dictator Somoza (Lancaster 1988). Those who think that only developing nations are prone to this kind of strategy need look no farther than the Bush administration's invocation of God and His power—both of which were on the side of "righteous" allied forces—in the Gulf War of 1991.

Using whatever relevant institutions, symbols, experts, and resources are available, this "reenchantment" of the world is often an effective way to attempt an authoritative ordering of cultural understandings and social orientations. Not only a matter of marking or enhancing the importance of what is symbolized, ideological orientations can also evoke and sustain an emotional commitment to what is decreed to be important (Needham 1979), though not all such efforts are successful and many are ambiguous at best. Still, it is possible for the social and psychological significance of even commonplace actions—such as making a fire for cooking, washing one's hands, or positioning one's body for sleeping—to be recast so as to resonate with cosmic or religious importance. To bolster, interpret, and maintain these values in the minds and practices of the people, "proper" ritual observances must be conducted periodically by legitimate figures of authority and transmitted far and wide. Early Confucianism held that the "natural" order itself would be put at risk should change occur in the social status or political role of individual actors such as the emperor or other significant officials. Therefore, it was better for each citizen to mind his or her own business, fulfill social responsibilities, and thus ensure the stability of the realm.

A growing number of scholars have come to see an explicit political connection between a religious institution and the social enactment of its practice. Politics refers to more than simply opportunism or imposing one's will upon others. According to Vivienne Kondos (1992), politics can provide an umbrella to assemble related activities that attempt to bring about desired transformations in persons, social relations, and natural or "supernatural" phenomena. To politicize the analysis of religious institutions extends the scope of possibilities for exploration. Each religion and the rituals it sanctions deal in some way with problems both existential and social: how to live, how to coexist with others, or how to access transhuman powers that are thought to animate all life. This broad-based perspective on politics is an essential referent for analysis because, as Asad notes, both micro- and macrolevel politics frequently impose the conditions for experiencing institutionalized religious truths in the first place (1983:245).

This has certainly been the case throughout the religious history of Japan, where ruling elites had the military capability to enforce social and religious practices consonant with their interests. What is thought of as Shinto in historical terms is, as Allan Grapard has pointed out (1991), a flexible combination of several religious systems that can be understood primarily through their rituals, which, in turn, are notable for their enhancement of political power. Citing the symbiotic relationship between Kōfuku-ji temple and Kasuga Shrine in Nara, Grapard notes that both were used by the Fujiwara family to legitimize and maintain their position as the dominant clan in the early Heian period. Grapard traces an intimate association between Shinto and Buddhism at the institutional, ritual, doctrinal, and philosophical levels (see also Kuroda 1981; McMullin 1989). Through most of Japanese history, he argues, Shinto and Buddhism were two aspects of a single sociocosmic reality, informing and shaping not only Japanese religious life but the culture as well. And yet, as Sonoda maintains, although there was considerable sharing, they never fused into one religion, nor is there a recorded case of an entire shrine for *kami*-worship being transformed into a Buddhist temple (or vice versa) (1990:4).[3]

At the time of Buddhism's arrival in Japan in the early sixth century C.E., it seems quite likely that Kamigamo Shrine was already in existence. With such a long history, a dominant feature of the shrine's present-day image of itself as well as its image in larger shrine and political circles is its status as an elite organization. Ranked second only to the Grand Shrines of Ise by the Imperial Household Agency, Kamigamo integrates folk beliefs, priestly expertise, and imperial affiliations into an ideology stressing (among other things) over 1,400 years of historical and institutional continuity. The shrine has been ranked second to Ise since the Heian period, and indeed it continues to receive imperial messengers *(chokushi)* at its Aoi Festival in mid-May. Although the shrine's founding date is disputed (possibly 678 C.E.), documents from the Nara period acknowledge its already considerable power and influence, and a highly popular festival *(keiba shinji)* wherein horses are raced for the entertainment of the Kamo clan's *kami*. It later became the tutelary shrine of Kyoto in the early ninth century, contracted by the imperial court to protect the region from flooding by controlling, through ritual and petition, its powerful *kami* of thunder and lightning, Wake Ikazuchi (see Inoue 1985; Tanigawa 1986).

The shrine has also served to block malevolent forces that were believed to enter the imperial capital from the inauspicious northeast. Based largely on ritual reenactments of alternatingly popular, historical, and mythic associations, allegiance to and alliance with the shrine becomes rich with status-enhancing possibilities for a variety of individuals and interest groups. These range from descendants of the founding Kamo clan, to community women's groups, electric utility companies, elementary schools, local politicians, Kyoto's famous tea ceremony schools, Boy Scout troops, and, most significant economically, the local tourist industry. Although in the pages that follow I do not provide extensive comparative data with other shrines, I believe that most major shrines throughout Japan provide similar legitimizing and status-enhancing opportunities.

But by far the largest of any shrine's many constituencies are "just folks" who turn to the gods in times of trouble, illness, indecision, frustration, or any of the other anxiety-provoking situations confronting human beings. While this theme encompasses much of the religious history of Japan and will therefore figure largely in the following discussions, one must keep in mind that the Japanese also turn to shrines in times of celebration or gratitude, to maintain a reciprocal bond established with the shrine's *kami* (see Reader 1991 : 27), or for leisure or cultural pursuits. One might also include transitional junctures (such as baby dedications, coming-of-age ceremonies, marriages, and so forth, with funerals generally the exception), times of tangible crisis (school entrance exams, launching new enterprises, casting out misfortune), or involvement in a shrine's annual festival. Although attitudes have changed from the Meiji (1868–1910), Taishō (1910–1921), and early Shōwa periods (1921–1945) when Shinto was promoted as a "national faith," participation by individuals with some part of a shrine's ritual cycle remains high among the general public, with an estimated 86.9 million people (72 percent of the entire population, 220,000 more than the previous year) turning out to visit shrines and temples during the New Year holidays of 1998.[4]

In contrast to conventional notions of ideology and institutions (as in Aston's elegy on Shinto earlier in this discussion), I will stress throughout this book how shrine Shinto's lack of centralized dogma, charismatic leaders, and sacred texts serves to promote both an institutional flexibility and a broad-based public participation. Neither doctrine nor institutional demand overshadows the sociocultural gardens of practice. History shows, however, that the same malleability that has empowered generations of Shinto priests is also responsible for a number of problematic identifications and associations that endure at any Shinto shrine in Japan, and especially one of high status such as Kamigamo. Not only do these associations and complicities endure, they must also be endured by those who regard the shrine from more traditionally religious (that is to say, pre-1868) or spiritually progressive perspectives.

For example, the question is often raised, both by scholars and through legal challenges in Japan, whether what goes on at a shrine is really "religious." Can public money go to pay for offerings at a ritual or festival benefiting the community at large? Can Shinto priests be used as functionaries in a municipal ceremony to dedicate a new airport by waving a wand of purification? According to a priest at Yasukuni Jinja (where the military dead are enshrined), rituals are sometimes "beyond" religion. Until recently, decisions by the Japanese Supreme Court in 1977 and 1988 ruled that certain ritual activities of shrines (such as land-claiming rites or offerings to the military dead) should be considered "social protocol" or "customary practices" (see Takayama 1990; O'Brien 1996). Though this decision was overturned in 1997, shrines could have been classified as institutions embodying secular folkways and thus become eligible again to receive governmental sponsorship of their agendas and affairs. To do so, however, would bring shrieks of protest from small but very vocal Christian, Korean, and other minority groups in Japan. Equally loud would be the outcry from many scholars, private citizens, radical students, and those in Asian nations Japan once occupied. All would be concerned with formal state-shrine ties that might summon from the past the insidious specter of state Shinto.

A sustained look at the shrine system in Japan shows that many of its priests (and especially its Central Association of Shrines in Tokyo, the Jinja Honchō) harbor strategies that would permit a more active and visual role in promoting national unity and prewar moralities. These attitudes and positions, expressed in a number of controversies since the end of the war, have encouraged a wide range of conservative and ultraconservative groups. They include causes such as resisting a governmental apology by Japan for starting the Pacific War, Japan's stance as a sovereign nation in international trade and territory disputes, the issue of "Japaneseness" fostered in part by millions of tourist and business-related encounters overseas, a revision of the constitution to allow Japan's military to protect its interests overseas, and so on. While highly vocal, well-organized, and sufficiently financed, these groups and the priests that support them do not make up a complete portrait of shrine Shinto's political dimensions. There are also many within the shrine system itself—priests young and old—who either remember firsthand the jarring experience of state or *kokka* Shinto, or who are embarrassed and feel constrained by the reputation of the wartime years from which shrine Shinto has yet to recover.[5]

Consider, for instance, the continuing relationship of shrine Shinto with the imperial household. There would likely be even greater controversy were more Japanese aware that the emperor remains the supreme Shinto priest for all shrines in Japan (see T. Lebra 1997). The trappings of imperial regalia (such as the lacquered clogs, the vestments, the headgear, and a number of important rituals) were adopted by important shrines such as Kamigamo during the Heian and Kamakura periods and, as I will show in the next section, help to bridge the centuries as well as the gap between the palace and the shrine community. In chapters 4 and 5, I will present in more detail the mixed feelings of Kamigamo priests and local historians about this association. Just as priestly emotions vacillate between attraction and resistance at a shrine whose long history is intimately involved with the imperial court, so do the sentiments of the general population.

Thanks to the present emperor's younger sons coming of marriageable age and the media attention their weddings have generated, it can be said that the imperial family is enjoying the greatest popularity they have had since the end of the war.[6] However, other less adulatory feelings periodically manifest themselves in radical ways, as in the 1993 protest of Emperor Akihito's first trip to Okinawa. Although the trip was billed as a gesture of healing and reconciliation by a new emperor who personally had nothing to do with the war borne so heavily by Okinawa, a striking response emerged. Three imperially affiliated Buddhist temples and one Shinto shrine were firebombed in Kyoto in the early morning hours of April 26. It is difficult to gauge the public reaction this attack was supposed to generate (no group has yet come forward to claim responsibility), and it was downplayed by the major papers. Although two of the temples (Ninna-ji and Sanzen-in) are national treasures, many Japanese viewed the attack with cool equanimity. After reading a *Yomiuri* news article highlighted by a photo of Nakata Shrine's totally incinerated outer hall of worship, one woman said casually, "Well, at least there wasn't much damage." When I remarked that the photo in front of her pointed otherwise, her response was: "I mean damage to the temples. What do you expect with a shrine? The real question is why they didn't bomb the old imperial palace (*Gosho*)."

ASSESSING THE GUISES OF SHRINE SHINTO

As a way of coping with the associations of shrine Shinto, a majority of shrines and the priests in their employ have assumed, created, or revitalized a number of guises for operating in rapidly changing sociopolitical climates. Looking at some of the ramifications of the term "guise" itself helps clarify an array of shrine Shinto's institutional characteristics and managerial strategies, rendering it less "anthropologically mysterious" (Pye 1989:188). The *Oxford English Dictionary* (1989) says a guise is first of all a "manner, method, or way." The characters for Shinto mean literally "the way of the *kami*," a concept borrowed from Chinese Taoism in the sixth century to distinguish local *kami*-worship from Buddha-worship. Like many traditions, ethnic groups, or ideologies, Shinto is often defined in opposition to what it is not. It is the "way of the *kami*" and not of the Buddha or the Tao; it is involved with enhancing the vitalism of life through particular practices conducted by priests in special sacred places (Brown 1993:10−13) but avoids as best it can life's mortal impermanence; it is a term first used by people in the sixth century to express their self-awareness and promote local traditions (Sonoda 1987:15) but with apparently little recognition of the origin of these practices in the Korean peninsula, China, the southern Ryūkyū islands, or the northern regions of today's Tōhoku and Hokkaido.

Though attempts have been made to set forth a specific ideology or doctrine (Ueda 1991), Shinto has been centered on ritual practices aimed to attain pragmatic benefits for imperial, state, clan, or communal petitioners. Shrine Shinto's second guise in historical as well as contemporary society is "a characteristic manner, custom, habit, or practice" that is marked by a certain "carriage or conduct" (*OED* 1989). Characteristics associated with ritual such as propriety, formality, and etiquette are all basic to Shinto-style acts of reverential or respectful behavior toward the *kami*. These acts may manifest themselves along a wide spectrum ranging from idiosyncratic spontaneity to strict priestly codes handed down for centuries. Norbeck suggests that etiquette is found in its greatest elaboration in societies such as Japan, where individuals have long functioned through distinctive and hierarchical social categories (1977:73).

How one acts, the way one carries and directs one's body into certain formalized gestures, and the overall environment of venerating the deities are other important features of shrine Shinto. These are in turn enhanced by its third guise, a "fashion of attire or personal adornment" (*OED* 1989). Using the imperial court of the Heian period as archetype, the vestments of priests and female shrine attendants have been altered very little. Colorful arrays of silken robes, pantaloons, kimono, and headgear distinguish Shinto ritual attire from the more somber, workaday garb of Buddhist priests. Not only the outward appearance of priests but the very public face of shrine rituals and festivals in general are posited (and usually marketed) as traditions representing Japanese cultural heritage and ethnic identity in relation to other Asian or Occidental peoples. Yet these events and the shrine itself complement the lifestyles of many men and women, adorning their individualistically motivated desires for entertainment, community involvement, or as opportunities and arenas to display social status.[7] Though clothes don't always make the man (or woman), the guise they provide fashions a continuity with the refinement and aesthetics of a romanticized high culture.

Finally, as "guise" is the root of the word "disguise," shrine Shinto has used its more apparent attributes to cloak a recent past and present complicity with nationalism, ethnic purity, and authoritarian means to enforce compliance within a hierarchy of rank and deference. Recent rulings by the Japanese Supreme Court (1997) regarding separation of religion and the state—based on cases concerning the legal status of ground purification rites and the state's enshrinement of familial ancestral spirits at Yasukuni Shrine—have only recently begun to problematize the relevance of postwar Shinto rituals to state interests (Nelson 1999). Thus, although each shrine appears to function independently of others, the Central Association of Shrines in Tokyo works behind the scenes to orchestrate and align the overarching structure of a shrine's yearly ritual practices, the *nenjū gyōji,* with patriotic agendas aimed to enhance national and communal solidarity.[8]

What appears a classic tension between internal and external forces, each representing different interests, will be shown below to be mediated and occasionally resisted by Kamigamo's leadership at the level of daily practice—often generating considerable controversy among the shrine's competing interest groups. There are also intermediate forces, such as local governments or tourist agencies, that (as in Kamigamo's famous hollyhock festival) have their own interests to promote through the activi-

ties of local shrines. I hope to engage throughout this book a tension between the structuring efforts, the "networks of communication, webs of
affiliation, and intimately shared cultural spaces" (Dissanayake 1996:xiii)
of these organizations and institutions, and the ability of individual actors
to exert personal desire and intentionality within these arenas.

Key to my discussion of agency and mediation are Kamigamo's fourteen male priests and two female attendants (as well as its groundskeepers and other hired hands), individuals who represent a cross-section of
Japanese society in all its complexity. Chapter 5 shows how the priests
in particular, as employees, salarymen and women, wardens of tradition,
and religious virtuosos, embody the shrine in the eyes of its parishioners
and visitors. And yet, during the time of my fieldwork, they were frequently at odds with decisions made by the elderly head priest (especially
those related to finances), with pressure from the Tokyo association of
shrines and its local representative, with priests from other shrines, and
with attempts made by civic, business, and political groups to sacralize,
legitimize, or otherwise authenticate their own agendas through formal
and informal association with the shrine. I will emphasize that a shrine's
viability and credibility as an institution is strongly influenced by the quality, intelligence, and inventiveness (to mention only the positive attributes) of the people in its employ. This influence does not, however, necessarily translate into social or cultural power to effect changes in a
Shinto-related manner in the community at large. For such influence to
be felt, very large sums of money or particularly close political alliances
would be needed.

But there are other ways to make a difference, provided an institution
can assume a tactical guise that not only suits its local environment but
responds to national discussions or capitalizes on social trends. A Shinto
priest or scholar may bristle internally at the questions of a young maga-
zine editor concerning which shrines his fashionable readers should visit
during New Year's, but suggestions will be forthcoming and the crowds
will come. A shrine visit that begins as "an accessory to modern life" (Sakurai et al. 1990) may, with time, assume a more central importance in an
individual's development as a social being. Ishida Ichiro has likened the
phenomenon of Shinto to a doll whose form remains basically the same
through time yet is amenable to having its outer accoutrements changed
according to the tastes (usually shaped by economic or political power)
of whoever plays with it (Ishida, cited in Brown 1990). That this "doll"
remains attactive, interesting, useful, and status-enhancing for many Jap-

anese indicates that their own symbolic repertoires have been influenced by a casual yet still significant participation in the ritual worlds and orientations of Shinto.

Since the end of World War II and the resulting push to modernize, many of the world's societies have seen their cognitive and cosmological maps slowly erode and in some cases finally collapse under the weight of what is now valued as new and essential. Once thought likely to share the same fate, especially immediately after the war, when much of the nation lay in charred and twisted heaps of rubble, Japan not only has managed to adapt to the present world system but is struggling to become one of its leaders for the future. Providing continuity and enhancing cultural identity as well as spiritual efficacy, Shinto ritual orientations might be considered inherently optimistic vehicles conveying the fundamental metaphysics of the Japanese people (Takayama 1988: 330). Notions of power as indefinite and always dynamic (the *kami*), of bilateral nonconfrontation as a part of an essentially harmonious unity (purity and impurity), of a situational rather than fixed conception of morality, the human body, and the sacred all lend themselves to a variety of contemporary contexts. Whatever one's scholarly interest in Japan, the dynamism and flexibility of this tradition so adept at reinventing and reimagining itself, and empowering men and women to see the cosmos as reciprocal and responsive, warrant further exploration.

A NOTE ON FIELDWORK

In many ways, as Clifford (1988), Geertz (1988), Marcus and Fisher (1986), Hastrup (1996), and a host of others have made abundantly clear, any ethnographic endeavor is skewed by the logistics of time and space; the personalities, politics, and defense mechanisms of one's informants and sponsors as well as oneself; and the pressure that the intersection of the above conditions exerts on what questions are asked, what discoveries are made, and what conclusions are drawn. The challenge of doing research in Japan occupies its own niche when placed under the umbrella of "anthropological fieldwork." One need not worry about being shot (unless hanging around gangsters), falling ill from epidemics, or any of the expected deprivations that fieldwork frequently entails in underdeveloped areas of the world that were, during the first half of the twentieth century, the site of most anthropological research. In Japan as well as other developed countries the researcher has telephones, computers, and copy machines at his or her disposal, not to mention a superb public transportation system, adequate shelter from the elements, and a highly developed infrastructure of institutions and funding. So where's the difficulty? one might ask.

As I make clear in my discussion of the priests of Kamigamo Shrine, economic factors weigh heavily upon their careers and activities. In my own case as well, I was daunted by the economics involved in conducting a long-term study in one of the world's most expensive countries. Because my family and I could not find affordable housing in Kyoto at the time we needed it, we opted to live some two hours distant from the area in northern Kyoto where the shrine was located. Graduate student one moment and "visiting researcher" the next, I simply did not have the funds necessary to make the large outlays of cash required for *shikikin,* or "key money," followed by the dreaded (because nonrefundable) *reikin,* or "thank you money." Nor did my family have adequate personal connections to those who might have been able to assist us in our search for housing. Although this strategy represents a departure from the traditional fieldwork strategy of living elbow-to-elbow with one's informants, I gained many insights into non-Kyoto Japan that have helped to reposition and qualify much of what occurred in the somewhat rarefied atmosphere of that ancient and once elegant city.

Thus, to "do research," I would wake at the crack of dawn, grab an umbrella and bag laden with tools of the observer's trade, then ride two trains and a bus during morning rush hour, frequently arriving only minutes before a ritual was to begin. Like the priests themselves, I would then enact my own transition from secular to sacred worlds, rushing behind a building to change clothes (if I had been rained on), put on a tie (an excruciating ordeal when one is drenched with sweat during summer or the rainy season), and attempt to smooth out an appearance ruffled from two hours of commuting. While hard for me, a two-hour commute is not unusual in the major urban centers of Japan. Needless to say, I did not come to the shrine every day.

Nor was it necessary or even advisable to be a full-time presence at the shrine. I mention this because of a double-edged sword I encountered early on. In one of my first interviews, I remarked on how little information and documentation there was for a shrine of Kamigamo's long history and high status. "Ah, well," the priest answered with a stern face, "that's because of the curse *(tataki)* that the deity inflicts on people poking around who lack the right attitude. Do *you* have the right attitude, Mr. Nelson?"

All I could do was nervously mutter something about how time would tell, but I acknowledged both the challenge and the threat.

At a shrine where the primary deity has at his disposal a formidable arsenal including thunder, lightning, and rain, the nature of the threat can be left to the imagination. The continual challenge was to conduct myself with the proper decorum when at the shrine so that the institution's wide-ranging constituents would not feel as if a bull had just entered their china shop, nor would the shrine's leadership be held accountable for harboring a disruptive influence.

As the first foreign researcher to have negotiated permission to conduct long-term research at Kamigamo, I was conscious of my ethical responsibilities as well as my hard-won privileges, neither of which I wanted to compromise. For example, on several occasions, a ritual mentioned to me by a junior priest as being worthy of my time and attention was made problematic simply because of my presence. Shortly before the appointed hour of 10:00 A.M., I would be rushing to take my place (always at the rear) in front of the shrine offices where the procession to the main shrine began. Suddenly, a designated priest would sidle up to me and say in a low voice that, because of the "difficulty" of the people involved today, would I please not participate? (*Kyō no sanpai-sha-tachi wa chotto muzukashii no de, Nelson-san wa go-enryo o shite itadakenai deshō ka?*). (The Japanese indicates it is not really a question at all.) To protest such a turn of events would have been worse than pointless. I would not only have demonstrated the bad manners and selfishness for which many Westerners in Japan are (not undeservedly) notorious, I would also have jeopardized the rest of my study by elevating my interests above those of the shrine.

Deference to authority is a sign of learning and loyalty, Confucius wrote, especially when that authority has the power to curtail completely or further one's own interests. I could never discern whether my periodic exclusions were a spur of the moment decision or whether the decision had been reached beforehand. I never asked for apologies or explanations, nor were any offered, other than that the sponsors of the ritual in question were not "regular" shrine patrons. Thus excluded from participation, I would watch from the innermost gateway and try to reconstruct the event from interviews with the priests at a later date. Fortunately, this situation did not occur often; in retrospect I must admit my gratitude to the priests for the considerable degree of access I was usually given.

The second side of the sword was the necessity to be aware that the priests' own positions and reputations could be called into question were they seen talking to me at the wrong moment (which is to say in any of the public areas of the shrine precincts) by, say, an influential and wealthy patron who disliked Americans. One must never think that World War II is completely a thing of the past or that, because of the number of foreigners in Kyoto, all are equally tolerated. The priest might be teased good-naturedly by his superiors (who would have heard about the incident secondhand) or by the accusing individual himself during a postritual reception at which sake and beer serve to free tongues and opinions — yet the coerciveness of the joking worked effectively to sanction future contact.

In part because of the position of Shinto shrines within Japanese society today and the defensive nature of many of those who gain their livelihood by working as priests, I never felt that, in spite of the considerable kindness I was shown on occasion, I had a protector or benefactor who would jump in to defend my interests. The vulnerability felt by many priests in trying to perform their tasks in front of a wide-ranging and highly critical audience that is increasingly willing and able to shift loyalties at the slightest provocation more than explains their defensiveness and caution. However, I was encouraged by a senior member of one of the shrine's lay organizations, which is frequently at odds with the administration, to "stand up" to the priests and assert myself more. When I suggested that such behavior could very well end my research, he promised that "his" organization would "back me up all the way."

Like many researchers in status-conscious Japan, I assumed initially that my institutional affiliations would imbue me with a kind of armor protecting my research interests. I soon discovered that while my connections with various sponsoring institutions (Kyoto University, the Fulbright Commission) gave my research an aura of legitimacy, there was little translation of this legitimacy into personal power relevant to those within the worlds of shrine Shinto. I found, for example, that the cooperation I was being shown at first was not consensual but coerced — younger priests were ordered to show me around or answer my questions despite their protests that they "didn't know enough" or that they preferred not to be seen with me on the shrine grounds.

I had assumed that, because of numerous letters and faxes between me and senior priests, my presence and research interests had been explained to everyone, but I found out shortly before the end of my research that again I had been mistaken. In interviews with both junior and senior priests as well as with members of lay organizations and people in the community at large, my requests for information were often (though politely enough) refused outright, stonewalled, or diplomatically deflected by taking the party line straight from *nihonjinron*-style ideologies. I could try to appeal to some objective "deity of research" (*benkyō no kamisama,* which actually "exists" in the form of Tenjin-sama) as a lighthearted attempt to elicit a response in an informant's moment of hesitation, but this tactic could easily backfire, such is the reticence of many Japanese to take a clear stand in dialogues liable to reach beyond spheres of influence within which they have control. Unlike some ethnographers in the past, I choose not to conceal these difficulties in my accounts of shrine affairs. Rather than seeing the challenges as impediments, I regard them as highly representative and instructive parts of an internal cultural debate about personal agency within institutions as well as tactics employed to maintain one's status and objectives in the face of a foreign researcher hungry for information.

CHAPTER TWO

FREEDOM OF EXPRESSION
The Very Modern Practice of
Visiting a Shinto Shrine

Cultural forms may not say what
they know, nor know what they say,
but they mean what they do — at
least in the logic of their praxis.
PAUL WILLIS,
LEARNING TO LABOUR

Why do people come to visit Kamigamo Shrine? Is it the allure of history and the chance to walk and worship where emperors and shoguns have passed? Is it the respite from urban pressures the shrine offers with its leafy canopies, winding paths, and murmuring brooks, framing buildings listed as "important cultural treasures"? Or are there powerfully personal reasons that dictate obeisance to and acknowledgment of a thunder deity once thought vital to the stability of the Japanese state?

Despite surveys, observations, and interviews with shrine visitors, it is daunting to propose one or two all-encompassing motivations for the continuing viability of the shrine in modern life. The quote from Paul Willis that opens this chapter points to the ways individuals shape and often transform the cultural forms they inherit — often interested, goal-oriented activity to be sure, but not easily reducible to rational calculations (1977 : 125). Were one to play with this quotation a bit and substitute "human beings" for "cultural forms," one would render Willis' concept a more suitable epigram for a discussion of visitations to contemporary Shinto shrines. The emphasis is less on the received norms, beliefs, or values (cultural forms) and more on how men and women render these resources into an experience of the world that, for them and no one else, makes some kind of consistent, coherent, and predictable sense. That the institution of contemporary shrine Shinto allows sufficient freedom for individuals to make such choices during their infrequent encounters with it is, I believe, absolutely vital to the continued relevance of this ancient yet in some ways very modern tradition within one of the world's leading industrial societies.

While considerable scholarship has corrected the West's assumptions about the development of ancient, medieval, and early modern "Shinto," surprisingly little has appeared about the present-day actors, issues, or cultural practices of the Shinto institution and its often novel uses of inherited or, some might say, invented traditions (see Ueda 1979). I have elsewhere discussed the institutional politics, cultural performances, and motivated actors within this broad tradition (Nelson 1996b, 1994, 1993a, 1992). Continuing one theme, I hope to show why this allegedly "crystallized" religious tradition (Grapard 1983) demonstrates a vital dimension of modernity: the assumed ability of average individuals to shape their own futures via subjective rationales and practices of the present. How seemingly traditional religious institutions such as Shinto have adapted to this aspect of the contemporary moment must be taken as seriously as the structures and practices that preceded it. Rather than imposing "the pure gravity of categories" sanctified by their embeddedness in the past, the contemporary religious institution, with all its complicated actors and orientations, is neither a departure from nor a betrayal of its traditions. It is, instead, "symmetrical" to them at every point of analysis (see Redfield 1996).

Just what is a Shinto shrine in this day and age of mass transit and cyberspaces? What is the cultural logic behind a shrine's operation and active players? What aesthetic, religious, or emotional salience does a shrine have for modern men and women? Since there are so many shrines in Japan (eighty thousand, according to "official" estimates) and because they are often central to the ways in which neighborhoods, urban centers, or rural areas have constituted themselves historically, politically, economically, and territorially, their physical presence alone provides a point of reference for a region's populace and an easy first answer to the opening question.

Particularly for local residents, a shrine is rarely referred to by its official name; instead, as if one were addressing an individual or personal acquaintance, the honorific "-san" is added after some derivative of the official name (for example, "Tenjin-san" for Kitano Tenmangū, "Suwa-san" for Suwa Jinja, or "Kamigamo-san" for Kamo Wake Ikazuchi Jinja.) Keith Basso has observed that places and landscapes "can be detached from their fixed spatial moorings and transformed into instruments of thought and vehicles of purposive behavior . . . eminently portable possessions to which individuals can maintain deep and abiding attachments" (1992:223). They may just as often treat these "possessions" in an offhand manner, but that they constitute and organize part of one's immediate social reality in Japan serves as a referential pivot grounding present to past in one's own neighborhood.

A shrine's presence is manifest most dramatically during periodic festivals of its yearly ritual cycle *(nenjū gyōji)*, originating in relationships among shrine, parishioner, community, and the natural world. As Ashkenazi has pointed out, festival events serve to promote community, to express common cultural idioms shared by a locale, to display power or wealth, to socialize newcomers into a sense of place, and to provide recreation and entertainment for locals and outsiders (especially tourists), all centered on the veneration of deities associated with a particular shrine (1993:146–148). At these times a shrine becomes a cosmos unto itself. There is heightened activity, a variety of management strategies and key players vying for strategic roles within the festival, and considerable financial gain to be supervised and redistributed among participants and priests.

But a shrine embodies a set of dynamics and practices that serve to discipline activity and exact a kind of social compliance from those entering into its cosmos. One of the key features of a shrine is the way in which its landscape is organized both to embody and symbolize fundamental attitudes about the shrine's deity and to provide gradations of physical access (mediated by ritual as one gets closer) to this deity. The physical approach may be straight but often, as at Kamigamo Shrine, it meanders so as to deflect malevolent energies from approaching too easily (see Takahashi 1991; Nelson 1993a).

Erving Goffman (1969) has discussed the "accessibility" and "communicability" of a setting and those who participate within it as a dialogue that follows unstated yet predictable rules of engagement, dependent on but not determined by an individual's conscious interpretations. Within shrine precincts, the architecture of the buildings, the scenic attractions of the shrine grounds (the trees, streams, signs, and so forth), even the shadowy regions of the deity's temporary dwelling place serve, to borrow a

Kamigamo Shrine, circa 1840.
Artist unknown.

term from Denis Cosgrove (1986), as a "visual ideology." A shrine's priests would no doubt support Foucault's notion that the physical layout of a place serves not only to discipline activity but to discipline awareness as well, often bypassing the individual's own representations of what she or he thinks the encounter entails (Foucault 1980 : 183).

Central to this dynamic of observer and object are the spatiotemporal practices (hand washing, strolling, shaking out fortunes from a container, bowing, throwing coins into a coffer, and so on) that provide modes of interaction. I am not suggesting these practices create an environmental determinism that robs people of their intentionality; rather they work to structure what appears as a natural environment. Like a road map, the layout of a shrine is a technology of power leading people into behavioral practices often unexpected and unanticipated that have the potential to give expression to inner mental or emotional states. In a similar vein, Allan Grapard has asserted that sacred geography should be thought of as a political geography. Since specific deities were considered to protect particular geographical areas, the meaning of sacred spaces must be seen as sociopolitical products, intimately related to power and epistemology (Grapard 1994:372–381). According to this perspective, then, even the natural environment found at a shrine, one of its prime attractions for visitors, serves as a legitimation as well as an expression of the institutional power that has preserved it (Friedland and Boden 1994:34).

Because a visitor's interpretations are, like any perception, culturally constructed and may not occur at a conscious or verbal level, it is a complex and problematic task to present findings concerning the activities of visitors to Kamigamo Shrine, or any other religious institution in Japan for that matter. Like researchers elsewhere, I have used questionnaires, interviews, observations, and histories. Yet, because the answers these methods yield are grounded in the changing dynamic of practice rather than rigid constructions of structure, they must be taken as tentative and fragile—"solid objects that dissolve under a steady gaze" (Geertz 1988:22).

For example, though I use the word "visitor" in referring to those individuals one finds strolling through the grounds of a shrine, in the eyes of the priests, there are no visitors. Anyone coming to a shrine is a *sanpaisha,* or "worshiper," whose physical presence on sanctified shrine grounds constitutes an act of reverence whether he or she knows it or not. From a less emic perspective, people may indeed be worshipers, but they may also be local residents taking a shortcut home, casual or highly motivated sightseers, or people seeking a little peace and quiet. Since the categories themselves usually overlap during the course of a single visit, using "visitor" as an analytic term encompasses without restricting these shifting possibilities. Thus, even when religious elements appear to dominate, it is best to think of shrine visits as multifunctional (Rinschede 1992:53).

While generalizations can be made based on empirical observations charting the course of individuals, as I have done for 112 visitors to Kamigamo Shrine, two precautions are advised. First, from simply watching people, there is no empirical way to discern whether a visit is predominantly spiritual, habitual, or recreational. As a number of scholars have remarked, much of what we think passes for Japanese "religious" behavior is a thoroughly syncretic blend of the three (Reader 1990, 1991; Davis 1992; Earhart 1984; Graburn 1983).[1] One cannot overemphasize the importance Japanese place on action, custom, and etiquette rather than on belief and structure (see Omura 1988). Many activities that appear to be evidence of religious belief to the outside observer—such as bringing the hands together, bowing before a statue or building housing a spiritual relic,

making an offering, or purchasing an amulet—may have alternate interpretations if the individual performing these actions is queried at length.
Even then, interpretations of these actions remain problematic. An individual bowing deeply before each subordinate shrine en route to the main
sanctuary may indeed be devoted to the deity, but she may also be performing these actions out of habit or propriety, all the while thinking
about whether or not she turned off the stove before she left home. I say
this not to belittle what may indeed be genuine piety, belief, or devotion,
but as a cautionary brake on those who would have subjective observations serve as a vehicle for generalized theories about the religiousness of
the Japanese.[2]

A second point concerns making definitive statements about the motivations behind an individual's visit even when face-to-face interviews are
conducted. Personal narrative is imbued with an importance and imme-
diacy that can be both liberating and constricting, but those conceptual
openings provided by and through language must constantly be contextualized, reevaluated according to the social positioning of the individual,
and weighed for symbolic or political content mitigating the apparent
factuality of what is said. Whether a person came for the beauty and calm
of Kamigamo's environs in general, because the shrine was en route to another site in north Kyoto, or for a specific "spiritual" purpose, motivations often remain obscure even after talking to visitors.

As Winston Davis has pointed out, measuring the "religious" or "secular"
attitudes of people by "simple sociometric techniques" in a cross-cultural
setting is complicated by the Japanese capacity for "self-effacement" and
the aversion many have to committing themselves in public to any kind of
ideological viewpoint, whether religious, political, or social (1992: 232).
A researcher can come away from observations and interviews with general ideas about why people do what they do, but to elevate the empiri-
cism of method in order to validate a body of data does not further an understanding of the issues at hand.

"Facticity is a status, not a state," Graham Watson reminds his readers,
"and the distinction between 'facts' and 'interpretations' is social rather
than epistemological" (1991: 87; see also Fardon 1990). This statement
(here I risk sounding like an antirevisionist defender of the Japanese "way")
is generally true in Japan, where situation and context tend to override
blanket applicability of mores and ethics, and where nuance and under-
statement are valued in certain situations as a sign of one's status, up-

bringing, and education. To posit a "reality" based on observation alone risks collapsing two different historical/temporal and spatial processes, of cognition (a visitor's intention) and of the social setting in which it is realized (see John Thompson 1991 : 16). So, while my observations, descriptions, and interpretations provide convenient means to think about the experience of Japanese people at a specific place, they are not intended to provide closure by the rhetoric of their presentation alone. Instead, like a mountain meadow that is different each time one visits, this rendering of cultural practices must point beyond the printed text to ongoing social processes given shape and meaning by culture, constantly in flux.

SHRINE VISITOR OPINIONS AND MOTIVATIONS

In a discussion of tourism and music, Ishimori asserts that for third- and fourth-world countries blessed with beautiful natural environments, the populace willingly commodifies this resource for economic gain (shizen no shōhinka) in attracting tourists (1991 : 24). Soon after this step is taken comes the subsequent commodification of a particular country's cultural characteristics (bunka no shōhinka)—its music, festivals, or folk art, for example—again for the express purpose of capitalizing on a tourist market. Key to Ishimori's observations is the fact that local peoples realize the importance of culture-as-commodity not because they are smart enough to know what will or won't sell, but because of outsiders' values. These values educate local peoples into producing only certain practices, goods, and degrees of social and cultural access into their lives—all of which are exploitable for capital gain. Although Ishimori reminds the reader that he is not concerned with first-world countries (senshin koku), his description of the commodification of culture can nonetheless apply quite nicely to the booming industry in Japanese cultural heritage directly affecting religious sites.[3]

The Japanese domestic tourist industry (described in Graburn 1983, 1995, Beer 1995, Moon 1989, and Moeran 1989, for example) also "means what it does" (to revisit Willis) in fostering an awareness and nostalgia of cultural inheritance in cities such as Kyoto, Nagasaki, or Kobe (and will continue to do so despite the 1995 earthquake) or in the countryside, where a pastoral past that "never existed" is advertised, promoted, and marketed as "home" (see Robertson 1991). Such topics as the packaging-for-consumption of sacred spaces, archaic customs, and "high" culture

TABLE 1.

AGE AND SEX OF INTERVIEWEES

Age	Male	Female
55+	10	9
55 to 40	10	12
40 to 30	10	8
30 to 20	12	19
Under 20	10	12
Totals	52	60

TABLE 2.

VISITOR'S CITY OR REGION OF ORIGIN

Origin	Number	Origin	Number
Kyoto	36	Fukui region	2
Osaka	14	Okayama region	2
Nara	3	Shizuoka region	3
Kobe	7	Matsumoto/Nagano	2
Nagoya	8	Hiroshima	5
Wakasa	4	Tokyo region	26

in general; the reenchantment of tradition; antisocial acts of resistance and protest; public performances that shape social memory; and current writing on sacred sites as tourist or pilgrimage destinations all find ample expression via the nexus of a shrine (see Nelson 1996b, 1993a; Smyers 1999).

Faced with the challenge of trying to discover the intentions behind an individual's visit to Kamigamo Shrine, I used a random sample to elicit general moods and motivations. By prior agreement with the priests, I interviewed only individuals who had completed their visits and were clearly on their way out of the shrine. After first gaining their consent to participate in my survey, I asked fifty-two men and sixty women questions concerning their place of origin, the motivation behind their visits, their general knowledge about the shrine's principal *kami,* and their impressions of the shrine (see tables 1 and 2).

Interview question 1: Could you tell me your main reason for choosing to visit Kamigamo Shrine today? *(Kyō wa dōshite toku ni Kamigamo Jinja o eranda no desu ka?)*

    a.   No special reason (18)
    b.   It's a famous place (12)
    c.   It's recommended as a nice place (10)
    d.   It has famous festivals (9)
    e.   It's a good place to walk (8)
    f.   We were in the area (7)
    g.   It's traditional (7)
    h.   It's old (6)
    i.   We live nearby (5)
    j.   Photography (5)
    k.   It was recommended by the guidebook (4)
    l.   We're returning from Kurama (4)
    m.   We're planning a wedding here (3)
    n.   We were having lunch nearby (3)
    o.   It's our graduation trip (3)
    p.   We have a baby dedication next week (3)
    q.   We asked for harmony between us (2)
    r.   I asked for blessings for my company, which is poorly located (1)
    s.   It's a good place to meet people (1)
    t.   I saw it on television (1)

Interview question 2: Do you happen to know the name of the shrine's principal *kami?* *(Kamigamo Jinja ni matsurarete iru kamisama no namae o gozonji desu ka?)*

What might seem an unreasonably specific question was evoked by the name of the *kami* on virtually all the more detailed informational signs. Despite standing and looking at a sign for several seconds, visitors' answers to this question showed little awareness of the content of these signs. Of the 112 respondents, sixteen (14 percent) knew the deity's name while ninety six (86 percent) did not. When I mentioned this finding to the shrine's senior priests, they were not the least bit surprised. "I'm amazed," said one, "that 14 percent were correct. That's much higher than I thought it would be!"

Interview question 3: Where were you before coming to Kamigamo Shrine? Where will you go next? *(Kyō, Kamigamo Jinja ni irrasharu mae wa doko ni oraremashita ka? Korekara, dochira e irrashaimasu ka?)*

For one-third of all respondents, Kamigamo was the first place they had visited that day. For those coming from elsewhere, no real pattern could be discerned concerning a possible visitors' circuit. I had predicted that many of Kamigamo's visitors would be drop-ins en route to or from the better-known sites of northern Kyoto such as Daitoku-ji, Kinkaku-ji, Sanzen-in or Kibune/Kurama. However, when these sites were mentioned, they were usually to come after the individual or group's Kamigamo visit. Virtually all Kyoto respondents said they were either going home after the visit or were en route to other errands.

Interview question 4: Compared to other shrines you've been to, is there anything special about Kamigamo Shrine that makes an impression on you? *(Ima made ni irrashatta jinja to kurabete, nani ka toku ni Kamigamo Jinja de inshō ni nokotta koto ga arimasu ka?)*

    a.   Natural environment (40)
    b.   Streams (16)
    c.   Cultural (16)
    d.   Colors/color contrasts (10)
    e.   Brightness (8)
    f.   Architectural aesthetics (6)
    g.   High status (6)
    h.   Heian-style festivals (6)
    i.   Seen on television (4)

The information from these interviews points toward two general cultural trends. The first concerns a public awareness that shrines (and other religious sites) are indeed prime repositories of Japanese cultural heritage. Thirty-five percent of respondents mentioned some aspect of the shrine's history, culture, or tradition as having motivated their visits. The other trend, represented by 56 percent of the respondents, concerns an appreciation for the natural setting at places like shrines. Like many of its counterparts within urban areas, Kamigamo is well-kept, spacious, and quiet, accentuating the beauty of the streams, buildings, and the surrounding landscape. Thus, it is not surprising that more than half the vis-

itors responding to question 4 mentioned the shrine's natural environment as a particularly striking characteristic.

If the above responses are posited as representative of shrine visitors
nationwide, then the main draw of a majority of shrines is not their "religious" services but their complementary ambiance of nature and what I
call "heritage aesthetics." Yet this attraction works to the shrine's advantage as a religious site, since most visitors engage in activities that complement rather than detract from the institution's viability. Nostalgia for
the past or a reassertion of aristocratic aesthetics is promoted by the
shrines themselves, by local and national media, and even by politicians,
merchants, and architects. The work of Jennifer Robertson (1991) on the
conscious manipulation of shrine festival dynamics to promote community within urban housing projects, my own work on the tactics of shrine
administrators (Nelson 1996b), and even Isozaki Arata's borrowing of Ise
Shrine's stone spaces for the Disney Corporate Headquarters in Orlando,
Florida, epitomize the emotive, nativistic appeal of a shrine's physical
features, symbols, and layout to evoke appropriate and complementary
behavior (Isozaki 1992).

POSITIONINGS

Although Kamigamo Shrine has had the status of being a pilgrimage site
at alternating periods in the past—beginning in the sixth century C.E.,
when its Kamo Festival drew people from as far away as western Hyōgo
prefecture (Tanigawa 1986), and again during the war years, when it attracted crowds owing to its status as a "great shrine for the national front"
(kanpei taisha)—Kamigamo today commands little of the mass appeal of
shrines like Ise, Meiji, or Izumo, or even the centers of several of the "new"
religions such as Tenri-kyō, Omoto-kyō, or Gedatsukai (see Earhart
1989). In fact, many of the major guide books to Kyoto (such as Japan
Travel Bureau's Ace Guide, Pocket Guide, Tabi-no-nōto [Travel Notes], or the
Blue Guide series) mention it as occupying the hidden side, or ura, of
Kyoto—worth a visit if one has time (or combined with a local eatery or
speciality shop on a gourmet tour) but not really essential when compared
to other sites such as the Silver Pavilion (Ginkaku-ji) or Kiyomizu-dera.

Thus, to talk about Kamigamo Shrine as an "axis mundi," in Eliade's
phrase, as a "center out there" in Turner's, or as a "formal" or "popular"
center of pilgrimage (cited in E. Cohen 1992:36) would be to misrepre-

sent its status in the eyes of outside visitors and local residents alike. The former group, as my survey indicates, see the shrine primarily as a political-cultural attraction set within pleasing natural surroundings where one has the freedom to access the shrine's *kami*. Local residents tend to regard Kamigamo as a defining feature of their neighborhood and, in many cases, as a cultural marker of their family and region's identity. Too often the local perspective is overlooked and under studied in research on visits to religious sites, as if the people who actually live in the area and use the institution are mere bystanders or extras in the spectacle of mass-transit visits. In the latter part of this chapter, I will present a detailed look at activities and practices that center on a physical place as a kind of communal resource perceived and used in ways not always in line with officially sanctioned norms.

To set the stage for the issues I wish to raise later, some of the framing (rather than theoretical) concepts used in studies of religious tourism and pilgrimage can be applied profitably to shrine visitations in general, regardless of the visitor's motivation. For example, Eric Cohen's categorizations concerning motives for visiting a religious site—such as acquiring religious merit, making specific requests, or seeking beneficial powers to enhance one's life situation (1992:38)—can be extended to include those individuals who may have come simply to enjoy seasonal scenery, a festive event, or a moment of unhurried privacy. Less helpful are guidelines such as those proposed by Valene Smith (1989:14), who sees belief as the key element identifying the journey of the pilgrim-tourist and who straitjackets the visitor's motives into a sacred or secular category, as if these binary opposites were more than analytical constructs that, when grounded in practice, tend to quickly dissolve.

A term introduced in one of Victor Turner's earliest works on pilgrimage is helpful in understanding the present-day public status of Kamigamo Shrine (1973a:229). His discussion of a "religious-political center" corresponds to the Japanese institution of *saisei itchi*, or "worship administration," that has long been central to the sociopolitical dynamic of government in Japan (see Murakami 1970; Kitagawa 1987:118–120). Turner goes on to describe in a European context some of these once powerful centers (Chartres, Köln, Canterbury) as "ritualized vestiges" of their former grandeur. Turner's concept applies equally well to Kamigamo (as well as almost every other major shrine complex). Allied to state interests throughout the shrine's long history as a "nation-preserving" shrine, today Kamigamo's administrators carefully downplay and selectively forget those controversial periods. While a portion of the shrine's older clientele still harbor strong nationalistic sentiments, the public expression of these leanings have by and large become political liabilities that detract from attempts to capitalize and improvise on a selected set of more generic cultural assets without an over nationalistic subtext (see Nelson 1993a, 1994).

As a final framing concept, Victor and Edith Turner have discussed the "bureaucratic organization" of the pilgrim's experience (1978:7). As pilgrims move from a "mundane center" to a "sacred periphery" where they can "reflect on basic religious and cultural meanings," their passage is mediated by travel agents, tour operators, and travel itineraries. The shrine is situated to accommodate tourist buses easily, with ample parking and spacious grounds for the visitor to explore en route to the sanctuary. But from the moment visitors approach the shrine, another level of administrative mediation begins shaping their experiences representing those in charge of the site itself.

MARKERS AND MEASURINGS

Markers, signs, notices, and icons of representation at a shrine grab the attention of a visitor and influence behavior even before he or she enters the actual place. At the outer boundary of a shrine, one may find anything from a crudely lettered sign naming the site, to wooden replicas of Edo period notice boards, to intricately painted maps of the entire precinct seen from the height of a passing hawk (such as one finds at Shimogamo Jinja, Kumano Hongū, or Meiji Jingū). Public spaces in Japan—commuter train coaches, train and bus stations, and pedestrian thoroughfares—are generally awash in messages, announcements, and advertising of every conceivable product and service. Visitors to religious institutions are often granted a reprieve from these demands on their attention, and yet they would likely think it strange were a place to be totally lacking in markers. After all, as MacCannell has pointed out, there is a process of "sight sacralization" at work in places open to the public, whereby signs and markers serve not only to identify significance but to frame and elevate specific attributes in a way that "enshrines" their importance (1990:45). In other words, the visitor is rewarded by visual clues that not only has he or she come to the right place but that the place is important and thus worthy of a visitor's time, attention, and indeed money.

Books and viewpoints dealing with the phenomenology of religion frequently point out that religious institutions in Japan are sources of or gateways to power that is channeled through Buddhas, *kami,* or some feature of the site's natural environment, such as the curative or purificatory waters of a spring (see Sonoda 1990). This special attribute of a place is often but not always marked by a sign or series of signs that "signify to all who enter that they are moving from the ordinary world into something special, into the powerful presence of the spiritual realms" (Reader 1991 : 138). At Kamigamo, however, one notices several exceptions to this general pattern. Here, signs lack the sequential progression alluded to above as a way of informing visitors they are moving into a special, spiritual realm. In addition, some of the largest and most dominant of the on-site markers at Kamigamo perform decidedly nonreligious functions as well.[4]

The permanent on-site markers at Kamigamo Shrine fall into three basic categories. The first announces (and advertises) services performed by the shrine, the second instructs visitors on diverse subjects ranging from prohibitions on behavior to information about the deities, and the third appeals for contributions. I turn now to a more detailed analysis of these signs not so much as a way to analyze their content, but rather to explore these messages as announcements that reveal, in a very public way, an emic view of the institution's social and cultural role.

Like a lighthouse beacon above the turbulence of traffic, pedestrians, and shop signs, the brightly painted red characters of *yaku yoke* are visible at a distance of one hundred meters while crossing the Kamo River at the Misono Bridge. Shop fronts, tree branches, and a never-ending bottleneck of cars, buses, taxis, and motorcycles do nothing to detract from the two-meter-high sign announcing a purification for those at ages thought to be inauspicious.

At the bottom of the huge *kanji* characters runs the message *kakushu gokito—jichinsai hoka,* literally, "all kinds of prayers: *jichinsai* (land calming rituals) and so forth." Immediately the visitor is informed that she is approaching a place whose ritual repertoire has the versatility and breadth to meet the various needs of a wide-ranging clientele. This sign, as big as any highway billboard, constitutes both a service offered and a reminder that certain members of the community are at risk. It can also be seen in an educational, even proselytizing light, serving as an emblem for a cosmos in which modern-day individuals perhaps no longer believe but that just might influence their lives nonetheless. What would it hurt, after all, to have a five-minute purification performed at the ages of nineteen and thirty-three for a woman or at twenty-four and forty-two for a man? Interestingly enough, there is no clue as to the name of the institution offering these services.

As the visitor rounds the corner, dodging the taxis and buses that use part of Kamigamo's precincts as end-of-the-line staging points, she sees the first of the shrine's enormous torii gateways. Here, two markers vie for her attention. To the left of the torii and most striking of all is a recently constructed notice board of the finest quality *hinoki* wood built in an Edo period style, complete with roof and a low fence surrounding its waist-high stone pedestal:

Sadame	*Notice*
Hitotsu: Kuruma, uma o nori ireru koto	Point: Riding vehicles or horses
Hitotsu: Sakana, tori o toru koto	Point: Fishing and hunting birds
Hitotsu: Chiku, boku o kiru koto	Point: Cutting bamboo or trees
Migi no jōjō o keidai ni oite kinshi suru	These three things are prohibited [within] shrine grounds

Even though the sign is new, the quaint nature of these prohibitions reinforces the notion that the shrine is a kind of open-air historical relic. It also reflects the most fundamental of concerns for the shrine's administrators, that the landscape is in no way to be interfered with. However, another sign to the right of the first torii, as if to compensate for the naïveté of the first list of prohibitions, is functional in both its simple design of white-painted wood with black hand lettering and its straightforward message:

After this point is shrine property. Without permission, you can't disturb the beauty of the area or its scenery, or [do things that] impair the dignity of the place. In addition, the following activities are prohibited:

Putting up stalls for the purpose of selling
Handing out flyers, brochures, advertisements, or political or religious messages
Putting up posters or billboards
Public speeches
Bothering the worshipers

Parishioners' Group
Kamo Wake Ikazuchi Shrine

With these two lists of injunctions, before taking a single step inside the shrine grounds, the visitor has not only been instructed in proper behavior, she has also been educated concerning the importance of the shrine's natural surroundings and worshipers. All the same, the consumption of alcohol is not among the overtly stated prohibitions, nor are sports, public assemblies, sexual activities, or other likely candidates, all of which occur with regularity.

Once inside the first torii, the visitor is greeted with what is in modern Japan an unusual sight: the long straight worshipers' path *(sandō)* is flanked on either side by open expanses of well-kept grass. The largest of these is used for the running of horses during the important *kurabe-uma shinji* on May 5, but they remain accessible to the public throughout the year for picnics, frisbee playing, and lazy Sunday afternoons with a book and a blanket. More than any sign, these fields enjoin visitors to understand the quality of the area (or arena) they are entering: only a powerful shrine (or the imperial household's control of the expansive grounds of the Gosho palace) could command and maintain such green spaciousness. The visual ideology of the shrine's social power and status is thus conveyed by the physical emptiness of these fields.

Walking about one hundred meters, the visitor reaches the second torii, where another large *yaku yoke* sign, similar to the one by the bridge entrance, again dominates. On the opposite side, rarely noticed and even more rarely read by visitors, is the first of the purely instructional markers that delve into shrine mythology, history, and cultural significance. Most visitors merely glance at this elegant and densely lettered wooden placard, succumbing instead to the lure of the middle courtyard's graceful pavilions. Markers found within this area are scarcely noticeable, so thoroughly has their wood been weathered. Still, each structure has a small *tatefuda,* or "standing board," that names it and notes its status as an "important cultural treasure" *(jūyō bunka zai)* but offers no additional information. Approaching the inner courtyard, a visitor will see either of two instructional markers that recount myths, important festivals and rituals, and supposed founding dates of the main or subordinate shrines. Again, the visitor who takes the time to read through these signs is rare, as most prefer to continue strolling at a leisurely pace. As she passes through the Tower Gate (Rōmon) leading to the middle sanctuary and courtyard, the last of the large signs suddenly appears, accosting the visitor with a plea for money as she approaches the site of worship:

37

Shaden shūri hi no go-kishin o   Please make a contribution
onegai shimasu   for the repair of the shrine buildings

Announcements and appeals of this nature come either as directives from the chief priest or as suggestions offered by the lay organizations that, because of lobbying or influence-peddling, receive the chief priest's sanction. In the words of one senior priest, "Whenever an [instructional] sign gets too old or someone complains that it looks shoddy, we put up a new one, after soliciting for donations, usually copying what was already there." Rather than implementing new knowledge or interpretations, this practice perpetuates the ideas of chief priest Sawada, active just after the war, who was known for his erudition but not for scholarly objectivity.

The younger priests are aware of a problem with the instructional signs and indicate concern that few visitors stop to read them. One commented, "In this day and age, we need to have graphics on our signs or pictures that will catch a worshiper's eye. As they are displayed now, the information on the signs is too detailed (komakai) and hard to read." When I asked about specific points on several of the signs, particularly about an old practice of burying large jugs of water beside the stream, I could find no one capable of answering or explaining what function this practice might have served. "It's that type of sign," I was told without apology by one of the priests, "that needs to be made more contemporary. There are problems on almost all the signs, but I don't know who is capable of rewriting them in a way that is accurate and interesting."[5]

ADVANCES

According to the priests, who are schooled in ritual propriety and must demonstrate their expertise before they can be promoted, a "correct" shrine visit includes a certain approach, an act of worship before the kami, and a prescribed departure. Regardless of the size of the shrine or its location in Japan, the first stage of this process still begins with an act emblematic of a great number of Shinto's ritual concerns: a purification at the stone water basin, the temizusha. The water is used to cleanse hands (symbolizing one's deeds and actions) and mouth (words) before one proceeds.[6]

Following the Kamigamo priests' course, one should then cross the Negi Bridge (thus attaining an automatic purification, since traversing flowing water extracts impurities) and pay one's respects before the

Kamigamo Shrine, inner courtyard.

shrine of Tamayorihime, the mythical mother of the principal deity. One then crosses the final bridge (another instant purification) before entering the Tower Gate, climbing the stone stairs, and finally arriving at the Middle Gate (Chūmon). Here, while looking into the splendidly preserved inner sanctuary compound that is shielded from full view by sedgegrass screens, curtains, and low eaves, one might compose one's prayer or petition. Then, after tossing in a few coins (ideally, the priests say, one hundred yen) that serve as donations and as another way to cast out impurities, one enacts the hand-clapping gesture *(kashiwade)* of two bows, two claps, then a final bow, which supposedly distinguishes the act of Shinto worship from Buddhist practices. One then takes a single step back, bows ever so slightly to inform the deity that one's business is completed, and walks back down the steps, turning before departing to enact a last bow of farewell and gratitude.

The final station on the "correct" course includes a stop at the shrine's information and amulet counter, the *juyosho* ("place of bestowing blessings"), to purchase a talisman (¥800), amulet (¥500–800), set of postcards (¥600), telephone calling card (¥500–2,000), or some other item to remind one of the shrine and one's visit there and to incur the protection of the deity. Legally speaking, the shrine does not "sell" these objects lest it endanger its tax-exempt status; a visitor makes a "donation" and receives these objects in return.

After all is said and done, it is hard to imagine why anyone should follow or even be able to follow the priests' course of visitation and worship. At Kamigamo Shrine, like the majority of shrines in Japan, visitors are on their own to do the right thing, since there are neither visual markers nor written instructions about what constitutes a correct course, nor do people have the opportunity (were they so inclined) to talk to priests to find out.[7] With the administrative offices outside the central shrine compound (and for good reason, too, since, as one priest said, "not all that goes on in an office do you want the *kami* to know about"), there is a high likelihood that many visitors will not even see a priest during their visits, not to mention have an opportunity to talk to one. Additionally, were a visitor to peruse all the available literature about the shrine available at the amulet counter, he or she would find nothing on the topic of ritual propriety for visitors.

To doctrinally minded Western clerics or missionaries, this laxity of prescribed practices would seem a breeding ground for all sorts of "heretical" or "illicit" religious behavior. Yet, contemporary Shinto's toleration of innovative and highly personal forms of worship, some of which will be explored below, is one of its most important characteristics.

WHOSE VISIT IS IT?

If an archetypal visit can be constructed based on data from my observations, most individuals coming to Kamigamo are sightseers first, what one might call "exchange practitioners" second (see Befu 1980), and frequently but not always "worshipers" last (the reader will recall the opening discussion of this chapter and remember this word is used to describe outward behavior only). The first group participates by a slow amble through the sumptuously cared for grounds, pausing at various buildings to glance briefly at the marker indicating the name but rarely lingering to read the entire description. The second group, although they do not engage in acknowledging the deities, may nonetheless want some pragmatic interaction with the shrine and so purchase a fortune *(omikuji)* or amulet *(omamori)* as part of their visit (see Ikkai 1988).

But by and large the third group is the largest and most complex, combining the activities from all three groups yet more conspicuously exhibiting some form of outward gesture of genuflection, deference, or acknowledgment that they have come to a place requiring a certain kind of behavior. Whether they do so because some feel the *kami* is present, because their sense of ritual propriety requires it, or because it is simply an acceptable social form of interaction with the place, I am still reluctant to assert that observations of and conversations with these individuals reflect their true religious beliefs or that social practices are functionally equivalent with inner dispositions. Once inside Kamigamo's inner courtyard, visitors labor up the rather steep stone steps until reaching the Middle Gate, through which only priests, ritual participants, and authorized individuals may pass.[8] Before this final barrier, on a gray limestone platform some three by six meters, a wide variety of actions and styles of what appears to be worshipful behavior can be observed.

The principal activity signifying what Catherine Bell calls "interaction [with the deity] from the bottom up" (1992: 201) and which most Westerners would recognize as the only private moment an individual has at a shrine—is the *kashiwade* (more formally, *hairei*). About half the time, visitors make a small monetary donation into a large wooden coffer-box, then, after bowing twice, raise their hands to chest level and clap twice more. In standardized practice, taught at the training universities for priests, performing *kashiwade* is straightforward and simple, taking no more than fifteen seconds. However, the manifestations and transmutations of this basic gesture are many and varied, some of which are multiple hand claps interspersed by moments of prayer, multiple bows of varying angles (it would appear that the deeper the bow, the more intense the petition), a prolonged prayer (much as one might do in front of a Buddhist altar), and claps arranged into a rhythmic sequence.[9]

Once again, there is no normative pattern of worship prescribed by the shrine and promoted as such. The priests have been educated in upholding the propriety of certain ritual gestures, but, as specialists, they do not impose these traditions on the visitors. While the majority of people simply toss a coin, clap their hands a couple times while bowing, then move on to the next site, there are other regular performances at the Middle Gate. Described below are three frequent visitors to the shrine who illustrated some of the possibilities for what may constitute a shrine visit in contemporary Japanese society. Their dramatic and apparently sincere behavior, rather than being considered aberrations, should be located along a continuum of ritual practices that find common motivation in conveying to spiritual entities a highly personal agenda:

Mr. N., from a suburb of southern Kyoto, comes regularly in the morning on the fifteenth of every month to petition the *kami.* A rather tall man of sturdy proportions, twenty-five to thirty years of age, he is always immaculately dressed in a double-breasted suit, with slicked-back hair and shoes shined to a sparkle. Bypassing the font for cleansing one's hands and mouth, his first station is the middle of the Tower Gate entrance, where he plants his feet wide apart and enacts the *kashiwade* with sweeping gestures that indicate an affection for sumo wrestling. Then, he ascends the stairs and finds two stones in front of the Middle Gate, positioning his feet in a manner not unlike a baseball player stepping up to the plate to bat. Legs wide apart, he flexes his knees, rolls his shoulders, and clears his throat before fixing his gaze in the direction of the inner sanctuary. Pulling a folded piece of paper from a suit pocket, he opens the first of many folds and begins his own invocational prayer, modeled on the *norito* prayer format given by a Shinto chief priest while seated before the altar. At first the words are slow and distinct: "O great *kami,* hear the petition of N., from X, who addresses you in awe and gratitude." However, soon after the prologue, the speed doubles, then triples, until Mr. N. is ripping along like a Buddhist priest during a rite to say the *nenbutsu* a million times. Even with this speed, his petition usually takes ten minutes to deliver. The attendant of the upper amulet counter adjacent to the Middle Gate says that Mr. N. is always on time, always stands in the same place, and always leaves without acknowledging anyone. His monetary offering to the shrine is discreetly slipped into the wooden coffer at the beginning of his petitioning and never placed in an envelope that might give away the identity of its donor.

Mr. H., a man in his late fifties, makes the trip from Yokohama to Kyoto once a month between the first and the fifth (the bullet train both ways costs around 23,000 yen or, as of this writing, around U.S. $210) to pay respects to the power of Wake Ikazuchi. Unlike Mr. N., he is quite open about his motives for making this journey:

> I believe this *kami* to be great and fearful, largely because I was granted a
> vision at Kōyama [the shrine's sacred mountain] shortly before the terrible

typhoon of 1991. It was a beautiful day in early August, still and hot, but not sticky like it usually is, and I had gone to the mountain as is my custom. Suddenly, even though there was no wind, the thick growth of trees and vegetation on the southern face of the mountain became agitated, as if moved by a great wind. However, there was no wind at that moment — so how did it happen? The very next day, typhoon nineteen hit Japan — eventually extending from Kyushu to northern Honshu — causing damage like we haven't had from a single typhoon in years. The *kami* of thunder and lightning gave me a message, and I've been trying to ready myself for the next one ever since. I do *misogi* [purification by flowing water] daily and have formed a group of people in Yokohama to talk, study, and experience this austerity so that we might be closer to the spiritual world.

He performs the *kashiwade* not once but three times in succession. On completion of his worship, Mr. H. always makes it a point to visit the priests at the administration building and keep them up-to-date on his group's activities.

Mrs. S., age seventy-plus from Ōtsu city, struggles up the steps to the Middle Gate twice a month, then sits on the stone *seiza* style (with legs tucked under the buttocks as the knees and shins support and carry one's body weight). There, hands held together in the Buddhist-style *gasshō,* she mutters a prayer of some five minutes while gently swaying back and forth. I am told that she is not the only woman who sometimes kneels on the stone, but for a man to do it would be "very unusual" or, in the words of another priest, "out of the question." One day, on her way back to the bridge over the river, she picked up little red berries on the path beside the Mitarashi stream, bowed to the hillside the berry bush grows on, then found a suitable spot to kneel beside the gently flowing water. She cradled the berries in one hand and, beginning what seemed to be a prayer, methodically tossed them one by one into the stream. Despite the soft morning rain, she did not wear a jacket or carry an umbrella. When the berries were all gone, she bowed to the stream, walked across the bridge to the second torii, turned and bowed once again in the direction of the inner sanctuary, and slowly ambled away.

From the above accounts, it is clear that despite the exalted rank of Kamigamo's principal *kami,* Wake Ikazuchi, and the fact that there is no physical representation of him offered to the public eye, many people supply their own religious framework and establish what may loosely be termed a patron-client relationship with the deity.[10] Requests cover an entire range of human problems and hopes, and are most conspicuously on view at the racks where one hangs an inscribed wooden placard, the *ema*.

Ian Reader has called *ema* "letters to the gods" that "offer a channel whereby Japanese people may therapeutically liberate their feelings in an individual way that enables them to transcend the restrictions of their social milieu" (1991:45). He has given a full analysis of the practice of buying and presenting *ema* plaques. I might only add that if one surveys even a few of the petitionary messages written on the reverse of these colorful placards, it becomes clear that "turning to the gods in times of trouble" *(kurushii toki no kamidanomi)* extends from toothaches, to wayward husbands or uninterested girlfriends, to an upcoming entrance examination. *Ema* provide another means whereby an individual can participate with and become a part of a shrine in a physical way. To externalize one's hopes, desires, troubles, and anxieties on a piece of wood and then leave it in the company of hundreds of other such placards is to join a community of petitioners. Often, an individual reads a number of *ema* before placing his or her own, as if surveying the neighborhood where one's request will best fit in. And while one cannot know for certain what degree of belief accompanies such actions, as they occur within a religious context, are often accompanied by bows, and specifically address the *kami,* I would agree with Reader that they serve as reminders, commitments, and insurance factors in an uncertain world.

While the above examples are public expressions and performances of subjective spiritual practices thought appropriate to a shrine and its deity when visiting, there are also occurrences of an off-stage, more private nature. To gain a full understanding of shrine visitations in contemporary Japanese society, one must also include situations and individuals operating within the shrine's spatial jurisdiction but outside its social norms.

OFF-STAGE RITES, CURSE CASTING, AND OTHER NOCTURNAL SHRINE ADVENTURES

In describing what happens on the grounds of a shrine at night, it is useful to note the work of Sonoda Minoru (1990, 1988), which provides a general discussion of Japanese festivals, or *matsuri*. The phenomenon usually translated into English as "festival" is actually a complex event composed of two parts, the first being "ritual" *(saigi)* and the second being "festival" *(shukusai)*. During unspecified "ancient times," Sonoda writes, the formal and solemn *saigi* was for the daylight hours, whereas *shukusai*—with aspects of carnival, bacchanalia, and even protest—was reserved for the cover of darkness. Night was "viewed as a world of visions, a time in which the order of day dissolved into darkness and various ancestral and other spirits freely traveled to and from the land of shade. The very act of humans awakening from that night and becoming active was a kind of offense against order" (Sonoda 1988 : 59; see also Iwata 1975).

Although written in regard to *matsuri,* Sonoda's distinctions can also apply to the individual in contemporary Japan (or in any other highly industrialized complex society) who seeks release and liberation from the solemn roles he or she must play during the daylight hours or the regimentation of behavior exacted by cultural and social norms. Although a shrine and its priests are regarded by many Japanese as examples par excellence of rigid and formalized behavior, some local residents nonetheless see the space and otherworldliness of the shrine precincts as liberating and empowering, especially when the priests and mainstream visitors are absent. Because the activities I am referring to occur outside regular working hours (8:30 to 4:30 in summer, and 9:30 to 4:00 in winter), away from the shrine's sacred center, and because the actors appear to be local residents who use the place for their own agendas and prefer not to be noticed by the shrine's priests, these activities have a secretive, even mysterious air to them. Like a detective who constructs a narrative based on circumstantial evidence, so can one piece together activities and people that add to the multifunctionality of a shrine's place in society.

Anyone familiar with the Japanese rural as well as urban landscape knows that it is still common to encounter statues of Buddhist saints, little shrines, and memorial marker stones scattered seemingly at random. Sometimes they are woefully neglected, especially in more sparsely populated farming areas, but where there are people nearby, one usually finds some thoughtful individual providing maintenance and care for the site. Periodically, as on the first or in the middle of the month, fruit such as apples, oranges or tangerines, persimmons, and bananas are offered at the doors of smaller shrines *(hokora, miya);* at the base of Buddhist *jizō* statues alongside fields, roads, or in cemeteries; and at grave markers at any time of the year but especially during the Buddhist holiday of Obon.

At Kamigamo Shrine, offerings appear not only at the subordinate shrines but also alongside the Nara-no-ogawa stream. Atop one of the many flat rocks flanking the stream, fruit is often set on a white square of lightweight paper, flanked by one small pile of uncooked rice and one pile of salt, and on occasion also some dried cuttlefish *(surume)*. Similar to the offerings presented by Shinto priests during important rituals as well as the prescribed offerings for one's *kamidana* altar at home, the rice, salt, fruit, and nearby water are thought to be the essential "meal" (with only rice wine missing) for numinous entities—whether they be Shinto *kami,* Buddhist departed ancestral spirits *(senzo),* or perhaps even the wandering malevolence of a vengeful spirit *(onryō)*. Beside the paper there is often a hardened pool of melted wax, the remnants of a spent votive candle, which is so much a part of Buddhist ritual and folk practices but plays little part in those of organized Shinto.[11]

Before waxing poetic about devotional practices that may or may not reflect belief in earlier cosmic orderings of the world and society, I introduce the shrine's groundskeeper (a retired clerical worker in his mid-sixties) as a reality check. He frequently finds similar arrangements on the steps to subordinate shrines, but disdains rather than condones these offerings for two reasons. First and foremost, the candles are fire hazards ("These people think they are doing something religious, but I'd like to see their faces if there was a fire and they were arrested and charged with arson!"). Second, the food offerings attract an even greater number of animals (particularly stray cats) to the shrine than already reside in or frequent its precincts. Rather than respectfully gathering up these offerings, he kicks them into the flowing stream below. Apparently the groundskeeper feels qualified to judge that these impromptu offerings have served their purpose and are no longer worthy of any special treatment. And perhaps he is right, for the donors of these nighttime offerings rely on the shrine's indulgence that someone will take care of them and clean the spot for future offerings and whatever petition accompanies their presentation.

Not everyone who comes to the shrine's shadows at night does so to petition the deities. Even as late as midnight, it is not uncommon to see a couple on a stroll or a single individual passing by for reasons unknown the closed gate of the inner courtyard. But, since only a very small part of the shrine's grounds is illuminated—with brighter lights found on the amulet-counter building of the middle courtyard and on the inner courtyard gate—the rest of the paths, subordinate shrines, and streamside groves are very dark. In summertime, several of these areas are still prime spots for viewing fireflies.

These are appropriate places to find one of the traditional Japanese equivalents of curse casting, the *ushi no toki mairi* or "shrine visitation at the hour of the cow." During the Edo period (1603–1868), when Japanese society was highly stratified according to military designs for keeping the peace, a practice developed of attacking one's enemies or social superiors by nailing a human form to one of a shrine's sacred trees *(shinboku)*. In a practice coming from the ritual repertoire of the *yamabushi* mountain ascetics, a woman dressed in white would visit a shrine between the hours of one and three o'clock A.M., the hour of the "cow" (according to the Chinese zodiac). Wearing around her head an iron "crown" holding burning candles, she would nail the doll-like cutout *(hitogata)* to a tree, all the while petitioning the deities to cause that person harm. On the seventh day after this visit, the curse *(noroi)* was supposed to have taken hold and affected the targeted individual (Ono et al. 1974:156).

During the fall of 1991, TBS television broadcast a murder mystery set in Kyoto *(Kyōto satsujin jiken)*. In one scene, the handsome detective discovers nails in trees at Kibune Shrine, formerly one of Kamigamo's subordinate shrines located north of the city. Soon after this broadcast, I noticed two trees in Kamigamo Shrine's outer grove sprouting nails driven through doll-like shapes, although these cutouts of unlucky individuals were made of leaves and not paper. Could it be that in the future, television will be the medium for conveying "traditional" practices to individuals seeking tools of empowerment? Freshly hammered nails in the trees of Kamigamo might indicate that the process is already well along, but it also indicates the continued inventiveness of men and women seeking methodologies for working their will against those impeding their progress through an increasingly complicated world. When I mentioned the nails to the groundskeeper, he noted them with a wary eye and, without comment, left them exactly as they were.

ISLAND IN THE STORM

As Kamigamo Shrine is located in the north of an urban area approaching a population of two million people, it should not be surprising that, after dark, the shrine becomes a haven for all kinds of activities having nothing to do with its normal functions. And, while these activities are not possible during the light of day, neither are they (according to the wooden notice board near the first torii) expressly prohibited. After one of the two priests on overnight duty *(shukuhaku)* makes his final stroll through the grounds between nine and ten o'clock P.M., the shrine returns to the public domain or, to use current terminology in the literature of popular resistance, is "reappropriated" under the cover of night and priestly inattention.

Because shrines have large open spaces that are unsupervised yet accessible at night, they have been used throughout Japanese history as clandestine meeting places for secret rendezvous. One need only think of the Noh dramas *Ikuta* or *Hatsuyuki,* or the Ashikaga clan's use of shrines (such as Iwashimizu Hachimangū) as staging grounds for military exploits in the 1400s, or contemporary television suspense dramas (where shrines are often treated as dramatic settings for protagonists to meet) to see evidence for this continuing cultural predilection. Kamigamo is used in a similar manner by contemporary men and women, except that today its nighttime visitors seem more interested in entertainment than in intrigue. In contrast with the surrounding area—the chic new stores along Kitayama-dōri, the constant din of traffic on Horikawa-dōri and Kitaoji-dōri—the shrine at night is for some a dark expanse of freedom into which city life does not intrude. For those afraid of malevolent spirits and *kami,* the shrine grounds are best avoided; but for those hoping to escape from the bright lights, cars, and pressures of urban life, the shrine is like an island of calm and quiet within Kyoto's economic storms of development and progress.

Two factors, both of them significant, contribute to the pattern of day and nighttime visitors to the shrine. The first involves the five different bus lines converging at a terminal just outside the grounds proper and the walking routes individuals take to and from the bus stops. In an American or European city, to walk through wooded, unlit pathways in a city of 1.7 million would be courting disaster; but in Japan, with one of the world's lowest crime rates, a shortcut through the shrine remains merely a way to get home more quickly. Second, a large university student population in the area frequently rides the city bus lines and also uses two of the shrine's outer areas as parking lots for their bicycles or scooters. These areas are congested with around two hundred bicycles or scooters daily, resulting in extra work for the shrine's maintenance personnel, who must clear hastily parked bikes away from the main access road leading to the administration building. For students going to Kyoto's Sangyō University (whose current president happens to be an important patron of the shrine) a special service is provided: the school is permitted to run a shuttle bus departing from the front parking lot.

With this frequency of human and vehicular traffic, it is perhaps little wonder that the shrine attracts people at all hours. Although I did not engage in systematic sampling of nighttime activities, some of my more interesting encounters (during the course of numerous late evening strolls) were

- a radio-controlled car club racing their miniature vehicles at astounding speeds across the large parking lot at 10:00 P.M. (November)

- people hoping to see fireflies at 10:00 P.M. (July)

- a group of motorcycle bikers *(bōsōzoku)* in the front parking lot at 1:00 A.M. taking a beer break from the hard work of disturbing the peace along Shirakawa-dōri (May)

- a group of bird watchers looking for nocturnal species at 11:00 P.M. (April)

- a drunk salaryman weeping by the banks of the stream at 11:30 P.M. because he couldn't remember how to get home and if he didn't get home his angry wife would leave him, thus reasoning that it would be better just to drown himself and be done with it (September)

- three old men in their underwear illegally seining the Nara-no-ogawa stream for the delicacy *ayu,* or sweetfish (August)

By and large, however, the most frequently encountered group at the shrine at night was a group of two—a young man and a young woman. Thirty years ago, these couples were called *"abeku,"* after the French *avec,* "to be with." Today, they are more casually called *"kaapuru"* after the English "couple," implying a degree of intimacy that may or may not have sexual connotations. The shrine provides aluminum benches at several locations, most of which are in the darkest part of the grounds (and, in warmer months, the most heavily infested with mosquitoes)—as if encouraging couples to pause and refresh themselves during their visit. However, most couples I noticed were more interested in conversation than intimacy and so preferred more open venues, such as the steps of the pavilion just inside the second torii or out on the grassy fields. And, while there are those who use the shrine for sexual escapades, a number of "love hotels" along the banks of the Kamo and Takano rivers commodify security and privacy in ways the darkness of natural surroundings does not.[12]

Concerning all these comings and goings over which the shrine has little control, the groundskeeper makes his opinion clear:

> I don't mind most parts of my job, but picking up after people who do things they shouldn't really makes me mad! I find empty bottles of beer, whiskey, sake—what have you—thrown here and there on the grass. I find motorcycles, scooters, and bicycles that people don't want any more and think they can just dump at the shrine because we have a lot of unused space. Under the drooping cherry tree I have found used condoms. Worst of all, I have to clean up the droppings left behind by people's dogs. I hate it! The new signs prohibiting dog walking don't seem to make any difference. It really is bad manners to treat the shrine in such a way. I don't know why the priests don't patrol the grounds more frequently at night. They would if *they* had to clean up what people leave behind!

The only security the shrine musters to defend itself—other than the nightly watch of two priests—is an antiquated system of electronic eyes that, if crossed, alerts one of the priests on duty in the administration building. These electronic barriers are positioned in the middle and inner courtyards, largely because of an incident some years earlier concerning a thief who attempted to loot money from the offering boxes inside the Main and Middle gates. The story goes that he had brought his own ladder to scale the walls, but, whether from drunkenness or sheer ineptitude, he made so much noise in the inky darkness that he was overheard and apprehended before he could break the rusty locks. So common were thefts of this nature throughout Japanese social history that there is a special name for this unique kind of thief: "a coffer-box thief" (*saisen-bako dorobō*). The priest who recounted this incident added as an afterthought, "When I think of how unprotected the shrine is in general—from terrorist attacks in particular or other really destructive individuals—it makes me shudder. We've been lucky so far, but who knows what will happen in the future."[13]

CONCLUSION

The preceding discussion has traced several patterns in the practices of visitors to Kamigamo Shrine and has suggested a number of these as relevant for shrines nationwide or, by extension, for many religious institutions worldwide. The first is the multifunctional nature of visits that may or may not combine sight-seeing with some kind of what is to Western eyes religious activity. Observations showed that a majority of individuals coming to the shrine do interact in some way with the spiritual and visual ideology of the site, yet few of these individuals would describe themselves as "worshipers." The signs and on-site markers as well as the layout of the shrine serve as subtle rather than controlling influences on a person's visit, especially since few take the time to read the densely worded signs in detail.

And yet most people interact with the place in ways congruent with its cultural logic. With a variety of approaches to the innermost sanctuary and with no guidelines for what constitutes a "correct" course or the "proper" way to pay one's respects to the deity, visitors have relative freedom of choice in how they structure their visit. Thus, a variety of styles and manners of performing the *kashiwade* hand-clapping gesture were observed, some that took a few seconds while others were elaborate and dramatic. Daytime visitors have ample opportunities to interact with the shrine in physical ways—walking through its grounds, cleansing their hands at the *temizusha*, tossing coins into a coffer, or purchasing a fortune, amulet, or *ema* plaque. Some nighttime visitors performed many of these same acts but others, under the cover of darkness, enacted a different set of practices, some of which resisted behavior officially sanctioned by the shrine's administration. It would be a mistake, however, to judge these activities as violating the "sacred" nature of the place, since "sacred" and "profane" are not seen as categorical opposites in Japanese society (a view held by Winston Davis [1992 : 246] among others). Making love under a blooming cherry tree on the shrine's outer grounds may not be socially acceptable during the solemn daylight hours, but at night it takes on a dimension of *shukusai* or "festival" behavior and resonates with the mythic antics of the *kami* themselves as found in the 712 C.E. "Record of Ancient Matters," the *Kojiki*.

I have tried to build evidence supporting my claim that the creative, flexible, and laissez-faire practices the shrine's priests allow are essential to the social position of Kamigamo Shrine in Kyoto. This public freedom of expression is inherent to the structural longevity of the institution of shrine Shinto and evokes an individual's desire for similar freedoms as he or she goes about life in the modern world. Because shrine offices are generally distanced from the ritual center and priests are engaged in clerical work for most of the day in those offices, their authoritative presence as ritual specialists is largely absent from the shrine grounds and thus does not interfere with the highly subjective ways in which people choose to interact with the site. In a highly structured and normative society such as Japan, this freedom of choice coupled with a lovely and peaceful setting provide a breath of fresh air, especially nourishing to the urbanized social body.

TOWARD AN IDEOLOGY
OF SACRED PLACE

In the sensuous rush of visual, audible, and tactile stimuli transmitted during a visit to a shrine or through one of its rituals, often overlooked is the medium that permits their expression: the nature of the place itself. The previous chapter described the various activities enabled through the medium of a shrine in contemporary Japan. This chapter takes a closer look at the historical momentum, cultural proclivities, and geographic contours that make the place what it is for those who interact with it. Many priests and Japanese Shinto scholars are fond of saying that shrines are situated where they are because of some innate Japanese aesthetic about the beauty or sacredness of nature. Features like ancient trees, distinctive rocks, waterfalls, scenic overlooks, or an association with some ephemeral manifestation of *kami* (a white deer reported at the edge of a forest, for example) are indeed all part of legitimating processes for the qualifications of a sacred place. However, one must also consider a site's strategic significance: was it founded near a trade route? does it control water rights to agricultural areas? is it on the side of a mountain so that more fertile land below can remain free for cultivation? Again to take Durkheim's notion of the sacred and profane as a point of departure, there is nothing that is inherently sacred or profane in itself; yet most tribal societies, the early Japanese included, had concepts and social correspondences concerning what did and did not qualify for inclusion.

Sakurai Katsunoshin, a noted Shinto scholar, says to think of Shinto as worshiping nature or as reverencing natural objects because of some innate quality of sacredness is a profound mistake. Instead, it was the propensity of *kami* to take up temporary residence within natural objects that must be recognized as fundamental in the development of attitudes toward the natural world. Thus, the second character of the word for shrine, *jinja,* does not refer to an organization (as in *kaisha*) but to a forest (*mori;* Ono et al. 1974:1294). The vegetation may be native to the place, or it may have developed in a particular area that came to be considered sacred because of the periodic presence of *kami* (Sakurai et al. 1990:62). Believing the *kami* could appear at any time as well as when summoned during rituals, people felt compelled to leave that place alone.

The tendency to assign a permanent relationship between a place and *kami* saturates much of the literature written by non-Japanese, where one reads frequently that Shinto shrines are "a place where divinity has manifested itself and made its dwelling" (Grapard 1982:197). From the perspective of priests, however, prolonged habitation in this world by a *kami* would threaten its vitality with a gradual depletion of energy—one of the symptoms of *kegare,* or "defiling pollution." For the community as well, the prolonged presence of *kami* would create other problems, not the least of which would be having to manage, entertain, propitiate, and control a powerful and inherently unstable other. So, to be renewed and recharged with the life-enhancing energies so crucial to human existence (and prevent any depletion or inversion of this energy), the *kami* must arrive and depart, aided by priestly or ritual expertise in summoning them to specific places at specific times.[1]

In early Shinto, after divination, geomancy, and political considerations designated an area as suitably sacred, it was usually covered with pebbles *(tamajari),* surrounded by stones *(saniwa),* and marked off by a rope *(shimenawa)* linking four corner pillars. Here, participants' attention could be directed to see that the water they purify their hands and mouths with was not the same water that lay fetid in their rice paddies, nor were the words spoken, the actions performed, the food presented, or any other observance the same as what might have occurred outside the sacred place. For the participants of a ritual held in this place, the world "pivots" (Van Gennep 1965 [1908]:16), so that the ordinary becomes infused with power and significance. All that is required for this transformation to begin is a place that a majority of members in a society, from the head priest down to the lowliest farmer, have recognized as set apart and that is marked accordingly with objects or emblems denoting sacredness.

This sacred area served as a kind of landing place for the descending numina, who were thought to alight upon a single tree *(himorogi)* or other elevated object at the far end of the enclosure. At first there seems to have been neither altar nor image to worship, only a cleared-out place to accommodate the presence of the *kami.* The double nature of the place— at once local and physical (with rocks, trees, perhaps a stream nearby) while at the same time linked to a distant and vast cosmic geography from which the *kami* issue forth—provides participants with a stage from which they can address the concerns that have prompted the ritual event. (Chapter 7 will describe how the priests continue to employ this cosmology for one of Kamigamo Shrine's principal ritual events, the *miare-sai.*) Though the archetypal pebble and rock clearing was eventually formalized into more permanent structures that are now called *jinja, taisha,* or *miya* (for which the English word "shrine" is currently thought to be a misnomer by some Kokugakuin University scholars), it is still maintained at many sites, remaining central to contemporary notions of sacred space and the ritual practices that occur both within and outside the main shrine buildings.

THE MOUNTAIN COMES TO US

There are few relationships more fundamental than those of human beings to their bodies and of their bodies to place. Human spatiality (the body) and the space of the environment (the land) are always integral parts of the stories people tell of their experience in the world (Ross-Bryant 1990:335). For most tribal peoples, the early Japanese included, maintaining a relationship with unseen yet tangible presences was as essential for life as was potable water or food sources, largely because physical sustenance was causally linked to what is too easily termed "supernatural" sources. Early human activities and habitations as well as the uncharted terrain of mysterious inner worlds and dreamtime were often fashioned to acknowledge, appropriate, or in some cases protect against the fluctuating energy of place through a rich variety of ritual practices and techniques.

What is now called Shinto has roots in this tradition of paying particular attention to the "vitalism" of a place (Brown 1993). Because the natural world was thought capable of embodying *kami,* those features dominant in or integral to a landscape held special significance for human societies organized around hunting, fishing, and rice agriculture. Natural landmarks were seen as representing (or as having the potential for) infusions or manifestations of extra-ordinary power. With power thus deeply implicated in this most fundamental of social relationships—people living in a geography (Thomas 1993 : 28)—it should not be surprising that stone rings from the late Jōmon period (dated to around 2400 B.C.E.) demonstrate a strategic orientation to the intersection of earth and unseen forces, both of which were deemed receptive to ritual intervention (Kidder 1993 : 76).

Partially because of the practice and promotion of land-calming rituals, community and territorially inclusive festivals that enhance solidarity and identification with place, and rituals synchronized with those in the imperial household (and these in turn with the cycle of rice production), many priests in contemporary Shinto posit a direct correlation between the institution today and its ancient predecessors. For instance, a visitor or participant will frequently be told as a matter of fact that a particular ritual is a thousand years old (or older). While nurturing a sense of continuity is important for the identity of contemporary Shinto, as I discussed in the Introduction, this guise tends to obscure important influences and innovations on liturgy and "Japanese" conceptions of the cosmos. Taoism (fifth and possibly fourth century), Buddhism and Confucianism (sixth century), and probably later elements of Christianity (seventeenth century) as well have all provided symbols, practices, organizational structures, and other contributions (Shimode 1980).

Thus, when looking at a contemporary shrine's buildings, history, or treasures, appearances are frequently deceptive. Complaining that, "language and images have become enigmas, problems to be explained, prison houses which lock understanding away from the world," art historian W. J. T. Mitchell could hardly imagine how appropriate his words are for those of us trying to understand the "opaque, distorting, and sometimes arbitrary mechanisms of representations" (1986 : 2) that shrine Shinto so elegantly employs in its various representations and practices.

The shrines seen today have endured not so much because they were deemed and maintained as sacred by generations of Japanese but because they managed to survive two major shifts in twentieth-century political power: first the Meiji government's radical shrine merger program from 1906 to 1915 (Fridell 1973; Sakurai 1992) and second the postwar Shinto directive of 1945 (Creemers 1968), which, among other sweeping changes, reapportioned shrine landholdings. A contemporary shrine's buildings, history, or well-guarded treasures may be prominent in its brochures or in how its public reputation as a religious institution is perpetuated. But preceding and underlying those elegant surfaces are more fundamental orientations regarding a relationship to place that is pragmatic (in the sense of managing a primary resource) but also philosophical and political. These orientations not only constitute one of the dominant characteristics of contemporary shrine identity but also foster a relationship to land and territory that provides ritual practices capable of accommodating and in some instances promoting the political agendas of a variety of sponsoring organizations or individuals. I am thinking primarily about the *jichinsai,* or land-calming rituals, which extend throughout Japanese society from elite corporate headquarters to humble family dwellings. Since I have described these practices as well as their political associations in detail (Nelson 1994, 1996b; see also O'Brien 1996), I will instead try to provide a sense of the geographical, political, and cultural locale of Kamigamo Shrine and how these combine to provide an ideology that sacralizes, authorizes, and legitimates particular alignments of meaning and power.

Any location, whether deemed sacred or not, can be thought of as a deeply layered text to be decoded at each level or (to use Lévi-Strauss' geological metaphor) as composed of underlying layers (structures, strata, and encrusted meanings) some of which are immediately accessible to the eye while others require excavation. In other words, place involves an appropriation and transformation of space and time into culturally bounded dimensions, all of which richly intertwine social, ecological, and, depending on the people's perspective vis-à-vis the cosmos, transhuman relationships and influences. Whether concerned with local sites or those of a global nature, the social ontology of a particular place has a scale all its own and is not self-evident in the same way as the appearance of its physical features (Hastrup 1996 : 66).

In trying to assess factors influencing the placement of Kamigamo Shrine, location is much more than an ecological environment with which generations of human social arrangements have interacted (J. Smith 1987 : 46). Following Alan Baker's lead (1992 : 2), place is situated and constituted by culturally specific ideologies. The historical record becomes important less for the exact dates it provides than for its serviceability in forging explicit connections between particular places and a sense of regional or national consciousness and community. For example, after effort and political will has negotiated and constituted a symbolic correspondence between a place and its sociocultural referents, the mere mention of its name (Ayodhya, Ise, Runnymede, Valley Forge) evokes values, emotions, or concepts promoted by certain groups or even the state. Useful in helping to constitute local or regional identities, places can also be used to enhance an association with the "surplus of legitimacy" usually afforded the nation (K. Thompson 1986:60).[2]

Landscapes and places rarely "speak" to us of their own accord. People interact with places through the shaping and mediating influences of cultural forms: local stories and limited personal experiences, public land-use architects, accounts from social historians, or images conveyed through the media. In these ways, the understanding of land and place is ideological because it "connects to a quest for order, to an assertion of authority, and to a project of totalisation" (Shils in Baker 1992:4). One's understanding of and relation to any ordering of reality "necessarily establishes silences that suppress generalizable interests that run counter to the particular interests an ideology serves" (Ooms 1985:294). The stone visages of four presidents at Mount Rushmore continue to stir feelings of pride and patriotism in a majority of Americans visiting the site, but this is possible only because the shameful story of the possession of this land through broken treaties and state-sponsored genocide of native peoples has been effectively silenced.[3]

As mentioned in the opening chapter of this book, positioning ideology within any understanding of historical or contemporary Shinto illuminates those social and political dimensions easily obscured by the rituals and ritualists themselves. The banner I am waving here (to mark a position and not necessarily to draw hostile fire) is emblazoned with the assertion by Jonathan Smith that the ways in which places considered sacred speak to human beings are political first (in a broad sense that invokes intentionality) and cosmological second (1987:17). This is not to deny other possibilities in the ways human beings perceive place. There may be very real and influential telluric forces (generated by magnetic fields, water courses, or tectonic shifts) or unseen dimensions of energy that, like breakers on a shore, lap at human minds as yet unable to perceive their presence consistently or benefit from their positive effects.

As important as ideology is, one must guard nonetheless against seeing religious sites and practices as determined through their operations.

Instead, the patterns these institutions embody are like independent variables extending through time. A particular agenda or idea may employ expressive strategies at the outset that, after mediation by historical circumstances and a succession of individual actors, appear very different several centuries later. For example, Kamigamo Shrine has an abundance of symbols and icons related to sexual reproduction and fertility "which symbolize an achieved harmony between human life and the hidden order of creation" (Cosgrove 1988 : 265). But these are no longer part of the shrine's carefully managed public image. Cultural artifacts—whether religious institutions, their rituals or surrounding landscape, or even those social processes through which cultural values gain expression—should be seen as communal and ecological assets, available to a wide range of interpretive possibilities regarding their use. While they may appear as "end products of a series of decisions and intentions," they are instead "temporary closures" in a long story awaiting new cultural twists of plot (Alles 1988 : 3).

One might look for comparison at the Athenian Parthenon or the Indian Kandariya temple, two renowned structures created at certain junctures of political will and historical circumstance. Their religiopolitical representations of mythic themes, deities, or historic correspondences were, like early Shinto shrines, not wholly determined by dominant ideologies and symbols. Instead, these structures and their encompassing landscapes represented different configurations within which local peoples and elites saw power operating (Alles 1988 : 31).[4] As political fortunes rose and fell, new manifestations, metaphors, and commemorations of political and social power gained currency and iconic representation. While the Parthenon sits contained on the stage of a massive rock outcrop above Athens, and the Kandariya is framed by a flat, level field, these structures call attention to and celebrate themselves.

However, the primary relationship of Kamigamo is to the cosmic, social, and spiritual dimensions of the landscape itself rather than the periodically renewed structures on it. Before the sixth-century state's agenda of "Shintoization," most local rituals involved no permanent shrine architecture; they were centered on little more than temporary ritual sites surrounded by natural groves of trees (kamutsumori) or stone borders (iwasaka) (Sonoda 1987 : 19) . Place was primary, buildings and other human innovations supplemental; together they were considered the arenas within which divine power operated and earthly religiopolitical power had to respond. To put it another way, "sacred geography became a kind of political geography, since specific deities worshiped in shrines were considered to own and protect discrete geographical areas" (Grapard 1994 : 381).

These concerns will remain central to the following discussion of contexts surrounding the founding and institutionalization of Kamigamo Shrine. But in order to frame and inform that discussion, I must first skate lightly over theoretical and historical ice of varying thickness concerning the spiritual geography of place.

JAPANESE SPIRITUAL GEOGRAPHY

When thinking about the development of Japanese cultural and social institutions that have influenced religiously inspired versions of land and its relation to the cosmos, it is crucial to remember the headwaters of these traditions within Chinese civilization. By the seventh century C.E., at a time when the fledgling Yamato imperial state in Japan was struggling with immigrant clans and the ascendancy of Buddhism, China had already experienced more than two thousand years of urban life (Wheatley and See 1978 : 115). A sophisticated cosmology (now conveniently called "Taoism") had developed out of the syncretist philosophy of the Han school of naturalists and diviners. It was believed that the success of any human endeavor depended on the degree to which it was in tune with the *ch'i (ki)* of the physical universe, an energy flowing through the heavens, earth, and the bodies of human beings (Feuchtwang 1974 : 103).

A philosopher of the early Han period, Tung Chung-shu (179–104 B.C.E.), noted that human beings are not only located between heaven and earth, but are in correspondence with the natural order. To borrow a simile from Gary Seaman, this interrelation resembles the strings of a piano vibrating in sympathetic harmony when they are struck (Seaman 1986 : 1). In one version, the human being was seen by learned elites as a microcosm whose flesh and bones corresponded to the texture of the earth, whose ears and eyes were the sun and the moon, whose five internal organs were similar to the five elements, and whose four limbs were the four seasons (Yoshida, cited in Seaman 1986). In another study of Taoist correspondences, Kristofer Schipper (1982) details the complexities of the human body as the image of a vast country: a chain of mountains runs through one's head, the nose is a valley, saliva is associated with interior waterways that wind through an immense interior landscape in which can be found constellations, the kidneys as sun and moon, and a Cinnabar Field, source of a human's "vital spirit." With these and other correspondences espoused by scholars and priests, traditional Confucian ways of looking at society and the world were supplemented and expanded by the systematization of Taoist teachings in the court, especially after the Yellow Turban rebellion in 184 C.E. usurped the Confucian court elite with one more sympathetic to Taoism.

It is difficult to pinpoint when the practice of geomancy that is today popularly known as *feng-shui* developed into a self-defining metaphysical system, but its influence is evident in the layout of ancient cities such as Lo-yang and Ch'ang-an in Han China, Buyō in Korea, as well as Heijōkyō (Nara) and Heiankyō (Kyoto).[5] Although many accounts posit a cause-effect relationship between *feng-shui* and the construction of these cities, Jeffrey Meyer cautions that the geometric spaces of these cities, with their grids and straight streets, conflict with early *feng-shui* principles (1978). Rather than situating entire cities, the *feng-shui* of the time was designed to determine the strategic placement of graves, houses, and smaller structures. Since a city covers many square miles, the flow of positive and negative influences forms a complex field so vast there would be no way for a geomancer to deal with it as a whole. Meyer thinks of these cities as "existential spaces" rather than geometric ones (p. 142), spaces designed as stages on which diviners and other religious specialists could enact a religious "language" of *feng-shui* and other practices "to deal with the reality of personal and communal fortunes, and to harmonize with the cosmic and chthonic powers of heaven and earth" (p. 152).

Thus, at the center of early Chinese imperial cities could be found the state altar to the god of soil, open to the elements and accessible to the influences of heaven and earth (Wheatley and See 1978:117). Despite this openness, however, the boundedness of these altars symbolized human-constructed as well as transcendental orders. The epitome of these orders was the city itself as a center for meaning and stability, fortified by massive walls against the chaotic forces of terrestrial and supernatural demons (Tuan 1977:133).

In determining an auspicious location, notions of astrology, yin-yang correspondences, and five-phase philosophy were imposed on the prominent features of a landscape: those that could be traced as lines (mountain ridges, alluvial formations, watercourses) and those with definite shapes such as mountains, boulders, ponds, and pools. A *feng-shui* practitioner then selected from this array of correspondences and symbolic relationships those best suited to the immediate sociopolitical situation. Generally speaking, a site was thought to be auspicious when mountains encircled it to the right and the left, when its principal orientation faced south, when waterways flowed to the south or east (never north), when the land drained to the south, and when spiritual protection (either by talisman or institution) defended both the northern and southern approaches.

When principles of yin-yang philosophy (called *onmyōdō* or *onmyō* in Japanese) found their way to early Yamato elites via cultural exchanges and immigration from the continent, the ancestors of the Yoshida and Shirakawa priestly guilds helped establish them as an institution, what would later be called the Onmyōryō in the period of the Taihō Code (645 C.E.). Little is known about the degree to which *onmyō* was accepted or rejected by commoners, but Felicia Bock (1985) believes that influential Chinese texts had been introduced to the court as early as the beginning of the fifth century. Like so many other continental cultural imports, the *onmyō* system was merged into the amalgamated cosmos of Japanese-style *kami,* Confucian, Taoist, and Buddhist practices, eventually complementing rather than conflicting with them.

Taoist practices in particular, such as observation of the heavens and of signs and portents, timekeeping, and *feng-shui* practices were experimented with and then adopted by degrees into official court ritual practices. For example, not only were the twenty-four compass-point directions important in determining the most auspicious location for siting a palace, so were the five elements (water, fire, wood, metal, and earth), their corresponding planets (particularly Mars, Venus, and Mercury), mythic, domestic, and wild animals, natural phenomena (equinoxes, growing cycles, and local flora and fauna), and the patterns of human domestic and social behavior. In China and later in Korea, the *feng-shui* specialist was not attached to institutions of worship, nor could he ever be proved wrong since interference from human factors or by heaven itself could account for his failures (Feuchtwang 1974:176). In Japan, however, these diviners were local practitioners as well as government officials of exalted rank, such as the chancellor of the Council of State, whose unenviable task was to harmonize governmental policy with Chinese yin and yang principles (Brown 1993:233).[6]

The layout of early Japanese capitals showed an awareness of two sets of orientations, encompassing the surrounding physical and social land-

scapes. The first awareness reflected but was not determined by cosmological and philosophical influences of early *feng-shui*-style alignments,
while the second indicated a need to create monuments to imperial authority and to provide for trade and defense. Although the capitals at
Naniwa (645) and Omi (667) had buildings of Chinese design, Fujiwara
(694) was the first full-scale Chinese-style capital, modeled after Lo-yang
in the Chinese kingdom of Wei. The palace faced south and was protected
by Kagu mountain to the east, Miminashi-yama to the north, and Unebi-
yama to the west. When the capital was moved to Heijōkyō (Nara) some
fourteen years later in 708, three auspicious mountains were again important for positioning the palace, although strategic considerations (such
as transportation and river travel) and maintaining an alignment with the
layout of Fujiwara were also important factors (see Brown 1993:243).

When trying to visualize or imagine the "new" capital, Heiankyō, it is
important to remember that the original site of Kyoto's imperial palace
was approximately two kilometers west of the current imperial palace
(Gosho) (see frontispiece map of Kyoto). With today's Senbon-dōri serving as the axis on which the city was oriented after its move from
Nagaoka, a number of significant geomantic and yin-yang principles are
in operation.

First, the Kyoto basin is ideal as a general site because it is open to the
auspicious south but surrounded by mountains to the north, east, and
west. The Chinese identified yang and yin with the eastern and western
quarters of the sky, associating a blue-green dragon of spring with the east
and a white tiger of autumn with the west. In the Kyoto basin, the dragon
hills can be thought to correspond to the Mount Hiei ridge to the east,
with its boldly rising yang elevations in the north, and the tiger to the
more gentle ridges of Arashi-yama in the west.[7] According to *feng-shui*
preferences, the yang mountains of the dragon and the yin of the western
tiger should meet in mutual embrace to the north, a topographic correspondence to the spread legs of a woman, just as a literary mention of "wind
and water" (*feng-shui*) refers to sexual lovemaking (Yoon 1983:222). The
mating of these mythical beasts was thought to bestow fecundity and
prosperity to all dwelling below the site of their union. Heiankyō's surrounding topography was virtually made to order for adhering to the
Chinese model.

The original imperial palace was further protected to the immediate
north by the small but strategic Funaoka-yama (which today bears a

shrine to Oda Nobunaga on its top). Further north, the higher mountain ridge of Daimonji-yama and Fune-yama extend far enough to the east to establish another viable defense against the inauspicious north, which was augmented to the northeast by the powerful Kamo Shrine. Later, after Saichō founded Enryaku-ji atop Mount Hiei in the ninth century, a more distant line of defense was thus established to protect both the palace and the city from the northeast. The concern concentrated on this direction, by both Chinese and Japanese imperial courts, concerns its yin nature associated with cold, winter, and the unknown. More important, a succession of threats and invasions from tribal nomads to the northeast were a constant source of anxiety to a long succession of Chinese dynastic courts. Likewise, the early Yamato and Fujiwara rulers' expansionary movements into central and northern Honshu were resisted and harassed by the Emishi, a feared tribe of people that are today thought to be of Ainu origin (see Sansom 1958 : 19, 90). Although the southern *urakimon,* or "back demon gate," was thought less dangerous than the northern gate, approximately four kilometers directly south from the old palace's central gate on Senbon-dōri, one finds the Shingon temple of Tōji, an institution established in the ninth century by Kūkai, a powerful priest who combined religious doctrine and magical practices, and then made them serviceable to the state.[8]

By the late twelfth century and the advent of the Kamakura regime far to the north, the cultural value once given to the protective defenses of a *feng-shui*-style system had been transformed by calamity and political change. According to Abe Takeshi's account, the capital was in decline, with robberies carried out in broad daylight by wandering thugs and the mansions of the aristocracy plundered and torched (1983 : 122). At the imperial palace itself, two of the central government halls had burned to the ground: the Burakuden in 1063 and the Daigokuden, from which the emperor provisionally governed the country, in 1177. The emperor's quarters suffered outbreaks of fire sixteen times between 960 and 1227, with restoration no longer attempted after the latter date owing to the ever-strengthening power of the Kamakura shogunate following the 1221 Jōkyū rebellion. It was not until after the devastation of the Onin wars in the sixteenth century that reconstruction commenced, thanks to Oda Nobunaga and later Toyotomi Hideyoshi, who began to restore the imperial capital. The imperial palace was moved to its present site by the Tokugawa in the eighteenth century.

Murakami writes convincingly that after the revolution in 1868, which ended centuries of feudal rule, the new Meiji government saw this ancient topomantic tradition as another means to help legitimate its authenticity and further centralize its power (1970:159). In an effort to systematize widely practiced land divination and land-calming rites, it wrested sect-specific rituals away from Buddhist (Shingon, Jōdō, Shinshū, Nichiren) and Shinto (Yoshida, Shirakawa) organizations alike. The Meiji social architects were following the lead of Aizawa Yasushi, who (in 1824) proposed in somewhat Machiavellian terms that the best way for the government to clarify the national essence *(kokutai)* to the people (and make them respectfully submit without asking why) was to devise government-sponsored religious rituals that played upon their awe of the *kami*. The five categories he advocated included (1) The emperor worshiping the *kami* of heaven and earth, (2) honoring the sun deity Amaterasu by worshiping one's own ancestors, (3) worshiping the *kami* of the Yamato plain in order to pacify the earth, (4) worshiping the rice *kami* called Ukemochi to show concern for the agricultural foundation the growing of rice provides, and (5) worshiping the *kami* of nature and all creation (Wakabayashi 1986:264, 267). Though nearly half a century passed until Aizawa's suggestions were implemented in government policy, the "new" land-calming rituals of the late 1800s were meant to serve and unify all constituencies within the context of a revitalized body politic centered on the emperor.

CONTEXTUALIZING KAMIGAMO'S FOUNDING

In a pattern repeated in virtually every society on earth, the moment a new regime establishes political ascendancy, out come a dazzling parade of strategically appropriate symbols, decrees, and legitimizing rituals to bolster and extend the new leaders' power. What better way for a "fundamentally arbitrary structure" (McMullin 1989:16) to control and attempt domination than to couch its workings in a sanctified dialectic of historical traditions, religious practices, and institutional supports? The Taika reforms of 645 were meant to impose "new" Chinese models of bureaucracy and centralized state control on the people and land of Japan in ways different and more effective than those attempted earlier in 603 (a twelve-court-rank system) and in Shōtoku Taishi's 604 seventeen-article "constitution" (Brown and Torao 1987:34). Thus, in order to understand the placement of Kamo Shrine and why it was moved from the base of

Kōyama mountain (some two kilometers north of its present location), it is informative to look at the historical events of the period rather than to postulate a rationale dominated by *feng-shui*.

A selective reading of major occurrences leading up to the official 678 founding date of the shrine yields this list (Brown and Torao 1987; Yoshinari 1989; Brown 1993):

645 Soga Iruka assassinated by Naka no Ōe and Kamatari. Capital moved to Naniwa (now Osaka). Imperial authority reinforced with Buddhist rites.

646 Imperial decree outlines Taika reforms.

656 Capital moved to Asuka Okamoto.

658, 660 Military campaigns waged against northern tribal people (Emishi, Mishihase).

661, 663 Two expeditions sent to assist the Korean kingdom of Paekche against Silla and T'ang forces. Paekche forces fall at Hakusukino-e.

664 Establishment of twenty-six court ranks; coastal defenses bolstered against fears of a T'ang invasion.

667 Capital moved to Ōmi (now Ōtsu) for defense purposes.

668 Defeat of Koguryō by T'ang and Silla forces.

670 Household registration system begun in response to fictive genealogies (see Chapter 4).

671 Ōmi civil code, followed by succession wars (*jinshū no ran*, 672) between sons of Emperor Tenchi.

673 Tenmu becomes emperor; capital moved to Asuka Kiyomihara.

674 First mention of a Kamo shrine.

675 Imperial order for abolition of *be* system; imperial officials in provinces permitted to wear weapons.

678 Silla envoys come to Yamato; Kamo Shrine officially founded as principal religious site of Yamashiro-no-kuni (north Kyoto basin).

Although the year 678 C.E. is recognized by the shrine as the date of its official founding (based on the no longer extant sources *Honchō getsurei, Nenjū gyōji hishō* and *Ukan shiki,* which mention its establishment as the shrine of Yamashiro-no-kuni), it seems likely the shrine was already in its present location in 674. The local historical account of the *Atago-gun sonshi* notes the construction of a Kamo shrine building in 674, but Fujiki points out that it is unclear whether the shrine was then being rebuilt or built for the first time (1992:22).

It is the location that gives the first clues to solving this puzzle. In its former location at the foot of Kōyama, the shrine was close to the source of its divine power (as well as to the forest resources that initially provided the economic base of the Kamo people and those they assimilated), but, primarily for reasons of defense, it was set back from the wide open expanse of the Kyoto basin. After Tenmu gained power and moved the capital back to Asuka in 672, the Kamo clan officials *(agatanushi),* by prior treaty or by expansionist design, increased their territory both northward in the direction of the former court at Ōmi and southward to the Kyoto floodplain. One can only speculate on the reasons for this shift, and I would like to propose three.

First, by relocating the shrine two kilometers to the south, it came to command a sweeping view of the entire basin and increased its influence over the upper Takano River watershed to the east and the trade route to Wakasa Bay, the Wakasa-kaidō. After the fall of Paekche and Koguryō, the country was swept with fears of a foreign invasion and had fortified Tsushima, Iki, the northern Kyushu coast, and other potential points of attack. While Kamo Shrine was not instrumental to the capital's defense (as the southern Iwashimizu Hachimangū would be later), its relocation provided both an observational vantage point and a potential staging ground for troop movements from the north if necessary. Inoue and Brown (1993) note that Tenmu's strengthening of the military base for his new regime included improving highways, such as the Wakasa-kaidō, for greater troop movement. However, they also highlight the fact that local clan power and clan interests played a decisive role in shaping these plans.

A second motivation behind this move may be attributed to continental religious influences brought to the area by refugees from the Paekche and Koguryō diasporas on the Korean peninsula (in 660 and 668 respectively). Inoue and Brown note accounts in the *Nihon shoki* indicating an influx to northern Kyoto of four hundred immigrants in the year 665, followed by two thousand the following year from Paekche and later seven hundred more, including two former ministers of state (1993:210). This last group was specifically relegated to the Kamo district of Ōmi province. Even allowing for exaggerated numbers, it is likely that these immigrants were influential in local sociopolitical affairs because of their superior skills and learning. Since the *Nihon shoki* notes that some of them were devotees of *onmyō* philosophy, it should come as no surprise that the Kamo Shrine came to specialize in *onmyōdō* or yin-yang-style rituals. Perhaps because of the influence of Buddhism and the accessibility of temples within a community, it had become advantageous to construct a proximate spatial relationship between shrine and community rather than between shrine and sacred mountain. Similar moves were enacted in the same period at Miwa, Isonokami, and Kasuga shrines, to name but a few.

As a third possibility, whether the 674 expansion of Kamo territory and the relocation of the shrine was authorized by the court or not, I would argue that the court's recognition in 678 of Kamo as the principal shrine of Yamashiro-no-kuni was an attempt first to accommodate and later to appropriate a powerful clan and their deity into the imperial pantheon at a time when state centralization, fortification, and (thanks to the skills of the new immigrants) urbanization were moving at an accelerated pace.

As I will show in more detail in the next chapter, this general approach proved highly successful for several centuries in solidifying Yamato hegemony over wide regions—a lesson not lost on the leaders of the Meiji revolution more than a millennium later. Although the control of local resources, strategic military placement, and the need to serve a growing clan-affiliated population figured prominently in the relocation of Kamigamo, the *feng-shui* and *onmyō* dimensions of the shrine's placement and layout, and the principal iconographic symbols still in use today also provide clues to the shrine's early cosmological and political orientations.

KAMIGAMO SHRINE: ORIENTATIONS AND PLACEMENTS

The entrance to Kamigamo Shrine displays both compliance with and resistance to the totalizing processes of imperial power. The main walkway (*sandō*), running between the grassy fields from the first to the second torii, is on a straight compass line (as are the torii themselves) with the original imperial palace (see Appendix 1 for a map of the shrine compound). Although the construction creating this alignment is difficult to date historically, it can be thought of as a very public acknowledgment of a period of shrine-court cooperation. As tutelary shrine of the city and protector against *kimon* influences from the northeast, Kamigamo enjoyed for many centuries a close and profitable relationship with the court, to be detailed in the following chapter. However, once inside the second torii, a subtle shift begins northward toward the center of Kamo power, the sacred mountain of Kōyama. The first hint of this imperial displacement is in the *tatesuna,* or standing sand cones, symbols that evoke important and fundamental relationships that precede as well as take precedence over those with the courtly rulers. The worshiper's path to the inner sanctuary then zigs and zags, first over one bridge and then over another, characterizing one of the *kami*'s dominant powers, the lightning bolt. But there is also a *feng-shui* influence that avoids straight lines whereby evil influences can penetrate.

Another resource for asserting Kamo hegemony is found in the second half of the "wind and water" combination that is *feng-shui.* As a deity of thunder, storms, and lightning, Wake Ikazuchi was ritually petitioned to intervene on behalf of his clan and influence the flow of the river.[9] Similar practices had been under way in the floodplains of China for a very long time, with the earliest treatise on the subject of rainmaking (the *Ch'un-ch'iu fan-lu*) dating to 160 B.C.E. According to Cohen (1978; see also Bownas 1963), there was a five-stage progression by which Chinese leaders tried to communicate with the rainmaking deities. First came either prayers, petitions, or requests, followed by shamans performing a rain dance. Ritual exposure of these individuals came next, apparently to activate the deity's sympathy for a naked body exposed to the burning sun. The fourth stage was more aggressive, in which a shaman or magistrate prepared to leap into a burning pyre. The last and most desperate attempts to evoke rain involved violence against the deity's shrine, such as exposing the deity's image directly to the sun or even destroying the shrine itself. Beyond these, sympathetic magic also played a role in China as well as Japan, as in the whipping of yin-yang stones or defiling the image of a deity (or a sacred place) with dirt (or manure) so the deity would send rain to cleanse it.

Further upstream, from the mid–Heian period onward, Kamigamo came to control the ancient Kibune Shrine as a kind of base camp leading into the higher spiritual elevations and recesses of deity-dwelling watersheds (Shirayama 1971). Therefore, the last finger of high ground—overlooking the point at which the Kamo River enters the floodplain—was positioned strategically as a visible and auspicious location to remind the lower-valley dwellers (including the court) of the authority of Kamo

Shrine (with its access to a powerful deity). In the early years of the Heiankyō court, messengers and representatives visited often with good-will offerings they hoped would promote bonds of reciprocity and mu-tual assistance. Even with this precaution and the levee-building activities that extend as far back as the eighth century (Abe 1983), the neighbor-hoods west of Kamigamo and north of today's Kitayama-dōri were noto-riously prone to seasonal flooding.

The pragmatic nature of the relationship between water and Shinto ritual is most evident in its effect on rice agriculture. Ishino writes that rice-growing communities observed ritual techniques aimed at control-ling both water supply and volume, and used rivers for purifications in the third century C.E. While these were predominantly local customs, they may have been influenced by relations with the Taoist Wei court be-ginning in 239. For example, shallow pits discovered beside the Miyamae River near the ancient city of Makimuku (third to fourth century C.E.) in-dicate offerings similar to those of first-harvest festivals in China. Groups in both China and Japan worshiped river deities, but Ishino delineates these forms of worship from riverside burial practices and from Japanese purificatory rites aimed at warding off illness and calamity. In the lat-ter practices, objects were first floated downstream in rivers, with fifth-century aqueduct systems serving as later innovations bringing in pure water to be sacralized then used for exorcizing defilements (Ishino 1992 : 197). Likewise, rituals for fields involved placing offerings in clay vessels at water spouts or irrigation channels and then entrusting them to the downstream current. At the Hieda River, now buried on the south side of the Heijō capital, more than one hundred items of pottery, horse-shaped clay figures, wooden blades, miniature ovens, and *hitogata* (small human effigies of wood) serving this purpose have been excavated (p. 205).

Nor should the myth of Izanagi and Izanami be neglected when assess-ing the cultural significance of water, since a purification in the Tsukushi River was instrumental in restoring Izanagi's creative powers after his near-disastrous encounter with Izanami in the netherworld. Matsumae (1993) sees the origin of this myth stretching from Japan to Southeast Asia to Polynesia, recounted for centuries by peasants and, more signifi-cant, fishermen. It was not until the late sixth and early seventh centuries, however, that water lustrations became politically relevant for Yamato state legitimation. Grapard notes that, beginning with the *Kojiki* account, purification rituals come to encode and encompass the human body, but it is a male body (1991 : 9). Izanagi's washing enables a number of *kami* to spring forth, including Magatsuhi, *kami* of misfortune, and Naobi-no-kami, deity of purity born from the water (Matsumae 1993 : 5). The most important of all the *kami* is Amaterasu, but all were central to the state cult of classical Japan and subsequent regimes as important cultural symbols (Grapard 1991 : 8).

The location of the Kamo Shrine within a spiritually and politically charged landscape in the seventh century corresponds to several of the practices above. The shrine's founding myth, for instance, begins with a princess purifying herself at one of the shrine's streams, in which a magic arrow floats mysteriously by. She retrieves it and the metamorphoses begin. Although the last time an arrow appeared in the shrine's streams was during a 1987 NHK television reenactment of this myth, there are twelve stone stairways providing streamside access for purifications of every sort ranging from simple hand cleansing to total body immersion. As part of the yearly ritual cycle, the shrine continues to conduct such rituals as the ancient rice planting festival *(otaue-sai)* in which consecrated seedlings are tossed into the Nara stream and carried downstream to waiting farmers for planting.

As protective and purificatory shields, shrines were often sited at the confluence of two rivers to benefit from the protective quality of water and to enable the ritual control of downstream flooding. Shrines built according to this orientation are scattered throughout Japan—at Shimogamo Shrine, Kumano Hongū (Kumano), Ōkuni Jinja (Aichi), Iwashimizu Hachimangū, and others. Shrines at a river's entrance to a floodplain were commonly called *kawai jinja,* or "river meeting" shrines. Likewise at Kamigamo, though on a smaller scale, the inner sanctuary and its surrounding courtyards are nestled between the Mitarashi-gawa on the west and the smaller Omonoi-gawa to the east.

Water was thought of as a yin energy (cold, changing, passive, unpredictable) that could deflect or carry away impurities or the malevolent "secret arrows" of *feng-shui*-style misfortunes. However, stagnant or sluggish water near a site was deemed the antithesis of life-enhancing *ch'i* energy and was to be avoided at all costs (Skinner 1982 : 28). Washing one's hands and rinsing one's mouth are still integral parts of the preparations for ritual participation or worship at shrines today, but few realize that simply crossing over moving water is thought to have a similar effect.[10]

As a barrier to misfortunes and an aid to purification, the properties of water were and continue to be essential in Shinto cosmology. Floods did occur in the area, however, necessitating an architectural style and technology for the middle courtyard structures that harmonized with rather than obstructed the flow of water. Visitors are frequently struck by the airy lightness of the inner spaces of the Tsuchinoya, Hashidono, and Hosodono. In one sense, they are open-air stages, buildings without walls (or a floor, in the case of the Tsuchinoya), representing a type of architecture found at shrines throughout Japan, though rarely with as much elegance as these national treasures at Kamigamo. However, there is a utilitarian dimension to their positioning and architecture as well. Each building has hooked iron rods that can swing down from below the eaves of the roofs when threatened by flooding. If these rods are anchored to pitons buried just below the gravel of the courtyard, the pavilions can withstand the current's pressure against their pillars by allowing it to flow through their interiors. In the great flood shortly after the war—caused in part by a massive felling of trees and clearing of groundcover to make a golf course north of the shrine—these buildings (whose present incarnation dates to 1628) emerged with little damage, as their massive roofs, like peaked islands, hovered calmly above the waters.

The above example points to one of the synthesizing qualities of Kamigamo Shrine's architecture and its placement within the physical landscape. Like sacred architecture in many parts of the world, the shrine encompasses the metaphysical and physical worlds and shows they are not at odds (Khanna 1991:61). Natural watercourses are neither dammed nor diverted; trees on shrine precincts are thought to span earthly and heavenly spaces; even the walkways, bridges, and entrances resonate with symbolic significance concerning purification or the balancing of yin-yang energies. One of the distinctive characteristics of any place constructed by humans, according to Christian Norberg-Schulz, is found in its degree of openness to its surroundings (1980:58). Since the ability to bestow vitality or restore it where depleted is one of a shrine's defining characteristics, its architecture should both convey this property and empower the process to occur unimpeded. The structural boundaries of a shrine's physical layout and buildings may appear solid at first glance, but, as I will show in the next section, they often accentuate other dimensions that are hidden behind or within the forms themselves.[11]

Like sacred architecture in many parts of the world, Hindu temples, Hopi kivas, Catholic cathedrals, and Shinto shrines are physical manifestations of ideas, some elite and others popular, replete with iconic signs and values that give expression to the fundamental worldview of a social order (Khanna 1991:53). Shinto addresses both folk and elite concerns about channeling, restoring, and revitalizing energy to depleted physical and spiritual conditions. The deity of a shrine may be of either gender (see Mayer 1992), but yang predominates in the type of benefits sought after and promoted. The shrine's landscape and symbolism are made to comply generally with its functions. It is time now to locate this compliance within larger political and cultural contexts, where meaning is further shaped in accordance with and in deference to the dominant forces of a particular historical era.

A "NATURAL" GENERATIVE ICONOGRAPHY

Imagine for a moment a young priest, fresh from a four-year course in a training university and three months of internship, starting his first day on the job at Kamigamo Shrine. He is delighted with his position and status because this 1,400-year-old institution is ranked second only to the imperial shrines at Ise. Some months pass, and then one day, while cleaning the inner sanctuary with a fellow priest, he is asked what he thinks of the shrine's "hollyhock" style of architecture. Somewhat embarrassed by his ignorance, he begs to be instructed and thus learns the astonishing secret of his new workplace: from top to bottom, it is imbued with sexual iconography and symbols! Indeed, the entire sacred landscape as well as its architectural structures comprises an elaborate sexual metaphor reflecting a model of and for the world. "But don't worry," he is told by the older priest, who has seen the look of panic before, "you won't be embarrassed, nor will the shrine, as long as you don't tell anyone."

Early social groups in Japan shared with tribal peoples elsewhere concerns that directly affected the survival of the group: security, cyclical growth patterns, the fecundity of the natural world, and perhaps most important, the fertility of humans and animals. The archaeological record provides evidence of ritual artifacts associated with these themes, such as phallic stone and clay rods some thirty centimeters in length *(sekibō)* made roughly five thousand years ago, abstract clay figurines of the female body, and pottery utensils with phallic spouts (Matsumae 1993; Czaja 1974: 164). Artifacts found in mountains from the middle Jomon period (3500–2400 B.C.E.), also connected primarily with birth and regeneration (Kidder 1993: 70), not only symbolized a knowledge of human fertility but extended it to the sustenance people received from a systematically productive earth.

In the landscape, architecture, and iconography of Kamigamo Shrine

Hosodono pavilion of the imperial
priestess and *tatesuna* sand hillocks,
on the night of the shrine's most
secretive ritual, the *miare-sai*.

these themes are grounded in three principal sources from which life-
essences were thought to issue: mountains, human beings (women as life
givers and men as life sustainers), and the vegetative world. Venerated
throughout the long history of Shinto ritual practices—especially at the
level of village or folk Shinto—these sources are today emphasized in
varying degrees, ranging from overtly obvious aspects of the sacred landscape (mountains) to the covert fundamentals of social reproduction
(sexuality). In the latter case, which is at present knowingly consigned to
the background by the shrine's priests, an inherited tradition is deemed
embarrassing or at odds with a carefully constructed image the shrine's
priests want to convey to their constituencies. Although further research
is needed to reveal how this symbolism of Kamigamo Shrine's landscape
and iconography was employed historically, today the content of the
shrine's sexual iconography is rarely mentioned or written about in any
shape or form, nor are most visitors to the shrine even vaguely aware of
an all-encompassing sexual dimension to the tradition they so casually

participate in. Of all the various "guises" of contemporary Shinto, this one is the most cryptic yet its overtness is breathtaking.

For example, a visitor emerging from the open grassy fields and passing through the second torii at Kamigamo is struck by two beautifully symmetrical cones constructed of off-white sand, both about 120 centimeters high, standing in front of a graceful, open-air pavilion, the Hosodono. One could assume (as I have overheard on occasion from tour group guides) that they symbolize the "breasts of mother earth," but a nearby sign indicates nothing of the sort. It says instead that the *tatesuna* (standing sand cones) represent Kōyama, the sacred mountain of the Kamo clan, where the *kami* was worshiped before the present-day shrine was developed. While generally accurate, this too-brief explanation is only a small part of the larger picture. Here, then, are three priests explaining the two *tatesuna* cones that, like miniature pyramids, are pivotal points of reference for the landscape of the outer courtyard and key symbols representing the shrine in photos and brochures.

A: These cones represent the sacred mountain Kōyama but also signify the act of gathering sand on top of the mountain at the site where the *kami* are thought to descend *(himorogi)*. This act is performed to steady the bamboo branch that is put up into the sky for the *kami* to alight on. The purpose of the cones here is different from the four little cones within the inner sanctuary (Honden) area; those are to create a sacred place within which the chief priest delivers his invocational *(norito)* prayer.

B: These cones are placed here to symbolize the *himorogi* in the days when there were no shrine buildings. The sand is pure and thus can be used in front of a person's house or in one's garden. The sacred tree of this shrine is the pine, and so the pine needles [sticking out of the top of the *tatesuna*] symbolize this as well as the pine forest on Kōyama, a place where no one is allowed to go. These cones are also yang and yin, so you'll notice that on the left is the "male" *(on-matsu)* with two needles while on the right is the "female" *(me-matsu)* with three. Their merging *(gattai suru)* creates the power of life.

C: These cones symbolize not only the original sacred mountain, Kōyama, but also the generative power of yin and yang, male [left cone] and female [right], that Shinto regards as worthy of veneration. Another aspect of this special sand is in purifying an area, and visitors may purchase some to take home and use in their gardens or in other areas.

From the perspective of ancient Shinto (and its Chinese predecessor, Taoism) mountains have traditionally been like lightning rods for *kami* descending from Takamagahara, the High Plain of Heaven. To simplify a rather complex story (more fully addressed in Chapter 4), the Kamo clan of the sixth century C.E. acknowledged and petitioned their local deity *(ujigami)* through a mountain to increase and restore the vitality of their tribe, its individual members, and its food resources.[12] More animals to hunt or rice to eat meant additional food to support more people; likewise, more people meant greater political and military standing vis-à-vis other clans in the area, such as the Hata. In many ways, this ancient ritual orientation still holds for the cosmology of Kamigamo Shrine, since once a year the priests revisit the mountain to invite the deity to descend for the Aoi Festival (see Chapter 7, May 12).

So, although for public consumption the *tatesuna* portray a triad of humanity, nature, and *kami,* the fact that there are two cones is a subtle reminder that it is the sexual pairing between male and female, yang and yin (Japanese *yō* and *in*), that provides the fundamental engine for all social and political organizations. On closer examination, one sees that the "male" cone has two pine needles projecting from its apex while the "female" cone has three, corresponding to the respective sexual organs of each gender.[13] Social architects, whether in the fifth century or today, know quite well the long-range demographic, economic, and strategic implications of a low birth rate. One need only listen to the ongoing cry from contemporary Japanese politicians and media commentators, imploring women to have more than the average 1.5 children to understand the anxiety elites feel when sex among their constituents does not necessarily lead to the birth of future workers, taxpayers, or soldiers.

The second dimension of the shrine's sexually inscribed landscape regards the power of women in ancient Japan. In early agriculture, according to Ito, "woman, fertility, sexuality, and nudity were so many centers of sacred power, so many starting points for ceremonial drama" (cited in Czaja 1974:165). Perhaps because of this awesome power, women were granted ritual responsibilities that later translated into religiopolitical power *(matsurigoto).* Tanigawa mentions the Southeast Asia–influenced system of the Ryūkyūs (now Okinawa), where kings dealt with political matters and queens controlled ritual (1985:21). The *Kojiki* begins with the female deity Izanami giving birth to an assortment of elemental deities, but its late date (714 C.E.) should alert modern-day readers that earlier social orderings had already been influenced considerably by continental

Chinese patriarchal models, not to mention immigration from those so-cieties. Izanami soon dies after delivering fire to the world and descends to the nether land of Yomi, after which the narrative subordinates any further creative power by having Izanagi generate the rest of the deities.

Yamaguchi notes that during this period the emperor himself fulfilled a procreative role (1987:6, 8). He was expected to be sexually vigorous and even promiscuous, performing the ritual of cosmic marriage with his wife but also with the daughters of clan chieftains affiliated with the court. Perhaps it is not surprising then that a parallel to this cultural trend, whereby male power comes to subordinate that of women, is found in the cardinal myth of Kamigamo. According to the large sign beside the national treasure of the Tower Gate: "The *kami* enshrined here is Wake Ikazuchi. The shrine worships this *kami* because of a mythological event in which Princess Tamayori was playing beside the little stream called Mitarae-gawa and noticed a white-plumed arrow drifting by. She took it back to her palace and then put it under her pillow and eventually delivered a baby boy. Later on, this little boy, while worshiping, ascended to heaven via a hole he broke through the ceiling and became the great *kami* of thunder, lightning, and rain." As in many other cultures worldwide, an incident of impregnation (which, in this case, is thought to be rather scandalous, since the basis for the myth seems to be the seduction of a Kamo princess by a prince from the rival Hata clan) receives ambiguous treatment (Kyōto-fu Bunka-zai Hogo Kikin 1980:58). Here, in language Freud would have enjoyed, a penis becomes a "floating arrow" and sexual intercourse becomes the act of putting this arrow under a woman's "pillow." Matsumae (1992) raises the possibility that this event could be based on an old ritual in which a female shaman entered a stream or river to wed the deity of the water in order to better control it. Not unexpectedly, the shrine sells little red arrows at its information and amulet counters. Those who purchase them mistakenly assume that they are a miniature version of the arrows sold at New Year's to dispel bad fortune and ensure good luck. They proudly attach the metamorphosed phalluses to their keychains or place them on altars at home.

The historic connection of Tamayorihime (the so-called mother of the deity at Kamigamo Shrine) to the Kamo clan is difficult to document. The name appears in other mythological contexts (for example, as the wife of the legendary emperor Jimmu) and may be thought of in an archetypal sense that suggests elemental features about women: *tama* signifies "soul," *yoru* indicates "possession," and *hime* is usually equated with "woman" or "princess." Historical records, such as the Chinese *Wei chi* (ca. 297 C.E.), show that women were once quite powerful in the Japanese archipelago. Epitomized by the third-century leader Himiko, many served as skillful shamans who, through magic, possession, and divination, wielded considerable political clout (Tsunoda and Goodrich 1951; Yusa 1993). While further in-depth historical referencing of Tamayorihime remains to be done, it appears that, although not a clan leader, she was an inheritor of this political and religious tradition, and she is thought by historians to have functioned in administrative and divinatory roles. Hishimura states flatly that the Kamo people had to change to accommodate the dominant political power of the period (1987:82), and yet it is too easy to say the shrine was coopted completely into the imperial system.

The historian Inoue Mitsusada boldly attributes considerable importance to women in the affairs of the shrine (1985:108–109). He sees, as in the Okinawan example, a double system of administration *(nijū ōken)* whereby women administered religious rituals and were more important than bureaucracy-controlling males. To this day, the shrine's priests first announce ritual events at the shrine of Tamayorihime before carrying them out on behalf of her son in the upper sanctuary. The shrine is, however, outside the central courtyard protected by the Tower Gate and surrounding walls, and is on the other side of the Omonoi-gawa. Its placement within the sanctified landscape of the shrine reflects fifth- and sixth-century forces that relegated women to secondary, though still influential, religious and political roles.

Despite the importance of Tamayorihime and women in general within the social order, the Kamo clan's political stance was determined by warriors and horsemen who, following continental cultural trends, worshiped a male deity associated with powerful natural forces of vital importance to rice agriculture. Thus, the Kamo shrine's male *kami* dictated in an oracle how he wished to be represented—by one of the flowers in Kamo territory, the "hollyhock" *(Asarum caulescens),* or *aoi.*[14]

While today the *aoi* is increasingly difficult to find, the early Kamo people liberally decorated themselves and their horses with it and had races when entertaining the *kami* at major ritual events in the sixth century (Chapter 7, May 5 and 15, will detail this history). That their clan deity should "choose" this foliage as symbolic of a powerful, male-dominated lineage is somewhat surprising to modern-day sensibilities: while there are two leaves at the base of a single, long stem with a slightly reddish, bell-shaped flower, it does not stand erect. In fact, only in May dur-

The predominant *aoi* motif on shrine
buildings.

The *aoi* motif on Kataoka-sha.

ing blooming season does the flower even vaguely approach its iconic
representation.

Rather than seeing this symbol as expressive of male dominance, I suggest that its botanical metaphor, when placed within the tradition of early
Kamo nature/mountain veneration, indicates that male power is generative (Alles 1988 : 32). And yet, as Bynum (1987) notes, when a symbol is

79

structured around the social and biological experiences of human beings, it does not simply or mechanically determine the self-awareness of men and women as gendered. Looking again at the shrine's iconographic and architectural attempts to strike a balance, one finds on the railings of buildings, atop roofs, and woven into fabrics a variety of *aoi* designs. In places having a strong yin principle—such as the Hashidono pavilion over the stream or the Hosodono (where rituals, purifications, and divinations were conducted by a succession of imperial daughters for about four hundred years from the mid-Heian to early Kamakura periods)—the *aoi* has a thick, erect flower.[15]

Perhaps in deference to the status of Wake Ikazuchi's mother, the shrine of Tamayorihime, Kataoka-sha, has a stunted central flower stem at the crest of the roof's central ridge beam. However, the railings of the shrine are decorated with metalwork having the same powerful and upright flower motif found at the other yin sites. The contrast in flower designs between roof and railing suggests that, mother of a deity or not, Tamayorihime is still a woman and (at least for public viewing) must be circumscribed by the Kamo/Yamato ideology of the dominant male.

Farther into the shrine at the the Middle Gate, where most people say their prayers and perform the *kashiwade* hand-clapping gesture (which also carries a yin-yang resonance according to many priests; see also Davis 1992 : 237), one finds the *aoi* crest woven into two cloth curtains shielding the left or right side of the entry. Since this site is much closer to the central male deity in the Honden, one would expect an erect flower here; instead, its central stem appears taut, neither erect nor limp. The leaves are the plant's dominant features; and, if one looks closely at their inner design motif, a powerful central "pillar" emerges, supported by two curious shapes at its base.

Priests at the shrine say rather embarrassedly that to have the "strong" design on the Middle Gate's curtain would be, in this day and age, somewhat less than refined *("Chotto, hin ga nai . . .")* even with the general public remaining unaware of its significance. Yet, after an individual says his or her prayers, drops a coin in the coffer, and turns to depart, he or she must pass an attendant selling a variety of talismans and charms. Dominating these items is the phallic *aoi* on the shrine's principal amulet *(omamori)*, sold as an all-purpose talisman for eight hundred yen.[16]

Once again, the central flower assumes a dominant, erect position with its flower only slightly smaller than the leaves (which are also taut and symmetrical). Here, the protective side of Japanese phallicism emerges

The *aoi* motif at the Middle Gate.

The *aoi* motif on shrine amulets
(*omamori*).

alongside its procreative one, as both combine to prevent disease and over-come the finality of death by continually generating new life. Coming to islands formed by a jeweled spear (or, in the words of Kato Genichi, the "celestial penis, root of heaven and earth" [cited in Czaja 1974: 162]), Izanagi and Izanami begin their procreative journey by traversing a phal-lic column. Later, after Izanami is tricked by Izanagi in the underworld, she screams her curse on humankind: "I will each day strangle to death 1,000 of the populace of your country," to which Izanagi counters, "if you do this, I will each day build 1,500 parturition huts" (Philippi 1968:66).

The *aoi* motif provides one further dimension of the sexual landscape at Kamigamo Shrine—namely, the striking architectural layout of the in-ner sanctuaries.[17] Constructed in the *aoi* style, or *aoi-zukuri,* the main and secondary halls are said to represent the leaves of the *aoi.* Shrine archi-tecture usually places the main sanctuary on the left and the secondary or additional ones to the right. At Kamigamo, however, because each build-ing is a leaf of the *aoi* and the leaves of this plant grow in a twisting fash-ion, the locations of the buildings are conceptually as well as structurally reversed.

The "leaves" are now in place, but what of the erect "flower"? Rather than pointing upward, the flower's stamen is inverted downward as the walkway between the buildings, used in every ritual as the stage where priests kneel before performing their duties. Although there is also a side walkway said to represent the less-than-erect flower (the place from which the head priest delivers his invocational prayer), the central walk-way is oriented to be on a direct line with the summit of Kōyama. The importance of this mountain is such that the priests say the shrine's in-nermost sanctuary is not really the object of worship. Until the 1628 re-construction of the shrine, the Honden had doors on its northern as well as southern side through which the *kami* could enter. No one knows quite why the larger doors were replaced with much smaller ones, unless new conceptions of the *kami,* less anthropomorphic, deemed Wake Ikazuchi entirely capable of negotiating his own passage. So while priests present offerings, bow, and deliver prayers before this sanctuary, the holy-of-holies *(goshintai)* is still the mountain some two kilometers distant.

The unknowing visitor, standing in front of the walkway at the Middle Gate, may think he or she is bowing to a sanctuary that enshrines a pow-erful deity, as one does at shrines all over Japan. But from the perspective of those privileged to understand the shrine's layout, floral iconography, and founding myths, the visitor is positioned directly in line with an ar-

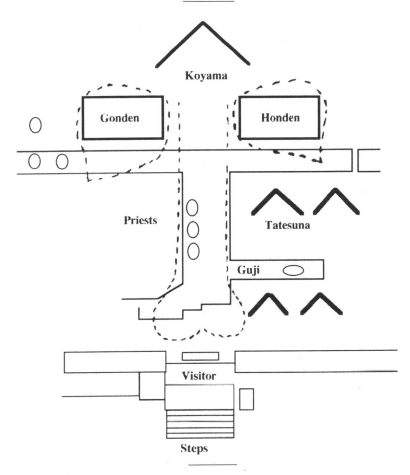

Koyama

Gonden

Honden

Priests

Tatesuna

Guji

Visitor

Steps

The inner shrine's "hollyhock"
architectural design.

chitectural rendering of the *aoi* phallus. The revitalizing energies the visitor seeks originate from the sacred mountain, but they are channeled through the two sanctuaries that are simultaneously leaves and testes. Could one conclude, then, that every blessing received and all energy revitalized is, thanks to the poignant symbolism of the *aoi* construction, a kind of spiritual ejaculation that sanctifies the worshiper? The priests, not surprisingly, are hesitant to comment on this possibility.

It is often the case that the myths and dominant symbols of a premodern era evoke metaphors for fundamental human experiences. These, in turn, can be made to serve as "prescriptive ground(s) for the inscription of social codes" (Grapard 1991 : 18), such as the imposition of a powerful male *kami* into shamanistic practices once dominated by women. Yet, one must be careful not to ascribe too quickly the social codes of an earlier period to present-day contexts, especially when the former emphasize sexuality. The priests I spoke with were highly uncertain what the consequences would be if these themes were stressed in brochures or on signs. In an age when every monetary contribution counts, they say it is better to preserve the status quo and not risk offending anyone. One may speculate, however, since Japanese religious practices have historically mirrored social and cultural realities, that the time will someday be ripe for letting the *aoi* flower carry its message about the sacred dimensions of human sexuality to a wider audience. Since a shrine is an arena in which religious and sociopolitical power operates, the authority enforcing its current symbolic ordering is a careful blending of ritualized nature veneration placed within a deferential context encompassing Japan's current political orders: the Liberal Democratic Party, big business, the imperial family, and millions of stodgily conservative elderly and middle-aged men and women. As long as shrine Shinto's overarching metaphors of cultural heritage and national identity remain associated with economic, political, and imperial structures, the little hollyhock's veneration of a sacred symbiosis between sexual energy and the natural world will have to wait its turn.

CONCLUSION

This chapter's meandering tour through continental and Japanese cultural history has highlighted a number of shared practices of geomancy, religious iconography (via Taoism, Buddhism, and elite as well as folk versions of *kami* veneration), and ritual acknowledgment of primordial forces. In assessing the presentation of the sacred via the particulars of Kamigamo Shrine, it has explored social, political, economic, military, and other deeply cultural factors that combine, often in apparently contradictory ways, to create a web of symbolic, material, and even cosmic associations. In trying to present a well-rounded portrait of what might have gone on in the creation of a sacred site, I am left with the suspicion that the list of adjectives above, from "social" to "cultural," are if anything too simplistic and totalizing, as if the world could be folded in on itself until there is but a single adjective remaining. As Jeremy Thomas has pointed out, the "immediate world is characterized by its inconspicuous familiarity," so that when one does try and represent the space of a particular place—through distribution maps, air photos, satellite images, geographical information systems—all are "distinctively specular." Not only do these methodologies imply a distance between the subject and the object but using them "presents a picture of past landscapes which its former inhabitants would hardly recognize, like a corpse under the pathologist's knife" (Thomas 1993 : 28, 25).

The approach to place I have patched together here—part ethnographic, part historical, part geographic, and part political—can be thought of as spokes in a wheel that have the shrine at the hub. All move and support the ongoing institution in its various spiritual and religiopolitical agendas, yet all are localized in the multilayered character of the physical place. How they fit together, complement, or conflict with each other—as well as how they are perceived by priests, parishioners, and the public at large—depends on a variety of strategies of presentation and meaning. These in turn find expression through ritual occasions held at specific sacred sites, all of which employ a highly visual yet opaque symbolic iconography.

Certain presentations gain greater currency at different times and in different circumstances, becoming "guises" that embody or reflect the designs of administrators and other elites. One must not, however, posit a functional equivalency between human intent and those physical representations the viewer might read as pregnant with imposed meaning. Interpretations vary from person to person and from one historical period to the next, with only the place and its environs maintaining a semblance of continuity—although here too changes regularly occur. A splendid new torii gateway, gleaming vermilion in a grove of trees; a fresh wooden sign in the style of Edo period governmental decrees at the entrance; a patch for a leaky cedar-shingle roof, a new receptacle for burning trash, or ten elegant wooden lampposts to better light the shrine grounds at night—each appearance and disappearance among the physical features composing a particular place is itself amenable to the kind of mapping I have attempted with the shrine as a whole.

But to close this discussion with an analogy to maps is perhaps less than helpful for, as a koan from America points out, "the map is not the territory." What the territory of Kamigamo Shrine *is* can only be approximated, like reality in general, through various methodologies, technologies, and analytical strategies, each a product of situation and human intent. Of a place dedicated to the veneration of a powerful thunder deity for more than fourteen centuries, only the most arrogant researcher or cynical priest would have the temerity to say he or she has exhausted the possibilities and truly knows the place for what it is.

KAMO MEMORIES AND HISTORIES

It was—*but what it was is harder to
say. Think the best, but don't make
me describe it away.*
IBN MU'TAZZ,
CA. ELEVETH CENTURY

Tradition—custom—history. These are fighting words to people in
many parts of the world where battles rage over the legitimacy of institutions, social practices, and the control of territory or resources. In
postwar Japan, the fight has thus far been waged largely with images,
words, and symbols instead of bullets and invasions, yet the persistence
of a discourse about both recent and distant "histories" remains one with
far-reaching economic, political, and social implications.[1] Kimono retailers live and die depending on the public's response (or lack thereof) to
marketing campaigns extolling "traditional" or "neotraditional" Japanese
fashion; advertisers and companies jostle to capitalize on a yearlong television series (produced by state television, NHK) that dramatizes famous
warlords and heroines from some critical moment in Japanese history;
and where would sumo be without its "traditional" training, hierarchies,
and etiquette? The domestic tourist industry in the historic city of Kyoto
alone, with thirty-nine million visitors in 1997, thrives not because of
restaurants, discotheques, or natural scenery; it is, rather, the quaint, "authentic," refined, and, as I will argue, potentially coercive atmosphere of
the "past" that seduces visitors.

What concerns me in relating this information to case material I will
present in this chapter is, as Connerton pointed out (1987), the question
of how to distinguish social memory from the act of historical reproduction and reconstruction. In both cases, thanks to the workings of culture,

individuals are supplied with interpretative frameworks within which to localize and personalize their understandings about identity, significant situations, and social order in general. Whether these memories reference specific actions and behaviors or specific networks of ideas, they share one important characteristic: they must be articulated before transmission can occur (Fentress and Wickham 1992). While easy to say and common-sensical, the articulations of social memory can range from legitimating a single word in a line of text to staging massive public commemorations, all with the intent of mediating consciousness about one's identity, social reference group, and sense of continuity with previous traditions and people.

While efforts have been made to create and promote these associations at national levels in Japan,[2] a focus on Kamigamo Jinja will show how associating with a once powerful but still famous institution is used to sacralize the symbolic capital and social standing of several important groups (ranging from the shrine's priests to Kyoto's industry in "cultural heritage"). A large festival, for example, while originating at a shrine where its ritual enactment is an extension of a priest's daily chores, may become a vehicle for one group to authenticate its identity or challenge its social status, or as an opportunity to accumulate tourist yen. I will show in this chapter how a group of local residents affiliated with the shrine draws on statuses and privileges of centuries past that, although no longer binding legally or institutionally, capitalize not on textual authority but on sentiments evoked by a renewed national and international emphasis on "tradition."[3] Thus, ritual events can be targeted as strategic ways for conveying particular agendas and for traditionalizing consensus, but the staging of these events can also challenge and renegotiate the very basis of what the sponsoring actors hold to be "traditional."

On a sultry September day in the early 1990s, Kamigamo Shrine hosted representatives of three groups that, had they crossed paths on a similar day in a certain period of the past, would have been immediately at each other's throats. The first of these groups—a tour of Korean-Japanese taxi drivers (speaking Japanese) from the southern city of Fukuoka—would certainly have put the priests on edge had they known of their presence. Owing in part to Japanese school textbooks obscuring cultural connections to and the twentieth-century military occupation of the Korean peninsula as well as a recent Korean-based nationalism antagonistic to almost anything Japanese (see Hata 1986), there continues today an antagonism among Koreans, Japanese-born Koreans (who are denied Japanese citizenship), and Japanese on a variety of economic, cultural, and political fronts that is perceived to stretch back to at least the sixth century C.E.

One of the main culprits in this scenario is the military leader Toyotomi Hideyoshi, whose brutal scorched-earth campaign (beginning in 1592) to subdue the Korean kingdoms has yet to be forgotten or forgiven by the Korean people. Thus, the leader and guide of the taxi-driver tour group had taken the group earlier to the "Ear-Mound" memorial (mimizuka) wherein lie buried thousands of severed ears brought back by Hideyoshi's samurai as proof of their victories. Commenting animatedly about the "hidden" and "suppressed" history of Korean influences in Kamigamo Shrine's development, the guide went on to say, "They probably don't know it and certainly don't want to know it, but the Kamo people that built this shrine were originally Koreans!"

As the taxi drivers strolled through the shrine, they gaped at a dress rehearsal of the Crow Sumo Festival, an important "registered intangible folk and cultural treasure" wherein young boys in loincloths engage in sumo matches in front of the shrine's symbolic sacred mountains, reenacting one of the Kamo clan's myths of origin. Oblivious to the stares of the visitors around them, older men and young boys hovered around the periphery of the ad hoc sumo ring (dohyō) as finishing touches were being made to its boundary.

While the Kamo group was rehearsing, some fifty meters distant at the shrine's administrative offices, the assistant head priest was busy entertaining a representative from the Imperial Household Agency (Kunaichō). Over tea and sweets, the two were discussing the last details for implementing in a new context a practice last seen in Kyoto eight hundred years ago whereby women from the imperial court served as priestesses at Kamigamo and Shimogamo shrines. Now, however, the woman would be "imperial" and a "priestess" not only for the Aoi Festival in May but also for the occasion of the Crow Sumo Festival, thus lending courtly elegance to an event once staged primarily by farmers. The relationship between Kamo and court, as I will show in a moment, has not always been so cordial. Largely because of historiographic representations, ritual reenactments, and the selected "forgetting" of incidents still charged with a potential for conflict, an accommodation has been reached in the service of forging local, ethnic, and national identities.

ORGANIZING KAMO ORIGINS:
DISTINCTIVENESS, NEAR AND FAR

Scholarly work in societies around the world has shown a cross-cultural tendency to reassert origins and identities in the face of rapid technological innovation and social change. In looking at the long-term continuity of village political institutions in rural Spain, for example, Ruth Behar (1986) found that the most-asked questions among villagers were how their community came into existence and who its first settlers were. Similarly, though Japan has had over a century since the Meiji period to cope with the tension of being "modern" and "Japanese," writers in the 1970s and particularly the 1980s have reinvigorated questions concerning national origins and identity. Born partially out of a need to resurrect national pride after the disastrous defeat in 1945 and the subsequent foreign-aid handouts, legal codes, and soldiers of the occupation, many early works criticized Japanese cultural tendencies thought to have contributed to prewar ideological blindness.

By the mid-1970s, however, these approaches (see the discussion of *nihonjinron* in Chapter 1) were being revised in favor of more positive assessments. That the astounding economic development and growth of the 1970s and 1980s was accompanied by a turning to the past should by now come as no surprise. Writing in the *Mainichi shinbun* newspaper, art critic Kurita Isamu went so far as to attribute the renewed interest in tradition to the "international flavor" of the Japanese lifestyle, whereby "traditional Japanese arts appear quite alien and exotic," thus fostering a perspective similar to a foreigner's love for Japanese culture (1983:131). As Wright (1985:18) and others have argued, the modern advances of technology and science have no moral capacity to give meaningful sanction to individual or social orders. Thus, "an imagination of the past is required for the construction of the future" (Robertson 1988:135).

Attempts by city planners and the national government's social architects—for example, orchestrating citizen rather than shrine-sponsored festivals to enhance community and place commitment in the concrete suburbs of Tokyo and other major cities—can be seen as conscious techniques to deal with the effects and consequences of rapid urbanization and social change. Robertson's examination of Japanese-style nostalgia (what she terms *furusato* or "native place" ideology [1988]) also helps to reveal some of the complex strategies and motivations behind the search for origins and communal values. Closer to the themes of this chapter, her work demonstrates how social memory depends in part on selective appropriations of antiquity and tradition that are of use to various interest groups and local residents, all with unwritten charters to "preserve, protect, and propagate" a past suitable to their purposes.[4] If history is thought of as "an intellectual process to establish the truth of earlier events," the past becomes what J. H. Plumb calls a "mythical complex inherent in the present as a created ideology with a purpose." But, he cautions, neither is the past strictly ideology or illusion; it can become an "established public institution with historical materiality" (Plumb 1970: 17), such as Japan's Furusato Jōhō Senta (Native Place Information Centers) or Britian's National Trust.

Nowhere is this theme more evident in everyday practice than at Japan's major Shinto shrines. Not only are they among the very few visible reminders of an archaic past in Japanese society, their centeredness within cities and neighborhoods makes them ready "stages" for a variety of actors and performances. Shrines control and, in the eyes of some urbanites, "waste" vast amounts of space and property, frequently within areas of a city where land prices were, during the height of the economic bubble, astronomically high.[5] Their buildings are more often than not from another century, as is the dress of the priests who work within them. And while a shrine's employee parking lot may be filled with the latest four-wheel drive vehicles and even chic Italian Vespa scooters, its public image is flowing sleeves, baggy bloomers, and *zōri* sandals or wooden clogs. And yet, all this is *atarimae,* the normal, common, or matter-of-fact so what—ness around which neighborhoods have developed, transportation networks have intersected, and political intrigues have sought shelter or alliance for centuries.

Seen in historical perspective that highlights their legitimizing role, shrines have frequently (some would say always) served to authenticate and sacralize political agendas coming from outside their precincts. The conquer-and-appropriate strategies of the Yamato, the restorative cultural practices of the Meiji government, and, more recently, the fascism of ultraconservatives responsible for the Pacific War have all used shrines (and Buddhist temples as well) in their efforts to consolidate power. As Weber (among others) has pointed out, any powerful religious institution — whether Catholic church, Hindu temple, or Muslim mosque — will find itself entangled less by ideas than by webs of interactive and interlocking social, political, and economic rationales, not all of which are harmonious.[6] What makes the case of Kamigamo Shrine of particular interest is the way in which all of these forces come into play in the attempt to service a nationally promoted image of community that does not wholly translate into local concerns. Below I trace some of the historical trajectories leading up to the superficially harmonious reconciliation of court, Kamo, and Korean-Japanese worldviews on that day in September.

Fortunately for the priests of Kamigamo shrine, visitors on the whole do not take the time to read the densely lettered signs scattered throughout the grounds. Were they to do so (as is the luxury and obligation of visiting researchers), visitors would face a casually constructed labyrinth of history and legend, fact and surmise that is offered for public consumption. By compiling information found on several signs, one learns of the shrine's founding in 678 C.E., of its long association with the imperial court, and of the Kamo clan who may have been here before the shrine's founding. But there is neither interrelation nor explanation of these important "facts." The festival of "Crow Sumo" is mentioned as an "important and unusual" event, but its centrality to both the shrine's founding legends and the identity of the Kamo people is not mentioned.

There are a number of written accounts that address these issues, although they are relatively scarce for a shrine of Kamigamo's long history and importance. Returning to the question of the community's origin, historians have looked to early genealogical records of the ninth century as "authoritative" textual evidence that permits the tracing of a story whose ending they already know—the Kamo clan's "charter" as founders of Kamigamo Shrine. The earliest mention of the name "Kamo" appears in the *Shōsōin monjo* (ca. 708 C.E.) and simply describes the residential locale of one "Kamo no Kurohito." From this shred of textual documentation, claims are made that there was only one Kamo Shrine (while today there is an "upper" and a "lower," a split that is still the subject of controversy) and that it was located in the place Kamigamo occupies today. Commentaries on another text, the *Yamashiro-no-kuni fudoki* (which no longer exists) are also said to have provided evidence about where the early Kamo people lived, and thus, by extension, arguments are made for the existence of one "upper" shrine (Inoue 1985:100).

The actual "upper" Kamo genealogies (or *keizu*) date to around the early 1300s, when, because of rising civil warfare, imperial favor and patronage toward the Kamo shrines was gradually waning. While these genealogies are considered valuable (in the sense of "irreplaceable") documents by priests, parishioners, and historians alike, it is probable that these scrolls are attempts to legitimize entire families of priests for future reference, promotion, and economic subsidies. The "lower" shrine (Kamo

Mioya Jinja, or more commonly, Shimogamo Jinja) is especially interesting, since (like the *Kojiki*) its genealogy begins with the legendary ancestors of the families before moving on to people who actually existed (Inoue 1985:98).

From a broader historical perspective, it is known that claims of authenticity from "invented" lineages were extremely problematic in early Japan, so much so that the early Yamato government ordered a compilation of families to serve as an equivalent of today's Burke's Peerage. The *Shinsen shōjiroku* (815 C.E.) recounts that a problem arose when "Korean" immigrants from primarily the Paekche and Kudara kingdoms—who had been coming to Japan ever since the fourth century to flee invading forces of the Hsiung-nu from the north and Silla from the east—claimed bloodlines that elevated their social status (Ōwa 1986:18). For their contributions as social and cultural consultants in writing, medicine, calendar making, ceramics, astrology, and a host of other skills, they must have thought the early Yamato bumpkins at least owed them a legitimate name, especially when years of intermarriage and occasionally adoption into "native" households had already altered their foreignness.

And yet many of them (as well as local Japanese) were subjected to the *kugatachi*, an ordeal whereby claims to legitimacy were verified by having the claimant's hand plunged into a cauldron of scalding water. Depending on whether or not claimants were burned (or what degree of burn resulted), the record of thirty volumes and 1,182 names was eventually systematized enough to satisfy the court (Torigoe 1988:138). Three orders of descent were thereafter promulgated: the *shinbetsu* for those families connected to the original deities, the *kōbetsu* for those of imperial descent, and the *banbetsu* for "foreigners-now-living-in-Japan" (ibid.). Entries were arranged by residential proximity to the new capital's palace, beginning with Sakyō and Ukyō, and followed by Yamashiro (the area of Kamigamo), Yamato, Settsu, Kawachi, and Izumi. Additionally, loyalty to the regime was rewarded with four political rankings that came to constitute the "new nobility": *mahito* for members of the imperial clan, *asomi* by clan leaders with imperial blood links, *sukune* and *imiki* for leaders of nonimperial but loyal clans, and four other titles *(michi no shi, omi, muraji, inaki)* for chieftains of nonimperial clans having potential for imperial affiliation (Inoue and Brown 1993:225). A final policy was the household register *(koseki)*, begun in 670 and strengthened in 689 under Empress Jitō.

The *Shinsen shōjiroku* placed the Kamo within the first category as being connected to the original deities; but this is hardly surprising in view of the political reality at hand at the date of the document's writing. After recently moving the capital from Nagaoka to what is today Kyoto in 794, the imperial court (controlled by the powerful Fujiwara family) was still in the process of solidifying their power and had, to these ends, been currying favor with the Kamo shrines from as early as 780. Through elevations in status, gifts of land, plus the fostering of intimate ties by having imperial daughters serve as priestesses at the shrine, Kamigamo Shrine became the tutelary protector of the court and city, providing a spiritual force field against attacks of vengeful spirits *(onryō)* issuing from the dangerous northeast.

Later historians—whether for fear of linking the Kamo clan to Korean immigrants and thus incurring disfavor from the Original Parishioners' Group *(dōzoku-kai),*[7] the upper and lower shrines, and perhaps the imperial household as well—say nothing of the historiographic nature of both early and later genealogies, only that they exist as documents from which accounts may be constructed. In fact, the Korean question is not even raised. Continental influences and cultures are not now nor have they ever been politically aware in Japanese scholarship on Shinto. Like the farmers in Spain studied by Behar, Torigoe (1988), Inoue (1985), Ōwa (1986), Bock (1970), and Fujiki (1992) want to know how the Kamo shrine community of *northern Kyoto* came into existence. Their inquiries are thus neatly bounded from the first stroke of the brush.

A second level of investigation begins with attempts to reconcile mythical accounts about the Kamo found in the *Shoku nihongi* of 698 with later genealogies. To summarize these tales briefly, the legendary emperor Jimmu, after a long journey from southern Japan, was finally led to the Yamato homeland by a magical, three-legged crow *(yatagarasu)* who also showed him the best place from which to begin his attack on the residents of the region. Mission accomplished, this strange bird then transformed itself into a human being, one Taketsunomi-no-mikoto, and became founder of the Kamo clan and grandfather to the principal deity of Kamigamo Shrine. The *Engi shiki* of 967 reports that Taketsunomi-no-mikoto settled near Mount Katsuragi in the Nara plain, but it says nothing about the establishment of the shrine and its community.

How then did the Kamo people get to northern Kyoto? Although the distance is negligible when compared with other migrations, the terrain and contested territories they had to cross makes it seem much farther away, both in distance and historical time.

Inoue's account is careful to avoid speculation about the Kamo migration, focusing instead on an early-sixth-century political organization, the *agatanushi,* in which the clan already had an imperially granted status. Later, however, in part because of a reorganization of the central government (645 C.E.) and the redivision and renaming of units composing the "nation," the newly imposed codes of the Chinese-style *Taihō ritsuryō* (701 C.E.) caused the *agatanushi* to be absorbed within the new system. Inoue believes that the Kamo made use of one of their principal assets, the Kamo Shrine (which, at this time, had not yet been divided into upper and lower branches), to establish a monopoly on priestly succession and thus retain some political influence.[8] One of his more daring assertions is that "Kamo" is not a place name, as is usually the case in *agatanushi* titles, but that it comes from *kami* (1985: 113), the word for those deities enshrined in what is now thought of as a uniquely Shinto cosmology. Thus, when faced with a political change that would have essentially undercut their legitimacy as rulers, they turned to the shrine, consolidated their political acumen with the shrine's religious clout in the northern valley, and ended up retaining privilege and power despite their initial losses of land and title.[9]

Inoue then backs up to an earlier point in history more germane to the original question concerning the founding of the first community. He introduces the possibility that "Kami/Kamo" was originally taken from the area of north Kyoto called "Kazuno," using references in a text no longer extant, the *Yamashiro-no-kuni fudoki,* to support his claim. Although he does not say so explicitly, there is little room for doubt that he believes Kazuno Agatanushi was the original name of the Kamo people when they moved into the region. Following the Yamato clan's style of centralizing power, they appropriated (or were assigned) the area, its name, its sacred centers, and its *kami* as well.

Ōwa further develops this claim (1986: 14), but with two important additions that Inoue seems to omit studiously. According to Ōwa, when the Kamo moved to Okada, then to Otokuni, and finally to the Kamo River area in the late fifth century, they did so alongside the Hata clan. The *Nihon shoki* refers to an incident in the north Kyoto area whereby an official of the title *miyatsuko* (in an administrative system centered on shrines rather than villages) had been assassinated. Even though no additional information is provided, one might assume that this was one of the many flareups of local clans trying to reassert their autonomy against the Yamato court. Ōwa believes that, as a means of controlling this area and stabilizing the political periphery, the Kamo and the Hata were sent by the court from Katsuragi to Kyoto (1986:16). Scholars of early Japanese history rarely agree on a single interpretation for anything, yet in the case of the Hata there is complete consensus concerning their Korean origins. Important shrines in the south (Fushimi Inari Taisha) and west of the Kyoto basin (Matsuo Taisha) trace their founding to the Hata.

So influential was this clan on the culture of precapital Heiankyō that one of the important sources for the origin of the Kamo Festival is not, as might be expected, a Kamo document but rather one from the Hata, the *Hata-shi honke-chō*. In it, one of the clan's shaman-priests, Tobe-iki-wakahiko, divined that the reason for a terrible period of inclement weather and pestilence was the anger of the Kamo divinities. Although evidence of associating with the Korean-originated Hata is circumstantial from a critical perspective, there is enough for Felicia Bock (1970) to state the Kamo people are a subgroup of the Hata clan. Likewise, but with a lighter touch, Ōwa implies a Kamo identity that, by association with the Hata, has its roots in the elite immigrant culture of the exiled Korean kingdoms (1986:14). Certainly the taxi-driver tour group at the beginning of this chapter would be a receptive audience for this information even if present-day Kamo descendants would not.

Like Inoue before him, Ōwa says that when the Kamo moved to northern Kyoto in the late fifth century, the area was occupied by the Kazuno Agatanushi. However, unlike Inoue, Ōwa says the Kazuno people too had come originally from the Nara area. And, because textual evidence points to their sharing a common ancestor in the "crow-man," Taketsunomi-no-mikoto, they are thus one and the same with the Kamo (1986:15). The eminent historian Ueda Masaaki is cited to support this view. He too reports in local customs of that time a practice whereby family histories (and names) were made to overlap as a way of legitimizing new members and leaders, the very practice that led to the judgment by scalding water some two centuries later.

Ōwa goes a step farther in relating the clan now known as Kazuno-Kami-Kamo to another less clearly defined group of people, the Yamabe and Yama-no-moribe. The former refers to the guild in charge of mountains, and the latter (subordinate to the first) to the guild in charge of the area's mountains and forests. They, in turn, were part of the Yamashiro-no-kuni-no-miyatsuko, the same group whose leader was assassinated. This group is mentioned in the *Hata-shi honke-chō* and the *Yamashiro-no-kuni fudoki* and thus, from Ōwa's perspective, impossible to ignore.

For the first time, then, a distinction is made between the Kazuno-

Kurabe-uma shinji, horse races to
entertain the *kami* with Mount Hiei in
the background.

Kurabe-uma shinji, horse races to
entertain the *kami.*

Kami-Kamo group and the "original" inhabitants of the area, the Yamabe.[10] In Ōwa's opinion, when the deities of the Yamabe were appropriated into the Kamo's ritual practices, they were neglected and thus became vengeful, causing prolonged rains and strong winds that threatened the harvest. The festival that was then staged to appease them, the "Kamo-sai," used the name of the new settlers but was an "invented tradition" that employed the hunting ceremony of the appropriated Yamashiro-no-kuni-no-miyatsuko's deities.

The festival was exuberant and even violent. From the perspective of new ritual specialists in the Yamato court—where continental influences such as Confucianism, Taoism, and Buddhism were gaining a foothold—its unrefined character may have been deemed necessary to appease equally rough nature *kami*. Hunters donned wild boar masks, fixed bells on fast horses, then ran races on the grounds of the shrine, creating an atmosphere of excitement and spectacle that drew people from as far away as eighty kilometers by the middle of the sixth century. A good harvest resulted, the deities were placated, and the Kamo-sai was institutionalized.[11]

I judge Ōwa's account (which the priests at the shrine were unaware of) to be the most accurate rendering and summation of all the various possibilities. I have summarized it at length so that I might compare it with the official version recently published under the auspices of the shrine and its Original Parishioners' Group.

The Kamo clan descendants at the end of the twentieth century—beleaguered by outmarriage and occupational dislocation, dwindling in numbers, and yet still influential in the affairs of the shrine—continue to take pride in the history of their lineage as well as its integral role in creating and promoting the Kamo shrines (see Chapter 7, October 27). Though he is not its official leader, the *dōzoku-kai* has been influenced strongly for some years now by Mr. Fujiki Masanao, a former administrator in the Osaka police department. In his role as self-appointed historian, he compiled the book *Kamo kannushi honnin-shi*, ostensibly a history of the shrine's priestly lineages (Fujiki 1992). The book's intent of recording, transmitting, and thereby preserving status and privilege is not very different from earlier attempts of the eighth and twelfth centuries. Working from a scroll called the *Kamosha negi hafuri keizu*, or "Genealogy of Chief and Secondary Priests at Kamo Shrine," which is some fifty centimeters wide and 19.5 meters long and which dates to the early Kamakura period in 1200, Fujiki sets out page upon page of family trees with historical incidents at the bottom, very few of which are referenced. The reader must take it on good faith that these correspondences—such as the date 785 paired with the founding of the Kamo *agatanushi* (when the evidence I've just considered makes the founding at least two centuries older)—are correct, aided but not always corroborated by the historian Suma Yoshi-hiro's essay at the end of the book.

When considering historical accounts, Hayden White (1973) has argued that it is necessary to recognize "the writer's problem of representation, exhibiting emplotment, argument, and ideological implications." Keeping these themes in mind when following the Fujiki-Suma text is particularly important, because what is stated on the page is not always the message. The book exemplifies a situation where individuals have no language to talk about their society because they can only talk within it (Bloch 1977:281). I hope to show how this text, important enough to warrant an expenditure of some two million yen of Original Parishioner funds (with an additional million from the shrine), establishes a landmark for the ideology of continuity vital to both shrine and *dōzoku-kai* identities. A number of writers have shown how "tradition" has been seized upon as a "fortuitous political device" as people worldwide struggle with issues of nationalism and independence (Horner 1992:2−3). Of concern here is its application by local peoples to their own conceptualizations of identity and heritage.

THE FUJIKI HISTORY OF KAMIGAMO PRIESTS

In conversations with Mr. Fujiki, I learned something of his reasons for compiling this book, few of which have anything to do with the academically oriented scholarship characterizing the accounts of Inoue or Ōwa. During World War II, he had the misfortune of being assigned to Hiroshima shortly before that fateful day of August 6, 1945. The night before the atomic bomb fell, he had a dream of white horses running on the grounds of Kamigamo Shrine in the Kamo Festival and was so moved by this dream that early the next day he took leave of the barracks and went to the countryside. The bomb detonated at 8:15 that same morning, killing most of the soldiers in his unit. Fujiki developed stomach cancer as a result of digging for comrades and civilians among the radioactive ruins of the city, but he attributes his survival to the dream "sent by the deity." He was extremely grateful to be alive and yet puzzled about why he had been the recipient of such a message.

His discharge and return to Kyoto brought the opportunity to learn more about the Kamo people that were his ancestors. He uses the word "apprentice" in describing his relationship to one of the shrine's elders and oral historians, Bamba Hirofumi. After years of teacher-disciple instruction and friendship, Fujiki assumed his work as a historian on the death of his mentor. Now that he himself is getting older, and being without anyone to whom he could convey his formidable storehouse of anecdotes and knowledge, he told me with an air of resignation, "The only choice was to do a book, even though I am not a writer and have no education." While passing on this knowledge is important, he acknowledges that it was his obligation *(on)* to his teacher that weighed most heavily on his conscience. "It's all due to his taking the time to teach me. I wanted to be able to visit Bamba-sensei's grave and present a copy of this book."

A close reading of the text shows it is concerned with a local culture— priests from Kamo lineages, their descendants, and the powerful parishioners' group—that is constituted both internally and externally as an elite. This ascription as well as the parishioners' group itself must be reproduced over time lest it decline and be subsumed within the increasingly impersonal (and non-Kamo) bureaucracy of a shrine. I use the word "impersonal" here with care to convey a deeply felt sense by the *dōzoku-kai* that the shrine's administrative and ritual components have been usurped by "outsiders." Studies in the field of ethnic identity have shown that the "otherness" of outer-group difference is a key component when defining intergroup similarity, especially when a group is oriented to the past (see R. Thompson 1989). For the parishioners' group to continue to call themselves "Kamo," several essential resources must remain under their control. These include the genealogical scrolls mentioned earlier; paraphernalia required for rituals such as Crow Sumo, the running of the horses, or the famous hollyhock festival; and their ability to designate social and cultural factors (such as expectations and norms about general appearance, deportment, and interaction) that distinguish themselves as unique, historically significant, and integral to the shrine—all subsumed in the name "Kamo." Especially threatening for Fujiki is when priests "presume to tell us what to do, as if they know better than we do!"

While it is tempting to present verbatim many of the fascinating accounts in this book about the shrine's past, I will focus only on two parts as they inform the previous discussion of origins and how these relate to the tension underlying the Crow Sumo Festival. Fujiki has enlisted an academic historian, Suma Yoshihiro, who, one might infer from his affiliation with Nanzan University in Nagoya well outside the Kyoto-Nara area, presents an "objective" perspective. Suma, in turn, looks to the prewar work of Higo Kazuo (1941) on the Kamo legends and finds that the grandfather of the principal deity at the shrine as well as the "crow man" of early myths was not a real person but a "sky *kami*" that was neither place nor clan specific. The Kamo believed they were descendants from this heavenly *kami (ten-no-kami)* and thus, like with like, "allowed" it to be appropriated into the Yamato clan's myths of legitimation (which are also centered on powerful sky deities).

Unlike Inoue and Ōwa, however, Suma argues that the Kamo people's migration never happened. To him the original inhabitants of the area were the "Kamo" (whom Inoue calls Kazuno Agatanushi and Ōwa terms the Yamabe). This local tribe of mountain people was aware of the reputation of the southern Kamo and so forged an alliance with them, assimilating their name and legends over time. Suma says nothing about what happened to the southern Kamo, but he believes, like Higo, the northern clan's longevity is attributable to a sensitivity garnered from protecting and maintaining their assumed identity. Political alliances could be formed (as in the *agatanushi* system), but allegiance to Kamo identity always came first (Suma, in Fujiki 1991 : 195).[12]

The early association with the Yamato and later Fujiwara clans paid off handsomely in the early centuries for the Kamo Shrine and its priestly families and parishioners. True, their huge Kamo Festival had come increasingly under imperial control in the years 698 (no shooting arrows during the running of the horses!), 702 (only Kamo people can participate!) and 708 (an imperial governor, the *kokushi,* will dictate proper protocol!). But this situation is hardly surprising when a movement was under way at the time to reorganize the entire country under the Taihō code that granted the central government sweeping powers over its periphery. When the capital was moved to Nagaoka, after a period of intense court infatuation with Buddhism in Nara, Emperor Kanmu revitalized the court's fundamental concern with *kami*-worship by beginning negotiations with the Kamo shrines (now two, after a separation in 781 of an upper "original" shrine [Kamigamo] and a lower "branch" shrine [Shimogamo]) to become protectors of the imperial court. This arrangement was in line with his general policy of revitalizing the imperial institution by furthering ties with the Ise shrines. One year later in 782, the Kamo shrines were given a status second only to Ise (Suma, in Fujiki 1991: 196)—a ranking still in effect. When the capital was moved again in 794 to what is today Kyoto, imperial messengers visited often to enlist the aid of the deities to protect the city and court. Shrine brochures still give prominence to the fact that Kamigamo was (along with the ninth-century monasteries atop Mount Hiei) the main line of defense against harmful spirit forces issuing from the northeast.

To foster an even closer association with the shrine, in 810 Emperor Saga began the *saiin* institution in which daughters of the emperor were dedicated to serve the Kamo deities as priestesses, divinators, and, at the festival of the *miare-sai,* conjugal partners to the *kami* as well. He was following the lead of Tenmu, who had reinstated this practice at Ise roughly 140 years earlier so an imperial priestess could worship the sun deity Amaterasu on his behalf. Saga was likewise interested in divine intervention (particularly that of Wake Ikazuchi and Taketsunomi-no-mikoto) to put down an attempt to reclaim the throne by the former emperor Heizei (Kamens 1990:50). Based on a similar tradition of high priestesses (*saiō* or *saigū*) at the Ise shrines, there was an attempt to flatter the *kami* with imperial attention and service in which divinatory arts and ritual performances—carried out under the supervision of Kamo male and female priests—could be combined with a certain amount of politics.[13]

Successful in this and other court-related concerns, the shrine continued to gain favor until, in 819, the annual Kamo Festival was treated with the same respect and veneration as a ritual within the court (Suma, in Fujiki 1991:199). The *saiin's* appearance in the Kamo-sai procession was a great crowd pleaser, and her residence at Murasakino was noted by the author of *The Tale of Genji* as a place of "perfect elegance," where the women could "keep to themselves" and develop the literary talent for which they were highly renowned. Over a period of four centuries, thirty-four imperial daughters served as embodiments of refined living and poetic sensibilities, although it must be noted that not all of them were happy about their duties and the sequestered nature of their lives (Kamens 1990).[14]

CROW SUMO AND THE CROW PEOPLE

One of the opportunities to convey clan heritage as separate from the shrine, to reassert boundaries between who is and is not Kamo, and to provide a ritual atmosphere in which socialization of these agendas is attempted occurs during the Crow Sumo Festival of September 9.[15] As the first big event staged by the shrine since June 30, it punctuates the dol-

drums of the stifling Kyoto summer with shouting elementary-school-age
boys and the excitement of team rivalries. There are brochures describing (but not explaining) the event from the perspective of the shrine:

> Every year, on September 9 in front of the Hosondono, "crow jumping"
> is demonstrated by the *tone*. Then children perform sumo in this rare rit-
> ual. When the first emperor, Jimmu, went to the east from the high plain
> of heaven, the grandfather of Kamigamo Shrine's *kami*, Kamo Taketsunomi-
> no-mikoto, became a strange big crow, the *yatagarasu*, and led Jimmu to
> Yamato. This was a very important event. For that he was rewarded the
> northern part of Yamashiro-no-kuni. Later on, his descendants built
> Kamigamo Shrine. The story about the *yatagarasu* and the ceremonial
> sumo both drive out evil *(akuryō)* that gives people bad luck for the har-
> vest. The traditional sumo event was held in the imperial palace [today's
> Gosho], but these three events became connected and the "Crow Sumo"
> started. The original date is not known, although there is a mention of the
> Crow Sumo in the *Kagen nenjū gyōji* from the Kamakura Period, seven
> hundred years ago. (Kamo Wake Ikazuchi Jinja, no date)

In my interviews with the sole Kamo descendant and last of a long line
of priests at the shrine, the message and meaning behind the Crow Sumo
appears straightforward: it is a performance aimed at instilling a particular kind of collective memory: "We are the descendants of the Kamo
people and so this sumo reminds us that we are strong, have power, and
have helped the emperor. We show this in front of the *kami* in a kind of
ritualized dance that is the sumo. All of this is a way of reminding ourselves
of our uniqueness. Since there is nothing really written down about this
ritual, changes are being made year by year, but the basic shape of the ritual stays the same. It is a symbol of power *(kenryoku no shōchō)*." Scholars
of ritual might see these comments the way a gold miner surveys a rich
deposit of ore—loaded with symbols, political alliances, and ritual rein-
ventions all awaiting extraction through analysis. For the sake of brevity,
I will leave most of this labor undone and dwell only on those aspects that
resonate with issues of identity and continuity.

As a vehicle for expressing the symbolic power of the Kamo descendants, the *karasu sumō* ritual both compels and manipulates its performers
to reenact the most basic tenets of Kamo social solidarity. The priest's
perspective is a privileged one, informed by selected representations of
history and myth, his association with the shrine, and his lineage as a Kamo

Participants in Crow Sumo *(karasu sumō)* entering the inner courtyard.

descendant. But it cannot be assumed that the other principal participants, the young sumo wrestlers, know or care anything at all about the mythic message they enact. Promoting self-aware or self-critical perspectives within a ritual context, what is often termed "reflexivity," has come to define rituals worldwide. A ritual event "distributes its many participants along a continuum that ranges from total engagement to casual disengagement" (Kapferer 1984 : 189) and may promote participants to be an audience to themselves as well as to others.

But does this diversity of participation necessarily undermine what the priest sees as the ritual's ideological goal? According to one boy, the ritual's message does have an impact on awareness and highlights it as an event set apart, traditional, and of significance for the shrine: "Our baseball club teacher asked if we wanted to do sumo at the Kamo Shrine, so we thought it'd be fun, all of us together. Of course, it's important too. . . . We heard that the shrine does this every year as one of their traditions. I'm looking forward to seeing the old man hop like a crow. It'd be fun if we could do that part too!"

The boys are divided into two teams, with the *hori-gata* (on the right) representing the east and the *negi-gata,* the west. At 10:00 A.M., after a perfunctory purification of their hands and mouths (the same one done before all shrine rituals), the boys leave the administration building and follow their two team leaders *(tone)* behind a procession of priests, elders, and, for the first time ever in this ritual context, the *saiō* priestess-proxy and her two attendants. Her twelve-layered silk kimono, imperial coiffure, and red-lacquered paulownia wood clogs are as sumptuous as the gangly boys' white loincloths (*fundoshi)* are meager. Seeing them together in the same procession, one can hardly miss the visible distinctions of class—one imperial and the other common—announced by their attire. All proceed slowly to the inner courtyard of the main shrine at a speed dictated by the mincing steps of the head priest's eighty-eight years and the *saiō*'s fifty-five-pound burden of silk.

Once within the upper shrine's gate, a short ritual is held in which a number of food and drink offerings are presented to the *kami.* The chief priest then intones a *norito* prayer announcing the festival of Crow Sumo is about to take place, that spirited young men will be serving the deity, and that everyone wishes the *kami* to bless the proceedings and safeguard a rich harvest. Although the majority of *norito* are extremely difficult to understand by simply listening, that of the Crow Sumo is delivered in a more contemporary and accessible Japanese. There are other

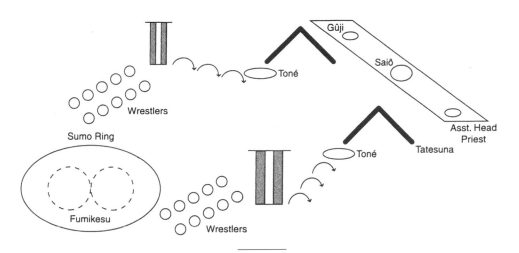

Layout for the Crow Sumo ritual.

occasions as well in which the shrine deems it important to modernize the language of the *norito*, thus attempting to accommodate and enfranchise participants, many of whom may be participating on the inside of a ritual for the first time in their lives. Interestingly enough, the chief priest does not ask that any particular notice or recognition be given to the clan for which this entire event is a legitimation of status and origins. Within the prayer of the shrine ritual, then, it is the community at large that is emphasized, although this emphasis should not be construed as a neglect of or domination over the Kamo dimension. So complete is the hegemony the Kamo organizers feel in this rite, they can afford to be self-effacing and magnanimous before the deity, elevating communal rather than clan concerns and thus, from their perspective, unselfishly promoting harmony and social solidarity at a time of the year when cooperation rather than conflict has been essential to bring in the crops.

At 11:00 A.M., the group emerges from the shrine and returns to the outer courtyard, where the boys sit in two groups of ten in front of the standing sand cones, and the *saiō* takes her position on the dais in the Hosonoden pavilion, accompanied by the chief priest to her right and the assistant head priest to her left.

At the *dohyō* ring where the sumo matches will be held, a priest (rather than a member of the Original Parishioners' group) makes with his scepter what appears to be a figure eight in the sand while mumbling inaudible words. This is *fumikesu,* a kind of magic to prevent enemies from coming into Kamo territory. The figure eight represents a pairing of *in* and *yō* (yin and yang) spheres of influence and balance, the joining of which creates energy that is said simultaneously to increase and protect one's territory. A senior priest provides the briefest of descriptions over a poorly functioning public address system and calls these circles "charms" *(majinai).* I am told later the accompanying incantations are not prayers but spells *(kotodama)* designed to enlist spiritual forces to "gain ground" against opponents — a handy tool if, for example, a group wanted to encroach upon rice fields in the domain of another shrine.

Another priest then comes forward and, standing on the place where the two circles meet in the *dohyō,* reads and then presents to the *saiō* a scroll noting the names of the two groups' participants. Acknowledgment is thus made of the imperial presence at the event, symbolizing the shrine's relationship with the court, although this is done through the priests and not the parishioners. Next, the *tone* from each group emerges from two standing enclosures, each draped with white and blue bunting. Both are holding a bow and arrow, though their appearance is anything but warlike, since their skinny legs and bare feet are exposed from the knee down.

For the first time, the crowd sees a "crow" jumping toward the sand cones, as the *tone* on the left first hops three times, then rests while his counterpart covers the same territory in an identical manner. The *tone* rest their weapons against the side of the sand cones representing the two groups and then hop back to their respective bases. The trip to the enclosure is made two more times, first to bring out a sword, which is also placed against the sand, and finally to produce a single fan and straw mat. Taking up a position on this mat and flapping his fan, the *tone* on the left cries *"kaw, kaw, kaw!"* and is answered by his counterpart some two meters away with *"ko, ko, ko!"* After repeating this cycle three times, they both rise and follow the same alternating jumping pattern, returning to their enclosures, where they stay until the end of the ritual.

The boys then stand and follow their group leader to circumambulate the standing sand cone of their respective group in a clockwise motion, bowing each time around to the *saiō,* the chief and associate head priests, and to the shrine's main *kami,* Wake Ikazuchi, sequestered behind them all. Ritual preliminaries completed, the matches are ready to begin. Unlike in professional sumo, there are no elaborate warm-ups, mental games with opponents, or salt-tossing purificatory magic. The boys simply enter the *dohyō*, bow to each other and assume crouched positions, then spring into action when the word is given. As in professional sumo, some matches end almost as soon as they begin, but what the boys lack in skill they make up in enthusiasm. A tally is kept by the officiating "referee," and the wrestlers get at least two turns each.

When all matches have ended, a champion comes forth from the leading side and battles all comers in succession until he too is knocked down or out of the ring, restoring a sense of victory to the losing side and, I am told, circumventing grudges that might linger after the match.[16] The priest at the microphone then announces that the sumo is finished and thanks everyone for their attendance. Most people linger in the shrine for twenty to thirty minutes, some going through the side gardens, others paying their respects at the innermost courtyard, while others line up for sips of sake poured from ornate vessels in which float yellow chrysanthemum flowers. The photographers descend on the *saiō* as she moves toward a waiting car that will take her back to the imperial palace dressing rooms. Thirty minutes after the closing announcement, the folding chairs are gone, the temporary canopies removed, and the sumo ring has merged again with the sand of the courtyard. Only an occasional hired hand walks across the ground where the "crows" have ritually reclaimed the territory of their clan for another year. The next section will explore why rituals like Crow Sumo may have originated.

THE "UNHEARD OF DISTURBANCE" AT KAMIGAMO SHRINE: A HISTORICAL CHARTER FOR INSTITUTIONAL LONGEVITY AND CONTEMPORARY CULTURAL IDENTITY

As weaknesses of the old *ritsuryō* system were exploited, leading to less centralized control and more autonomy in developing the *shōen* landed estates (with their classic feudal structuring of authority, patronage, defense, and hunger for territory), Kamigamo's cozy relationship with the court slowly began to unravel. Part of this change was due to the enormous economic power and independence — seen by the court as rivaling its own — that the shrine had managed to accumulate through "donated" land.[17] But there are also powerful personal elements, most notably when an emperor's third son, adopted into the Kamo priestly lineage, began a cycle of divisive confrontations between the priests and the parishioners. I will discuss this process in detail because in it lie the seeds of a centuries-old distrust between the present-day parishioners' group and the priests as well as the frequently sanctimonious righteousness felt by the parishioners in their dealings with the shrine.

I have said a good deal about Kamo inclusiveness and attention to clan identity. These fit within a range of particular historical contexts, all of which influence contemporary clan and cultural identity in alternating local and national allegiances. For many ethnic, tribal, or other socially defined groups in the world, present-day claims to authority and continued social status arch backwards in time to a seminal historical incident. With nearly 1600 years of history to select from in formulating contemporary Kamo identity, the *dōzoku-kai's* leadership has seized on a strategy that juxtaposes two periods. The first is the shrine's golden age from the early Heian period to well into the Kamakura. According to Suma, from the year 796 forward, money was regularly offered to the shrine by the court; by 819 shrine rituals were afforded the same importance as those within the court compound, and every problem affecting the state was addressed through rituals at the shrine (in Fujiki 1991 : 199). Later, the shrine was under the protection of Minamoto no Yoritomo, though his patronage could do nothing to stem a slowly escalating series of incidents during a time of tremendous social conflict and turmoil, culminating in the mid–fifteenth century. An account of this conflict provides the second component of the juxtaposition and assumes central importance in the Fujiki history of Kamo priests. What begins as an intimacy with the court and all the trappings of imperial power ends with that same power responsible for severed Kamo heads displayed near the ruins of a burned-out shrine.

At the height of shrine and court goodwill, when Emperor Gotoba played kickball with Kamo chief priest Yoshihisa (1214–1221), a pact to mingle imperial lineages with those of the Kamo priests was carried out. One of the emperor's sons, Ujihisa, was adopted into the Kamo lineage, making him as well as his descendants Kamo priests. Yoshihisa organized a party to celebrate this joyous event, wherein Kamo fortunes would be even more closely allied with a popular emperor's agenda to restore imperial power after the beginning of the Kamakura military government *(bakufu).* However, chief priest Yoshihisa's brother (a senior priest at Kibune Shrine, a powerful Kamo subsidiary shrine along the upper Kamo River) boycotted the event, warning that it would only increase the power of the court at the expense of the Kamo. Not only did he predict "discord" *(fuwa),* but he ominously announced the likelihood of a battle between priests and parishioners in the future.

A conflict soon came, although it took a different form from the one Yoshihisa's brother forecast. In 1221, intending to restore imperial rule and make the military subordinate to the emperor, Emperor Gotoba tried to usurp power from the Kamakura military government in a disastrous rebellion now called the Jōkyū-no-ran. He vastly overestimated the strength and loyalty of his allies and failed to secure key defections to his camp from the Kamakura league, with the result that the attempted restoration ended in bloody defeat at Uji Bridge in south Kyoto. As Gotoba had enlisted the help of everyone he could find, including the Kamo shrines' militias, his fall precipitated a short-lasting but nevertheless hard time for the shrines. Suma points out that priests had to curtail by one-third sacred food offerings to the deities and even to eat the leftovers (instead of burying them, as was and still is customary) (in Fujiki 1991 : 205).

Despite the arrest of those priests who had participated, the shrines were able to retain most of their landholdings so that the hardships experienced after the rebellion were only temporary. Rather than attributing this good luck to divine intervention, political connections, or the *bakufu*'s forgiveness, it must be connected to a sudden outbreak of lawlessness in the surrounding countryside and outer provinces following the defeat of the imperial forces. Needing to restore order, the Kamakura rulers retained most governmental and courtly ruling systems, largely because establishing a new order would require considerable time, effort, and expense before stability could be attained. As a part of the traditional authority of the imperial system, which could not be dismantled without risk to the *bakufu*, the *shōen* estates were left largely intact (Mass 1990 : 71).

The Jōkyū-no-ran introduces two important factors that influence the rest of the Fujiki narrative. First, the priests at Kamigamo (like major religious institutions elsewhere during this period of interclan conflict) either had their own militia or had access to an armed militia. Second, the shrine's priests showed a willingness to enter into conflict for the sake of the imperial court, risking considerable land and status in the process. As violent confrontations between clans and estates escalated, old animosities were expressed and acted on in more confrontational ways, often with destructive outcomes.

Following Suma's account, in the fifth generation after the adoption of the imperial family's Ujihisa into the Kamo priesthood, another powerful shrine, Yoshida Jinja, had a rice field inside Kamo territory around the years 1470–1471 (Bunmei 2) (in Fujiki 1991 : 215). For reasons unknown, the farmers working that ground abandoned their obligations and left the area. When Yoshida Shrine tried to restore its workforce, six Kamo farmers banded together to harass the group and interfere with their cultivation, no doubt scheming to appropriate the land into Kamo holdings. It seems they were successful and took over cultivation but then refused to pay taxes to the land-owning shrine, a situation that prompted Yoshida administrators to bring suit against these Kamo farmers. Not surprisingly, the Yoshida priests had allies within the priesthood of Kamigamo. Because of an increasing spiral of intermarriage between the Kamo priesthood and women from other families as well as Kamo women marrying out to husbands in high places, the shrine was less "Kamo" than ever before. As a result, its administrators saw little to gain by siding with the farmers and turned to their considerable military and imperial court connections to discipline the farmers. The "defilement" of the Kamo priesthood warned against some 250 years ealier, which began with the adoption of an imperial son as a sign of friendship, was, from the farmers' perspective, now beginning to show its true colors.

Despite the formidable array of forces aligned against them, the farmers did not meekly submit. As in other areas of Japan during the fourteenth and fifteenth centuries, the Kamo *ujibito* (clansmen) had developed a social organization called *sō,* a kind of guild village consisting of 140 households charged with managing the production of certain shrine lands *(orai* or *iryo den)* within the *shōen* estate of the shrine. The effect of *sō* organization was to establish a structure of interlocking commitments and obligations whereby a council of elders *(shukuro)* guided the rest of the *ujibito (wakatonobara)* into a community preoccupied with self-preservation and defense. They not only "claimed control over internal matters but created administrative bodies and codes to regulate them" (Berry 1994:42).

The Yoshida Shrine claim can be seen as a test case for the effectiveness of the Kamo *sō* and whether it could withstand the forces of assimilation and appropriation that were gobbling up smaller entities all over the country. Members of the *sō* households proudly considered themselves "Kamo," just as members of the priestly enclaves did, and set their rules into written codes that, in content at least, were agreed to by all the households involved. Although this system of self-government had in most places become a relic of the past by 1500, at Kamigamo the *sō* continued until the first part of the Meiji period (1868), an impressive structuring of social relations lasting some three hundred years.

A select summary of guidelines relevant to the 1470s illustrates the tightness of the group as well as the troubles of the times:

1. *ujibito* must live in certain places and cannot be moving around
2. fields cannot be sold or put in hock
3. no working for samurai or rich people
4. no informing or betrayal to outsiders about the activities of the *sō*
5. arguments are to be decided by the council of elders of the *sō*
6. no stealing, no arson, no hoarding of money
7. no trapping fish in the rivers, no gambling, no dogs
8. don't bother merchants going in and out of the shrine
9. fields and bamboo groves can't be used to graze cattle
10. no kidnaping women off the road
11. those going against these rules may be ostracized or killed

(Suma, in Fujiki 1991:215)

In response to bullying and threats from the priests to pay taxes and return the contested land, elements of the *sō* staged a "disturbance" *(sōran)* inside the shrine grounds on September 2, 1475. While a number of priests were away at the imperial court, the farmers first broke into the administrative wing and stole valuables, then tried to remove the sacred essence *(goshintai)* from within the shrine buildings. Members of the shrine's militia successfully defended the inner sanctuary, and the perpetrators escaped into the surrounding mountains (Suma, in Fujiki 1991 : 215).

This incident resonates easily with modern imaginations and sympathies — given such events as the fall of communist regimes in Eastern Europe, the student movement for democracy in China, or popular resistance in Central America. But before analyzing the Kamo incident in terms of categories such as "resistance," "alterity," and "weapons of the weak" against corrupt and exploitative regimes, it is necessary to locate it within broader social and political contexts — ones that the Fujiki and Suma texts do not provide.

Beginning as early as 1298, cultivators of *shōen* and *kokugaryō* (public land under control of provincial administrators) in Ōmi province were banding together to form unified fronts against a variety of administrative afflictions (Nagahara 1990 : 286). The groups motivating the uprisings (known as *do-ikki* or *tokusei ikki*) demanded fewer taxes, exemption from the notorious labor corvées, and moratoriums on debts *(tokusei)* owed proprietors. When successful in having these demands met, local farmers gained influence and wealth, some of them to the point that they were called *jizamurai,* or "(armed) warriors of the land." Thus, in 1408, the farmers of Kamikuze-no-shō, an estate of the powerful Tōji temple in southern Kyoto, began a series of successful demands and protests for the lowering of taxes that lasted until 1437. In 1428, there were widespread peasant uprisings in Ōmi, Yamashiro, and Yamato provinces that continued until a devastating famine in 1430−1431 affected the entire area. In 1441, a unified front of cultivator groups in and around Kyoto forced the military government to issue an edict granting an abrogation of debts. In 1447, a major *do-ikki* rebellion destroyed parts of the city, leading to widespread unrest and lawlessness that continued sporadically for over fifty years.

This sampling of socially disruptive incidents shows not only how tenuous the old order (whereby peasants generally deferred to authority) had become, but also the very real political power the cultivators' groups had attained in defending their social and economic interests. In an ongoing social climate of unrest and conflict, what Elizabeth Berry calls the "culture of civil war" (1994), the following sequence usually occurred. First, negotiation between allied public groups sharing a common goal (reduction in taxes, debt cancellation, and so forth) tested their own resolve as well as probing the resolve of their enemies. Next, if an alliance proved resilient, a mass public witness, often highly theatrical, was accompanied by selective displays of violence (usually involving fire). Because the organization of these uprisings tended to follow horizontal rather than vertical relationships, they displayed new social configurations that often transcended the norms of class, religion, occupation, or locale. Finally, with political elites challenging the constraints that once ordered the medieval polity (such as legal statutes, precedents, institutions, and attachment to one's lord and family) and using coups, assassinations, personal assaults, physical destruction, arson, and looting to further advance their agendas (Berry 1994:13), the populace followed suit. From this perspective, it is not as surprising (or as heroic) as the Fujiki and Suma texts would have it for the Kamo *sō* to stand up not only to the military government and the Yoshida Shrine but to the demands of their own proprietors to return the disputed farmland.

Following the disturbance inside the shrine grounds in 1475, the priests' militia captured and arrested two of its ringleaders. With neither trial nor appeal, they were beheaded the next day beside the Kamo River.

Word went out that the priests considered this act of justice to have ended the confrontation and that the other *ujibito* would now be forgiven. According to Fujiki's account, however, the *ujibito* were preparing for the worst—even drawing up a document *(okibumi)* that formalized their opposition to the priests and their vow to take revenge for the murder of their kinsmen. The document also showed how the "wrongs" of the priests were manifold: cutting down part of the sacred grove of trees, building at great expense a mansion for entertainments, leading a life of dissipation, using the shrine as their own institution (rather than representing the Kamo community at large), and failing properly to carry out their ritual duties. Fujiki reports that word of the *ujibito* preparations somehow reached the priests, who then adjourned to the mansion to plan a preemptive strike of their own (1991 : 84).

Since both Fujiki and Suma are telling the same tale to the same audience, it is revealing to see how each structures the specific incidents in accordance with his sentiments, agenda, and background. Fujiki, on the one hand, is clearly aligned with the *ujibito* and takes pains to set the stage for their actions, basing his account on journals and an "official" history of the area, the *Atago-gun-sonshi*. Suma, on the other hand, attempts objectivity in using these same sources but glosses over details that provide important motivations for behavior related in the accounts.

Both relate that the priests were indeed planning for their militia to attack in May of 1476, yet only Fujiki explains that the Buddhist monk-in-residence at the Kamigamo mansion (who also produced the journal *Chikanaga kyōki* from which this information is taken) informed the *ujibito* of the priests' plan. Suma's account (subtitled a "summary") nonetheless incorporates considerable detail that Fujiki's does not, such as noting that another *okibumi* pact was drawn up by the younger *sō* members in which ninety-one men made provisions for the transfer of property in case they were killed. He also gives an important aside that introduces an element of internal conflict within the *sō* that Fujiki does not wish to include: fearful for their lives, several *ujibito* ran away from the group and sought shelter in the mountains to the north (in Fujiki 1991 : 216).

The *sō* group set off for the priests' mansion early in the morning on May 19, 1476, with seventy armed men, fifty of whom attacked from the front and twenty of whom attacked from the rear. In the ensuing mêlée, several priests were trapped inside and five were killed. The main villain of Fujiki's version, chief priest Katsuhisa, whose duplicity in matters be-

tween court and *sō* had caused much of the trouble and misunderstanding, "unfortunately" managed to escape. Fujiki states that the *ujibito* "won"
this conflict and went back to their houses to inform the *sō* council of elders, who, in his account, seem to have been unaware the attack had
taken place.

Immediately, efforts at reconciliation and a truce were initiated by the
elders. With the Buddhist priest Chikanaga serving as an intermediary
between Kamo and the priests, petitions were made to convince the imperial court that the attack was in revenge for the unwarranted execution
of the two men the year before. This approach proved successful, because
the court then intervened to reduce the risk of conflict. On June 12, 1476,
eighty-eight *ujibito* signed a document of peace produced by the court and
prayed at the shrine to have no further hostilities. The very next night,
however, two ne'er-do-wells from the *ujibito* (Fujiki's text includes the
priest Chikanaga's comment about one of them having "a good head for
evil things") went to the Shinkō-in Jingūji temple located within the
shrine compound and killed the son of chief priest Katsuhisa. Suma makes
no mention of this crucial incident nor of the fact that the *ujibito* group con-
demned the murder and tried again to make the new peace treaty hold.

Fujiki provides a more complete version of what happened next
(1991:85). Katsuhisa and his allies made a pact with the imperial court
that if the murderers were given up for execution, there would be no re-
taliation against the *ujibito*. Through their spy network, however, the
ujibito learned of this agreement and, in a crucial meeting in early August,
discussed various alternatives: If all-out war against the priestly enclave
developed, there would be no way to win, some noted, so why not occupy the shrine and seek official redress against Katsuhisa's group for their
wrongdoing and mismanagement? Others said that Katsuhisa was an evil
person and could not be trusted, yet a frontal attack on the shrine would
not be productive. The two murderers of Katsuhisa's son must be given
up for execution and then, under the imperial court's supervision, "peace
could again be restored after misfortune" *(wazawai o tenjite fuku to nasu)*.

Even as these deliberations were taking place, the priests' militia in the
Nishikamo area was recruiting an additional force from Kyoto's ready
supply of samurai warriors; the message went out that once assembled,
they would attack the *ujibito*. Rather than surrendering and thus acqui-
escing to the priests' demands, the two murderers of the chief priest's son
chose to commit joint suicide by stabbing each other with their swords
(sashi chigae), followed by decapitation at the hands of a second. The *sō*

council of elders ("weeping" Fujiki says) then collected the severed heads and, along with a formal letter identifying them as the murderers of Katsuhisa's son and also pleading for further hostilities to be avoided, sent them to the Nishikamo priests' militia. The priests were pleased and did not order their militia to attack; they even drew up a new treaty of peace that was signed and delivered to the *ujibito*.

But, as Fujiki implies (drawing upon the perspicaciousness of his readers to recognize the Japanese cultural type of an "evil priest"), with head priest Katsuhisa in the background, the *ujibito* should have known better than to be lulled into believing this gesture of reconciliation was genuine. In the early morning of August 23, 1476, Katsuhisa's militia and samurai allies attacked the *ujibito* community, killing an unspecified number and setting many dwellings on fire. The *ujibito* rallied at the shrine and fought to secure the inner compound at the Tower Gate, losing many people in this effort. Although the inner compound was successfully defended from frontal assault, the use of burning arrows by Katsuhisa's men, despite a storm of heavy rain and wind (implying that the *kami* himself was involved in the shrine's defense), eventually led to the farmers' undoing.

During the battle and the storm, the inner sanctuary's sacred object (*goshintai*) was removed from the burning buildings and spirited away to a location behind the sacred mountain, Kōyama. Those defenders that stayed eventually were either killed outright or captured, or committed suicide, with thirty-six heads displayed in a row by the victorious forces in what is today Yamamoto-cho. (Suma lists the total *ujibito* casualties as between forty and fifty, whereas Fujiki mentions only the thirty-six heads.) Fujiki reports that on the same evening, after the militia forces had returned to the Nishikamo area to celebrate their victory, they were attacked and several were killed by remnants of the now devastated *ujibito* settlements (1991:84).

In the end this striking and "unheard of conflict" (*zendaimimon*) between a shrine's priests and parishioners eventually turned to the latter's advantage. Chief priest Katsuhisa was removed from his post by imperial order and a neutral party was installed (one who is listed in the genealogy, significantly enough, as "father unknown"). The shrine itself lay wasted and ruined for an unspecified time, becoming "an empty field, overgrown with weeds" (Suma, in Fujiki 1991:216). Even the all-important and highly secret ritual of the *miare-sai*, in which priests "call down" the numinous spirit of the Kamo clan's deity to revitalize the community and its fields, was not carried out the next year (Fujiki, p. 85). Yet the imperial

court was insistent that this shrine, which had protected its vulnerable
northeast direction from evil spirits since the late eighth century, be rebuilt, ordering materials to be secured by razing one large house from the
priests' community and one from the *ujibito*'s (Suma, p. 217). Among the
many documents passed back and forth between the two factions, one of
the few that still survives is a scroll signed by 133 *ujibito* and eight priests
affirming a mutual intent to abide by the conditions of a peace treaty and
to work for the good of the shrine.

It was not long after these events that a succession of the three great
"unifiers" of the warring feudal states—Oda Nobunaga, Toyotomi
Hideyoshi, and Tokugawa Ieyasu—imposed upon the *shōen* estates a vast
reorganization within larger and more stable political systems. Although
the shrine lost much of its holdings, through compromise and skillful negotiations it did retain six communities in the immediate vicinity that,
with reapportionment and careful supervision by the *sō* administration,
provided adequate income for the *ujibito* and for shrine affairs until further rebuilding efforts could be initiated.

Suma posits several factors that allowed the *ujibito* of Kamigamo Shrine
and their administrative organization the *sō* to remain viable over time
when similar organizations elsewhere in Japan had died out or were being assimilated into more powerful administrative units. The first of these
features is a shared purpose in serving a shrine closely linked to the preservation and protection of the imperial court. In some ways, this sense
of purpose is similar to the enchantment that nationalism gives to the
lives of common people who, touched by the "luster" of its symbolism, feel
connected to and empowered by a transcendent cause (Wright 1985:
24). Second, he mentions the ability of the *ujibito* to keep outsiders from
encroaching on a "Kamo" sense of territory that is both physical (in the
case of the estate's rice paddies) and symbolic (the priesthood and clan
identity). The awareness this group had of its histories and traditions
(*dōzoku-ishiki* in Suma's phrase [p. 218]) also provided a strong cultural
and social cohesiveness that positioned the present within the sanctified
context of the past. In addition, Suma notes financial independence from
the rice fields as another factor in the parishioners' ability to weather
change.

But perhaps most important of all were the fairly "flat" horizontal status relationships that were maintained assiduously within the 140 households composing the *sō*. Although effective during this period of conflict

(described as *"issha no sōran,"* or a "riotous disturbance") in fostering a unified front to meet challenges from the priests, on other occasions the *sō* was unable to extract compliance from all its members in coordinating tactics representing the best interests of the group. The brash murder of the head priest's son at the very moment a peace treaty had been agreed on seems inconsistent with the picture Fujiki and Suma present of the inner hierarchies and authorized actions of the *sō*. If one is to accept the accounts' portrayal of these events—recalling that the Chikanaga journal was written by a Buddhist priest who straddled *sō*, priestly, and court interests, and that the *Atago-gun-sonshi* was rewritten at the order of the Meiji government in an effort to systematize and streamline shrine-related affairs (see Fridell 1973)—their representation must be placed within the context of the Fujiki shrine history.

Marshall Sahlins has commented that any historical event—whether it be an uprising or the publication of a text—is best thought of not as an entity bounded by beginnings and endings but as a relation between something that happens and a sociocultural structure (in Ohnuki-Tierney 1990:15). Fujiki is most concerned with the structure of parishioner identity as Kamo descendants and leaves no doubt that his book, although ostensibly about the priests, is an attempt to preserve and reconstruct events that have shaped this centuries-long process. He himself has selected, ordered, and (through publication) frozen into a particular narrative shape a variety of social and cultural associations that value positively his own ordering. He has also formed a symbolic ecology of crucial dates, events, and personages from the past that will, he hopes, influence and enter into future shrine-parishioner interactions, recalling the good as well as the bad times in which the shrine was an axis mundi where lives were at stake and whole neighborhoods prospered or met disaster vis-à-vis this sacred center.[18] The Kamo identity so valued by Fujiki (and others) is one that has been fashioned to stress its links to the earliest nature spirits of the land and sky, to the imperial court and Kamo protection of its northeastern spirit channel, and to ancestors who suffered great injustices and conflict in order that their descendants could prosper. Fujiki is implying that as long as Kamo descendants know the stories in his book and thus stay conscious of their histories and traditions, they will not be swallowed up by the forces of modernity, social change, and internationalization. It seems fitting to add, however, that the shrine's priests have recently commissioned several respected authors to compile their own version of history, one that will, no doubt, present the priests in a more sympathetic guise.

CONCLUSION

Catherine Bell says of "tradition" that, like a tree, it must be "pruned for a clear profile" and, like farmground, it must be "softened to absorb revitalizing elements" (1992:123). An active hand is at work in the maintenance of cultural practices, and it is part of the task of scholars to see which tools are used and which techniques enacted as well as which are avoided. While this analysis may appear subversive to those involved in the creation and promulgation of these practices or texts, the clarity and richness of a picture can emerge only when its background and frame are established. I have tried to show in this chapter how the appropriation of external cultural forms worked to the advantage of earlier productions of state and nation in Japan. There was also, however, a considerable reshaping of malleable domestic institutions, as evidenced by the serviceable posturing of a Shinto shrine. That this reshaping of traditions and realignment of priestly lineages with the court led to a disastrous conflict between a shrine's ritual specialists and its parishioners underscores the tendency of many researchers to see an overabundance of compliance and harmony in the religious history of Japan.

And yet, contemporary performances of Crow Sumo appear to bring together effectively the formerly conflicting institutions of Kamo and court, largely because the message of the festival is left at an implicit rather than an explicit level. Crow Sumo thus takes on an aura and characteristic common to other shrine rituals: performance, not preaching. At no point in my observations or interviews did I hear or see anyone extolling the virtues of Kamo heritage or history or, conversely, calling for secrecy about the meaning of the event. The boys received instruction about the details of their performance, but they were not lectured to concerning its significance within larger historical or political processes. Likewise, on the day of the ritual, the assembled audience was guided only in rudimentary ways concerning what they were seeing. Rather than stressing the symbolism of Kamo hegemony implicit in the performance, the narrator adhered to the pamphlet's description of the ritual as "magic for a good harvest" and "sumo to drive out evil." After waiting patiently in steamy heat for the inner-shrine ritual to end, the audience of over four hundred mostly middle-aged spectators took obvious pleasure in the spirited exchanges of the boys' sumo matches. To them the ritual was (to use some of the words heard in interviews) "interesting, splendid, amusing," and "traditional," leaving them satisfied that they had seen what they had come for: "crows," sumo, and spirited young boys—which, in a way, represented part of the cultural heritage and history of all Japanese.

But was the ritual they "saw" the same as the event staged by the Original Parishioners' Group and the shrine? I suggested at the beginning of this discussion that the staging of ritual performances such as the Crow Sumo—which, to its ritual specialists, serves to promote communal benefits regarding the upcoming harvest as well as furthering Kamo hegemony at the shrine—can renegotiate "tradition" just as easily as promote it. Any performance wherein a tradition from the past is staged before a contemporary audience will necessarily face this dilemma because of the number of perspectives possible for those engaged in the event as well as for those who are not. Not only can participation by both audience and performers be charted along a continuum of engagement and disengagement, so can the meanings of multivocal symbols such as the crow, the sumo ring, and even the *saiō* priestess (see Kapferer 1984.205).

In short, public perspectives of ritual events and festivals such as the Crow Sumo are no longer anchored in one system of cultural meanings, if indeed they ever were (see Fox 1990; Gerholm 1988). Rather than lamenting the fragmentation of culturally consensual meanings (as is common among the priests and inner-circle parishioners), one might note instead a revitalizing reciprocity operating within these multiple perspectives. All appear to find what they are looking for. This reciprocity, along with the nonrhetorical nature of Shinto ritual practices in general, helps prevent the Crow Sumo Festival (and other Shinto rituals as well) from becoming a heavy-handed ideological exercise as those framed by the military government in the 1930s and 1940s. Although contrary to the designs of its principal sponsors at the shrine and in the parishioners' group, this multiplicity of perspectives constitutes a primary reason for the continued success and public appeal of Shinto festivals and shrines in general: people have the conceptual liberty to construct meanings appropriate to their expectations and preconceptions. Religion and its ritual practices have always depended on addressing both the tangible and the intangible needs of human beings, including one's social and cultural identity as a subject within a domain of political power. If Shinto ritual performances can continue to address and sometimes satisfy these needs with a minimum of spoken commentary, texts, and preaching, the institution will ensure for itself a role in any future Japanese society.

WARDEN + VIRTUOSO +
SALARYMAN = PRIEST
The Roles of Religious Specialists
in Institutional Perspective

At age forty-seven, Ishida Haruo is at the point of no return.[1] A Shinto priest for seventeen years, he knows at this stage there will be no career change, no drastic improvement in his lifestyle, and certainly no promotion to head or even associate head priest. And yet, when listening to him discuss his work and career, one does not hear complaints. "When I come to the shrine in the morning, I have a secure feeling. I know what I am supposed to do and I know how to do it with a minimum of effort and stress. Not too many Japanese can say that about their jobs! *I* certainly won't die of overwork *(karōshi)!*" he says with a laugh. Each morning he parks his aging Toyota in the same spot, enters the shrine's back door by the kitchen, and goes into a four-mat tatami room to change into white *samue*-style work garments if office work or grounds maintenance is scheduled or pale blue *hakama* bloomers if dealing with the public or participating in a ritual.

At first glance, his career as a self-ascribed religious specialist and keeper of traditions appears to separate him from the mainstream of Japan's workforce. He is, to many, one of the charming anachronisms that give modern Japan a gentle reminder of its spiritual roots and historical heritage. People imagine his task to be the preservation and enactment of religious customs that have been around for centuries, some of which, they argue, help structure the very foundations of Japanese culture. As part of the institution within which these traditions have credence, he guards this unique heritage from despoilment by socially amalgamating forces the same way a game warden protects what is natural and fundamental. Were casual observers to look more closely and in a more sustained way, they would see that the hats he wears as a warden of tradition and religious virtuoso are only two emblematic markers for the many roles he plays during his career.

In this discussion contemporary Japanese Shinto provides the basis of a preliminary attempt to realign and expand scholarly perceptions of the role of priests within modern or modernizing societies. The preconceptions about religious specialists described above are likely to be familiar to scholars working in a variety of disciplines and social contexts. Confucians in Hong Kong, Buddhists in China, Caó Dai priests in Vietnam, Hindu brahmans, and Islamic imams in Malaysia alike are compelled and coerced (like everyone else) by the tense interplay of rapid social change, political economies of institutional development, and religious heritage. The easy stereotyping of these individuals comes not necessarily through negligence or errors of approach but through what Takie Lebra calls "an exaggerated uniformity produced by viewing things from a distance" (1993:17). The following pages provide an intimate portrait of Kamigamo Shrine and its priests in order to elicit a greater appreciation of one way of accommodating tradition and modernity and, by extension, to provide paradigms applicable for research within other social and cultural systems throughout Asia.

Like any employee, a modern-day priest has certain responsibilities and obligations that must be fulfilled lest inattention to duty reflect badly on the institution. One might even compare him to an archetypal salaryman, with lifetime employment, bonuses, health and insurance coverage, and incremental advances in status and pay assured the longer he remains. As in the world of the traditional salaryman, the more seniority one gains, the less work one actually does, with the burden of administrative details falling on the shoulders of the junior priests. But, as is true for Mr. Ishida, head of one of the shrine's inner departments, he is held almost entirely responsible for the tasks he delegates to others. As if to drive this point home (and to convince his interviewer that he really does have worries despite his uncluttered desk and relaxed smile), Ishida relates the tale of a priest before the war who did not carry out his duties and suddenly found himself transferred from Kyoto to northern Hokkaido. Today, with the Jinja Honchō in Tokyo involved in personnel appointments as a control against greater autonomy for individual shrines, the likelihood of a similar occurrence is extremely remote. Still, he wants me to understand that

Senior and junior priests,
Tsuchinoya pavilion.

he is under the watchful eye of powerful individuals who could make his
life very difficult.

INSTITUTIONS

Even though I will talk about institutions in general and shrines in particular as if they had agency, it is important to remember that this is only a
technique to personify what would otherwise be an abstract and bland
descriptive category. I agree with Mary Douglas that "institutions cannot
have purposes. Only individuals can intend, plan consciously, and contrive
oblique strategies" (1986:92) that come to stand for, embody, and sometimes subvert the "life" of institutions. I will have more to say later about
the priests and parishioners involved in this process but would first
like to sketch a conceptual portrait of institutions en route to describing
the particulars in operation at Kamigamo.[2] This attempt to understand
the roles of priests within a single shrine must be connected with larger
cultural systems that are, by and large, already constituted; what gives
"drama, pathos, and depth" to a single social context comes in observing
"how individuals originate and experiment with ideas about society and
their place in it based on existing cultural meanings" (see Fox 1991:108).

The word "institution" is used so widely in contemporary society that
it applies to everything from the hospital downtown, to the International
Red Cross, to (as the media is fond of saying) the "institution of marriage." And yet a precise definition that encompasses all possible situations, organizations, alignments, networks, and so on is, like a definition
of "democracy" or "religion," impossible to achieve. There are approaches,
however, to thinking about the term in creative and advantageous ways
that can make it easier to negotiate the distance and terrain between
signifier and signified.

The word's Latin root, *institutum,* refers in the *Oxford English Dictionary*
to a "purpose or design," which becomes in its final form *institutio,* an
"arrangement or establishment" (*OED* 1993:1382). A family is an institution, but so is a game, a ceremony, or Sony, Inc. What all of these phenomena have in common is the legitimation of a particular social group-
ing that starts (sometimes innocently enough) with rules of thumb and
norms but that can end, according to Schotter, by storing all useful information relevant to its survival and perpetuation (in Douglas 1986:48).

But institutions concern themselves with much more than information. John Thompson notes that an institution is "not a particular organi-

zation but a relatively durable set of social relations which endows individuals with power, status, and resources of various kinds" (1991:8). This perspective broadens the frame of reference to include a field within which the particular institution must operate, depending in large part on how the individuals envision that field and devise strategies (not always consciously) to mediate their interaction with it.

The apparent durability of institutions, then, leads one to think of them as "entropy-minimizing devices" (Schotter in Douglas 1986:48), which define a degree of sameness in the world as a way to perpetuate institutional stability and continuity. Experiences, objects, phenomena, and other human beings are assigned to classes and categories, then colored with moral and political attributes depending upon how they impinge on or extend the life of the institution. Bourdieu tends to see this process as an act of social magic, "creating difference out of nothing" (1991:120), yet institutional "magic" can be made all the more powerful and lasting by creating analogies having similar categorizations in natural and supernatural worlds (see Douglas 1986:63). Characterizing women as natural "caregivers," human aggression as "predatory behavior," or certain religious practices as continuous with mythic precedents furthers institutionalizing categories. When effectively maintained through social codes, religious values, and cultural practices, "institutions systematically direct individual memory and channel our perceptions into forms compatible with the relations they authorize. They fix processes that are essentially dynamic, they hide their influence, and they rouse our emotions to a standardized pitch on standardized issues. Add to all this that they endow themselves with rightness and send their mutual corroboration cascading through all the levels of our information systems" (Douglas 1986:92).

Although Douglas is not referring to religious institutions in particular, the general terms of her argument are amenable to religious contexts as well. In a construct somewhat like Geertz' definition of religion that stresses moods and motivations, models of, models for, and blueprints for reality, one can think about institutions, whether religious or not, as ideological and practical constructs that systematically endow their authority with moral and ethical parallels.

SHRINE SHINTO

One can see a prime example of Douglas' archetypal institution in Japanese shrine Shinto since the Meiji period. When shrines came under state control in 1868, the place-specific nature of local and regional deities was gradually (and controversially) standardized into a broader set of formally codified cultural meanings such as filial piety, Confucian mores, and a linkage of the imperial line to the sun deity, Amaterasu. It is by now widely known how well this overhauled Shinto eventually served the state's goal: to unify the country through an administrative network linking local and national shrines, and to implement a system of emperor worship and patriotic self-sacrifice. Japan's defeat in the war and the eviscerating effects of the Shinto Directive of 1945 (which removed state support from all religious institutions) should have, in the eyes of many, put an end to this system once and for all.

One of the more recent assessments of the institutional history and effectiveness of shrine Shinto since the war sees little chance for its survival. Specific charges are leveled regarding the current state of "decay" afflicting the institution (Hardacre 1989 : 142). Shinto is described as "ethically and intellectually bankrupt," an "empty shell" seen by the Japanese public as having been discredited by the loss of the war and the "absence of state patronage." An additional shortcoming is seen in the commercial enterprises (such as wedding halls) that shrines have opened to compensate for dwindling parishioner support. The blame for this sorry state of affairs is seen as resting with the priests, whose "feeble and ineffectual" efforts have not met challenges such as the growing prestige of science, the secular disposition of society, and "the media's tendency to ignore or ridicule religion" (pp. 142–143).

While these charges may have been valid during the period in which the source material was published (Norbeck 1970; Morioka 1975), considerable changes took place in the 1980s that necessitate a reevaluation of this assessment. It is not that society has led the way and the Shinto priesthood scrambled to keep up; instead the innovation, creativity, and long-range, systematic plans of a number of priests in particular as well as the alternately guiding and coercive hand of the Jinja Honchō in general have responded to (with varying degrees of success) the challenges that were brought up.

First, Japan's increased economic prosperity of the 1970s and 1980s gave wealthy individuals the means to influence or sponsor activities and institutions that extol national and local history as well as cultural or communal pride. Research institutes (such as Nichibunken), museums (such as the Sagawa Museum of Shinto History at Ise), and publicity campaigns (the late Sasagawa Ryōichi's "helping hand" commercials or his largesse to a number of academic institutions to help further his quest for a Nobel prize) all served to promote and memorialize their sponsors' frequently hand-picked agendas. Many of these individuals, socialized and educated during the prewar period, have returned to shrines in their moneyed later years as important patrons for maintaining and repairing shrine buildings, funding the staging of major festivals, and permitting shrines to use their business and political networks for fund-raising. In exchange, they are often given what they see as potential access to national status hierarchies connected with the Jinja Honchō, the imperial household (in the case of Ise), and other elites. A shrine elder in northern Kyoto said of one wealthy individual, "Whenever we're short of funds, we can always rely on him for a million yen . . . but it's important not to ask too often." Affiliation with a major shrine (or Buddhist temple) is not an "empty shell" but often a protective or decorative one, sought by many individuals for self-promotion (of one's status, heritage, or lineage) and entrepreneurial gains that extend into business and social networks.

Second, an interest in the past (the so-called *kodai būmu*) has burgeoned since the mid-1970s, stimulated by extensive media coverage given to the excavation of imperial tombs (Takamatsuzuka foremost among them), by archaeological sites such as Yoshinogari in north Kyushu, and by the proliferation of books addressing the "wheres", "hows", and "whys" of Japanese culture and history vis-à-vis the rest of the world. Yoshino terms this phenomenon "secondary nationalism," a process through which national identity is enhanced and preserved according to a changing set of characteristics creating a distinct group (1992 : 5 – 6). What better place is there to see the "real" Japan (one often aligned to resonate with some archaeological record or precedent) than at a local neighborhood festival? Usually (but not always) sponsored by a neighborhood shrine with private and corporate financial backers, these events are increasingly promoted by local and often national media as encoded discourses about a community's identity and thus about inclusion and exclusion, about identifying "Japaneseness" with local cultural events, and about surrendering the right to define local culture to agencies beyond the community's control (see Herzfeld 1986; Nelson 1996b).

Growing out of the second trend, there has been a general shift in Japanese media perspectives on religion and religious institutions. Japan's mainstream religious traditions are portrayed in a sympathetic and normative manner as embodying essences belonging to the mysterious "heart" of Japan and its people. Mountaintop temples and shrines, seaside sacred places, even inner-city religious sites are frequently featured in television travelogues as places rich in history and culture that are easily accessible to the urban domestic tourist. As Graburn has noted (1983, 1995), the boom of domestic tourism has carefully nurtured and exploited linkages between regional and national transportation infrastructures and an abundance of "significant" historical, cultural, and religious attractions (made accessible and comprehensible by a plethora of guide books).

Also part of this network are numerous shopping opportunities for tourists with ample travel budgets, which encourages more rather than less participation with shrines and temples and the public activities they sponsor. A tourist can see a shrine (or temple), eat regional delicacies, and shop in nearby boutiques or arcades all in the space of an hour or two. With advertising campaigns on national television that capitalize on such trends or use "traditional" religious themes, images, and events to promote a product (sake, household cleaning tools, automobiles, coffee), the public is fairly saturated with positive and enticing images associated with "traditional" religious institutions within Japanese society. It is possible that the publicity associated with the Aum Shinri Kyō subway gas attack in early 1995 will further enhance the cultural legitimacy of Japan's mainstream, nonproselytizing religions, especially when contrasted with the radical fringe of bizarre cults and sects.

Shrines may have lost governmental financial sponsorship after the war, but with this loss has come more freedom to determine their own affairs. The Jinja Honchō in Tokyo still figures prominently in a shrine's appointments, in the certification of priests, and in promoting selected political agendas through its weekly newspaper, the *Jinja shimpō*. But, according to its Kyoto representative, it has no legal authority to exact compliance should a shrine wish to follow an alternative course. Although a shrine could, theoretically and legally, do so, the nature of the national association of shrines and the networks of interlocking acquaintances, reputation, and finances do a great deal to constrain individual shrines to follow the national line a majority of the time. Ostracism, public criticism, or private censure is a price few Japanese are willing to pay for an independence that would, in the long run, be detrimental not only to the shrine but also, in Robertson's analysis, to the efforts of municipalities to reclaim the "indigenous village within the city" (1988 : 124).

As Haley discovered in a study of law in Japan (1991 : 196), what appears to be an outward submission to authority does not necessarily entail a diminution of community or individual freedom. Western observers are quick to assume that with authority also comes coercive power, yet throughout Japanese society there is a tendency to have pyramidlike hierarchies within organizations where power derives from consent and consensus. The trade-off, Haley argues, is between submission and autonomy, with outward deference to authority ensuring greater freedom from regulatory control. By maintaining order and stability, containing conflict, and promoting consensus whenever possible—all characteristic of the Japanese workplace and general shrine administration—direct intervention by outside authorities (state agencies or the Jinja Honchō) can be avoided and autonomy preserved. It is not that shrines meekly submit to all guidelines or directives—they have frequently gone their own stubborn ways, indicative of their regional power base, financial and patron support, and the idiosyncrasies of different managerial styles.

INSTITUTIONAL ELITES

Individuals (and groups) shaping, modifying, and directing institutional processes from within and without are found along a continuum of status and influence. At the elite end of the continuum are the administrators, policymakers, and other interested individuals who have maneuvered or been born into positions of rank and power. The exclusivity of their personal agency to formulate agendas as well as their interlocking relationships with individuals at other institutions provide venues for influencing and sometimes shaping policies. However, the term "elite" is one they do not necessarily apply to themselves, since it depends largely on a public perception that someone within the institution is acting in conspiratorially discreet backstage arenas that are invisible to nonelites (Marcus 1983:11; see also Lebra 1993). While they may have formally defined functions, offices, or controlling interests within an institution, these are all modified by the creation of a domain of personal relationships and tacit practices that extend their influence into other nonofficial realms (Marcus 1983:42).

The problem becomes how they justify their acts and interpersonal networks without appearing conspiratorial, self-serving, or, even worse, corrupt. In a study of Latifundist Sicily, Schneider has shown that acts of charity, philanthropy, patronage, and hospitality are not only characteristic aspects of elite behavior, but necessary to justify their concentration of power both to themselves and to others (in Marcus 1983:160). The Rockefeller, Mellon, Annenberg, and a host of other corporate foundations operate in much the same way.

Elites involved with a religious institution may see their activities as expressions of devotion rather than exercises of power, but, again, interpretations of their acts of generosity are not exclusively theirs to make. A wealthy patron of Kamigamo, for instance, gave nearly $25,000 in 1991 for the construction of a new Shinto torii at the shrine's eastern entrance. Even though there was nothing structurally wrong with the existing torii, the shrine was only too happy to accept his donation, since the periodic rebuilding of wooden structures is fundamental to Shinto notions of purity and renewal and since part of the money could be applied to other maintenance projects. That this particular torii was selected was not happenstance — it is the principal approach both to the shrine and to the bus terminal for local residents in the historical neighborhoods east of the shrine. The patron himself said he frequently gives donations to the shrine as a way to express gratitude for all the good things that have happened to him. But to local residents, the strategic location of the torii and the commemorative plaque that stands before it reminds them of the patron's wealth and power rather than his devotion. "If I had that kind of money," one elderly man remarked, "I'd use it for myself instead of giving it to the shrine. He [the patron] must have so much money he doesn't know what to do with it all!"

This example points to what is perhaps the most effective way for neutralizing and redirecting public biases against elite behavior — the manipulation of established cultural codes.[3] Just as a modern nationalist consciously wills his or her identification with a culture (Gellner 1987:10), so do modern elites will an identification with institutions whose underlying cultural and social codes they interpret to be resonant with their own and thus, over time, perhaps amenable to their intentions.

Appadurai has examined the ways in which elites associated with a Hindu temple in southern India attempt to maintain and promote their hold on certain key rituals that they feel enhance identity and status. Their strength within the temple, he says, depends on the "kind of past they can credibly marshal in defense of their collective interests" (Appadurai 1983:210). So too do the elites of the shrine employ a repertoire of publicly visible and historically referenceable symbols (torii or building maintenance and reconstruction), activities (the sponsorship of festivals and rituals), and organizations (the original parishioners' group, board of regents [riji-kai], or parishioners' council [ujiko sōdai kai]) as means through which to enact personal and collective ends. Shrines assist in these ends by posting names and the amounts of donations on a large display board that is displayed prominently for everyone to see. In circumstances where a formal, institutional approach is not sufficient to further and legitimate their power, they can turn to social networks made by intermarriage, friendship, political alliances, and residential proximity.

SHRINE SHINTO'S RELIGIOUS VIRTUOSOS

Caught between these lay organizations and elite patrons are the priests, who struggle with a surprising lack of power in dealing with self-serving interest groups. Before elaborating on the tenuous and awkward middle ground that a shrine's religious specialists occupy, it may be useful to summarize briefly what they are not.

There is an assumption among many Westerners that religious specialists in Japan, Shinto and Buddhist alike, are celibate as part of their "vows." Shinto priests have never had celibacy as a qualification for serving a particular shrine, although temporary periods of abstinence *(imi)* from sexual intercourse are required before certain major rituals. So important is the family structure to Japanese social life and institutions that the monastic tradition in Buddhism was forced to adapt to Japanese sociopolitical environments (of the sixth and seventh centuries C.E.) in which families were religiously validated through affiliation with tribal (or *uji*) tutelary deities. Perpetuating the lineage, and in later years what came to be known as the household *(ie)*, was a primary responsibility of every individual. Today a growing number of women are entering the priesthood for precisely this reason (see Nelson 1996b). As Lancaster has shown in a Buddhist context (1984:16), applying in many cases to Shinto priestly families as well, married priests remain within the family's kinship system, creating a regular family life "centered on the continuity of the father-son control of the temple" or the shrine (where sometimes a father-daughter, or even grandfather-granddaughter transmission is found). The way one gains self-fulfillment is not by a religious separation from society (as traditional Buddhism idealized) but by developing higher and broader abilities of awareness about the meaning of one's relationships and social interaction (see De Vos 1976, 1984; De Vos and Sofue 1984; Kumagai 1984).

Another misconception is that Shinto priests live at shrines. History shows that communities of ritual specialists once lived in close proximity to the institutions they served. Kamigamo Shrine's famous and well-preserved neighborhoods to the east, now called *shake machi* in the tourist guidebooks, were once such a place. In order to maintain ritual purity before an important shrine event, priests would take back alleys through these neighborhoods en route to the shrine lest they meet someone coming from a funeral or someone handicapped, or lest they see a fire—all of which would compromise their preparedness and force them into another period of abstention (kessai).

In smaller shrines, it may indeed be the case that a priest and his family live on shrine property. However, unlike the residences of many Buddhist priests that connect to the main hall of worship through long corridors or immediately adjacent buildings, the residence of a Shinto priest will be separate from the Honden where rituals are performed. In line with an apparently functional separation of sacred and secular affairs, one not always translating to actual practices, the mundane world of the family should not physically impose in any way upon the sacred space of the deity. In the case of Kamigamo, only the head priest lives on shrine property, in a residence considerably removed from the central sanctuary. All other priests (save those trainees or junior priests in residence) must commute to and from the shrine, often considerable distances.[4] Land, house, and condominium prices in the immediate vicinity of most urban shrines have skyrocketed far beyond the purchasing ability of priests with very modest incomes. These contemporary social, economic, and demographic realities have a direct bearing not only on the attitudes of priests toward their workplace but also on the priests' degree of involvement with the shrine's immediate surrounding community.

Max Weber considered priests "religious functionaries" who have specialized knowledge and vocational qualifications rather than a magician's self-promoted charisma (Morris 1987:71). Even though he notes that all religions contain aspects of magic, he says it is the function of the priesthood to develop doctrines that systematize a religious ethic that can function independently of magical and other nonrational causalities (Weber 1964 [1922]:22). Weber might have succeeded in integrating this rather narrow definition into his theory had it not been for what was going on in Japan. Because of the example of Shinto, he stops short of making doctrine a defining characteristic of the priesthood. Shinto, he says, unlike all the other religious systems he has considered, does not have a "revelation" on which to base a "stable, consistent doctrine" giving rise to a "systematic and distinctively religious ethic" (p. 29). Instead, determined to include even such oddities as Shinto, Weber forges a definition of priesthood as "the specialization of a particular group of persons in continuous operation of a cultic enterprise, permanently associated with particular norms, places and times, and related to specific social groups" (p. 30).

As far as this definition goes (and despite the problematic and ideological nature of the terms "cultic" and "enterprise") Weber is pointing in the right direction. He has located an institution within specific contexts of place, society, and social groups—the "fields" spoken of earlier—rather than positing it as a monolithic structure functioning independently of social circumstance. However, his all-encompassing developmental scheme—which relegated Japan's "traditionalist and magical" religion as theoretically detrimental to the development of capitalism—simply was not true. Nor is the notion of a "cultic enterprise" accurate when examining the function of priests.

Generally speaking, it is possible to supplement and amend Weber's influence on current thinking about religious specialists by following Bourdieu's advice and looking first at those features of a religious institution that authorize an individual to pronounce certain things in certain ways (1991 : 111). Such features are not restricted to doctrine or institutional practices. An institution also tries to determine the ways in which its specialized discourses are received, the analysis of which spirals outward into social and political spheres.

Following Catherine Bell, whether or not a priesthood operates within literate or nonliterate traditions, its first and perhaps most important function is to adjudicate the relations between human and nonhuman powers (1992 : 134). From this mandate, priests can rank ritual activities according to importance, significance, and efficacy and, consequently, have considerable impact on the structuring of social relations as well as the social calendar. What might seem to be the unmitigated power of an individual to dictate the means and ends of ritual activity is in fact mediated by the specialist's office. In other words, the power to perform the ritual resides not in the person but, as Bourdieu suggested, in the institutional framework of his office. Correctness of performance can promote and maintain the expertise of a specialist, but judgment is continually passed on this performance by fellow specialists as well as other groups (elite patrons, parishioners' groups, even long-term local residents) integral to the operation of the institution.

Within the context of shrine Shinto, a priest has the training, experience, and status to intervene with nonhuman forces on behalf of local communities and individuals, thus maintaining what Weber calls a "cultic enterprise." At Kamigamo, in order to satisfy local audiences a priest must know the shrine's way of performing rituals (see Ashkenazi 1993:110), which may be different from the tradition he or she grew up with at the family shrine, what was learned as correct in a training university, or even what was taught about the shrine's rules and regulations on ritual propriety *(sahō)*. A priest's tenure at the shrine depends in part on the reputation he or she builds based on local ritual performances, but appointments and advancements come from the Central Association of Shrines in Tokyo. So, while a priest may be well liked and respected by superiors and colleagues, he or she must also be on guard concerning relations with the shrine's trustees, the shrine's elders, the women's group elders, and other affiliated individuals who contribute to the operation of the shrine. An adept religious virtuoso learns how to "play" these different dynamics so as to maximize their resonant components, harmonize dissonance, and even improvise on particular themes based on the perceived authority of his institutional agency.

Whereas Appadurai sees Hindu priests as "isolated from power" (1983:215) and "linked to peculiar and separate sources" (p. 214), for a Shinto priest power relations are multifaceted and often diffuse.[5] In tactical or organizational structures, power occurs most pragmatically as it controls the ritual and bureaucratic settings in which people show their potentialities and interact with human and nonhuman others (see Wolf 1990:14). Performative occasions such as important ritual events may appear to be instances where priests exercise their full powers as religious intermediaries, yet they may have been coerced or compelled to play their role by the administrative structure within which they operate.

In the internal workings of a shrine's departments, power is alternately concentrated and diffuse, so that figures of authority are often not the locus where institutional power accumulates and orchestrates shrine policies. At social and cultural levels within Japanese society, however, priests know that they are imbued with a formal authority other men and women do not possess to stage rituals, uphold certain traditions, and address spiritual entities that were once deemed awesome in their power. Unlike many Buddhist priests who are easily spotted in public by their clerical attire, Shinto priests do not flaunt their institutional garb in public, preferring to dress as any other person does when dealing with the secular, profane world. Their understanding of religious symbols and how the meaning of these symbols is managed (as in the case of the shrine's hollyhock, or *aoi,* crest) is a somewhat less important but still viable source of power. An ability to control scarce resources—whether they be finances, ritual participants, or the costumes and props necessary for ritual events—also contributes to a priest's effectiveness and off-stage authority. Often, in order to make the most of these resources, interpersonal alliances, networks, and control over informal organizations and individuals affiliated with the shrine must come into play.[6]

Priests able to manage, manipulate, and maneuver the opportunities and challenges presented with a deft but gentle touch are rare indeed, largely because they must do so, as in other institutions in Japan, within a spiraling hierarchy of rank and seniority. "If only I were fifteen years older," said one priest aged thirty-four with a sigh (a sentiment I've heard in other shrines as well), "I might be able to get something done around here." A brief look at the details of the shrine bureaucracy will provide an orientation to the social and political fields a priest must acquire some mastery of en route to fulfilling his or her obligations on the ritual stage.

STRUCTURING THE PRIESTHOOD

Among the many high-water marks along the banks of the river that is Shinto history, the Meiji revitalization of the priesthood continues to influence the course of shrine Shinto. The detail that follows may tax the reader's patience, but to omit it would compromise understanding and appreciation of the structural and institutional fields a priest must operate within and constantly negotiate during his or her career.

Until the Meiji revolution, according to Abe Masamichi (1990), a centuries-old system of rank and title traceable to Nara period documents divided priests into a top-down hierarchy beginning with *daigūji, hafurishi, ōuchibito, tayu, oshi,* and ending with *sendachi.* Not all shrines had enough priests to fill all these ranks, but the larger ones, such as Kamigamo, Ise, and Miwa certainly did. From the Meiji period onward, however, these ranks became known at the imperial shrines of Ise as *saishu, daigūji, shogūji, negi, gonnegi,* and *gujō.* At all other shrines the ranks were *gūji* (or head priest), *gongūji* (associate head priest for those shrines large enough to fill this position), *negi* (or senior priest), and *gonnegi* (or junior priest). The principal task of Shinto priests, according to Abe, is the continual study of how to mediate between the *kami* and human beings (1990:154). To these ends, training *(shugyō)* and manners or propriety *(sahō)* are integral to developing a proper attitude and practice. Abe notes in an aside that priests also have duties in shrine administration and maintenance of the grounds, but he quickly adds that these tasks come between the main work of providing food offerings to the deity in the *niku-sai* ritual at morning and evening.[7]

According to 1998 Jinja Honchō statistics, there are 21,393 certified Shinto priests in Japan; of that number, only around five thousand actually work full-time as religious specialists at a shrine. Among the outside occupations profiled by the June 1992 "Statistics Concerning Activities at Nationwide Shrines" (Jinja Honchō 1992b), only those concerned with some aspect of education receive mention: high school teachers (491) and civil administrators (445) are the most numerous, followed by retired teachers serving as probation officers (418), junior and elementary teachers (301 and 247), and many others ranging from school superintendents (140), members of educational committees locally and regionally (106 and 147), public defenders (114), directors of public halls (98), city and prefectural officials in charge of education (14 and 25), and museum or library employees (39 and 15). These selected statistics show Jinja Honchō ideology at work, assigning an overt complementarity between these "educational" occupations and those of priests, but making no effort to represent occupations connected to business.

Economic factors effectively prohibit most licensed priests from practicing their profession full-time and discourage many other men and women from studying to become priests. The average salary of priests nationwide is 155,000 yen per month (U.S. $1 = ¥110, U.S. $1,409), totaling 1,860,000 yen ($16,909) yearly without summer and winter bonuses (1992b Jinja Honchō figures). With this salary, an individual must either have a strong predilection for the priesthood and its lifestyle, strong family pressure, a wife with a career, family money, a supplemental job, or landholdings belonging to his family's shrine.

Compare the above figures with a 1996 Ministry of Labor survey (Keizai Kōhō Center 1997) of 286 companies having more than one thousand employees, with an average fixed salary of 296,000 yen per month ($2,690). At a yearly rate, this salary alone (which excludes bonuses) exceeds 3,552,000 yen ($32,290), or 1,691,910 yen ($15,381) above priests' salaries (excluding bonuses).[8] Clearly, the Shinto priesthood is not a profession for those interested in monetary gain and material payoffs based on salary alone.

Additionally, a formidable process of certification awaits the candidate not only at the start of his or her career but when moving through the ranks of the hierarchy. From lowest to highest, the rungs of the ladder to the position of head priest are *chokkai, gonseikai, seikai, meikai,* and, at the top, *jōkai.* These terms are not used in public, where the more simple *shinkan* or *kannushi* (literally "master of worship" [Kitagawa 1987:151n.]) is preferred when referring to priests in general. Nor would a priest introduce himself to a lay person as holding one of the formal ranks listed above, not only because it would have no meaning to one unfamiliar with shrine appointments but because advertising one's particular social or professional status is considered an indication of one's need to enter quickly into a strategic or advantageous situation. The etiquette, timing, and circumstances of bestowing business cards fills this function quite nicely for priests as well as salarymen in Japan. However, instead of the formal distinctions of rank listed above, one finds the more familiar terms of *gūji, gongūji, negi,* and *gonnegi* printed clearly beside the name of the shrine. Distinctions of rank using the *-kai* system come up frequently in conversations between priests, as when former schoolmates discuss the careers of their classmates or priests from different shrines note one of their colleagues' promotions. In ways more precise than the business card system, the formal titles are not only indicators of status, they also signify erudition, position the ambitions of individuals within their respective institutions, and hint at political adeptness in maneuvering through a hierarchy of gender, seniority, and social alliances.

The Japanese face examinations at nearly every stage of their lives, beginning at kindergarten and culminating in company hiring exams, and the Shinto priesthood is no exception. In his book on festivals, Ashkenazi remarks that priests "are not 'ordained' but merely trained" (1993:112). While I agree with his assessment concerning ordination, to imply that the training process for all *kannushi* is somehow insubstantial does not do justice to the complexity and rigor facing them at each career turn. In order to pass from one rank to the next, a succession of tests covering three broad areas—Shinto studies, ritual performance, and speaking ability— are administered periodically throughout the year by the Jinja Honchō. For the *chokkai* level, graduation from one of the training universities or accreditation centers is all that is required (although an eight-thousand-yen fee is charged for the actual certificate). To reach the next two successive ranks, examinations covering three days test one's knowledge in the following areas:

Gonseikai: (Day 1) General knowledge about shrine Shinto, Shinto history, the *Kojiki* and its interpretations, shrine rituals, ritual etiquette, and ritual performance. (Day 2) Shrine Shinto's old customs and ritual practices, interpretation and composition of invocational prayers *(norito),* Shinto educational curriculum and bylaws, and Japanese religion. (Day 3) Japanese history, ethics, and Japanese literature. Exam and certificate cost: ¥10,000.

Seikai: (Day 1) Knowledge of shrine Shinto, shrine rituals, Shinto theology, and Shinto documents, and interpretation of the *Nihon shoki.* (Day 2) Interpretation of invocational prayers from the *Engi shiki;* knowledge and performance of shrine rituals and etiquette, prayer composition, general knowledge of world religions. (Day 3) General knowledge of philosophy, psychology, Japanese literature, and Chinese literature. Exam and certificate cost: ¥15,000.

Meikai: (Day 1) Shinto, shrine Shinto, Shinto history, rituals, and Shinto theology. (Day 2) Interpretations of the *Kojiki, Nihon shoki,* and *Engi shiki* invocational prayers, and shrine etiquette and ritual, followed by a graded ritual performance. (Day 3) Shinto documents, ancient rules and traditions, prayer composition, Shinto tenets for public dissemination, laws relevant to shrines. (Day 4) Religious studies in general, the history of religion, the history of Japanese religion, Buddhism, and Christianity. (Day 5) Japanese history, Japanese literature, philosophy, psychology, ethics. (Day 6) History of the world, some knowledge of a foreign language. Exam and certificate cost: ¥20,000 (half price for second and subsequent attempts to pass).

Jōkai: No tests are given to achieve this rank. It comes through recommendation and appointment by the Jinja Honchō. Many younger priests I spoke with feel this level should also be attained through examinations of codified knowledge rather than networking, reputation, and politics.

After one has passed the written and performative tests, there is a period of training that supposedly allows priests to contextualize their newly certified knowledge and skill. *Gonseikai* priests must go for two weeks to a *jisshū jinja,* or "training shrine," especially designated by the Jinja Honchō as appropriate to the individual's general level of skill. *Seikai* level priests' training period extends to an entire month but can occur at a *kōbetsu jinja* or any shrine belonging to the nationwide Jinja Honchō system. The *meikai* level priests have the same requirement as *seikai* priests, but they must also go for an unspecified period to a *jingū jisshū* such as Ise, Meiji, or Iwashimizu, where, according to the brochure, their "faith can become stronger." Finally, a mentor is introduced into the training process in the *chūō jisshū* training period, where *meikai* priests are taught and supervised for three days by a single individual, usually more advanced in age, so as to affirm the *senpai-kōhai* dynamic found in Japanese society from junior high to the corporate world.

It is important not to overemphasize what occurs at the larger shrines. Until the Meiji period, the Shinto priesthood could be inherited from one's father without leaving one's natal community. With the advent of national certification of priests, instigated by the Meiji state (1871), additional study and training has served as a kind of internship for those aspiring to this career. Today, for families operating rural or smaller urban shrines, inheritance can still be passed on to a son, son-in-law, or even a daughter provided he or she has proper certification and training.

Although Ueda criticizes the inherited priesthood's easy access to status as "lacking passion" (1979 : 326), it is easy to see how the economic and social advantages of continuing what may be an asset-rich religious institution deeply embedded within the social relationships of a community compensates for what is, when judged by the standards of Japan's high-tech consumer society, a financially marginal occupation. The right to conduct rituals at a particular shrine, whether it is in one's family or not, is legitimated by attendance at one of the training universities (or an accredited regional training center) and performing an internship at a larger shrine. Several of the younger priests at Kamigamo (as well as at the other shrine I have studied, Suwa Shrine in Nagasaki) were "apprentices" (*yatoi*), studying (as they put it) "with the best" before returning to the shrine their family owns or has been allowed to run by a local shrine guild (*kōjū*, formerly *miyaza;* see Davis 1992) for generations. And while apprentices do acquire status during their affiliation with a larger shrine, they must also endure low pay and hard work in much the same way a doctor suffers through the exploitation of his residency or aspiring artists or athletes follow the character-building strategies of their seniors in order to become skillful adepts themselves.

On graduation, a young priest often has little choice but to go wherever a place is found. Assisting in this process is the placement service of the Jinja Honchō, which fields requests from shrines nationwide for new employees and matches them with lists of coming graduates provided by the universities. However, having an important patron at a particular shrine is thought to be essential, since the acquaintance of this person and the recommendations he or she provides will serve the graduate as a kind of protection later on when he or she is relegated to the lowest rungs of the shrine hierarchy.[9] The indignities and initiations of a new priest are made bearable for most by the knowledge that they will return to their family shrines within three to five years and there assume positions of real authority.

However, for those individuals who have come to the priesthood as a second career, an escape from the pressures of salaryman existence, or (in rare cases) a spiritual calling, the first years of socialization and training within this new world are critical. Very much outsiders, these individuals are hired on a trial basis to see whether they will fit in with a shrine's existing personnel and way of doing things and, even though they may be permanent employees, are given the same status as other trainees (or lower, because they lack the networks of another shrine and its community).

As trainees, the younger priests are not expected to know or internalize the history, sacred qualities, or other "essences" composing a shrine's public identity. They serve in rituals on an alternating basis with other priests, yet always wear green *hakama* indicating their lowly status. While they shed the green vestment within a year, it may take another five years before they are offered a permanent position. Unlike the rural shrine trainees, these "rootless" individuals have freedom to move elsewhere should they find their sponsoring institution or its personnel intolerable. It is safe to say however, based on conversations with a number of priests, that such individuals will not risk being characterized as "difficult" or contend with unfavorable recommendations from senior priests, preferring instead to exhibit what De Vos (1973) has identified as the preeminent character trait of Japanese, endurance with the hope of delayed gratification.

I have discussed to this point how priests are situated within local and national networks of power, elites, and institutional structures. But rather than claiming that the stage of shrine Shinto is full of heavy, immovable props, I will show in the next section how priests from all ranks are often able to configure certain scenes so as to allow room for individual expression and creativity. At any time and in any social situation, individuals are presented with choices, struggles, changing circumstances, and unforeseen pressures to which they must react, often without the luxury of careful consideration. Or, having the time to scheme but lacking decisive tactics, intelligence, or sufficient resources with which to influence strategic and beneficial outcomes, they put their reputations (not to mention their occupations and livelihoods) at considerable risk.

It is in situations charged with opportunity and hazard, according to Abu-Lughod (1991 : 154), that detailed ethnographic observations can inform and redirect ideas about culture as something homogeneous, coherent, and timeless. When problems raised by individual choices are acted on and collectively answered by a social group of which an individual is part, cultural innovation leading to social change can occur (see Fox 1991 : 107). Though such innovation is generally the exception rather than the rule, it happens frequently enough to subvert structural arguments seeing individual action as reinforcing vast systems that people are powerless to change. As Robert Smith points out, rather than seeing individuals within institutions as marionettes to be manipulated, a closer and more sustained look provided through an ethnographic encounter shows they are actors who have been taught a pattern within which they "demonstrate their individual virtuosity" (1985 : 43). In short, it is important to establish a perspective from which it becomes apparent that social structures and the practices of their actors are both the outcome and the source of one another (Pred 1986 : 27). One might think, based on its rituals and seemingly antiquated façades, that the organization and institution of shrine Shinto has changed very little; but I will show in concluding this discussion how the guise of Shinto has incorporated radical cultural and social change.

A traditional Japanese workplace, whether shrine, factory, school, or office, is not composed of separate individuals laboring for separate goals. Instead, as many authors have pointed out, it is a collective institution to which individuals belong.[10] Collaboration, cooperation, mutuality, even a village-style communalism have all been posited as characteristic features of Japanese companies. While all of these are usually prevalent, these harmonious features tend to obscure the inevitable personal and systemic discord within organizations. As in the case of the aspiring priest seeking a patron (see note nine), there is a strong paternalistic dimension to company life that has positive, negative, and ambivalent attributes. The deference required to operate in this type of environment is a culturally and socially learned skill, but it does have its rewards if one can delay immediate gratification and endure periodic indignities. In the following discussion, I will deal with these aspects of shrine organization through specific practices and examples. I will conclude the chapter with a further examination of their effects on overall institutional effectiveness.

For the younger priests, each day begins with a cleaning (called *seizō*) of the outer and inner courtyard areas. In this, they are not much different from Buddhist novitiate priests who have as part of their spiritual training *(shugyō)* tasks like polishing wooden floors, cleaning sacred objects and images, and generally making the temple environs spotless. The younger priests are given this job because they are low in the hierarchy, but there is a borrowed element of Buddhist-style spiritual training involved as well. "By sweeping and cleaning and raking the grounds, we're to think that this is happening in our own hearts as well," said one Shinto priest of five years. But do you, I asked? "Well, usually we're just anxious to finish the work as quickly as we can so we can go back and have tea and a cigarette before the morning meeting.[11] Also, since there aren't many worshipers *(sanpai-sha)* at that time of day, we usually joke around. It helps make the work go faster."

The morning meeting (or *chōrei*) is the principal assembly (the other one being lunch) for everyone involved with the shrine on a daily basis. Like the phenomenon of *chōrei* all over Japan, its function is to define roles, activities, and responsibilities within a formal institutional structure, all the while passing along official information. While there are many aspects of meetings that evoke normative settings and principles of organization that resonate cross-culturally (such as people coming together, projects to be discussed, deference shown to the leader, and so forth), other characteristics are specific to place and context so as to render the term "meeting" problematic if used without care. To draw attention to the culturally constructed character of the shrine's morning meeting, I will use the Japanese term.

Since the *chōrei* involves people in an institutional hierarchy, it serves as an occasion whereby individuals are reminded of a number of important subtexts in addition to the set agenda. First, in a physical sense, where they sit in the room reminds them of their rank and status within Kamigamo (see the following diagram). Next, with rank come varying degrees of obligation and duty, delegated to the younger priests based on seniority, ability, and even creativity in successfully carrying these out. Obstructions do appear, however, and so the morning meeting is also a daily reminder of whose interests and personalities may stand in one's way. Work assignments are generally given with some sensitivity for existing relationships, but interpersonal dynamics can change quickly and subtly in ways a superior is not always aware of. Finally, the *chōrei* reminds shrine personnel of the strengths and limitations of the institution itself. Only certain events and agendas can be realized, while others, perhaps too expensive or grandiose, or requiring more manpower than is available, are tabled with a pronouncement of "We can't do it" *(dekinai)*. Were the shrine larger, richer, more centrally located, better managed, better networked, or any of a hundred other tactical possibilities, its sphere of influence in the community and region could grow and, with it, the priests' status and salaries. All of these factors are in play before the *chōrei* begins. Thus, more than a meeting, it reminds the staff in unspoken ways of their complex, interlocking webs of influence, codependence, and power.

In the winter Kamigamo's *chōrei* begins at 9:15 A.M. and in the summer, at 8:45. The official workday begins fifteen minutes earlier in both seasons, but most staff are present at least a half hour before, even those who commute considerable distances to reach the shrine. The contemporary image of people working at desks evokes an office environment of computers, multiple telephones, fax machines, copiers, and so on, and in many of these regards the administrative office (Shamusho) is in step with modern business practices. There are several laptop computers on which all printing, finances, and recordkeeping is done, one fax machine, and a copier. However, the scene of the meeting is a fifteen by thirty foot room, two sides of which are sliding glass shutters (to call them windows is stretching the concept) that look out on the access road and foliage. Built around the turn of the century, there have been few improvements other than three overhead fluorescent lights. What is noteworthy about this office is its organization into three rows of low, legless desks *(suarezukue)* as areas for beginning, junior *(gonnegi),* and senior *(negi)* priests. Desks located closest to the door and windows, that is, with the most public access, are for individuals of lower ranks. Thus, it is not surprising to find the shrine's female employees by the windows in the row closest to the door, the most junior priests by the window in the middle row, and so on. The room is old and dreary, although providing plenty of cross-circulation in the humid Kyoto summer (the complaint "We are the last office in all of Japan that doesn't have an air conditioner!" was no longer true as of 1995) and kept stifling by two large gas heaters, and clouds of cigarette smoke, during the damp, bone-chilling winter months. At any time of the day, work may be interrupted by deliveries, businessmen making courtesy calls, or shrine visitors wishing to make a contribution,

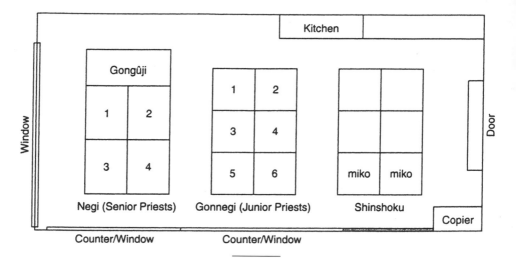

The shrine administration
office layout.

chat with priests they know, or schedule a private ritual in the Gokitōden. If a visit is scheduled or the person of sufficient status, he or she will be invited into the shrine for tea in a private reception room and tended to by the associate head priest or the most senior of *negi* priests.

Having an office's spatial arrangement reflect status hierarchies within an institution is a ubiquitous feature of work environments in any culture. The morning *chōrei* is likewise found in most institutions, since it provides a chance for everyone to focus on the tasks of the day and be reminded of their roles in helping the institution function properly. To use a summer *chōrei* on June 10 as an example, by 8:30 A.M. the morning tasks have been completed. The first ten minutes in the office, when everyone is present except the head priest, are spent simply chatting, enjoying tea (served by the female attendants) and smoking. At 8:40, the clamor of conversation diminishes as the arrival of the head priest from his private office in the rear of the shrine grows near; by 8:45, the *gūji* has entered the room and all are silent as he takes a cushion on the floor. The most senior priest (after the associate head priest) announces it is time to begin the meeting, then turns the floor over to the priest in charge of office affairs, the *shomu-ka* head (or *shunin*).

Referring to a large chalkboard, the general affairs chief reminds everyone what is planned for the day. The following day, June 11, the head and associate head priests as well as the *gūji's* secretary were scheduled to attend a reception given by the emperor for representatives of the major *choku-sha* shrines in Japan or those that receive messengers from the imperial household during their main yearly festivals. On this particular morning, a fairly important ritual of rice planting, the *taue-sai* (classified as a "middle-ranking" rite) is scheduled for 10:00, but no further mention is made at this time of who will participate or what preparations need to be made final. The *shunin* next names those priests who will serve as *tōban* (also called *tantō*) for the day and the night. These two individuals will remain at the shrine for the next thirty-six hours, putting in two full days of work and administration as well as a night of watch duty before they return home for a much cherished day off. With only fourteen male priests at Kamigamo, the overnight duty (or *shukuchoku*) appears on everyone's agenda at least three times a month. For the younger unmarried priests, however, and especially for those apprentices living at the shrine, duty can come more frequently if circumstances (such as a Tokyo trip for a senior priest) demand. No overtime is paid, since *shukuchoku* duty is as much a part of being a priest at the shrine as is performing the various rituals.

If there are no questions after the naming of the *tōban,* the meeting ends with an expression from the *shunin* ("Sore ja . . . " or "Sore dewa . . .") that signals "Well, that's it for now." On this day, however, an insurance salesman and his wife are present to explain vacation policies for Kamigamo employees' yearly excursion sometime in July and August when no major rituals are scheduled. Usually a hot spring resort is chosen, but this year, keeping in pace with contemporary social trends that see nearly twelve million Japanese traveling overseas every year, the two-night, three-day trip will be to Hong Kong. Asked about the reasoning behind this first-time-ever foray overseas, I was told jokingly, "Shinto shrines too have to do their part in internationalization." To my surprise, even the chief priest, at age eighty-eight, and his wife were planning to go. While the employees are responsible for personal expenses and supplementary insurance (thus the salesman's pitch about the muggings, murders, and mayhem that can happen overseas), the rest of the bill is paid by the shrine.

SHRINE ADMINISTRATION

Since a majority of individuals living in highly industrialized countries are members of what Morgan calls "organizational society," gaining objective distance with which to gauge the depth of knowledge and cultural practices required by office workers challenges social scientists (Morgan 1986:123) much in the same way that the Heisenberg Principle confounds physicists. Like any corporation or company, the organization of a shrine's administration depends largely on the size of the institution and the number of people in its employ. For very large shrines such as Ise, Meiji, or Daizaifu, employees may be relegated to the same department for an entire career. At Kamigamo, however, with its fourteen salaried priests, the departmental heads shift every two years, thus gaining facility and experience in all aspects of shrine operations. The person in charge of coordinating and supervising all the branches of shrine operations is the associate head priest, who serves as the general affairs manager *(shomu)*.

Just as in a company, the business of various departments is channeled upward in a pyramid structure of responsibility, authority, and status. Theoretically, the associate head priest approves or modifies proposals, actions, expenditures, and so forth that are submitted to him for scrutiny, with his seal *(han)* going on documents before being passed along to the head priest for final approval and stamping. In one way, this kind of decision making is similar to a corporate-style *ringi* system, where each document builds momentum rather than pointing out a specific direction for the institution to follow. Because the decision-making process at a shrine is vertical, only rarely will the associate head priest recirculate plans to the department chief that issued it, as is done in a classic *ringi*-style system. The decision-making process at the shrine is begun collectively but concluded individually, with the head priest assuming full accountability even though he may know only a tenth of a particular plan's implications.

Currently, there are five principal areas that Kamigamo's leadership feels are essential to the expeditious operation of the institution. Were there suddenly to be a windfall of income allowing more employees to be hired, the departments would probably diversify to ease the workload in each area. Likewise, a change in leadership could also alter the existing structure of shrine operations. In interviewing the priests one by one, I asked each for a ranking of the shrine's various departments and found general consensus for the following order:

1. *Saiji-ka,* or "ritual affairs": Officially the most important of all, this post concerns the correct staging and performance of ritual events. Its concerns include doing things "the way they've always been done," food offerings for important rituals, and paraphernalia required for ritual

participants who are not priests. A story is told about a priest during the prewar period who could not find the reference book needed for the *nagoshi-barae* "festival of great purification" held in summer. Even though everyone remembered all the words for the prayers as well as the order of the proceedings, this unfortunate priest was reported and demoted because he did not fulfill his responsibilities properly. "But we would never do that now," the storyteller informed me. "Times have changed since the days when our shrine was a branch of the national government and all the priests were government employees." (For more on the history of shrines under the control of the *naimusho-jinja-kyoku*, see Haga 1981; Hardacre 1989.)

2. *Yōdo-ka,* or "supplies and operations": Like a quartermaster in the military, the *yōdo-ka* is responsible for keeping things running, whether it be supplies for the kitchen, for the refurbishing of shrine property, or office supplies.

3. *Kaikei-ka,* or "financial affairs": Although it is ranked third, perhaps to deflect attention from its real importance, money makes the ritual world go round in fascinating and deliberately veiled ways. Budgetary matters, donations, fund-raising, salaries, expenses, and so forth are all managed on one of the laptop computers.[12]

4. *Shomu-ka,* or "general / miscellaneous affairs": This department is a kind of catch-all managerial post that helps facilitate the smooth operation of the shrine by coordinating the above departments. The priest in charge must be able to see all aspects of shrine operations but also the bigger picture of their place in local and regional communities. Thus, he is the liaison between Kamigamo and the local branch of the Jinja Honchō, the Kyoto Jinja-chō. The *shomu ka* head is also in charge of producing the shrine's quarterly newsletter as well as supervising news releases or inviting the media to certain events ("but they don't always come since there are so many shrines and festivals in Kyoto"). He also conducts business at the morning meetings, to name only a few of his responsibilities.

5. *Keidai-ka,* or "grounds and maintenance": A shrine is, in the eyes of the public, primarily a place available for leisurely strolls, seasonal festivities, and reveries of nostalgia for the "old" Japan (see Nelson 1996a). Its grounds and buildings are direct evidence of the care bestowed on maintaining appearances as well as the financial health required to do so. Thus, keeping the grounds in a way that, in the words of the cur-

rent chief, "honors the shrine that has been handed down to us from ages past and ensures that we can do the same for subsequent generations of priests" is a responsibility fraught with worry and vigilance.

> You might think that all I do is walk around and look at buildings before I go home in the evening, but I am constantly concerned with important questions. Does the roof of a subordinate shrine leak? If so, are there funds to repair it or should we risk public ridicule by putting plastic over it? Are termites attacking the steps of the main sanctuary? Should we take down a big torii so that an important patron can put up one with his money? And how about the coming retirement of the groundskeeper? Who can fill his shoes [he says with a smile] so that there is less work for me?

> Under the *keidai-ka* is the *bōsai-kankei-sha,* or "person in charge for the prevention of disasters." Actually, this position is filled by whomever is the senior priest on night duty, but its overall monitoring comes under the jurisdiction of the grounds and maintenance department. Two priests are necessary for night duty because, in the event of a fire or a crime, one priest must staff the telephones while the other is out directing emergency or law enforcement personnel. Kamigamo has been extremely fortunate since the last rebuilding of the central shrine's sanctuaries in 1628, having suffered no major disasters (other than the postwar flood) or conflagrations. But the priests know there is no guarantee this good fortune will continue and therefore must organize events like a yearly "Fire Prevention Day" in which fire trucks and firefighters swarm over the shrine, rehearsing for a "worst case scenario." Which is what exactly, I asked? Earthquakes, lightning, terrorist attacks? "All of them," I was told. "It doesn't matter where the disaster comes from, only how we control and contain it so it does the least damage to our cultural treasures."

The chief of each department has two junior priests subordinate to him. They assist him in all aspects of his job and, as is the case in many other workplaces worldwide, frequently do the real tasks for which their superior receives credit. Thus, for example, on orders from the director of the *keidai-ka,* younger priests will turn into groundskeepers to clean up the shrine after the New Year's rush. Or, because they know their responsibilities overlap with those of the regular groundskeeping staff, the younger priests will do a lackluster job of raking, knowing someone with lower status than themselves is there to clean up what they may "inadvertently" leave behind. Still, I heard few complaints from the priests about being called on to do a variety of tasks. Virtually everyone felt that being involved in all aspects of running a shrine was an opportunity rather than a burden, and an opportunity of which their friends at large shrines were envious. With this involvement comes not only expertise and knowledge but, according to one priest, a deeper understanding of the significance of Kamigamo's place in history.

> I can't explain it well. Sometimes we [priests] forget just how old this shrine really is. It has survived wars, conflicts of all kinds, natural disasters and financial hardships, but it is still here. Priests from bigger shrines with lots of employees are jealous about the variety of our work here—being called on to do this and that, with every day different from the one before. Personally, I feel like the more I do, the more I'll understand this place. But this kind of understanding is different from research or studying books. How can I say it? I want to know about the life of this place *(kono jimen no inochi)* in the way that priests from the old days did.

As a way of reminding the priests (and other employees) of their duties and roles at Kamigamo, on the first of every month a formal vow *(shokuin no chikai)* is made before the *kami* during the ritual of *tsukinami-sai*. After the regular ritual and postritual reception have been completed, the entire staff—from priests, amulet counter attendants, and female attendants to groundskeepers, cooks, and janitors—all assemble in two rows (according to the status of their position) just inside the innermost gate. One priest stands in front as the group's leader, and, with some reciting from memory and others looking at printed papers, the following vow is delivered before the inner sanctuary (although the deity is "sent back" at the conclusion of the ritual):

1. We will carry out shrine rituals with full sincerity and seriousness.
2. We will make an effort to promote the *kami* to our parishioners *(ujiko)* and deepen their faith *(shinkō)*. They should know how great *(erai)* the *kami* is. We will try harder to win parishioner respect.

3. We will keep the grounds and buildings in good shape: we should care about the property and shrine administration and guard against fire and disasters. [Let us] dash forward to keep the shrine's dignity and good fortune high.

4. We should make new plans for the shrine and make an effort to realize them.

5. All staff members should study diligently about Shinto, be a good example to others, and work together harmoniously.

Even though the context is set for these words to have an impact in a public forum, the priests I talked to felt coerced into having to profess "do's and don'ts" before the eyes of strangers. Still, similar vows of loyalty, forthrightness, and sincerity are part of many organizational codes of ethics, and some organizations go through them as a part of each morning's *chōrei* meeting. One can summon forth images of automobile factory assembly lines, where workers face each other and follow their floor supervisor in repeating company slogans, or bank employee meetings, or even those of trainee nurses at the start of their shifts (see Rohlen 1974; Kondo 1990). A profession of one's duty on a regular basis is a socializing and disciplining technique to exact compliance and agreement with an institution's ideology. The vows have also been suggested to be an outgrowth of the religious tradition of *kotodama* in which words are powerful not only in themselves but in their place "within a system of associations" (Plutschow 1990:11).[13]

However, these verbalizations are attempts rather than faits accomplis at disciplining behavior and thought. At Kamigamo, for example, the "employee's vow" is a recent innovation on the part of the associate head priest. Because of his status and experience with larger organizations (though not necessarily because of his seniority), he was able to convince the head priest to implement the vow as part of the monthly *tsukinami-sai* ritual process. The vow is particularly unpopular with priests whose tenure predates the recent arrival of the associate head priest. Unlike the younger priests and some of the more devout staff members who have memorized it in its entirety, several senior priests either read from papers or simply stand there at attention until the vow is completed. The recitation is ragged and unpracticed and, from an outsider's perspective, appears to highlight cleavages indicative of deeper conflicts rather than the solidarity and "harmony" everyone professes in the vow.

CONFLICT AND CONSENSUS

Mary Douglas begins her book *How Institutions Think* by remarking that in writing about the cooperation and solidarity inherent to institutions, one must also cover rejection and mistrust (1986:1). Indeed, writers such as Nicholas Dirks (1994) suggest that order, stability, and continuity have been foisted upon the social sciences as the dominant paradigm of a Western worldview when actually disruption, chaos, and disorder deserve center stage when tracking social history. Chapter 4 described an extreme example of this hypothesis in dealing with the shrine's, and Kyoto's, period of civil unrest and violence. Today at Kamigamo Shrine, as at institutions elsewhere that function through interdependent administrative departments, one should not be surprised to find individuals who, operating through the authority of their position, meddle in the affairs of other departments, trying to subvert intentions and plans so they can gain credit, exact revenge, or advance their own agendas. March and Simon assert that the potential for conflict is greater, not less, when there is a shared sense of interdependence (cited in Krauss et al. 1984:382). Anyone familiar with farming communities in general and Japanese villages in particular knows that despite the bucolic pastoralism of their surfaces, there are real and enduring schisms that pit individual against individual and family against family, sometimes lasting for decades.

The aspects of an agricultural community incorporated by Japanese organizations are especially relevant for a shrine, where the institution's common vested interests (and not those of individual priests) are expected to predominate and influence consensual decision-making. However, when consensus itself becomes one of these vested interests, its preservation and top-down implementation frequently drives conflict into realms that are secretive and destructive. Linda Smirchich's study of insurance company executives shows how a genial and mild-mannered president who began policies encouraging his managers and employees to work together in a positive spirit of cooperation and harmony actually paralyzed his company. Rather than providing outlets for disagreement and conflict, his policies drove them underground. The public and private faces of the corporation were so radically different and oriented in such different directions that even simple problem-solving techniques were ineffective in responding to change in the industry. As a result, the company entered a managerial gridlock, eventually being absorbed by the parent corporation to prevent further disintegration (Smirchich, cited in Morgan 1986 : 123).

Kamigamo Shrine has weathered a variety of climactic changes in managerial style. By far, the predominant characteristic has been mutual interdependence and cooperation among priests, shrine, and community, as well as between shrine and national leaders. However, a major incident that does not fit this pattern was still very much in play during the period of my fieldwork. While it is sensational and anomalous, by looking at variances from the predominant pattern one can better understand the urgency sensed by current administrators to uphold and promote consensual solidarity. While there are a number of other, less dramatic but equally revealing contemporary examples I could relate along these lines, to protect the identity and confidentiality of my informants I will gloss over the particulars of current close-quarters conflict within the administrative offices.

The system of administration at Kamigamo is set up to give the priests a good deal of latitude in daily affairs but also to provide a wider scope of consensual decision making that draws on elders from the surrounding precincts. A four-member board of trustees (riji-kai) meets regularly with the head and associate head priests. The group is, not surprisingly, entirely male, with the youngest member fast approaching his late seventies. But rather than the term riji, one hears these individuals referred to by the title sekinin yakuin, or "responsible official." The head priest is also considered a yakuin official of the shrine, but since he represents the priests, his title translates into something resembling "official representative," or daihyō yakuin. The trustees are ranked in a hierarchy of status and authority, with the head person going by the title of sōdai, or "principal delegate of the trustees." Titles and positions are all-important markers of identity and power in Japan, so that a person serving as head of the board of trustees to the shrine would have on his namecard "Kamowake Ikazuchi Jinja Riji-kai, Sekinin yakuin, sōdai" or, roughly translated, "Principal Delegate for the Board of Trustees Officials, Kamowake Ikazuchi Shrine." The simplified block model below illustrates the structure of shrine organization.

Now that the principal agents have been located within a somewhat oversimplified structure of shrine administration, a major crisis during the 1970s will set things in motion. Following these motivated players will reveal how institutional policy, strategy, and individual memories continue to influence shrine affairs, not to mention the importance of interpersonal relations between priests, trustees, and the Original Parishioner's group.[14]

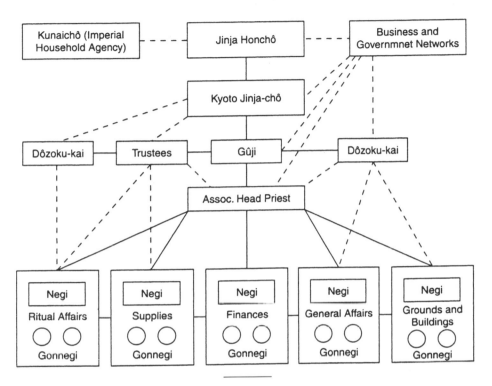

Shrine administrative positions
and affiliations.

Iide Masakazu, who served as head priest from 1967 to 1971, was one
of the more influential and energetic priests the shrine has had in the twentieth century. By all accounts, he worked hard to make the shrine more
active in the community and to restore some of its social status following
the new laws of the Occupation, especially the Shinto Directive's separation of religious institutions from state interests. Because shrines were in
difficult financial straits stemming from the 1945 Shinto Directive's pro-
hibition of all state sponsorship of religious activities, even twenty years
later Iide was constantly searching for money from a variety of parish-

ioners and patrons. Largely successful in keeping the shrine viable and even in repairing some of the buildings, he turned to his personal affairs and what he felt was the need for a new residence for the head priest. No doubt he saw this residence as a reward for his efforts and a place where his family could live comfortably after many years of deprivation. He may also have thought such a residence was appropriate to his status, since Kamigamo is second in rank only to Ise and until the end of the war served the government as a *kanpei taisha* (shrine receiving imperial offerings). Unfortunately, Iide tried to solicit funds for his residence not as an official shrine project but as a private one.

Priests and officials I spoke with were still unsure why Iide felt he had to follow this course of action. Visiting the head of the Ura-senke tea school, which (along with its counterpart, the Omote-senke school) had been a part of shrine rituals and social networks for centuries, Iide announced his project and the need for funds. However, he claimed to have been divinely informed by none other than the principal deity, Wake Ikazuchi, that he was to get his money from the tea school's director. The shocked director sent the head priest on his way as courteously as he could with the promise of a donation. When not enough money was forthcoming, the head priest visited him again, threatening divine retribution *(tatari)* from the deities, who he said were now acting through him as an intermediary.

This time, however, the director informed the shrine's trustees that the head priest was coercing donations through his office. Allegations were made, heated arguments and counterarguments were hurled back and forth, and the local office of the national Jinja Honchō was called in for consultation and mediation. But the head priest went ahead with his plans and secured funds for a new residence (which still stands today). He might have survived this incident had he not then pressed for another dwelling for his son, again claiming divine sanction and retribution to anyone interfering with his plans. Here, however, laws were already in place regarding private dwellings on shrine property. It was, in the words of a trustee, "completely out of the question." He continued: "We were sure he had gone mad." And yet, Iide insisted, flaunting the trustees' admonitions and provoking them into open disagreement in a social arena usually noted for the absence of conflict: the formal, public arena of in-group relations.[15]

At this point, the trustees had little choice in dealing with Iide. Because of his adamant disregard for their point of view and the damage he was causing to the social position of the shrine, and because he would not listen to the local representatives of the national shrine association, they could either submit to his plan or ask him to resign. The latter course was put into effect, but Iide refused to cooperate. By doing so, from a structural perspective, he elevated the stakes of this confrontation to the level of total defiance of the authority of the trustees. And yet, as the Kyōto Jinja-chō director pointed out in an interview, the fault was not entirely the head priest's. Had the head trustee (sōdai) been slower to anger (which is often accompanied by total silence), more decisive in taking action, willing to settle the case out of court, and thus less concerned about individual and communal "face saving," perhaps the explosiveness of this situation could have been defused.[16] By refusing to resign and by continuing to occupy the new residence, Iide flaunted the decision of the trustees and appeared (however briefly) to "win." Once the battle expanded beyond in-house means of managing conflict, the trustees turned to the legal establishment as a last resort, filing suit against the head priest for violation of trust and abuse of office.

Upham's discussion of law and social change in Japan points out that discrete grievances (such as the trustees had against the head priest) can gain broader appeal only if there are suitable political allies, if the disputants have adequate commitment and political resources, and the underlying issues (the integrity of the shrine) have a degree of normative appeal (1988:3). The trustees certainly had all of these points in their favor before initiating court proceedings. Members of the dōzoku-kai were not pleased at the trustees' handling of the situation but rallied behind them because of the threat Iide posed to their own group's reputation. Powerful patrons turned against the head priest when it became clear, in the words of a trustee, that "his religion was more important than the shrine." As a result, Iide lost not only the court decision but his position, his residence, and his dream of providing for his son. From the point of view of the Jinja Honchō, Iide had wantonly provoked the entire situation into this unhappy conclusion and thus had sole responsibility as the shrine's daihyō yakuin to receive suitable punishment. Thus, he was divested of rank and position (hakudatsu suru) and essentially barred from serving as a priest again.

In the case of any overt conflict resulting in clear-cut winners and losers, those who win feel vindicated and righteous, while those who lose try to minimize damage to their positions and reputations by distancing themselves from the instigator. Iide did have his supporters both within and outside the shrine, but after he was removed from office many of these individuals either quit, were transferred by the Jinja Honchō, or endured the indignities of remaining at their positions. Those most affected within the inner circle of shrine administrators were the trustees; seventeen years later, the trustee-shrine relationship can be characterized as one of extreme caution, mutual defensiveness, and skepticism. However, owing to the presence and influence of the remarkable man chosen to replace Iide, the shrine is well on its way to restoring its reputation.

After the departure of Iide, the shrine was without a head priest for almost two years. According to shrine protocol, it takes five *yakuin* officials to choose the next head priest. Since there were only four at Kamigamo (the departing head priest would normally make up the fifth position), the trustees asked the Jinja Honchō to send an appropriately qualified person. Abe Makoto was seventy-two years old at that time and ready to retire after a lifetime of service as an official in the regional shrine administration of Fukushima prefecture. As he tells it,

> I had been in the Jinja-chō for six terms, a very long time. On my retirement, I finally had time to myself. I wanted to travel around and see other shrines, visit people, and do grave visitations *(ohaka mairi)*. One of my former students in Fukushima said he would drive me anywhere I wanted to go. All the plans were made when suddenly I got a call from the Jinja Honchō asking me to go to Kamigamo Shrine and take over the job as head priest. I said, *me?* Go to a splendid shrine like that? The *sekinin yakuin* doesn't know me, and it'll be bad just to drop in like that on the Kamigamo people. Also, of course, I had heard about the problem there with the head priest. So, naturally I refused. But they kept up the pressure and so I went down for an interview just so they would leave me alone. The first thing I asked for was to fail the interview. I left my résumé behind and went back to Fukushima, relieved that the trip was over. But soon, I got a call from the head of the Kyōto Jinja-chō, who asked me to come. Well, I refused, still thinking they couldn't really be serious. The calls kept coming and I kept refusing until, a week or so later, I got a call from my *daisenpai* [elder or senior advisor]. He told me that I was giving everyone a hard time and that I had to say yes or no about this job in two seconds and be done with it. OK, OK, I'll go, I said, but if I make a mistake, I'm leaving.

His apprehensions about taking the position were not unfounded. First and most pressing among the problems he faced was to return the shrine to a semblance of normal administrative functioning in order to regain the confidence of its parishioners, patrons, and visitors. Second, because of the way the shrine's reputation had suffered during court proceedings (not to mention citywide gossip and innuendo), the new head priest had to reempower the shrine's demoralized (because publicly shamed) priests. Third, even though the trustees had complied with the Jinja Honchō's recommendation and appointment, he nevertheless faced a suspicious inner circle of men his own age (or older) who would not be intimidated by his status. Finally, he was expected to reverse the economic decline of the shrine and make it once again a splendid place for worship.

On a visit to present his credentials at the Imperial Household Agency in late 1977, one official remarked to Abe that he had gained a certain fame for his stubborn but intelligent refusal to take the job. Another confided quietly: "The situation there is very difficult. Whatever are you going to do?" The righteously indignant trustees and especially the head *sōdai* were adamant about doing anything to repair the rift between the shrine's lay organizations and priests caused by misunderstanding, poor communication, and different views about the shrine's agendas. The long history of antagonism between these factions, as seen in Chapter 4, usually worked to the advantage of the parishioners and strengthened their influence in shrine affairs.

It is fascinating, then, that one of the first acts of Abe gūji as head priest was to submit a plan for showing formal appreciation for the long years of service and real contributions that the disgraced former head priest had made to the shrine. The problems leading to the scandal were, in Abe's (and the Jinja Honchō's) opinion, separate from the service the former head priest had rendered. Although the *yakuin* were against any form of recognition, "we reached an agreement with our lawyers to make a final payment to Iide gūji." I did not inquire about the sum, nor did the amount seem to be generally known, but informants speculated it was fairly generous, probably around two million yen (about U.S. $19,000.) "This was very calming to me," Abe remarked, "and my wife too was satisfied that we had done the right thing even though it risked alienating the *yakuin* from the very start." By Abe's own account, the complex array of social, legal, and political problems generated by the scandal took four and a half years to resolve. Because institutional memories are long, the reputations of individuals and shrine, once sullied, take years to recover. Thus, the healing process is still very much under way.[17]

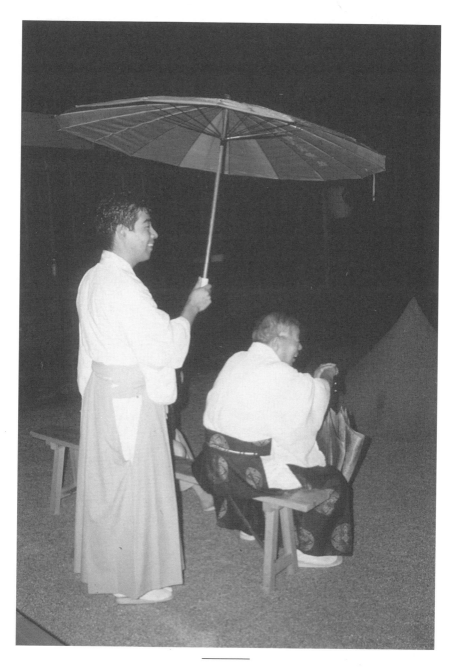

Former head priest Abe and senior
priest Yamada.

Abe was not, however, paralyzed by the problems and controversies facing him. Soon after becoming head priest, he went to the head of the parishioners' group—which had gained considerable face and empowerment among its members following their victory over the former head priest and his allies—and asked that those participating in rituals make an effort to be on time. The tendency for ritual participants to show up seconds before the rite's procession, or even come late, and dispense with the hand-washing purification simply would not do. He also requested that the parishioners stop treating the shrine's priests disrespectfully, for example, by "gesturing with one's chin the way an imperious ruler might do." Reminding the trustees that they had repeatedly asked him to accept this position, he explained it was "only natural" *(atarimae)* that he make every effort to improve the reputation of the shrine; and one of the ways to achieve this was by having those who participate in its rituals show proper decorum. Knowing well that even respectful requests such as this could generate more tension between priests and parishioners, he made a point soon after this meeting to schedule a party for the inner circle of lay officials and priests. Calling this occasion a *bureku* (from the English "break"), the idea was to stage a Gluckmanesque "rite of rebellion" whereby ample alcohol and food allow "anything" to be said without fear of recrimination.[18] Likewise, he made sure the lay groups knew about "housecleaning" activities within the shrine, taking some of the priests to task for certain indulgent tendencies they had developed:

When I came to Kamigamo, I asked the staff people directly, now who likes sake? Even though I knew there were some big drinkers in the room, no one raised his hand. I said that there was a time and place for drinking sake and suggested that we have a big party four times a year: after the new year's rush, after the Aoi Festival (in May), once in August, and once in December after all our end-of-the-year cleaning and work is finished. Everyone liked the idea. After that, we never had a problem with drinking on the job again.

The challenges faced by Abe gūji and the other priests at Kamigamo were formidable and riven with conflicting interests, and yet they managed to find common ground on which to restore to respectability the position and reputation of the shrine. Perhaps the height of this achievement was marked by the official visit of the emperor and empress in 1995, in honor of the shrine's periodic rebuilding and repair of its principal structures.

Asked to explain the philosophy behind his success in dealing with people and institutions during six decades of service, Abe speaks calmly and without hesitation: "It's simple because I have three mottos. First, don't flatter powerful people or those with authority over you. Second, be willing to talk with and listen to anyone, regardless of class or status. Finally, always be honest with yourself and others." Amid celebration and acknowledgment, Abe gūji retired in 1995, saying two years before that, "I want to leave a wide clearing into which others may step smoothly." Following tradition, the assistant head priest, Mr. Takeuchi, has assumed the primary leadership role at the shrine.

It should be clear by now that a contemporary religious institution (such as a Shinto shrine) and the priests that give it institutional continuity and life are hardly just cogs in a system within which they have little control. So important are the managerial skills, institutional philosophies, political orientations, and interpersonal networks of a shrine's priests that it is fair to say the institution's reputation and economic viability rests squarely on their shoulders. Earlier I suggested (following Bell) that one of the attributes of a religious specialist's power was invested in his office and not his person, but I was referring to power in a *ritual* context. When one's gaze shifts from the enchantments of the ritual stage to the less alluring, less accessible, and even mundane aspects of maintaining institutional viability, individual agency matters a great deal. The institution of shrine Shinto continues to provide links between ritual and administrative power as it has always done, but never has the administrative end of the equation been so dependent on the creativity, planning, and foresight of particular individuals.

Religious historians may argue that priests have always responded to challenges and changing social and political circumstances. In the Japanese case, until very recently they have done so under the watchful eye and with the permission and financial sponsorship of military rulers, imperial officials, and regional warlords or landowners. With greater autonomy in the postwar period have come greater pressures on shrine leadership to survive a total withdrawal of governmental financial support by fostering economic and administrative plans not only responsive to but proactive of current or developing realities. Thus, shrines have built parking lots and rented out spaces on a monthly basis, built wedding halls, promoted and staged new festivals to attract greater community support, and often commercialized existing festivals to coincide with the boom in domestic tourism or to better accommodate the work schedules of their primary constituencies. In an earlier book on Suwa Shrine in Nagasaki, I showed how its new head priest completely transformed an institution in decline, making it one of the stellar shrines of the entire nation (Nelson 1996b).

In these examples, rather than subverting some monolithic and reified notion of "tradition," creative and strategically positioned efforts respond to, anticipate, and sometimes even invent the needs of a changing society. Although it is important to look carefully at a religious institution's symbolic capital of rituals, texts, teachings, and accoutrements, if one has a magnifying glass in one hand, one must also have binoculars ready in the other.

In the course of this discussion, I have raised in one form or another the following questions as relevant for all contemporary studies of religious institutions: What social and political forces have enabled throughout history the viability of a particular institutional expression of cultural religiosity? To what extent do these precedents display continuity with the present-day situation and are they amenable to change? What strategies and tactics, implemented in what way and by whom, have proved most successful in scripting the institution's ongoing social dramas? How and why do powerful elites align themselves with the institution? What social fields do the institution's priests and administrators operate within vis-à-vis society as a whole, and how does individual agency within these fields shape, subvert, refigure, and eventually implement policy in ways meaningful and advantageous both to the institution and to the people that make it work? Whatever longevity is imparted to particular religious traditions and institutions throughout the world, it is doubtful how resilient their messages and practices would be without the active management of their motivated specialists. For an institution to fail to respond to its surrounding environment is to risk stagnation and decay, conditions shrine Shinto (as well as many other religious traditions in East Asia) has so diligently avoided.

PERFORMING RITUAL

Readers might find it odd that I have deferred until now discussion of a shrine and its priests' ostensible raison d'être: those ritual events and performances said to embody the heritage, hierarchies, and myths of its primary *kami*. Since Japanese festivals are known the world over for their dynamism and pageantry (not to mention the expenditures lavished on them), they may seem a likely choice for center stage in a discussion of shrine Shinto within contemporary Japanese society. I opted for such a strategy of presentation in my earlier book on Suwa Shrine in Nagasaki, using that institution's ritual performances as points of access for issues that ranged from the invention of tradition to gender politics. In the current study, I have tried to establish a different logic, one more concerned with the personal agency, sustaining ideologies, and underlying practices that enable long-lived institutions to reformulate their identities within constantly changing social environments.

One of the most obvious ways this happens is through ritual performances. There continues to be enormous instructive potential in ritual and festival because a sampling of a culture's norms and values—usually in some kind of condensed or exaggerated form—occurs within a neatly demarcated frame of time and space constructed by the people under study and not by the observer (Brandes 1988). In choosing a specific site or event and then working up into larger institutional realms, this study has aimed at distinguishing between what Clifford Geertz calls "a religious attitude

toward experience and the sorts of social apparatus which have been associated with supporting such an attitude" (1968:8). While some religious historians and phenomenologists (such as Mircea Eliade) assert that
the sacred is an unassailable quality transcending human society, one of
the ways anthropology encompasses the phenomenon of religion is to
treat it as well as its activities of worship, faith, and the sacred as fundamentally social institutions and forces created from cultural repertoires
specific to certain peoples and places (see Geertz 1968:19).[1]

Anthropological perspectives on ritual and religion (even as early as
Hubert and Mauss' 1898 study of sacrifice) have long sought to contextualize practices deemed "religious" within specific social and cultural mi-
lieux. Such a perspective entails, however blasphemous it may sound to
some, trying to understand that the construction and implementation of
a religion's texts, the pronouncements of its virtuosos, and the institution
itself do not necessarily represent a religious universe. They are instead
highly evocative of the concerns, dilemmas, access to resources, and preferred social organizations of a particular people at a particular time.

Since the last part of this book deals with the rituals of Kamigamo
Shrine, I will first consider what David Parkin refers to as "culturally loud"
expression of these events within the context of contemporary Shinto.
Catherine Bell notes that the term "ritual" is a farily recent concept "heavily used to help differentiate various styles and degrees of religiosity, ra-
tionality, and cultural determinism" (1997:ix). It is not, she adds, a "universal phenomenon with a persistent, coherent structure" that works the
same way everywhere (1998:217). While ritual is a way of acting that
shares much with other kinds of human activity, there is a tendency to
privilege ritual activities as being different from other social practices.
Ritual can be characterized (but not encompassed) by its strategies of for-
malization and periodicity, the centrality of the body as it defines (and is
defined by) a specific environment, and the negotiation of power to appropriate opposing or divergent forces. By creating and maintaining a
context seen as sanctified by members sharing certain cultural norms, ritual can also legitimate common interests, empower selected individuals,
and negate or deny threats that challenge the legitimacy or survival of the
individual or group.

However, betraying a Western preoccupation with the individual, Bell
denies that the goals of the community, social solidarity, or conflict reso-
lution are the real reasons for ritual activity. Instead, she posits the "ultimate purpose" of ritual (what she calls "ritualization") as "the production

of ritualized agents, persons who have an instinctive knowledge of these schemes embedded in their bodies, in their sense of reality, and in their understanding of how to act in ways that both maintain and qualify the complex microrelations of power" (1992:221). Individuals gain through ritual an ability that is "relatively empowered (rather than conditioned or molded)" to "deploy . . . basic schemes in ways that appropriate and condition experience effectively" (ibid.). While there is much to recommend here for understanding contemporary religious activities in societies emphasizing the individual, Bell's conceptualization of ritual is historically shallow. It gives too little emphasis to the historically formed and highly interrelated social networks of a community. An individual's interpretations of his or her own feelings or thoughts are influenced significantly by collectively experienced, sanctioned, and negotiated worldviews. Through the mediation of relationships within a community, an individual comes to understand his or her place in the world as well as the forces impinging upon this orientation. If certain interpretations persist over time, it is because of a socially enacted consensus (which may be coercive as well) of local people to be bound by them (see Behar 1986). To put it another way, it has always been the case that "the way the world surrounding the person was mapped played a central role in the way people explained their destinies to themselves and to each other" (Sabean 1984:31).

While ritual addresses the concerns Bell mentions, its orienting and socializing influences for individuals embedded in communities must be recognized as primary. Reinforcing shared beliefs or promoting an ideology is not the issue here; while these aspects may frequently appear to dominate ritual activity, there are also ways to embody schemes that promote forces thought to work against social solidarity and control (Bell 1992:216; Dirks 1994). As presented in Chapter 4, there is a long and honored divergence between rituals thought efficacious by Kamigamo Shrine's Kamo descendants and those events related to the court's imperial hegemony. What must be stressed are the ways that Shinto rituals have worked to reinforce conformity and continuity within a specific community (its "particularism," in Delmer Brown's terminology [1993]) while bringing the social experience of group and individual into line with dominant (though sometimes highly local) conceptions of the cosmos.

No matter what concern a contemporary Shinto ritual might be addressing, it usually is carried out by following the same procedural "script," one that—like its many counterparts in tribal as well as complex societies—is frequently characterized by scholars as being "invariant" (see

Hobsbawm and Ranger 1983; Rappaport 1980; Goody 1961). When appropriate conduct of the individual or group is in doubt, when authority is questioned, or when the unstable nature of human existence produces anxiety, ritual can indeed provide consistent symbols of reference and support. And yet, recalling the earlier injunction about assigning belief too quickly, there is no guarantee that the participants in a ritual actually experience it as a legitimation of their goals. In an increasingly pluralistic and multicultural world, and despite the coercive effects of society, an individual must be afforded the possibility "of staying clear of the normative system" (Gerholm 1988 : 202). Depending on variables of the moment, his or her ritual participation takes place in a spectrum that might range from intense religious arousal to bored indifference.

There is also the possibility that participants might resist or actively subvert the "essentializing strategies" of a ritual (Bell 1992 : 207). Dating from Max Gluckman's "rituals of resistance" (1962) to the present, a number of studies have demonstrated that ritual does not always enhance communal harmony. Schnell's work on the "rousing drum" festival of Furukawa (1999) takes prevailing paradigms regarding festivals in Japan (as expressions of communal sentiment, as vehicles for promoting social harmony, as integrating institutions between the deity of a shrine and its parishioners, and so forth) and extends their perspectives to include class conflict, resistance to modernizing forces, and even "divinely inspired" violence directed at figures of authority. In the darkness, with masses of intoxicated people filling the streets, more than one community has seen a ritual occasion swing from prescribed formats to improvised social protest.

Just how is this local knowledge about rituals and ritual contexts communicated to the average person? The truism that shrine Shinto's basic orientations are "caught, not taught" (Ono 1984 : 94) seems the most ready explanation offered by insiders, as if by simply being a member of Japanese society and breathing its air one comes to assimilate certain assumptions. Or, to paraphrase one of the many priests I interviewed, as the members of a community are exposed to and participate in the ritual cycle of their shrine, they gradually come to internalize "not an idea but an attitude" concerning a general sense of ethics permeating the Shinto practices.

Needless to say, admirers of Foucault, Bourdieu, and Williams would have a field day dissecting these sentiments as "inscribed discourses," examples of "habitus," or "hegemonies" that discipline common sense. What is being "caught" are the cultural politics of a time and place, those "official symbolic representations of reality that prevail in a given social order at a given time . . . [and] seek to control the terms in which all other politics, and all other aspects of life in that society, will take place" (Ortner 1989:200). Social and religious practices have long provided key articulations or outward manifestations of culturally held values. Such practices may be as simple as a pledge of allegiance to a flag in elementary school, as entertaining as a community festival sponsored by major corporations and businesses, or as complex as a state-run campaign to win the hearts and minds of a populace (such as occurred in the United States during the 1991 Gulf War). Indeed, as George De Vos has asserted, there is in ritual a socially sanctioned "pleasure of propriety" gained simply from keeping the rules and performing them well (1992:48). Intentionality and efficacy aside, he believes there is aesthetic gratification, even a kind of self-righteousness, that ritual gestures impart. To see ritual as consistently framed by localizing cultural values, social needs, and secular events may irritate more theologically minded scholars, but it is a perspective that must remain in focus at all times when looking at religious practice.

Another part of the focusing mechanism through which anthropology views ritual has been called "cultural relativism." While frequently maligned as a doctrine rather than the method it is, cultural relativism initially helped anthropologists (as well as politicians, administrators, and even the general public) gain sensitivity about making blanket pronouncements concerning universal values. Especially relevant to discussions of religion and ritual are judgments about what a people do or do not "believe." Because of Christianity's influence on Western thought, belief is still seen by many as a requirement for membership and participation in a religious tradition. To Malcolm Ruel, however, terms such as "belief," "faith," and "truth," the meanings of which may appear evident to the outside observer, are actually abstractions specific to a privileged "monopoly of perspective." When applied to actual practices and cultures, these same abstractions tend to "bracket off" ideas that a people hold about the world from the world itself (Ruel 1982:29).

In Japanese ritual practices and in shrine visits especially, just what is happening inside the minds of participants is always a matter of conjecture. In an average ritual lasting forty minutes, only five are concerned with utterances that might influence a worshiper's thoughts or feelings (provided the person was able to understand the archaic language). Late-nineteenth- and early-twentieth-century "ethnographers" such as Frazer, Tylor, and Robinson-Smith may have fearlessly skated onto the thin ice of intellectual projection of beliefs to non-Western peoples, but contemporary anthropologists (or anyone dealing with religion) must trace ritual actions and orientations through a major range of social activities before venturing any hypothesis about what a people may or may not believe, or what the symbols of ritual practices signify (see Gluckman 1962:42).

Similarly, assigning an opposition between the expressive and instrumental ends of ritual seems a sociocentric imposition from Western models on societies that are likely to see no separation at all, let alone conflict (Nadel, cited in Goody 1961:149). Instead of thinking in terms of neat and tidy binary oppositions, I have tried to follow the advice of Jean La Fontaine and have attempted to locate ritual practices along "a continuum of action" stretching from what could be labeled technical to the symbolic (1972:161). In "traditional" Japanese society, for example, activities appearing to Western eyes as primarily technical, such as swordsmithing, pottery making, or weaving, were (and in some cases still are) frequently loaded with symbolic values. Langdon Warner writes that an artisan was once thought of as a kind of shaman, because, in possessing the mystery of his craft, he had a power over the "nature gods" through an awesome ability to fashion raw materials into finished products (1952:17). Empirical and expressive at the same time, the above example can serve as a metaphor for similar correspondences in Shinto ritual practices.

As long as the concept of a "continuum of action" is used as a guideline, one's analysis can avoid being overly restrictive about what constitutes ritual activity. However, I do not mean to imply that any repetitive action should be characterized as ritual. I frequently use the word "performance" to convey the progression of a shrine ritual, but I do not intend it to mean that ritual is unvarying, or that ritual activity necessarily provides a scripted model for what is or is not a ritual, or that the symbolic acts of a ritual necessarily invite or promote interpretation among those watching or participating in it. In short, following Rappaport (1980), ritual is not drama, although like any dramatic performance, ritual has elements of formality that must be enacted. Both "ritual" and "performance" are used as inclusive terms, referring to a specific occasion with specific actors, but the dynamics of these events both organize and distribute the participation of individuals along a "continuum of engagement and disengagement" (Kapferer 1984; also Gerholm 1988). To stress the performative dimension of ritual activities is to show that "ritual action does what it does by virtue of its dynamic, diachronic, physical, and sensual characteristics (Bell 1998:209).

To do otherwise by proposing, say, a structural model such as Van Gennep's tripartite scheme (in which, significantly, the liminal phase is not seen as sacred [Morris 1987 : 248]) would make aberrations of occurrences that are common in ritual practice but that do not work to uphold the analyst's reified structure. How would one account for a priest suddenly looking up from his ritual activities to watch for omens in a flock of birds overhead? Or interpersonal joking behavior between priests during what is supposed to be a solemn ritual? Or, at a time when each movement and utterance is sanctified in one of a shrine's biggest festivals, the elderly head priest losing one of his oversized lacquered clogs on the steps to the inner shrine and muttering loudly to no one in particular, *"Shimatta!"* (Confound it!).

What is *supposed to be,* to rephrase Blake's verse quoted at the opening of Chapter 1, is not always what *is* within ritual occasions. Ethnography, like religious studies, has for too long ignored the performative variability created through ritual occasions, as if babies crying, crows squawking from a rooftop, or an old man coughing were not part of the experience of the event.[2] What is often most fascinating about a ritual is not its symbolism, its performance, or the alleged goal it tries to bring about; rather, it is the tension between the rigors of an attempted invariant performance and the beautifully unexpected ways the minds, bodies, and actions of human beings intervene in spite of themselves. In the words of Johannes Fabian, an ethnography of ritual or any other social phenomenon must not "call the tune" but "learn to play along" (1990, in Hastrup 1996 : 82).

HISTORICAL STRUCTURINGS OF SHINTO RITUAL

This is not the place for a full discussion of the historical development of religious rituals in Japan.[3] As general background, however, two of the earliest documented accounts of ritual in the Japanese archipelago are the accounts of envoys from China in the third century (Tsunoda and Goodrich 1951) and the later mythological-genealogical narratives in the *Kojiki* and *Nihon shoki.* It seems fairly certain that the earliest rituals were performed in recognition of and gratitude to a simultaneously vague and yet powerfully immediate sense of the sacred specific to local peoples (Ishino 1992). Early animistic worship in Japan held the sacred to be anything mysterious, marvelous, uncontrolled, strange, or simply having the power to defy human comprehension. These forces and phenomena, called *kami,* were at first unnamed and amorphous numina in what Kato Genichi (1973) calls Shinto's naturalistic phase.

As society grew in complexity and scope from the third to fifth centuries and the Yamato clan gained dominance, many but not all *kami* acquired names and specific powers that imbued them with personality traits not unlike those belonging to human beings. They could be coarse and violent, causing earthquakes, typhoons, or surprise attacks, but they could be beneficent and refined as well. As with one's neighbors or enemies, certain ritual strategies were required to control a *kami*'s temperament and influence, thus maintaining a tenuous balance between human, phenomenal, and transhuman worlds. At the same time, these strategies needed to be flexible enough to appropriate whatever blessings the *kami* could bestow, especially those related to the management of wet-paddy rice agriculture, which in turn led to greater social stability and continuity (see Muraoka 1964).

Early Japanese ritual specialists learned well a Chinese precedent for fostering a degree of compliance among diverse groups: by imposing ritual structures (for example, the worship of the state cult of the emperor or the sun deity) that employed ambiguous symbols rather than dogmatic beliefs, a flexible means to address wide-ranging concerns could be promoted locally and by the state (see Watson 1985). Even a cursory reading of early Japanese history demonstrates how the Yamato clan preempted and condensed many of the myths of the clans they conquered. These revised myths were in turn woven into a charter for their own leaders' direct descent from the deity of the sun, Amaterasu. By this means, they were able to legitimate and sanctify their hard-won prestige to the ever-watchful dynasties in China and Korea.[4]

As Buddhism made inroads among the Yamato administrative elite in the sixth and seventh centuries, considerable amalgamation was occurring, with Buddhist divinities worshiped in Shinto rituals and the *kami* venerated in Buddhist ones (McMullin 1989:24). Ritual practices became more effectively centralized and consistent as administrator-priests focused on suitable historical events in an attempt to establish a "carefully designed continuity of authority" (see Hobsbawm and Ranger 1983:5) for their respective lineages. The "Record of Ancient Matters," or *Kojiki* (712 C.E.), cloaked these events in the descriptive imagery of mythical dimensions and characters. This imagery served not only to link the aristocracy (and, by extension, their subjects as well) to a deeper, primordial sense of reality sanctioned by the *kami* themselves, but resulted in effectively "blocking off explanation and questioning about the interpretable nature of the past" (Percy Cohen 1969:351). Nor was this practice lost on nonimperial clans that came to occupy the seats of political power, since they all divinized their own ancestors in order to legitimize their position with sacred authority (see Sonoda 1983 and Chapter 4).

MATSURI

Because of the ease and frequency with which public festivals can be observed by outsiders, *matsuri* have been a popular topic of research for years. General discussions usually focus on the dramatic and frequently ecstatic performances once the event has been committed to its lay participants. Littleton (1987:195) and Sadler (1976), for instance, concur that *matsuri* is ecstatic religious performance in the demonstration of community solidarity and economic power. Descriptions of material preparations, the mobilization of personnel and finances, maintaining harmony, or the interlocking social networks needed for a *matsuri* point in a linear direction toward the performance itself (see Ashkenazi 1993:7). Anyone who has seen one of these events comes away with vivid images of the spectacle of portable shrines powered by masses of high-spirited men (and more recently women as well) careening through narrow streets. The excitement and spontaneity are contagious, and one can easily find oneself similarly "possessed" by the "spirit of the *kami*" and absorbed into the mass of the shrine-carrying crowd.

The opportunity to loosen the bonds of workplace, social, or familial obligations and experience a brief, well-bounded, but nevertheless liminal stage of social existence is often welcomed within modern Japanese urban environments, even at the high-rise concrete blocks of "new towns." Similarly, rural communities threatened with demographic change have tried to revitalize old festivals (or create new ones, such as Fukushima's "belly-button" *matsuri*), hoping to stimulate local economies with a boost from tourism. Robertson (1987), Reader (1991), Graburn (1983), Inoue et al. (1979), and others have described these *matsuri* as events where individual and communal energies can be reaffirmed through what seems to be a convenient pretense of "serving the *kami*." To Sonoda the dynamic of contemporary *matsuri* is its bringing dream time into real time (1990:41, building on the ideas of Huizinga, Bataille, and Bakhtin).

Even though both the audience and the participants know a festival is based on what Sonoda calls an "illusion," *matsuri* can build in intensity until the mental boundaries that keep it contained as an illusion diminish and a profound sense of reality (often ecstatic and transcendent) is imparted to those involved.

Perhaps it has always been so to one degree or another. Murakami (1970) sees *matsuri* as a special characteristic of folk religion that has kept its basic structure through the centuries—providing the common person with a structured venue for channeling emotional energy in a positive light. Schnell has shown that even when *matsuri* are used to express class dissatisfactions—as when a portable shrine (akin to a battering ram) veered into a hated landlord's house or the local offices of an overly authoritative police—it is because the *kami* have "possessed" the participants, thus absolving them of responsibility (1999; see also Davis 1992; Yoshida 1984).

The "new" *matsuri,* in contrast, while tapping the energies and resources of the general populace for their success, are hardly examples of what Murakami posits as "folk" culture. Like many other scholars of the 1970s, he sees "folk" practices as insulated through protective mechanisms (afforded festivals, agricultural occupations, or rural residency) from dominating social forces. Now more than ever in Japan, the reach of state-oriented institutions and hegemonies extends into every nook and cranny of social life. NHK television's *Keizai Journal* broadcast mentioned in 1994 that 80 percent of housing complexes have developed summer *matsuri,* but only some are connected to the traditions of a shrine. The *mikoshi* portable shrines (many times paraded without any sacred essence inside) are used as a way to unite people rather than to bring the revitalizing energies of the *kami* into local neighborhoods. Children have their turn during the day at pulling their own style of *mikoshi* while adults have the night—a pattern that some see as divisive rather than uniting (Sakurai et al. 1990:200). Authenticity is also a debated issue, as one informant replied to a Japanese ethnographer about the City Hall–sponsored "invented" *matsuri* of a new town, "without *kamigakari* [spirit possession by a *kami*] festivals are no fun" (Matsudaira, cited in Robertson 1987:131).

At issue here are important questions about how members of highly industrialized and demographically mobile societies learn to identify with the places their occupations or life situations lead them to as well as how they become informed about and accept the "given" historical and spiritual dimensions of these places. Shinto shrines, through the public festivals they stage, serve to create a kind of short-term community. They encourage and permit instant membership in and identification with this community, and educate millions of people yearly through direct participatory experience about the historical, spiritual, and national significance of this "shared" community (see B. Anderson 1983; Herzfeld 1986; Gellner 1987).

If enhancing community is one of the primary issues in the staging, performance, and strategies of *matsuri* (as Durkheim once argued in a different context), then *matsuri* are, not surprisingly, of interest to the state. A frequent contributor to "insider" accounts of Shinto, Mayumi Tsunetada, an associate head priest at Kyoto's Yasaka Shrine (around which the famous Gion Festival revolves), mentioned the inspiration he received after encountering the ideas of Robert Bellah and Neil MacFarland at a conference on civil religion. He too sees the potential of *matsuri* to unite communities, advocating that shrines have a responsibility to do so by revitalizing old traditional festivals. However, he says, if such festivals are conducted without a religious dimension (as in permitting portable shrines without a transferred *kami*-essence to be carried), stronger human charisma will be needed to hold the event together. This practice, he believes, is dangerous, very possibly leading to the creation of new cults (Mayumi 1989:35). Thus: "Shrines are the only place where people get together to worship society and community and family and ancestors. That is *matsuri*. There is no other way to unite the Japanese people, and no other way for people to realize their identity. Shrine *matsuri* is the only thing capable to respond to that need" (p. 78).

Enhancing community is important, but there is another crucial dimension to *matsuri* which, if omitted from an understanding of their practice, leaves the phenomenon like a shallow lake in an arid region—glittering and refreshing when the sun is right but doomed to evaporate because it lacks depth. When I was beginning my fieldwork at Kamigamo Shrine, a priest from another shrine said bluntly: "Why do you want to work there? It's very complicated, and besides, their *matsuri* are the old style—slow, stately, and not very interesting." I soon discovered the "old style" of *matsuri* was, in fact, the more historically accurate, with the raucous festival coming into its own as a widespread social practice only in the last two hundred years.[5]

Sonoda Minoru has proposed two concepts for encompassing both the "old" and "new" aspects of *matsuri*. The first, *saigi*, is the ritual aspect of *matsuri* marked by reverence and solemnity toward an invoked presence of the sacred (1988:60). The original meaning of the word *"matsuri"* comes from both *matsuru* and *matsurau,* meaning to "serve one's superior with respect" (Sonoda 1987:9) as well as "to be with," "to attend to the needs of," and to "entertain" either the *kami,* the soul of a deceased person, or a superior of higher status (Kitagawa 1987:122). But there is also the aspect of *matsu,* "to wait," which evokes an attentiveness to the sudden manifestation of the *kami* into a ritually prepared space and time. During Shinto's golden age in the early and mid-Heian period, it was thought efficacious to conduct rituals at night, when the *kami* were believed to move about more freely in a liminal period unhindered by the profane activities of workaday human affairs. Kamigamo's *miare-sai* (detailed in Chapter 7, May 12) and Iwashimizu-Hachimangu's September 15 *taisai* festival are among the many that continue this tradition.

Sonoda sees the features of "waiting" and "service" as composing the essence of *matsuri* in its "true" historical sense. There is, however, one more element that must be added before the concept reaches full resonance. According to Kamishima Jiro, when the legendary emperor Sujin moved the shrine of the sun deity Amaterasu out of the imperial palace and into its own abode at Ise in the sixth century, an important transition occurred. The "attending" of close-at-hand *matsurau* became the "enshrinement," "worship," or "veneration" of *matsuru.* The *kami* was no longer part of the ruler's household but was now distanced to become a powerful other, whose needs were not only met but catered to with an institutionalized and highly regulated deference and obedience (cited in Kitagawa 1987:123).

From the *Taihō ritsuryō* of 701 C.E. to the late 900s, the imperial court attempted, based on Chinese models, a systematic correspondence between the domain of heaven and that of the court. Key to this agenda was *saisei-itchi,* or the unity of *matsuri* with governmental administration, also called *"matsurigoto"* when practiced as policy or ritual (see Wada Atsumu 1986). Although problems affecting the systematic practice of *matsurigoto* as state policy arose shortly after its codification in the *Engi shiki,* it has existed in one form or another throughout most of Japanese political life. It again became especially relevant during the Meiji era with the proclamation of the council of state (the Daijōkan) that the nation was being restored to a policy of general renewal and unity of worship and administration, as founded upon the achievements of Jimmu, the legendary first emperor of ancient Yamato (Brown and Araki 1964:204). This policy allowed state Shinto to harness the often dangerous energy of *matsuri* within a context linking even the most spontaneous actions or resistance with overarching themes of national unity and "modern" progress.

Previous chapters contain historical and contemporary examples of the importance of power in ordering a sacred place and its ecology of symbolism. For *matsuri* as well, the "sacred order" established is a reproduction of a "microcosmos which has immanent within it that mythological macrocosmos present on the national level" (Sonoda 1987:63). A sanctified chain of causality and connections established through the efficacy of time-honored ritual practices extends to and blends with the procession of the portable shrines through the town in the second, more festive, carnival movement of a *matsuri,* the *shukusai.* As I have suggested elsewhere, the alignment of secular political organizations so that they appear as extensions of a divine arrangement is one of the underlying characteristics of Japanese religious and social history (Nelson 1992:99). From *kami* to priest and from priest to parish, businesses, and local government representatives, hierarchical positionings put motivated parties directly in line for legitimation and sacralization.

RITUAL PRACTICE IN CONTEMPORARY SHRINE SHINTO

It is thought that the earliest rituals occurring before the sixth century were basically a two-part process: an opening purification followed by a petition to the *kami* (Kitagawa 1987; Ishikawa 1987). However, as the more highly structured ritual practices of Buddhism made inroads with the aristocracy beginning in 538 C.E., local clans such as the Nakatomi or Imibe specializing in *kami*-veneration refined specific ritual actions and orientations to better fend off Buddhism and its world-appropriating tendencies. These priests wanted not only to protect their status but also to ensure a greater efficacy of communication directed to the *kami,* as the Buddhists were seemingly able to do (though often for different spiritual ends) with their liturgical "magic" based on texts, chanting, and prolonged prayer-petitioning before statues representing various Buddhas, bodhisattvas, and ancestral figures.[6]

Nearly fourteen centuries of momentous events, charismatic and powerful individuals, and profound changes have passed since the early ritual systemizations of the seventh century. However, many aspects of contemporary shrine Shinto ritual practice, such as invocational *norito* prayers and priestly roles as life-enhancing ritual specialists, still correspond to these early periods. And (as I will discuss later) because ritual sacralization remains part of Japanese social and political practices, it may be said that modern-day shrine Shinto is still "in immediate association with its own historical depth" (Pye 1989 : 196), when *matsurigoto* was the norm.

Whether sanctifying the start of a new company, blessing a fire truck, honoring one of the shrine's *kami,* or purifying the entire nation, contemporary shrine rituals conducted by priests proceed in orderly, predictable rhythms, moving from framing techniques at the start to sublime closures at the end. A divergence emerges, however, between insiders and outsiders in the way these rhythms are understood and discussed. Much of what one reads or hears about Shinto rituals from a Japanese perspective reflects the education, training, and experience of individuals who are intimately involved with shrine affairs, either as priests or as scholars (many of whom are priests as well).

From this vantage point, a ritual has three parts, all of which are centered on a phenomenology of the *kami.* Using Misumi Haruo's perspective in *Matsuri to kamigami no sekai* as a representative example, a ritual does not really begin until the *kami oroshi,* or "descent of the *kami,*" is enacted by the priests (1979 : 80). Once the *kami* has been summoned and is considered present, the categories of ordinary reality become infused with a divine transcendence, where each action, offering, or word resonates with sacred significance. With humans and *kami* sharing the same moment and place, the "host" then acknowledges the invited "guest" in the ritual's second stage, the *kami asobi.* While the word *"asobu"* commonly means "to play," here it signifies an activity that placates as well as entertains. This second stage covers everything that goes on while the *kami* is present—the food offerings, the *norito* invocational prayer, the dance of the shrine female attendants (when appropriate), and the worship of priests and public participants alike. Winding up this ordering of a ritual is the return or "sending back" of the deity in the *kami okuri* (also called *"kami-age"*).

To many Shinto priests and scholars, the purifications that precede and the reception or communion that follows these three movements are separate activities that, because held in a different location, do not qualify as integral parts of a ritual. Yet they say when asked that a ritual is not correctly performed unless these framing activities are carried out. Several also acknowledge that some part of the *kami*'s power is engaged from the moment the first prayer is offered during the opening purification. Thus, while feeling very strongly that a ritual depends on the presence of the *kami* within the inner sanctuary, priests also hold that the *kami* is not bound to that place and time.

As an alternate reading of what may be thought of as a typical Shinto ritual, Robert Ellwood has proposed a four-part structure consisting of purification, presentation, petition, and participation (1978:151). It is consonant with my earlier discussion of ritual and encompasses both the preliminary and concluding framing activities as well as those when the *kami* is thought to be present. While each shrine imprints on its ritual traditions local readings and the personalities of its ritual specialists, there is still considerable continuity among shrines in the basic practices enacted in venerating the deities. Recalling that the privileged actions of a ritual try to establish and reinforce conformity among an individual's body, his or her place within a community, and the community's orientation to the power of the *kami,* one finds that Ellwood's four-part scheme accommodates all these dimensions simultaneously.

From the moment an individual or group receives a preparatory purification, this chain of causality and interconnection begins to operate, although it is never mechanistic in that certain actions are believed to produce predictable or agreed on results. Whether it consists of simply rinsing the hands and mouth with water, waving a wand of white paper streamers in the air over the heads of priests and lay participants, or readying a site for the *kami* to be summoned, purification is an essential first step for making visible participants and invisible environments conducive for receiving the *kami*'s presence. Priests say that the practice of purification is based on an event from the *Kojiki* in which one of the primordial *kami,* Izanagi, had visited his partner, Izanami, in the underworld after she died giving birth to fire. Breaking his promise not to look at her, he saw her decaying body and thus aroused her wrath, from which he barely escaped back to the earth's surface. He then washed himself in a river and (without meaning to, it seems) thus restored his original creative abilities, as *kami* sprung forth from various parts of his body (Philippi 1968).

Since water plays such an important part in the myth, not to mention its importance for agricultural communities growing rice, shrines have traditionally been located near some form of moving water: rivers, mountain streams, springs, or the sea. Because impurity is thought to be an external imposition and not a corruption of the heart or will of an individual (or *kami,* for that matter) it can be removed if one has *makoto,* an inner attitude of conscientiousness and sincerity to comply with ritual proprieties.[7] All those entering the precincts of a shrine should ideally wash their hands and mouths (signifying a cleansing of deeds and words) at a special font, the *temizusha*. Should they be participating in an event within the shrine, a similar procedure will be enacted first as the procession of priests leaves the preparatory staging area, then again in a special place closer to the shrine.

This opening step, called the *"shubatsu"* or (more commonly) *"harae,"* usually consists of waving a wand of purification (the *haraigushi*) over the bowed heads of the participants. At Kamigamo, however, the wand of purification is for most rituals a small and thin piece of wood, approximately eight inches long, with a tiny paper or hemp-fiber streamer *(onusa)* attached to one end. Each participating priest is presented with one of these *ogushi,* which he uses to purify himself at the same time the lay participants are purified by one officiating priest standing before the entire group. The little wands are then collected, broken with one swift motion, and tossed into the nearby Nara Stream, where their impurities are thought to dissipate into the ocean via a chain of hierarchically arranged female *kami.* Though not practiced at Kamigamo, a secondary *harae* is sometimes performed after the *haraigushi,* when droplets of water are scattered in four directions by a leaf from the sacred *sakaki* tree.[8]

Volumes could be written on the importance of purification for the Japanese as it developed from Shinto rituals. Citing textual sources from 1120 B.C.E. China, Ueda Masaaki sees the roots of the practice in the succession of emperors; each time a change occurred, a female shaman performed a purification with magically charged *tama* stones (1979:62). Kevin Reinhart (1990) has shown that in another religion concerned with pure and impure physical states, Islam, there is nothing inherently wrong with being impure. In fact, impurity is basic to living everyday life; the only time it really comes into play for the individual is when one has ritual obligations to perform. In the broad sphere of Japanese social life, impurity should not be thought of as the opposite of purity; rather, as Davis points out, it can be seen as a "withering" or "run-down" state of affairs for the community or for the productivity of its lands, animals, or households (1992:216).

While rituals distinguish between what is sacred and what is profane, both states of being are ever-present in group as well as individual life. Indeed, rather than elevating or separating the individual from group life, the sacred "binds him more tightly in a common destiny" to that of his neighbors (Koschmann 1978:9). Many scholars hold that religious purification practices thought to be specific to *kami*-worship were eventually dispersed enough in society to heighten even the common person's awareness about aspects of health, disease, food preparation, and bodily cleanliness (see Ohnuki-Tierney 1984:37), all of which distinguished one social-cultural order (as in the Kansai or Osaka region and the Kanto or Tokyo region) from another. Essentially, through the associative power of mythic, cultural, and social correspondences, purification rituals can be thought of as placing "proximate acts in ultimate contexts" (Geertz 1974:122).[9]

The next stage involves the presentation of offerings and entertainments, beginning after the participants move into the shrine buildings (occupying either the outer or lower Hall of Worship or the inner/upper Hall of Offerings) and, in their state of purity and readiness, present themselves through the person of the head priest before the innermost sanctuary, the Honden. Before the Honden doors are opened by the chief priest, he leads everyone in a single silent bow *(ippai)*. Then, riding the eerie sound of a single drawn-out vowel intoned by a nearby senior priest in the *keihitsu,* the *kami* descends from its "heavenly realm" to the shrine's *go-shintai,* a sacred object (such as a stone, a sword, a jewel, or mirror) sequestered within the Honden. I have already mentioned how priests and mainstream Shinto scholars believe the ritual begins at this point. Many say this movement is an "invitation" to the *kami* to join in the ritual, but one could also see it as a way of creating the *kami* ad hoc each time (Fortes 1987:294). By doing so, the priests ensure that the *kami*'s power will be efficacious because fresh and fully charged.

The second presentational phase consists of food and rice wine offerings *(kensen)* that make up the essential core of the attending priests' duties. Since the *kami* are, by nature, thought to be entities that arrive and depart much the way a guest does, the priests extend offerings native to the region as a way of fulfilling their obligatory duties as hosts during the *kami*'s brief period of attendance.[10] Rice, thought to be a gift from the *kami,* is offered first, followed or accompanied by water, salt, and sake, called *"omiki"* in ritual contexts. The offerings proceed to the Honden along a chain of priests arranged according to rank, with the head priest supervising the event from his seat. Each time a tray laden with vegetables, fruits, seaweed, or a whole fish is passed, the fingers of giver and recipient slightly overlap, signifying a continuity along each stage of the relay. Offerings may occasionally be more elaborate (silk, money, or utensils), as in the case of gifts made from one shrine to another, but the presentation consistently follows the same general structure and pace regardless of the variables of season, circumstance, or the numbers of participants.

The priests subscribe to the notion that these offerings are basically a spiritual meal presented to the *kami* through physical means. But a more operational perspective, such as that advanced by Fortes (1987:299), shows that not only are the food offerings a symbol of the basic vehicle of kinship mutuality—that of sharing a meal—they may also be seen to alter the dynamics of the relationship between the participants and the *kami* for the next stage of the ritual. While human beings are wholly dependent on the *kami* for most of the benefits and good fortune that the natural world offers, in this case the participants are subtly reversing the relationship by making the *kami* dependent on the participants for food. By doing so, they redefine themselves as being entitled to make demands on the *kami* in the next stage of the ritual.

Scholars vary with regard to whether the food offerings or the petitions constitute the most significant part of a ritual (Ono 1984; Kitagawa 1987; Ishikawa 1987). Most head priests, however, will answer unequivocally that the *norito-sōjō*, or "words spoken to the *kami*" (usually referred to simply as *norito*), is that place in the ritual where there is an intensification of attention directed toward the *kami* and is thus of paramount importance. Beautiful, correct words, intoned with reverence and awe, are intended to bring about good influences through the power of *kotodama*, a spiritual power thought to reside in words, or words arranged in certain magical formulas (Philippi 1959:3; Plutschow 1991). To make a mistake in the recitation or incantation of these vibrations bodes ill for the efficacy of the ritual.[11] There are parallels to this practice found all over the globe—from the early texts of the Rig Veda to the Catholic high mass—all of which serve as useful points of reference regarding the expertise and authority of a religious tradition's "virtuosos" to communicate with transcendent forces (Weber 1964:2).[12]

After the slow rhythms of the *norito*, a sudden movement to "center stage" of the female shrine attendants (or *miko*) marks the beginning of several participatory interactions regarding entertainment and offerings that involve everyone present. While not all shrines use the *miko* tradition, they are easily the most dramatic and accessible part of the event. (Kamigamo uses other dance forms, such as *bugaku,* when circumstances require.) Dressed in vermilion slit-skirt bloomers, spotless long-sleeved white kimono, and white gossamer *tabi* slippers, these young women perform a slow, circular dance (*urayasu no mai,* more generally called "*sato-kagura*") while carrying *suzu* bell wands in their outstretched arms as entertainment for the *kami*. Accompanied by ancient court music *(gagaku)*, which may be live or recorded, the young women's serenely timed shaking of the bells evokes a mythological incident when the sun *kami*, Amaterasu, had shut herself in a cave because of her offense with the outrageous behavior of her brother.[13] Only through music and dancing was she again lured out and sunlight restored to the world. This stylized entertainment has been reenacted as a part of Shinto rituals since the earliest records and, according to some scholars, provides the source of all forms of Japanese dance from Noh to Kabuki (Grapard 1983, 1990).[14]

The second phase of participation—where those in attendance rise to present offerings, bow, and clap twice—is formally called *"hairei."* It begins after the *miko* have returned to their seats (and the audience restores circulation to legs cramped and immobile for nearly thirty minutes). Leafy sprigs called *"tamagushi"* from the *sakaki* tree (the same species used in early rituals for the descending *kami* to alight upon) are distributed as emblems that are said to link the individual heart/mind *(kokoro)* to that of the *kami*.[15] Each designated person (often one represents an entire group [see Ashkenazi 1990]) follows the example of the head priest in the *tamagushi hoten,* slowly coming forward, bowing, and then presenting the little branch on a small table so that its stem, pointed first to the center of the individual's body, is now turned to point toward the Honden. Kneeling in some shrines and standing in others, the participants then bow twice before enacting the two hand claps of the *kashiwade,* followed by a final, single bow. In a large group of participants, only a few representatives will come forward; the rest remain in their places and mimic the leaders' actions.

The participation phase is temporarily suspended while the food offerings are removed *(tessen),* the doors to the Honden formally closed, and the *kami* sent back *(kami-age)* with another eerie yowl *(shōshin).* The ritual comes to a conclusion with everyone following the head priest's lead in a closing bow. Likewise, he leads the way out of the shrine in a procession of descending priestly ranks, with even the lay participants following this protocol by letting those in their group with seniority of age or status leave first.

The final—but by no means unimportant—aspect of participation occurs after the ritual has formally ended. In many shrines, the lay participants receive a sip of sanctified rice wine *(omiki)* on leaving the Hall of Worship, while the invited guests and the head and senior priests reassemble in an adjacent building's special banquet hall to partake of more substantial fare. Originally, only the same offerings made to the *kami* were consumed. But current practice usually supplements the offerings with a simple meal prepared in the shrine's kitchen or with catered box lunches. Whatever the style, the postritual gathering serves as a transition from what has been a space and time of intense mediation by symbolic values and structures to a more secular and relaxed state. Called *"naorai,"* the eating and drinking are also thought to be efficacious means of incorporating the *kami* (which has permeated these offerings with its essence) into the communal and individual mind and body.

Anthropologists as well as religious historians have documented a wide variety of manifestations of this practice, resembling the way the eucharist is used in the Catholic church or the "ancestor's beer" is consumed after a ritual by the Gisu of Uganda (see La Fontaine 1987, for example), with subtle reminders of the participants' social status reflected in the order of seating and serving. The junior priests and *miko* serve the senior priests and guests, although sometimes a senior priest will make the rounds with sake or beer bottle in hand, pouring drinks for important or wealthy visitors. The cost of the banquet appears to be borne by the shrine, but everyone knows that without being subsidized by the participants' contributions, there would be no *naorai* (and very possibly no shrine). With sake of the highest quality, the guests usually consume a prodigious amount in a very short time before going about the rest of the day's business.

A departing act might be to purchase a talisman or amulet *(ofuda, omamori)* from the information counter at the front of the shrine. This small object is said to connect the worshiper to the *kami* in ways more vast and potentially more propitious than he or she could ever be aware of, as well as extending ritual access to the *kami* to secular areas where its influence is needed (see Swanger 1981; Reader 1991). In his study of Islam, Geertz has commented that sacred symbols serve a dual purpose both in formulating an image of the world's construction and as a program for human conduct that are reflexes of one another (1968:97). And yet, the Japanese seem especially relaxed about this reflexivity, demonstrating the way that modern men and women negotiate meanings appropriate to their social and cultural environments.

Depending on the situation or crisis, there is, to foreign observers, a wild swinging by Japanese people from Shinto to Buddhist rituals with little regard for cosmologies that appear to the categorically minded as mutually exclusive or even contradictory. A survey conducted by the NHK television network and *Yomiuri shinbun* (1994) showed that, in such areas as belief in the *kami,* or the Buddha, or the soul after death, what is important is the participation in religious rituals rather than holding firmly to specific beliefs. The more devout parishioners of shrines and temples have altars in their homes (with 45 percent of the respondents reporting they had both Shinto and Buddhist altars in their homes), where they can make simple oblations on a periodic basis. Even those who interact infrequently with these traditions in a public setting may still apply the orientations of Shinto and Buddhism to their worldviews. If the nearly 80 percent of the Japanese population visiting shrines on or soon after New Year's is any indication, it is likely there is far more substance and reassurance in these activities than participants realize. For those who participate in shrine rituals throughout the year, as the following chapter will outline, a complex interplay of associations and meanings, at the very least, reinforce cultural identity and historical continuity, empower the individual or group in a variety of ways, and resonate with possibilities for renewal with and realignment to what it means to be human within Japanese society and culture.

KAMIGAMO'S YEARLY
RITUAL CYCLE

The following overview covers some of the thirty-eight rituals listed in
the *nenjū gyōji,* the official listing published by Kamigamo Shrine. According to some interpretations, only those events celebrated "for centuries"
should qualify as *nenjū gyōji* rituals. A criterion like this would problematize considerably the selection of rituals owing to the vast reogani-
zation and revitalization of shrine Shinto after the Meiji period. In selecting the rituals to present here, I worked with senior priests at the shrine
to select those of most importance (judging by either the difficulty in
organizing a ritual, its performative effect on the general public, or its efficacy for the deity). When one considers (as the priests did) the time, expense, public relations work, and human as well as material resources involved in some of the more recent rituals, it becomes clear that they must
be included with no reservations about suitability or, more absurdly, "purity of form." Since I have discussed the maintenance of ritual traditions
elsewhere (Nelson 1996b), I will here present the events, people, and,
when possible, historical background that contemporary ritual occasions
comprise, using examples from my fieldwork in 1991 and 1992.

Out of all the following events, large crowds representing the general
public can be found at only the *kurabe-uma-shinji,* the Aoi Festival, the
summer purification called *nagoshi-barae,* and the Crow Sumo discussed
in Chapter 4. All other rituals are usually held by invitation only, although
casual visitors may watch from a distance, take photos of the priests or

rites from outside the inner courtyard, and come and go as they please. While the recounting of rituals can be tedious, I have three main agendas in sketching these events: first, rituals serve as a site where complex economics, performative personnel, and administrative agents merge; second, it is worthwhile to pay attention to these performances since the yearly ritual cycle provides and encompasses the most public of the many guises of Kamigamo Shrine in particular and contemporary Shinto in general; finally, this compendium can serve as an ethnographic testimony to the longevity of a tradition that remains of religious, cultural, economic, and political relevance to many Japanese.

JANUARY 1, 5:00 A.M.
Saiten-sai (First Offerings of the New Year)

According to the shrine's official listing of ritual events, the *nenjū gyōji,* the first occasion to acknowledge the *kami* begins in the early morning hours. During the Heian period, many of a major shrine's most important rituals were held during the early morning hours, when the profane activities of human beings were minimal. Thus, while the form of the *saiten-sai* was established in the Meiji period's nationwide systematization of shrine rites, its early-hour staging elicits much earlier orderings. On a more pragmatic note, by 5:00 A.M., the crowds of the *hatsumōde* New Year visitations have temporarily subsided, giving the priests a chance to attend to the presentation of food offerings and words of praise and to petition the principal *kami,* Wake Ikazuchi. During the forty-five minutes this ritual requires, the shrine's innermost gate and courtyard (which has been open to the public since midnight) is temporarily closed.

Virtually all rituals at Kamigamo begin in front of the administration building (Shamusho) located outside the hedge-ringed enclosure of the first courtyard. The most direct route to the shrine would be to pass through the torii immediately opposite the Shamusho, but processions always advance to the front of the shrine. Since the second as well as the outermost torii are aligned with the imperial palace, the priests' route acknowledges the formal ties between the palace and a shrine ranked second to Ise. When the procession *(gyōretsu)* begins in darkness, an attendant is present with a burning torch to lead the group into the lighted areas of the shrine.

At 4:45 A.M., when the priests assemble in front of the Shamusho, it is very dark and cold. Visitors and merry-makers seem startled when eight priests and two formally dressed shrine elders suddenly appear en masse from out of the darkness, assembling at the Tsuchinoya pavilion for the opening purification. Once purification is completed, they cross the Hori Bridge and then bow slightly to the Kataoka-sha (wherein is enshrined the "mother" of the principal *kami*) before passing over the Tama Bridge immediately in front of the inner shrine's main gate. Thus, by the time they have entered the central compound, priests and participants have encountered one physical purification (hand washing) and three symbolic ones (the *ogushi* wand of purification, traversing Mitarashi-gawa on the first bridge, and crossing Omonoi-gawa on the second). These are the standard activities and routes for any formal ritual at Kamigamo.

Once inside the shrine's innermost gate, the Middle Gate *(nakamon)*, the senior priests take their positions on the central walkway (with the head priest closest to the inner sanctuary), the junior priests take theirs along the walkway to the area where food offerings are prepared, and the participants assemble in the eastern wing to the right of the Middle Gate. After the head priest opens the doors to the inner sanctuary (Honden), he returns to his seat and leaves the rest of the special offering placement to the associate head priest. The offerings are conveyed priest-to-priest, changing hands three times before the associate head priest receives them at the top of the Honden staircase. He then maneuvers behind the heavy silk curtain protecting the sanctuary's entrance from sight and positions these offerings on low tables within. Second in sheer number and variety only to the Aoi Festival, the new year's *shinsen* food offerings number around 120 different kinds of fruit, fish, vegetables, meat, rice, and rice wine *(omiki)* and are said to represent the bounty of the nation's mountains, seas, rivers, and fields. After the associate head priest presents the *omiki*, water, and salt trays, the *kami* is given special metal chopsticks *(ohashi)* with which to partake of the coming treats. Three trays of white radish are then followed by a freshly killed pheasant; its order in the hierarchy of offerings represents, according to the priests, the pre-Buddhist hunting ancestry of the Japanese people in general and of the Kamo clan in particular (see also note 17 on Aoi Festival *shinsen* offerings).

When these offerings are completed, the most solemn part of the ritual centers on the *norito* invocational prayer or petition. The head priest slowly moves to a part of the central walkway, veering eastward where a round straw mat awaits. Located slightly off center from what would be a direct line to the doors of the Honden, this position signifies deference on the part of the head priest as well as a defense against being in the immediate path of the shrine's powerful *kami*. He drops slowly to his knees,

New Year shrine visitation
(hatsumōde), Middle Gate.

sets his *shaku* scepter on the wooden floor, unfolds the *norito,* and begins a petition on behalf of shrine, community, and region. Everyone in the immediate vicinity participating in the ritual bows deeply, and no one rises until the last syllable of the prayer is completed.

At this point, all except for the head priest depart to worship at the various subordinate shrines. Once again, the group is led by a burning torch that, with its eerie and solemn glow, throws virtually no light for those priests and participants bringing up the rear. In addition to worshiping at the shrines within the precincts, bows and hand-clapping gestures *(kashi-wade)* are made to the shrine's important subordinate shrines *(sessha)* of Ota and Kuga. Between the Sawada and Nara pavilions, the group stops before a tree planted especially for this occasion: it aligns their acknowledging bows with the sanctuary of Ota Shrine about a half-kilometer to the east. Likewise, facing a tree planted on the south side of the Geheiden pavilion, the group acknowledges the two-kilometer-distant *kami* of Kuga Shrine. After these rounds are completed, the procession returns to the inner compound, where the first *naorai* of the new year is held in a long and narrow room to the left of the inner gateway. The priests will then return to the Shamusho, change from ceremonial vestments back to their working garb, and continue to attend to the rush of visitors that, by January third, will total some 145,000.[1]

JANUARY 4, 10:00 A.M.

Hatsu-u shinji (Ritual for the First Offering of "U")

According to the Chinese zodiac, January 4 was the first "day of the rabbit" for 1992. Because the zodiac changes in accordance with the heavens, the day of the Hatsu-u Festival also varies from year to year. Although the sound "u" (pronounced of *usagi* "oo") is homophonous with the sound in the festival's title, there is no direct correlation. "U" signifies an offering called *"uzue"* that, beginning in the Heian period, was presented to the *kami* by both the imperial court and Kamigamo. Now, however, the practice exists only at the shrine. The *uzue* is about thirty centimeters long and is a branch of the *utsu* tree (also called *"hikage-no-katsue"*) decorated with a sprig of red berries *(yabu kōji)* and a small paper streamer, similar in shape to the *gohei* altarpiece or purificatory wand whose function is to both receive and transmit the spirit of the *kami.* Thus, the *uzue* is a charm against misfortune *(yaku yoke no majinai)* and a life enhancing *(seimei-ryoku)* talisman because of the red berries that bloom in the dead of winter.

The ritual proceeds in a shortened version, distinguished only by the *uzue* offerings, which are presented first among the offering trays headed for the Honden. I would like to suggest two additional interpretations: since winter is a time of low energy in the natural world (extreme yin), the use of a tree whose name is homophonous with the Japanese verb *utsu*, "to strike," implies also a ritualized blow against the debilitating effects of winter. I see additional significance in associating a midwinter rite with an animal known for its fertility and reproductive abilities. To offset the sickness, lack of food, and most probably loss of life traditionally associated with the cold season, a ritual with undertones of striking back and procreativity, and with overt talismans to ward off misfortune in general, seems highly appropriate to usher in the new year.

JANUARY 5, 4:30 P.M.

Shinnen kyōen-sai (Ritual and Banquet for the New Year)

The importance with which the shrine views its patrons, benefactors, supporters, and behind-the-scenes advocates becomes clear on January 5, when a ritual and *naorai* feast of appreciation is observed for these individuals. Late in the day compared to most shrine events, the 4:30 P.M. starting time of the *kyōen-sai* signals deference to the busy schedules of these men and women. From 4:00 on, they assemble in the Chokushiden hall adjacent to the administrative offices. By 4:30, when the ritual procession begins, the group has grown to about sixty-five individuals of all ages—elderly couples and individuals, middle-aged salarymen occasionally with wives and children, even a TV entertainer and his attractive wife.

Bypassing any kind of ritual purification en route to the upper shrine, the group straggles along talking and laughing behind the priests. Only when they are seated within the chamber to the right of the Middle Gate does a younger priest appear with the standard *haraigushi*, waving it over the group before the ritual begins. The area closest to the front and thus indicative of status is the only area even marginally heated; an electric carpet provides meager warmth for the four elderly men of the shrine's board of regents. The rest of the group kneels on a thin red felt mat, sniffing, coughing, and shivering whenever a blast of icy wind sweeps through the courtyard. Many of the women are in kimono or warm winter clothes, but few of the men have their topcoats, which they feel are not appropriate for a formal ritual such as this. As if to acknowledge the situation, moments before the ritual begins one of the priests comes by and encourages them to sit close to the sliding paper screen doors (shoji) where, he jokes, "it is much warmer." It is obvious the priests are aware of everyone's discomfort, because they move quickly and present few offerings before the *norito* prayer begins. Because the audience is large and diverse but also important, the language of the prayer contains fewer classical forms and is thus more accessible to untrained ears than ordinary prayers. Predictably, the themes of the *norito* stress the importance of communal worship and interdependency with the shrine and acknowledge the power of the *kami* to bring everyone together for this event.

As soon as the prayer is completed, the main event begins: a *bugaku* dance with musical accompaniment.[2] To introduce the dance and its story, one of the senior musicians steps forward from the growing shadows of the grey afternoon. He announces that the origins of this particular performance reach to Persia and northern Pakistan, the same region from which the "horseriders" *(kiba minzoku)* swept into China, Korea, and Japan. Thus, he says, it is relevant to Kamo descendants and Kamigamo Shrine. The dance conveys the joy of a deity who is returning to his people, having escaped death in a duel with another deity high in the mountains. With great pomp and skill on the part of the masked dancer, it is splendidly performed. When it is finished, the priests remove the offerings from in front of the Honden, and the group follows the priests back to the Chokushiden, where the *naorai* feast will be held. The room is jammed with low tables and cushions, with each place set for a box lunch, beer and sake vessels, a small gift from the shrine, and the latest newsletter. Before anyone begins eating, however, the head priest addresses the group. He touches on key words dear to the hearts of many older and more conservative members of the audience —"*Nihon no kokoro*"(the heart of Japan), "*seishin*" (spirituality), "*yomigaeru*" (to return to or reinvigor), and so on— but then reminds the group of their good fortune to be Japanese. "We have a secure identity and a stable nation, unlike many people struggling to find their way in Eastern Europe. At this time of plenty and thanksgiving, we should remember them." He then thanks everyone for coming and requests their continued support and cooperation for the coming year.

The head of the shrine's parishioners' group then leads a toast, and the banquet begins. The associate head priest and most senior priests join with two younger priests in making sure everyone has a good supply of beer or sake, often partaking themselves as custom demands. Some individuals pick up their box lunches and gift and immediately depart; others accept the shrine's hospitality and indulge themselves freely, becoming red-faced and noisy, happy to be an insider at Kamigamo Shrine. The head priest stays for twenty minutes, then returns to his office. Like all good administrators, he knows that in his absence parishioners will feel less constrained to voice their opinions, and to this end the priests who have been serving are joined by others, who drink with the parishioners and hear their suggestions and complaints about the shrine.

JANUARY 7, 10:00 A.M.
Hakuba sōran shinji (Ritual of the White Horse)

The "white horse" ritual is a rich intermingling of continental, imperial, and local influences. The rite is mentioned in the *Kagennen nenjū gyōji,* dating to the late Kamakura period, but most likely is far older. It was observed originally in the imperial court in mimesis of Chinese customs connected with yin and yang, and auspicious days for purifications. In China, legend has it that if one goes to a green hill in springtime and sees seven young horses eating fresh spring grass, one can be purified for the whole year. Apparently, the rite was traditionally held on the seventh day of the second lunar month, but the adoption of the Western calendar moved it to January 7, so it now is associated with the *nana-kusa,* or "seven sacred herbs," which to this day are frequently enjoyed as part of seventh-day new year's observances (see Nelson 1996b: 199).

Eating is a crucial part of seventh-day activities and is the central event in the *hakuba shinji.* Evoking an earlier ritual hierarchy in which women were instrumental, one of the shrine's female attendants serves magical beans to the shrine's white horse, which has been led to the upper sanctuaries. Since horses are full of yang energy, the rite signifies the triumph of spring as the horse eats the (slightly cooked) hard, white, and round soybeans *(daizu)* that represent yin and winter. Soybeans, once eaten, are said to have powers to stop one from grinding one's teeth at night, to protect one from lightning, and, evoking the famous *setsubun* festival, to cast out demons. Unlike early European myths and ritual practices—where the functions of horses ranged from oracular powers ("out of the horse's mouth" meant a true pronouncement), benefits gained by sacrificing them atop mountains, or protection of an area by sculpting horse images into the sides of hills—the white horse has been primarily a vehicle for the *kami* to travel from the heavenly high plain of Takamanohara to earth. No wonder that during the war years Emperor Hirohito consistently appeared in public military reviews with or on a white horse.

Today, only two shrines in Japan beside Kamigamo have similar *hakuba* rituals, Sumiyoshi Taisha and Katori-jingū in Chiba prefecture, but the priests say emphatically that only at Kamigamo is the original rite preserved. This claim does not imply inflexibility, however, because adjustments must be made for the quirky personality of horses. For example, in 1991, the shrine's horse (named Kōyama-go, after the Kamo sacred mountain to the north of the shrine compound) refused to cross the lower bridge because of the hollow-sounding echo of his hoofs on the bridge's wooden floor. Despite considerable coercive measures, Kōyama-go simply would not budge. Thus, the priests were forced to bring tables, offering stands, and the all-important soybeans out of the inner compound to the bridge and to hold the ritual there. "Horses are fainthearted creatures," remarked one senior priest, "and you never know what they're going to do." To avoid a recurrence of these events in 1992, Kōyama-go was walked through the shrine several times to familiarize him with each step of the ritual. By January 7, he was docile and most cooperative. Not only did the ritual proceed without incident, but, thanks perhaps to the yang powers of the white horse to conquer winter, a beautiful spring came early that year.

JANUARY 14, 11:00 A.M.

Mitanae shinji (Offerings in the Shelf-Palanquin Style)

The *hakuba sōran shinji* illustrates that concern for good harvests begins quite early in the ritual cycle. The ritual on January 14 continues that general theme but is also representative of the late Heian period, when Kamigamo controlled considerable territory through the *shōen* estate system (see Chapter 4). In the year 1018, during the reign of Go-ichi jō, a reckoning was made about fields and property whose ownership was disputed by Kamigamo and Shimogamo. As a result of this decision, Kamigamo received the townships of Ōmiya, Kōyama, Ono, Okamoto, and Kawakami. The *mitanae shinji* resulted when the leaders of those areas presented elaborate food offerings to the shrine in acknowledgment of their newly ratified affiliation. (The word *"tana,"* found in the title of this rite, refers simply to the shelves within a palanquin on which the offerings were placed, with *"mi"* acting as an honorific.)

The six-shelf palanquins of the past have become a single-shelf one today, and it is prepared and offered entirely by shrine personnel. Filling the shelf are small carp and sweetfish *(aiyu)* from the Azumi River, and from the sea come bream, flying fish, red snapper, and mackerel. To protect the food and keep it pure, thin cotton curtains cover the entire palanquin. Leading the procession to the Honden is a single priest carrying a

large branch of a tree *(nara-no-ki)*. From its smaller branches hangs a lacquered container with unrefined sake inside, while perched above is a female pheasant—a standard offering in most middle or large festivals. After a short purification at the Tsuchinoya, the group crosses the Tama
Bridge and proceeds to the Honden, where the palanquin is placed at the
base of the steps leading upward. Additional food offerings are made by
the shrine priests before the *norito* prayer is given.

JANUARY 15, 10:00 A.M.
Mikayu shinji and *Tsukinami-sai*

Once again, food offerings figure prominently in the *Mikayu-shinji,* the
first of two rituals on the fifteenth of the month. *Mikayu* is a kind of rice
gruel prepared and offered to the *kami* for the first time in the new year.
However, preceding the presentation of the offering, a curious exorcism
is conducted on the structure of the Honden. Two of the senior priests
take long wooden chopsticks *(ohashi)* that have their ends wrapped in
white paper and begin tapping here and there, over and over in a regular
rhythm (tap-tap [pause] tap), on the open doors of the inner sanctuary.
From the doors they move to the railing along the upper level of the Honden, then down the railing flanking the steep stairs, and finally to the front
railing at the base of the sanctuary. They are especially careful to tap all
those sites where the hollyhock icon is represented in metalwork filigree.

The priests interpret the tapping rhythm, like the bows one makes
when performing *kashiwade,* to be symbolic of a yin-yang balance, with a
final yang tap to tilt the scales in the direction of positive life energy. As
seen in another ritual on January 16, even the new year is prone to impurities and defilement, all the more so because the shrine accommodates
public participation, petitions, and worship. Once the exorcism is completed, the ritual proceeds with the rice gruel offering (along with the
usual assortment of cooked and uncooked rice, sake, water, salt, vegetables, fruit, and dried sea products) positioned within the Honden. The
head priest intones the *norito* invocational prayer, and then the offerings
are removed. As soon as this is completed, the doors of the Honden are
closed and the *tsukinami-sai* begins.

The closest a shrine comes to a regular worship service is the monthly
tsukinami-sai. Usually held on the first of every month, the *tsukinami-sai*
can also occur on the fifteenth, when other more important ritual activities are given precedence at the beginning of a month. The principal intent of this ritual is to reaffirm the shrine's commitment to serving the

kami, to acknowledge the subordinate *kami* elsewhere on the shrine grounds, and, as a recent addition, to create an occasion for shrine personnel to state publicly before the *kami* (thus sacralizing activities most would see as secular in nature) that every part of their job is performed in service to the shrine, its *kami,* and the shrine's parishioners. To these ends, simple offerings are presented on an eight-legged table before the doors of both the Honden and Gonden sanctuaries, within which are enshrined Wake Ikazuchi and Takenotsumi. Additionally, a box of offerings makes the trip down the steps, over a bridge, and to Kataoka-sha, the shrine of Tamayorihime, the legendary mother of Wake Ikazuchi. In fact, the *norito* to Wake Ikazuchi never begins until an announcement is made before Kataoka-sha that a ritual will soon begin to honor the deity's son. Once the prayer to Tamayorihime begins, a priest positioned just within the Tower Gate shouts loudly that the Kataoka *norito* is under way, which then enables the *norito* to Wake Ikazuchi to commence.

On completion of both *norito,* the offerings are then removed to prevent their despoilment, and the priests proceed down the steps out of the inner compound. Their route takes them over the bridge by Kataoka-sha, in front of a sacred rock, and over the lower Hori Bridge. With the head priest at the fore, the group assembles in front of the Hashidono pavilion and presents bows and hand claps on behalf of all the subordinate shrines *(sessha* and *massha)* located both on shrine property and elsewhere in the city. The procession then returns to a side chamber near the Middle Gate of the upper shrine for the *naorai* — a ritual partaking of consecrated rice wine *(omiki)* and slightly softened but uncooked rice. The head priest sits closest to the inner sanctuary, and the other priests position themselves according to rank while they are served by junior or apprentice priests. The total silence is broken only by a single clap performed by each individual before he partakes first of the rice, then of the *omiki.* The last phase of the *tsukinami-sai* brings all the priests, as well as other shrine staff (such as the groundskeepers, female attendants, and sales personnel) to within the inner courtyard for a recitation and reaffirmation of their roles within the institution. For the text of this document, see Chapter 5.

JANUARY 15, 1:00 P.M.

Seijin-shiki (Coming-of-Age Festival for Young Adults)

When a young woman or man turns twenty in Japan, it is thought a significant milestone in that person's life. She or he is henceforth considered a full adult, with all the legal and civic responsibilities that accompany this new status. Since Shinto shrines attempt to maintain social relevance by providing rituals corresponding to life transitions, the *seijin-shiki* commemorates this important event at the beginning of the year. The ritual itself is a Meiji era innovation, but it draws on the standard practices and structures common to most shrine events (for another discussion of this event in a different location, see Nelson 1996b:212).

However, the *seijin-shiki* has become in recent years a civic assembly sponsored and promoted by the governments of local municipalities. According to Endo (1993), some 3,200 cities and villages nationwide have adopted this event for their purposes of encouraging citizenship and responsibility, usually through a series of speeches by local mayors or prefectural VIPs. However, only 5 to 6 percent of eligible twenty-year-olds attend these events, using them largely as a chance to show off their fine kimono or hairstyles and to frolic with present or former classmates.[3]

At Kamigamo, those participating in the 1992 *seijin-shiki* were members of the young persons' alumni association *(shōnen dōsō inkai)* affiliated with a local junior high school and the shrine. Each participant dresses in formal attire (kimono for women and suits for men) and follows the priests in a procession from the administration building. At the Tsuchinoya purification pavilion, everyone lines up and is purified with a standard, paperstreamer *haraigushi* instead of the usual wooden stick unique to Kamigamo. After a short ritual in front of the Honden, the group assembles in the western field to plant a cherry tree, each participant contributing one shovelful of soil to the process. The group then retires to the Chokushiden within the administration building for three formal speeches stressing gratitude to parents, the brevity of youth, and the contributions they will make to society, followed by a *naorai* reception that includes sake and beer.

JANUARY 16, 1:00 P.M.
Musha shinji (Casting Out the Last Demons of the Old Year)

According to the "traditional" ritual cycle (which began with the Meiji Restoration imposition of a Western calendar), New Year's celebrations used to continue until the fifteenth of the month. Even today, it is socially acceptable to wish someone a new year's greeting until the fifteenth but not after. The *musha shinji* is designed to purify the shrine after the rush of public visitors and petitioners have poured into the shrine during the first fifteen days of the month. I was told that each request made to the *kami* is "burdened" *(omoi)* with sacredness but that this condition can turn to a life-depleting drain on the shrine's spiritual energy if these requests are "misplaced." I interpret this to mean that not all requests for aid were delivered properly (in a formal petition before the central sanctuaries), and therefore there may be loose ends within the shrine, interfering with its purity or ritual functioning.

The ritual is thought to date from the late Kamakura period (an estimate based on the omission of this ritual from the *nenjū gyōji* text of the early Kamakura), when the syncretism of Buddhism and Shinto was firmly established in social practice. In order to dispel those "demons" lingering here and there within the shrine that other purifications may have missed, a target with a bull's-eye painted on one side and the character for "demon" *(oni)* on the other is set up in the eastern open field between the first and second torii. After a short ritual and *norito* in the inner sanctuaries' courtyard, the head priest, associate head priest, and five other senior and junior priests lead a procession of four shrine attendants and eight archers from a local archery school to the field.

The most senior of the archers begins the outer ritual by shooting an arrow with a ceramic tip that, because it howls on its way to the target, is supposed to frighten demons away. The head priest is next; although his arrow fell short in 1992, I was told that the year before he had miraculously hit a bull's-eye. The other priests then rise in pairs to take their turns. Finally, with great deliberation and stately elegance, the archers address the target; some of them even hit it. After two rounds of attempts, the ritual ends, and all retire to the Chokushiden for a short speech from the head priest followed by a *naorai* reception. Because this group of archers has close personal ties to the priests and the parishioners' group, the reception is a full lunch, with ample sake and beer. The target is rolled up by the groundskeeper and stored in the shrine's storehouse until the next year.

JANUARY 17, 10:00 A.M.
Shōjō-sai (Ritual Burning of New Year Talismans and Decorations)

The *shōjō-sai* ritual is held after considerable effort on the part of the groundskeeping staff and younger priests to separate, bundle, and box a substantial pile of discarded objects brought to the shrine for ritual disposal, stacked waist-deep in a side wing near the Tower Gate. People ususally make a small donation of one hundred yen for the service, leaving behind shopping bags full of a variety of objects they consider imbued, for better or worse, with some kind of spiritual energy. These objects include *ofuda* (paper tablets inscribed with the name of a *kami* and placed on or within the home altar [*kamidana*]) and *omamori* talismans—both of which should be renewed every year—entire wooden altars whose original purchase price was forty thousand yen (U.S. $330), replica torii, *ema* placards, representations in porcelain or wood of animals (horses, sheep, foxes, rabbits, tigers, and so on) associated with the Chinese zodiac, miniature rakes (to "rake in" good fortune), *daruma* dolls (often with only one of their two eyes painted in, indicating that a wish was not achieved), Western-style dolls, ceremonial chopsticks used in a wedding, small Buddhas on keychains, bells, *inkan* (personal seals), letters and postcards that carried significant news, certificates of achievement, calligraphy, photos of pets that died, clippings of human hair, bottles of unopened sake, dried *mochi* (rice cakes), numerous *chimaki* fan-shaped talismans composed of five oak leaves rolled up (odd numbers, because indivisible, are associated with strength), replicas of spears, swords, mirrors, and gold coins *(koban),* vestments from Buddhist temple pilgrimages (as well as books to hold seals from various temples visited, sashes, prayer beads, maps), smiling deities of good fortune (Ebisu), exquisitely carved wooden hawks from Kitano Shrine, and silk-embroideried dolls of prince and princess. More specific to New Year's are the orange arrows (*hamaya,* stacked head-high in twenty-six bundles), door-decorations *(shimenawa),* and pine branches, but only rarely a piece of bamboo that may have been in the *kadomatsu* decoration.

This amazing array of objects, all charged with what must be thought of as "unstable" spiritual energy of one sort or another, is painstakingly sorted. Those objects that do not qualify for inclusion in the shrine's ritual burning, such as plastic decorations, wrappings, Buddhist prayer books and ritual implements, and certain dried food offerings (other than dried fish, fruit, and beans), are relegated to a separate pile. The entire contents of the holding bin are then brought to what might be called the shrine's second most important administrative center (after the Shamusho offices): the groundskeepers' maintenance and supply sheds, located just inside the western torii facing the administration building. Common trash is thrown into the "secular" burning pit, while a specially constructed incinerator, made of new concrete blocks, is stacked with the selected "sacred" items. An eight-legged table, laden with food offerings, leans against the concrete blocks for stability, while a wooden box resembling a birdhouse shields a burning wick used to start the fire.

With the groundskeepers and other helpers standing in a semicircle, two priests in less formal *joe* vestments begin the rite, purifying first the offering table, then the incinerator, then the boxes and bundles nearby, and finally the participants. The second priest then intones the *norito* and stresses themes regarding the "sending-back" *(kami oroshi)* of heavenly generated power that these objects once had but that is now depleted. The fire is then lit by the first priest under wooden slats (*gomagi,* each three by eight centimeters) on which are written prayers and requests that smoke will "deliver" to the high plain of heaven, a ritual practice common to cultures worldwide but here most likely of Buddhist origin. During the first ten minutes of the burning process, the priest in charge of the opening purification and lighting the fire stands by himself, chanting the Nakatomi prayer of Great Purification. Once the fire is at full force, bundles of arrows and the other less flammable objects (such as the cloth talismans) are periodically put in together. Beginning at 10:00 A.M., the burning takes until midafternoon.

FEBRUARY 11, 10:00 A.M.
Kenkoku kinen-bi (Founding of the Nation Day)

A carryover from the Meiji era, *Kenkoku kinen-bi* became part of the Japanese national calendar cycle of public holidays in 1976, although it is not formally observed by government agencies. Its acceptance came after intense lobbying by the Jinja Honchō, the National Association of War Veterans, the Association of War Bereaved Families, and a nationalistic wing of the Liberal Democratic Party, the Seirankai (see Takayama 1988; O'Brien 1996). The holiday is controversial and contested because it commemorates the founding of the nation as stipulated by Meiji and later Showa ideologues, linking the past to the present by an "unbroken" chain of imperial rulers. At Kamigamo, unlike many other shrines, the affair is low-key. There is a procession to the Honden as usual, but on this day everyone stops en route at the flagpole beside the second torii. Here, while one of the younger priests raises the flag, another fiddles with a portable public address system until the Kimigayo national anthem blasts forth at ear-splitting volume. (On the day I observed this ritual, the sun burst through a leaden sky at precisely the moment the music started. Later, when I remarked on this fact, no one else seemed to have noticed. They did notice, however, a group of young adults who joked and laughed while the group was waiting for the song to begin but became silent during its playing. Later, while the group was in the audience chamber within the shrine, we heard a loud and well-orchestrated *kashiwade* from this same group.)

The upper shrine ritual follows the standard format, and the *norito* touches very briefly on the themes concerning the long line of emperors and the stability of the nation. In 1992 on the table for offerings in front of the Honden, several boxes with large red dots similar to the rising sun emblem of the Japanese flag were presented to the *kami*. When I remarked on this during the postritual *naorai* held in the shrine's main room for greeting important guests, I discovered the red circle was actually an apple; specifically, apples from the Tohoku region that had survived the devastating typhoon of 1991. Once I could see the boxes clearly, they said proudly *"Nihon no tsuyoi ringo"* / "Japan's tough apples." "Just apples after all," one of the shrine's elders teased, "so you don't have to worry [about us promoting nationalism]!"

FEBRUARY 24, ALL DAY
Sanyare-sai (literally, the Festival of Congratulations)

Sanyare-sai reflects folk rather than elite concerns about local young men coming to adulthood (defined differently than on the January 15 occasion). It also asks the *kami* of particular mountains in Kamigamo's eastern neighborhoods to come down to the rice fields. While the sixteen lineages once making up the shrine's priestly families participate in the Aoi and *kurabe-uma* festivals, this event is closed to them and thus may be thought of as a farmers' festival based on a *sō*-style organization's maintenance of community (see Chapter 4). Those households having a son turning fifteen (note that nothing was done ceremonially to acknowledge in public the coming-of-age of women in agricultural Japan) organize in honor of this transition small processions to Ōta Shrine, followed by a visit to the site of a neighborhood's tutelary mountain deity *(yama-no-kami)* and finally to Kamigamo. Older men play flutes while younger boys whack little drums and cymbals, singing out *"omedeto gozaru"* in a highly stylistic chant. The boy's father (or a community elder) leads the procession with a *sakaki* branch in his hand to purify and clear the way both of the procession and of the boy's course into his adulthood.

Central to this *matsuri* is the notion of work, that at age fifteen a boy carries with him the heavy expectation henceforth to fulfill his adulthood through work. The trip to the *yama-no-kami* is interpreted as petitioning the most local of *kami* to invest the boy with the same life-enhancing and perpetuating energy as they do the rice fields. To these ends, a branch of the sturdy *kashiwa* (oak) tree is presented for the *kami* to infuse with their power and is later buried in one of the paddies below. Today, since there are few remaining rice fields in northern Kyoto, in addition to the agricultural dimension of burying the oak branch, the *kami*'s revitalizing power is also asked to suffuse the occupational activities of the supplicants, whatever these callings may be, and to help them prosper. The final stop for the procession is the inner sanctuary's courtyard, where they are purified by a priest and present an offering to the deity. The group will then return to the boy's household, where all are treated to a feast composed of a variety of dishes and standard congratulatory red-bean rice *(akamame gohan)*.

MARCH 22, 10:30 A.M.
Mitama matsuri (Festival for the Ancestral Spirits)

Celebrated for the first time at Kamigamo in 1991, the idea for a *mitama matsuri* was introduced several years earlier by chief priest Abe to venerate the departed souls of the parishioners' ancestors as well as shrine personnel, much in the same way a Buddhist ritual would (see Morioka 1977). It was not until the arrival of the associate head priest, Mr. Takeuchi, that a person emerged who could handle the sensitive administrative and political details necessary to bring the event to life. Although the rite takes place within the symbolic framework of Shinto, it is done, according to Takeuchi, to "console, express gratitude, and petition these ancestral spirits for the future benefit of the shrine." Because of the impurity associated with death, this rite is held in the Chokushiden at the southern end of the administration building, wholly outside the torii-fortified shrine proper. Even so, many people both within and outside the shrine proper were opposed to the idea of conducting a *mitama matsuri*. Those of Kamo descent have their own ritual, the *sosen-sai* of October 27, but it was felt that a ritual was necessary to "calm" *(nagusameru)* the spirits of those involved with Kamigamo who were not Kamo people.

It is interesting to examine briefly how a major contemporary shrine goes about implementing a new ritual. First, the month and time of year are chosen based on a calendar noting days in gradations of whether they are auspicious *(taian)* or inauspicious *(butsumetsu)* days according to Buddhist reckonings. The spring and fall equinoxes are considered especially propitious days for ancestral rites, and indeed even the imperial household worships its ancestral *kami* on this day in the Kōreiden hall. After the date is decided, consensus is gained from the other priests, then the idea is presented to the shrine's trustees for approval. Once permission is granted, the difficult task arises of deciding who to invite and how much to request as a donation. For this first *mitama matsuri*, the heads of the parishioners' group, former employees, and people close to the shrine who had lost loved ones during the past year were invited.[4]

An altar was set up in an alcove *(tokonoma)* facing in the direction of Kōyama, appearing to validate one of Yanagita Kunio's assertions that the souls of the dead were thought to return to the mountain (see Hori 1972). The subject is highly complex, however, and hardly reducible to a single claim such as Yanagita's. Before the rite begins, the audience is warned that the *norito* will be longer than usual because of the names to be mentioned and history to be recounted; thus their patience is requested. After the opening bows *(shubatsu)* and purifications (first to the altar, then to the offerings in the hallway outside the room, then to the attendant priests and musicians, and finally to the audience), the *kōrei no gi* calls the *kami* to be present.

Unlike upper shrine rituals, however, this particular eerie call consists of two rising intonations followed by a very long rising and falling crescendo that is thought to bring the *kami* into the proceedings. Offerings are presented, then the associate head priest rather than the head priest reads a *norito* that he has composed. In very accessible language, it touches on the principal points of Kamigamo history—how its *kami* came to Kōyama, how the shrine's first buildings were erected, how it received status from the court, how the Aoi Festival was conducted, how imperial daughters became *saiō* ritual attendants, how temples were built on shrine grounds and later asked to leave, how rituals are conducted on behalf of subordinate shrines located elsewhere, and so on.[5] In short, the purpose of recounting this blending of myth and history is to frame the present-day ritual within a continuum of events made sacred by the *norito* and to establish its authenticity within the tradition of Kamigamo Shrine. The *norito* continues for nearly ten minutes, but few names are called out as the earlier announcement might have led one to expect.

The next part of the ritual departs from standard Kamigamo practice but is highly representative of shrine rituals elsewhere in Japan. Leafy sprigs from the *sakaki* tree *(tamagushi)* are offered before the main altar by representatives from the audience. Each person comes forward, performs the *kashiwade* bows and claps, and formally presents his or her *tamagushi* to the *kami*. This completed, the offerings are covered and the *kami* "sent off" in the *shōrei no gi,* although here the call is much less dramatic than the earlier one. Finally, a senior priest unrolls a silk curtain to conceal the altar within the *tokonoma,* and the ritual comes to an end. After a short recess, a *naorai* is conducted, which follows closely the pattern described for the January 5 *shinnen kyōen-sai*.[6]

APRIL 3, 10:00 A.M.
Toge-sai (Divination for Rice Planting)

Toge-sai is classified as one of the shrine's major ritual events *(taisai)*. The characters for *toge* are interpreted by the priests to mean "understanding the earth." Through several divinatory techniques, the priests discern the best time for planting rice seedlings. The ritual's adoption at Kamigamo is said to date to the Kansei period (1789–1801), although in form and intent it would appear to be much older. According to the head priest, this ritual, held for the benefit of agricultural pursuits *(nōsangyō),* has nothing to do with the government-influenced ritual cycle of the Meiji period (which most shrines continue to follow although with less emphasis on the emperor). After a ritual before the Honden, complete with formal offerings and *gagaku* music, priests assemble at the open-air Tsuchinoya for a simple purification, then take seats within the Hashidono over the stream. Small tables holding a variety of ritual paraphernalia have been positioned before six straw mats facing downstream.

After a long opening prayer by the associate head priest, each of the six takes a small hemp string and tears it with his teeth before tossing it over his left shoulder into the stream below. Next, a small paper *hitogata* figurine comes into play, rubbed first over the heart, then over the right breast, then in the center of the chest. Finally, each priest blows on the paper before crumpling and tossing it over his left shoulder into the stream. From unfired clay dishes on the tables, small squares of white paper are then scattered left, right, and center, using only the left hand. Next, salt is tossed in the same pattern. The priests then purify the scepters *(shaku)* they carry in all rituals by rubbing a small stick along their edges, and again toss the purifying agent into the stream. Finally, while the other priests begin the Nakatomi *norito* of purification, from which all the preceding purificatory practices are taken, two priests come to the forward railing, where each rhythmically shreds a white cloth into eight pieces. This completed, the fabric is then dropped into the stream and the preparatory purifications are completed.

The divinations are conducted by the head and associate head priests in front of the Hosodono pavilion while seated on round mats placed on a mossy buffer between the hall and the *tatesuna* sand cones. Each holds a grain winnower *(kokibashi)*, a small bamboo implement that strips grain from the head of the ripe rice plant. These grains are examined, then taken outside the second torii to the open grassy area, where they are scattered in four directions. The priests do not return to their seats but come to the Hashidono, perform *kashiwade*, and return to the administration building.

APRIL 10, 10:00 A.M.

Ōta Jinja matsuri (Ōta Shrine's Spring Festival)

As one of Kamigamo's principal subordinate shrines *(massha)*, Ōta Shrine provides access to the elite Kamo hierarchy for farming neighborhoods to the east of what were once the priestly residences in the *shake* enclave. On April 10, Ōta Shrine celebrates its spring festival by sponsoring a number of events lasting into the evening. At 10:00 A.M., the head priest and an attendant priest from Kamigamo come to Ōta Shrine to deliver a *norito* and present offerings. Not only do they worship before the main altar, they also go to each of the subordinate shrines *(sessha)* on the grounds, performing bows and hand clapping in front of each one. In a similar manner, people from the surrounding area come to pay their respects and ask for benefits (called *"onkei"* in this context) during this season of renewal. While the sacred performance called *"kagura"* is not performed at Kamigamo, Ōta Shrine promotes its *kagura* as the oldest in all Japan. In the morning ritual, Ōta's attendant priest (who is not called its head priest because of the shrine's close affiliation with Kamigamo) begins with an opening purification of offerings, *kagura* dancers and musicians, and participants from the neighborhoods. Several small trays of offerings are presented, a *norito* is intoned, and then *kagura* is performed to entertain the *kami*.

Rather than consisting of the elaborate and well-timed movements performed by young women, that are usually associated with this dance form, the Ōta Shrine *kagura* is performed by older women past menopause. As cymbals and a small drum (similar to that used in Noh theater) keep a simple one-two rhythm, the dancer stands in one spot, arms outstretched with *suzu* bell-wands in each hand, and slowly revolves in place. Although this *kagura* takes place during the day, it was traditionally performed at night (similar to the performance in Kyushu at Takachiho, the legendary site of the cave in which the sun deity Amaterasu hid herself) in order to gain greater access to the spirit of the *kami*. According to the priest, old women are more susceptible to receiving the *kami*, because they are no longer ovulating and have no impure blood to interfere. Also, the exalted status they achieve by performing this *kagura* reminds younger people (who are in need of spiritual guidance) that their elders have much to impart. Other aspects of the *Ōta Jinja matsuri* are a display of spring flowers, a tea ceremony, and a *naorai* in the evening to reaffirm the shrine's important public networks within a sacred context.

APRIL 21

Sessha, massha-sai

(Festivals for Primary and Secondary Subordinate Shrines)

Once spring is well under way, this simple ritual lavishes attention on the many subordinate shrines scattered throughout the grounds. Eight priests assemble in the Honden courtyard and receive wooden boxes holding cooked and raw food offerings that they then carry to the many smaller shrines *(sessha)*. The *kami* (sometimes more than one) are first presented with the offerings, then a short *norito* extolling their powers, and finally the *kashiwade* veneration. The priest then covers the offerings, picks up the box, and returns it to the Honden courtyard. To leave it at the subordinate shrine would subject the offerings to physical despoilment (as well as pilfering by crows and other animals) and thus compromise the ritual's efficacy.

MAY 1, 10:00 A.M.

Keiba ashizoroe-shiki

(Purification of Riders and Horses for the *Keiba shinji*)

Although preparations and training for the May 5 *keiba shinji* (also called *kurabe-uma shinji*) have been going on since early March, the *ashizoroe-shiki* is the first formal ritual enacted for the two teams of horseriders. Held in the Nara-sha pavilion (a national treasure), it acknowledges the agricultural *kami* enshrined at Sawada-sha in Kamigamo's northeast corner and evokes a long-standing dependence on ritual intervention to ensure abundant agricultural production. Riders *(norijiri)* are first purified by one of the main shrine's priests. Then they proceed to the Sawada-sha, where they purify their riding staffs *(sashi)* by rotating them left to right and then right to left (thus effecting a yang-yin balance) in the small stone-lined stream running in front of the shrine. A more elaborate purification awaits them at the Nara-no-ogawa stream, but they must first wait for the horses to have their turn. Nothing complicated is attempted here; a few scoops of water from an attendant's cupped hands are simply thrown on the horses' legs. The riders then take a stone stairway by the Jinji Bridge to the stream's surface, where they employ small wooden wands to purify their upper bodies, then dip heel and toe ever so slightly into the water. Finally, they dampen their bamboo riding staffs and touch them to their legs.

Once riders and horses are purified, they are presented before a select group of Kamo elders assembled at the Geheiden, who note the characteristics, including teeth and legs, of each horse, and try to pair it with an appropriate rider. The proposed matches are then run at full speed down the 150-meter course to test the compatibility of rider to horse. The day ends with a *naorai* reception in the Chokushiden, with even the youngest riders permitted to imbibe a little sake. I will elaborate on the horse-riding tradition at Kamigamo in the description of the May 5 ritual.

EARLY MAY (BEFORE MAY 12), 10:00 A.M.
Saiō-dai misogi (Purification of the *Saiō-dai*)

In 1956, after an interim of almost eight hundred years, the procession of the imperial priestess, or *saiō-dai,* was revived as part of the Aoi Festival. Since then, it has become one of the most popular parts of the entire event. Each year, a young woman around the age of twenty is selected from one of Kyoto's leading tea schools to play the part of the *saiō,* an imperial daughter selected by divination during the Heian period. Depending on the reign of the emperor (as well as other intervening factors), she would have served as a ritual attendant at the Shimo and Kamo shrines, a practice modeled after the *saigū* of Ise Grand Shrines. (I have discussed part of the history of the *saiō-dai* in chapters 2 and 4.) The woman selected to play the role of the *saiō* must not only be versed in tea but must also have a good academic record and come from one of Kyoto's upstanding families.

Since 1956, Shimogamo and Kamigamo have agreed to share the preliminary purification of the *saiō-dai* ("*dai*" indicates this is not the authentic person but a stand-in or proxy) in alternating years, although there is evidence the practice once belonged solely to Kamigamo. Not only was it the principal tutelary shrine of the court and the city, purifications were believed more efficacious if they took place upstream, as far away as possible from the profane associations of daily life and politics. While today the ritual is held within shrine precincts (at the pond of Mitarashi-gawa for Shimogamo and on the bank of Nara-no-ogawa at Kamigamo), it was traditionally held on the day of the horse at a site on the Kamo River determined by divination (McCullough and McCullough 1980:408). As in the coming Aoi Festival, a procession made its way from the imperial palace to the *saiō*'s residence at Murasakino and then on to the river.

Since style and elegance continue to charm modern-day Japanese just as they did their ancestors, it is likely that people are more interested in seeing the attire, makeup, and stately demeanor of the *saiō-dai* and her attendants than the extremely short purification ritual itself. The *saiō-dai* wears a twelve-layered kimono called *"jūni hitoe"* covered with a white outer robe, the *omigoromo*. Both are associated with Heian period courtly life as famously described by Murasaki Shikibu in the *Tale of Genji* and as depicted in the scroll paintings *(e makimono)* of that era. She carries a large fan *(hiōgi)* wrapped with many multicolored strands of braided silk. Most strikingly, her gold-plated headpiece *(saishi)* is said to evoke the crowns of early shamanic rulers both on the continent and in Japan: it is an upright tree whose branches are bedecked with silver plum blossoms. The tree is anchored by an upper half-disc of sun, which in turn is supported by a lower half-disc of moon at the bottom of the *saishi* just above her forehead. This design recalls the *himorogi*, or original sacred place of early *kami* worship (as well as the vertical universe of Siberian shamanism), while the sun and moon symbols speak of Taoism and yin-yang balances thought integral to the proper functioning of cosmic and human worlds.

The ritual of purification is quite simple and is neither preceded nor followed by a corresponding rite held within the upper shrine. After the *saiō-dai* and her entire entourage of ladies-in-waiting *(nyokan)* have been purified by one of the shrine's priests within the Tsuchinoya pavilion, the *saiō-dai* and two female acolytes *(warawame)* take their places on a platform built at the level of the stream. They are accompanied by a priest from Kamigamo (who looks over everyone's shoulders from a position at the rear), a male official from the Imperial Household Agency, and a woman who, like the puppeteers in Japanese *bunraku* puppet theater, is present but not supposed to be "seen." Hands moving constantly, she keeps the long silk train and heavy sleeves of the *saiō-dai* from interfering with her ritual duties.

As the priest almost silently intones the Nakatomi prayer of purification, the *saiō-dai* slowly leans forward from her kneeling position on the platform. She first sets adrift a single piece of tissue-thin white paper, which serves symbolically to "open" the stream to her as well as to purify

The *saiō-dai* (representative of the
imperial priestess), Aoi Festival.

the very spot she will soon touch. Then, with palms joined, she ever so slightly dips the tips of her fingers into the water and is thus partially purified.

To complete her ablutions, she and the other women ascend the raised platform of the Hashidono and perform a self-purification using wood and paper figurines. The wooden *hitogata* of the *saiō-dai* is similar in every way to those excavated from archaeological sites in Nara and farther south; she first rubs it on her chest in a left, right, center motion, then blows on it one time before tossing it over the railing and into the stream. While she slowly departs, the rest of her entourage take their turns at the railing, where they perform the same actions with paper *hitogata*. The highest-ranking women of the imperial lineage were from the *onnabetto* wing of the palace, followed by the *naiji* (from high-ranking but not imperial lineages), the *myōbu* (court attendants), the *munanori onna* (affiliated with the *saiō* as ritual attendants and *miko*), and finally the *nyoju* (associated with food procurements for the palace). The entire group, including priests, sponsors, attendants, and parents or friends of participants then assembles for an official commemorative photo. It is only the *saiō-dai* who must face the swarm of unofficial photographers as she attempts to return to her limousine. Her numerous ladies-in-waiting file out of the shrine and onto a large tour bus, hired for the occasion of transporting them from the imperial palace to the shrine.

MAY 5, 1:00 P.M.
Keiba shinji or *Kurabe-uma shinji* (Ritual of the Racehorses)

Of all the shrine's rituals, there is probably none so specifically "Kamo" as the *kurabe-uma shinji*. Where the *miare-sai* of May 12 is the sine qua non of the shrine's religious events and the Crow Sumo of September 9 reenacts early Kamo myths, the *kurabe-uma* is far more than a casual festival or an opportunity to encourage tourism. It conveys the essence of what it has historically meant to be Kamo: a stubborn fearlessness, sincere service to the *kami* Wake Ikazuchi, and a ritual expertise (originally involving horses) of vital importance not only to the clan but to the imperial state as well.

As outlined in earlier chapters, the ritual that later became the Aoi Festival in the sixth century is thought to have its origins in southern Kyushu near Miyazaki and the Osumi peninsula. With regard to the *kurabe-uma shinji*, Ōwa among others believes that in communities venerating mountains, certain hunting ceremonies for wild boars came to apply to rice production. He also associates the ritual with the southern Hayato people who opposed assimilation with the imperial clan from the very beginning (1986:19), a sentiment that has had periodic resurgence during the long relationship between Kamo and court (see Chapter 4 for discussion of a major conflict between these groups). The use of horses in the ritual came later, which corresponds to the archaeological record of horse-trappings, armor, and weaponry discovered in burial mound chambers from around the fourth century. Certainly, horses have been in vogue ever since their appearance in Japan, and they may have been part of the Kamo clan's political and military resources as they settled first in the Katsuragi area of the southern Nara Plain. When the Kamo later moved to the north-central part of the Kyoto basin, one might surmise that their horse culture merged with the hunting culture of the mountain-based people whose territory and deity they appropriated.

For many Kamo descendants, Egami Namio's theory (1964)—about a mounted invasion from the Asian continent into Japan—fits nicely conceptions of a man-horse symbiosis promoted with regard to the clan's origins. (Indeed, this link to the continent was the explicitly stated subtext of a dance performance on January 5.) Whether this conception is accurate is immaterial for those who choose to believe it: the possibility is so abundantly rich in political associations of power, conquest, and domination that it yields considerable pride and a feeling of distinctiveness for contemporary Kamo descendants.[7]

The opening segment of the *kurabe-uma shinji* on May 1 paired riders and horses. The next step is the *shōbu no ne awase* (iris roots game) on the morning of the fifth, taken originally from Heian period courtly games. The *shōbu*, "iris," becomes in this context *shōbu*, "competition." Riders from the left and right teams pair up as they will in the afternoon's matches and first record their names with brush and ink on official ledgers. Then they proceed to the area where the horses will be run *(rachi)* between the first and second torii. At the far end, a temporary shrine (Tongū) has been set up for the *kami,* complete with two small standing sand cones before it. Although the upper sanctuary's *goshintai* has not been physically removed for the ritual, the site is nevertheless the principal reason for the day's events: to entertain the *kami* and win his favorable intervention for the Kamo people. At the Tongū, the two senior riders each hold high a bundle of iris leaves bound with white paper at their roots; after comparing the length of the roots, they exchange the bundles and then toss them onto the roof of the Tongū. The other riders all have a turn, then proceed into the shrine, where only the senior riders repeat the ritual in front of the Tanao-sha by the innermost gate.[8]

A pamphlet published by the shrine in 1993 to commemorate what is thought to be the nine hundredth running of the horses highlights the following dates as being of historical significance:

1093 The shrine and Kamo descendants were awarded the exclusive privilege of running horses for the Aoi Festival from the court of Emperor Horikawa.

1191 A request for rain was made by the court to the shrine.

1255 One of retired emperor Go-Saga's mistresses was due to have a baby. So, to ensure a safe birth, Go-Saga ordered horses to be run on February 21.

1401 Ashikaga Yoshimitsu came. (Yoshimitsu was third shogun of the Ashikaga rule, builder of the Golden Pavilion [Kinkaku-ji] in north Kyoto.)

1574 Oda Nobunaga came.

All these events are centered on interaction with the imperial court or the military shogunate, once again indicating that internal group identities are often fashioned around recognition from or an encounter with powers outside the group. The Ashikaga shoguns (1338–1573) were enthusiastic supporters of the event and reportedly came every year. Likewise, Nobunaga patronized the event, sending messengers in years when he himself could not attend. At his last appearance two years before his assassination, he donated two horses equipped with saddles and stirrups inherited from Minamoto Yoritomo. The most skilled rider of the day rode the best horse and pleased Nobunaga to such a degree that he wanted to see them perform again. However, because a repeat performance was not in line with the form of the ritual offered in service to the *kami* Wake Ikazuchi, the Kamo clan elders respectfully refused.[9]

While today's race consists of equal parts display and action, earlier events were dangerous, violent, and often resulted in injury or death for the riders. The *Dai Nihon keiba-shi* (Great History of Horse Racing in Japan; cited in Kamo Wake Ikazuchi Jinja 1991) states that the Kamo way of riding horses in this festival was so dangerous because "wild" or "unbroken" horses were used. Since the races were in honor of the *kami*, the horses had to be fresh and untainted by previous victories or losses (not to mention labor or military service). Thus, the riders had only minimal time to acquaint themselves with their mounts.

Fujiki (1992) also notes that the horses of the past, while smaller and shorter than today's mild-mannered thoroughbreds, were also much more aggressive and high-spirited. In fact, those contributing horses for the event often found the wildest, most unmanageable creatures they could in order to challenge the Kamo riders and ensure a good return on gambling investments that accompanied the races. During the Edo period, the *shoshidai* military police would donate two horses that were always among the most interesting to watch. "Rank and status doesn't matter to a horse," Fujiki says, "and even the most skilled rider was often thrown off. But because he was a Kamo, he would get up and keep trying until he could ride the horse." With twenty horses appearing in ten separate matches, the riders, handlers, and patrons would have had their hands full. Although the specifics are no longer practiced (today's horses are re-tired thoroughbreds from a local riding school and far too valuable for any rough treatment), the preparation of horses for the ritual was formerly called *Kamo akuba-ryū,* or "the Kamo style [of training] wild horses" (while the character *"aku"* usually means "bad," here it implies "rough-ness" or "violent spiritedness").

The ritual is composed of four parts: an opening banquet and initial procession to the shrine, the upper sanctuary petition for victory and safety, the walkabout through the grounds, and finally the races them-selves. Below I present only an overview of each part. The reader should know, however, that the riders, their teachers and assistants (only one of whom is a priest at the main shrine), the wives of the teachers and assis-tants, and a constant flow of part-time helpers, well-wishers, researchers, photographers, and occasionally a curious non-Kamo priest from the shrine have all been working for almost two months to prepare for the af-ternoon of May 5. Some of the younger men who formerly rode in the event express regret that, because of their jobs and family responsibili-ties, they can no longer participate except as weekend assistants. "The *kurabe-uma* was one of the greatest events in my life," one man aged thirty-six said wistfully, "and I want to make sure my son has the same chance. My wife, however, is of an entirely different opinion—but then she's not a Kamo person, so I can't expect her to understand my feelings."

After the iris root game, the riders change into their formal costumes, which are modeled after *bugaku* dance apparel. The left team wears the *dakyūraku* "red" garments with silver inlay and the right team, the *komaboko* "black" accented by gold. When everyone is fully attired, they sit down to the *kanpai no gi,* a ceremonial lunch heavy with symbolism for the coming race. As with the double-entendres of the *shōbu* game, the meal features three puns to feast on. In a wooden tray before each rider, there are first the *noshi* wrappings common for money offerings or decorations; here, however, the word signifies *nosu,* "pressed or flattened down," commonly used in the phrase for subduing one's opponent *(aite o nosu).* Next are seaweed snacks of *konbu,* which play on the latter half of the word *"yorokobu,"* or the "happiness" one will feel after achieving a victory. Finally, a dried-chestnut snack *(kachikuri)* plays on the word *"katsu"* for victory.

Fortified with these and other treats, the two teams perform a hand-washing purification *(temizu no gi)* before leaving the building. They proceed to the horses and ride them a short distance into the surrounding neighborhoods to the east, then return to the first torii of the shrine. The horses in each team line up in formations resembling a square; when seen from above, it is apparent that this ceremony called the *"higatanori no gi"* has formed the character *"hi"* (day, sun). After some minutes, the teams move their horses into semicircle formation; when joined together in the *tsukigatanori no gi,* the two semicircles become the full moon. Thus, at the onset of the day's rough-riding and potentially violent events, the yin and yang of the Kamo cosmos (sun and moon, day and night) have been balanced and harmonized.

When the teams finally enter through the first torii, they are met on the main path to the shrine by one of the shrine's priests, who performs the *onnyōdai shubatsu no gi,* an all-purpose purification for everyone involved in the event. The riders then dismount, leave their horses in the hands of many white-clothed attendants, and proceed inside the main gate. In the last act they will do as a single group, they line up facing each other and perform a bow; then they separate into teams and enter the upper shrine courtyard. Here, the left or red team goes first in the *hōbei no gi,* a series of dramatic wavings of a one-and-a-half-meter-tall stylized wand of purification *(heigushi)* that petitions the *kami* for victory and safety.

In front of two small standing sand cones, each rider starts out on his knees on a round straw mat *(enza).* After standing, he swings the wand left, then right, then center while taking a step backwards with each swish of the wand. Pausing a moment, he then returns to the mat with the same gestures, ending on his knees as he began. With the *heigushi* held erect before him, the rider is completely hunched over, forehead nearly touching the gravel of the courtyard as he makes his silent prayer for victory. When all ten riders have done this, the group's elder representative *(daihyō)* per-forms the same gestures from a space between the innermost sand cones, then delivers an invocational prayer on behalf of his team. Once com-pleted, he slowly climbs the narrow steps to convey the *heigushi* to the ap-propriate side (the red team to the left, the black team to the right) of the open door of the inner sanctuary. There they will remain until evening.

The entire ritual takes nearly fifty minutes for both teams to complete, during which time a considerable crowd of approximately 1,500 people has formed outside along the runway of the "place of the horses" *(baba)*. Although there are heavy wooden poles to keep the public at a safe dis-tance from the galloping horses, people are constantly running across the open area. The groundskeeper responsible for keeping the way clear can find nothing better to do than to berate the guilty party, using language rarely heard in public. "These stupid people," he remarks, "know nothing about horses and how powerful and unpredictable they are. One kick and *pfft!* they'd be in the hospital. But then they'd probably try to sue the shrine, and no doubt it'd be my fault for not doing my duty!"[10]

The audience has been educated in the finer points of the event by Mr. Fujiki, who at one point likens the early *kurabe-uma shinji* to an Amer-ican-style rodeo's bareback riding. "The riders didn't have saddles like you see today; all they had was a strap *(hara obi)* around the horse's mid-section. As imperial and other patronage increased, there was competi-tion to see who could outfit the horses with the finest saddle and stirrups. One of our most prized possessions is the saddle and stirrups given by the daughter of Tokugawa Hidetada (one of the Tokugawa shoguns) more than three hundred years ago, whose mother just happened to be a Kamo person." He also points out that the preparation of the saddles, girth straps (woven by hand by Mr. Fujiki with assistance from others) and ad-ditional riding paraphernalia began on March 8 and continued unabated until the night before the ritual.

Once the riders have exited the upper shrine, they take their mounts and are led to the runway to begin the weaving back and forth that for-merly helped riders become familiar with their untamed horses. Judges and other officials, all of whom are dressed in Heian period attire, like-wise get into position. Some are at the starting line, some at the Gehei-den pavilion, where the race will be officially recorded on paper for the shrine's archives, and some (called *kōken*) on a three-meter-high platform to receive race results from judges at the finish line—marked by a single small maple tree. To the south of the Tongū temporary shrine is a small enclosure in which the head priest and several attendants watch the race.

Suddenly, moved by the spirit of the moment and without any formal announcement, the senior rider of the red team is thundering down the runway, shouting "ai, ai, ai!" at the top of his lungs while thrusting out his staff in the direction of the Tongū temporary shrine. Moments later, the black team leader follows suit, eliciting gasps from the onlookers with this dramatic *sashimuchi* style of running the horses.

Although I did not hear Mr. Fujiki mention Kōyama in 1991 or 1992, it is important to note that the horses run at full speed, aligned directly with the sacred Kamo mountain some two kilometers to the north. There is an element of reciprocity in the considerable energy directed toward the *kami*. Just as human beings petition the deity for the vitality needed to help their crops or lives, here they have a chance to generate and return decidedly yang energy in the direction of the *kami*.

The next running is supposedly a "real" match, but it is rigged from the start so that a "red" front horse *(saki uma)* wins handily over the "black" rear horse *(oi uma)*. (I have heard some priests say the red team represents Kamo, while the black is Iwashimizu-Hachimangū—the powerful and important shrine protecting Kyoto from the south just as Kamigamo does from the northeast—but have been unable to confirm this from a reliable outside or historical source.) Following this red team victory comes the *kyōchi no gi*, where riders are supposed to stay a distance of two horse-lengths apart and thereby arrive at the finish line at the same elapsed time, with neither winner nor loser. No one I spoke with was really sure why a "tie" is built into the structure of the matches at this point, unless a yin-yang rebalancing of the opposing sides was once thought efficacious. Back at the starting line where a raised dais holds race officials, light and dark fans are raised simultaneously to show both have "won" the *kyōchi no gi*.

All subsequent matches are decided according to the skill of the rider and the horse. Each contest begins with a slow cadence called the "*kanmuri awase*" (meeting of the *kanmuri* hats) whereby the horses appear to be paraded inside the runway. They finally come together at the south end and, with timing similar to that in sumo, are supposed to engage in competition at the instant they turn from south to north. In times past, this "meeting" often included one rider grabbing the bridle of his opponent's horse or grabbing the collar of his opponent and trying to throw him to the ground! According to Mr. Fujiki, acts like these were not deemed illegal, although they must have caused an uproar among those betting on the matches. Today, the *kanmuri awase* sometimes causes one horse to bolt and begin the race before reaching the appointed spot; when this happens the other rider can only try to catch up.

After each race, a single drum beat indicates that the finish line has been crossed. A signal then goes to the *kōken* officials atop the high platform, who in turn relay the winning side to the judges at the Geheiden. Even though only the winner reports to the Geheiden to have his victory verified, he is expected to feign ignorance and ask politely of the officials, "How was the race run?" They inform him of his triumph and present him with a short wand, which he waves twice above his head before returning to his team near the entrance to the shrine.

When the last match is finished, the ritual is considered to be completed, ending with little fanfare save an announcement over the loudspeaker system thanking everyone for attending. The onlookers then rush for the bus terminal and taxis. At the shrine, there is considerable work to do before anyone can relax: the horses must all be rubbed down before getting into their carriers; the riders must undress and prepare their costumes for dry cleaning; the groundskeepers must remove the poles and *zasoe* leaves and vines that have formed the racing compound; and the doors to the Honden must be solemnly closed. With the running of the horses completed for another year, the Kamo clan's descendants have done their part to ensure that, on May 12 when the awesomely powerful Wake Ikazuchi is summoned by the priests, he will arrive in a jovial and benevolent mood—just as he required.

MAY 12, 3:00 P.M.
Oharae (Great Purification), *Osōji-sai* (Cleaning the Sanctuaries),
Kanmiso-sai (Changing Seasonal Garments for the *kami*)

In preparation for the evening's main event when the *kami* is called down to earth, the most senior priests, all of whom are dressed in white robes, lead a procession to the Hashidono pavilion. The senior priests take their places on six round straw mats, leaving three junior priests standing at the steps leading up to the Hashidono stage, escaping the pouring rain (of 1991) under the eave of the pavilion. The ritual that follows is identical to that of April 3, with the exception that, at its completion, a large branch from the *sakaki* tree, festooned with *shide* paper streamers and small pieces of hemp cord, is waved over the bowed heads of the junior priests in the left, right, center motion characteristic of Kamigamo purifications. The branch is then broken in half and immediately jettisoned over the railing into the rapidly moving water below. The *norito* has been completed at about this same time, and, without further ceremony, the group enters the upper shrine to perform the next ritual of May 12, the *osōji-sai*.

This ritual entails the the actual cleaning of the inner sanctuary and is performed in a matter-of-fact way, preceded by neither offerings nor prayers (save those performed at the Hashidono). Whisk brooms are used on the doors of the Honden, with two priests sharing the duties on the outside while the associate head priest works inside the sanctuary. Tables and trays come out and are conveyed to the off-stage preparation area, where they are wiped clean and returned. (Although the associate head priest's status demands that he perform the cleaning duties inside the Honden, he whispers through the silk curtains to receive instruction and guidance from two senior priests who linger on the upper shrine's walkway.)

Once the cleaning is completed, the *kanmiso-sai* begins. Two sets of pearl-colored, padded-silk "winter" kimonos, folded into neat squares, are conveyed out of the Honden while thinner "summer" silk kimono (in two sets layered white, red, white, and purple) go in. When considered rationally, paradoxes abound regarding why a numinous presence should be thought to "need" garments of any sort. However, according to the priests' explanation, they serve more as offerings than as actual coverings for a divine "body," and they symbolize a human concern for the *kami*'s comfort when it blesses the earthly sphere with its presence and energy. I was unable to obtain an interpretation of why two sets of garments were presented to a "single" *kami,* yet I drew a parallel with an explanation given me concerning why two sanctuaries are necessary within the upper shrine: the yin-yang nature of the Kamo deity must be accommodated, as well as the "rough" *(nigimitama)* and "gentle" *(aramitama)* character shared by all Shinto *kami.*

Alan Miller (1984, 1991) offers additional interpretations for the connection between garments and *kami,* seeing the weaving process as a metaphor for the recreation of the cosmos and the garments symbolic of the cosmos itself. To support this view, he notes a ritual at Ise Shrine whereby Amaterasu is presented with a miniature sacred loom, thread boxes, spindles, and reels. Since weaving is a "disciplined, regular, orderly, and integrative activity of binding diverse materials into finished form" (Miller 1984:39), Miller sees weaving as a metaphor for the sun goddesses' control over the universe. It is possible that, with Ise as a model, the Kamo priests long ago adapted this ritual to their deity and local situation.

MAY 12, 8:00 P.M.
Miare-sai (Ritual for Meeting the Kami)

On the evening of May 12, regardless of the weather, Kamigamo priests go to a secret area in the direction of Kōyama mountain to invite the spirit of Wake Ikazuchi to the human sphere. It is this visitation, lasting three days, that motivates the Aoi Festival (or Kamo-sai) to be held on May 15. As on other occasions, the presence of a *kami* must be acknowledged with offerings, petitions, and entertainment. Of all the festivals held during Kyoto's long history, none has surpassed the elegance and longevity of the Aoi Festival.

But without the *miare-sai* to summon the deity to the upper Kamo Shrine environs, there would be no point to the Aoi Festival other than a frivolous display of wealth and status. There is consensus among priests, parishioners, and scholars (see Abe 1990) that the *miare-sai* is both the oldest and the most important of all the rituals at Kamigamo Shrine. The most important aspect of the phenomenon of *kami* is *miare,* which Sonoda Minoru translates as "hierophany" or sacred manifestation (Sakurai, Nishikawa, and Sonoda 1990:66). While the *kami* can appear seemingly at will, they are more inclined to be manageable and benevolent when summoned with offerings and words of praise. The word *"are"* means to be born or to appear, and *"mi"* indicates a retrieval or going toward the place where this happens (Shibata 1982:53). Since *kami* are inherently unstable and dynamic entities, the place where they might choose to manifest themselves is set apart, fearful, and charged with potentiality.

Because of the high status of the *miare-sai,* those familiar with the commercializing trends at other shrines or temples might expect it to have been tailored to attract a wide-ranging and financially rewarding public participation. However, this is not the case. As the most guarded and secret of the shrine's *matsuri,* it is held in complete darkness and is closed to everyone except the shrine's priests, a majority of whom have completed a twenty-four-hour period of abstinence *(kessai)* and other ritual purifications.

Many important rituals were originally held at night, because the *kami* were thought to move and appear more readily during liminal periods when human activity was curtailed by darkness (see Sakurai, Nishikawa, and Sonoda 1990: 86). At exactly 7:50 P.M., the priests form a procession that leaves the administration building. The procession is led by the groundskeeper, who carries a burning reed torch, the only light for the twelve participants. All wear short black-lacquered hats *(eboshi),* a short ceremonial garment resembling the standard *joe,* and straw sandals *(waraji)* without the benefit of *tabi* socks. They enter through the second torii, then cross the outer courtyard in the direction of the information booth *(juyosho).* Suddenly, as if swallowed by the night, the procession veers northward along a little-used path winding behind the walls of the inner shrine.[11] While the other priests continue their silent march into the area beyond the shrine compound, the head priest waits behind with an attendant.

After arriving at the *himorogi* site, which has been thoroughly shielded from view by a three-meter-high wall of pine boughs, the *kami* is requested to descend into a *sakaki* tree (called the *"miare-gi"*). According to the account of a dream in which Wake Ikazuchi appears to Tamayorihime (some accounts say Taketsunomi), the *kami* stated the conditions for his reappearance: first, a sash *(ama-no-hagoromo)* is needed, then bonfires must be lit, horses decorated (with the implication that they are also to be run on shrine grounds, thus the May 5 *keiba-shinji), sakaki* fetched from deep in the mountains and affixed to flags, and finally the decoration called *"aoi kaide"* (blending the *aoi* flower and the *katsura* tree as male and female symbols) is to be centrally positioned. When all these preparations are completed, the *kami* promised to be there. Although the priests would neither confirm nor deny my conjecture, I believe that during the *miare-sai* the *kami's* numinous energy is invested in an *aoi* flower, which serves as the "sacred essence" *(goshintai)* of the *kami.* Evidence is available in the shrine's iconography and architecture (see Chapter 3), the writings of a former head priest (Sawada 1973), and the *mikage-sai,* a similarly structured ritual held by Shimogamo Shrine.[12]

While the contemporary *miare-sai* (also called *kami oroshi* or *kami mukae* according to Misumi 1979) appears to concern itself primarily with conducting Wake Ikazuchi earthward and dates to the Kamakura period, the shrine's Aoi Festival brochure (1991) also mentions an earlier practice whereby the *saiō* priestess conjoined with the *kami* at the sacred site. Recall here the *niju ōken* dual administration of shrine affairs and the *saiō* system begun (from a Kamo perspective) at the late date of 804. The ritual practice of women receiving a male *kami* in a divine "marriage" was an early, established practice, conducted by priestesses of Kamo affiliation who were only later usurped by the imperial princesses for more pragmatic political purposes of the court. In a similar mode and as a part of the grand *daijō-sai* enthronement ritual, every new emperor conducts similar rites within the Yukiden and the Sukiden, where a kind of bed is provided for the female sun deity Amaterasu to commingle with the earthly body of the new emperor (see Fujitani 1992:847). Because of this close affiliation with the court, Gorai calls the *miare-sai* a ritual that enhances Kamigamo's efficacy as a shrine that can "calm and soothe" unstable spirits *(chinkon no tame no jinja),* thus helping to stabilize the affairs of the realm (1994:11).

The symbolism of the *himorogi* site is predominantly male: two poles protrude from the pine-bough enclosure, aligned with two *tatesuna* sand cones, each of which sprouts two pine needles from its apex, signifying (like the *tatesuna* before the middle courtyard's Hosodono pavilion) a *yō* or male correspondence (see Nitschke 1990 for a drawing of the site). The generative power of the *kami* to revitalize the flow of life for the Kamo people was and remains the main concern in this ritual. At the point when it seems everything is proceeding according to design, a crow call relays a message to the head priest waiting back at the main shrine. He then re-enters the shrine, where he will, upon the return of the procession, lead the investiture within the Honden of the newly revitalized sacred essence. The shrine is now ready to accommodate clan, community, and court concerns that will be discussed in relation to the Aoi Festival below.

MAY 15
Kamo-sai, Popularly Known as the *Aoi matsuri* (Hollyhock Festival)

The historical beginnings of the Kamo-sai, now commonly called the *aoi matsuri* (by everyone except individuals connected to the two Kamo shrines), have been discussed in chapters 2 and 4. To do justice to the Kamo-sai and what it has meant for the city of Kyoto, the court, and Japanese culture in general, one would need an entire book and several years of meticulous historical research (see Murakami 1980; Sakurai 1987). Here, I will only briefly allude to these themes and instead will focus primarily on the events themselves.

Generally speaking, the Aoi Festival is not a single festival event. The May 15 procession and rituals are preceded by the running of horses at Kamigamo (*kurabe-uma shinji;* horses are also used in rituals at Shimogamo) and the purification of the imperial princess *(saiō-dai)* on May 5. Both of these events are indispensable to the May 12 *miare* and *mikage* rites of the upper and lower Kamo shrines, respectively. Once all these preparatory rituals are completed, the Aoi Festival can begin. However, it too has component parts, which I will discuss after summarizing the event's historical progression.

To trace the origins and development of the contemporary Kamo-sai, one customarily begins in the year 567 C.E. According to the *Nihon shoki*, heavy rains had caused severe flooding and crop destruction, with a resulting famine of such magnitude that "in some cases men ate each other" (Shibata 1982 : 55). The emperor Kinmei asked for a divination to determine the cause of these rains and discovered they were punishment *(tatari)* from the *kami* of Kamo Shrine. Although most accounts of this story provide no reason for this punishment, Ōwa's research (1986, see Chapter 4) suggests an earlier people's hunting ritual (one having wide geographic distribution essentially in honor of a mountain *kami*) had been curtailed when the Kamo appropriated their area. Thus, after the divination, the festival was started again in the fourth month's second *tori no hi,* or "day of the cock," but it was conducted in the Kamo name and in service to the Yamato regime (ibid.).

Among the ritual's early characteristics were these: riders donned masks of wild boar (most likely the outer hide itself), decorated their horses with *suzu* bells, then raced them (often shooting arrows along the way) in honor of the *kami*. Also, elaborate food offerings were served to the deities, and the *aoi* flower festooned offerings, riders, horses, and temporary buildings. The local festival grew in popularity to such proportions that it attracted participants from a wide area, causing the Yamato court to see it as a threat to their policies for stabilizing the provinces.

Prohibitions against certain "rough" activities were handed down in 698, 702, and 708, with the result that a court representative, the *kokushi,* was assigned to administer the festival in either 708 or 711. However, the whole event was canceled in 738, because of its noise and chaos (Tanigawa 1985 : 20), but also as a necessary demonstration of the court's control over outlying areas. Subsequent festivals were strictly regulated by the state and given a new title, *chokusai* or *kokusai,* with those in attendance (other than Kamo people) relegated to the role of observers rather than participants. In 796 the festival's status was elevated when the shrine's *kami* became a primary protector of the new capital of Heiankyō. Interestingly enough, Tokoro remarks that although the shrine was prospering, the Kamo people worshiped their ancestors at Kuga and Kawasaki (no longer extant) shrines (1991 : 116), apparently sites of original Kamo habitation before they moved farther north.

The *chokusai,* or "court-sponsored festival," continued yearly until 1502 (Tokoro 1991 : 117). However, this date obscures the social and political disruption in Kyoto during the Onin wars and the 1478 conflict that left the main shrine in ruins (detailed in Chapter 4). When the festival was restarted in 1694 under Tokugawa auspices, it was smaller and did not have a *saiō* priestess. The waning years of the Edo period also saw a more austere Kamo-sai, but it appears to have been celebrated even in the momentous year of 1868, the beginning of the Meiji Restoration. However, the capital's move to Tokyo in 1869 together with new injunctions against hereditary priesthood (such as the Kamo *shake* houses) and a withdrawal of state financial support once again led to a break in the Kamo-sai tradition in 1870. Tokoro claims that persistent requests from priests at both Kamigamo and Shimogamo were instrumental in returning government sponsorship of the festival in 1885 (p. 117), but a closer look at the "new" political ideology of emperor worship more accurately frames the Kamo-sai's revitalization. One of the principal moments in the entire festival involves not the parade or the running of horses, but the message *(gosaimon)* conveyed to the Kamo deities by the *chokushi* on behalf of the emperor. A *gosaimon* from 1843 reads:

> We, in awe and reverence, do address Thine Augustness the Great Deity of Kamo, in trembling be thy name whispered. We beseech thee that by divine protection and help, the emperor may reign in peace, and that his realm may be free from internal troubles, and natural calamities. For this we petition, and in gratitude for thy unbounded benevolence, we do now send our trusted and well-beloved (name of imperial messenger) bearing, as in former years, rich and beautiful offerings,[13] and we do cause him to present these before thee, the priests and priestesses, and the running horses. Spoken in awe and reverence.

In 1885 the references to priests *(areotoko),* priestesses *(areotome/areonna),* and horses are deleted to add the following:

> We beseech thee to lend thy ear to our prayer that the emperor may enjoy fruitful and prosperous years, and that his officials, and the common people may one and all flourish like the abundant young branches of a tree.[14] (both passages translated in Ponsonby-Fane 1933 : 116)

This was the year in which the festival had its government patronage restored, as its new *kansai* ("festival receiving state offerings") status attested. Additionally, with the adoption of the Western Gregorian calendar, the date of the festival was changed from April to the middle of May (a time known to farmers for its heavy rains). Even with this sponsorship, there were still variations from the "traditional" form, such as curtailing certain food offerings, a part of the festival that was not regulated until 1926.

The last major disruption of the Kamo-sai occurred during World War II. From 1943 to 1952, the harsh realities of the war and its aftermath precluded any celebration of *kokka* Shinto associations, which, in retrospect, most people blamed as having betrayed them (see Woodard 1972). Even though Kyoto escaped being bombed, shrine Shinto had "estranged itself from the sympathies of a good many of the more progressively thinking Japanese" (Creemers 1968:xvi). The Aoi Festival, however, was much more than a shrine or imperial ritual—it was intimately tied to Kyoto culture and Japanese literature. The first postwar staging of the event was in 1953. By 1955 the *saiō* was once again part of the procession from the imperial palace to the lower and upper Kamo shrines, and the basic shape of the event has remained more or less unchanged since then.

KYŪCHŪ NO GI

The actual *aoi matsuri* consisted of four rituals until the Meiji period. The first *kyūchū no gi* was strictly for the Kyoto-based imperial court. The emperor would watch a variety of decorated horses *(kazari uma)* parade before him, then attend a dance performance *(iide-tachi)* before his envoy the *chokushi* departed with the emperor's message to the Kamo shrines. The initial communications between the Imperial Household Agency (Kunaichō) and the head priests of Shimogamo and Kamigamo shrines are carried out in much the same way as in the past. After the head priests send a joint document outlining the festival activities, one of the emperor's personal *kannushi* priests (called a *"shotenshoku"*) is selected and the shrines notified. The Meiji Restoration did away with the *kyūchū no gi*, but there is still a preparatory staging that takes place at the old Kyoto Imperial Palace. At 8:30 A.M. on May 15, the *chokushi* receives the *gosaimon* prayer from a representative of the Imperial Household Agency as well as the cloth offerings *(heihaku)* stored in large wooden boxes. Although there are other *chokusai* festivals where the imperial messenger participates, the Aoi Festival is the only event where the *chokushi* comes directly from the imperial palace.

ROTŌ NO GI

The second part of the festival is the procession, called *rotō no gi,* from the imperial palace grounds to Shimogamo and Kamigamo shrines. During the Heian period as many as eight hundred people participated along Ichijō Avenue; now, approximately 530 sumptuously attired men, women, and children walk the slow, winding route to the shrines. The procession comes under a shared jurisdiction of four organizing bodies: the Aoi Matsuri Gyōretsu Kyōsan-kai (procession support committee) and the Dentō Bunka Hozon Kyōkai (organization for preserving traditional culture) are composed of individuals representing both shrines and their lay organizations (particularly the *dōzoku-kai*). Also involved are the Kyoto Imperial Palace Administration and the Kyoto Kankō Kyōkai tourist organization, which sells for two thousand yen each tickets for seats to view the procession as it leaves the old imperial palace grounds.

Until the Meiji period, the *chokushi* was at the vanguard of the procession, preceded and protected by a unit of foot and mounted soldiers. During the Heian period he was an officer of the fourth rank permitted to wear the black military robe with red inner and white outer *hakama* (according to the *Engi shiki*), but he carried only a ceremonial sword and no arrows or bow, nor did he wear *kanmuri* headgear that might have signified his military standing. Following him, the court-appointed representative of the Kyoto area, the *kokushi,* was also well guarded. Today, three horseriders from Kamigamo's *keiba shinji* appear toward the front of the parade, preceding a stand-in for the traditional role of *kokushi*. Next come the bearers *(goheibitsu)* of the emperor's fabric offerings to the deities, who are also escorted by a military official, the *meiryō zukai*. The famous ox-drawn coaches (*iidashi-guruma* or, more informally, *gissha*) are the next principal attraction, creaking slowly along on their 1.5-meter-high spoked wheels. Imperial princesses, princes, and other officials once rode in carriages similar to these, as illustrated in the famous scene in Murasaki Shikibu's *Tale of Genji* in which Lady Rokujō was humiliated because her cart was given low status in the parade for the *saiō* lustration ritual (see the "Heartvine" chapter in Seidensticker 1987 and Field 1987:48 for a discussion). Today, however, these black-lacquered carriages are usually empty.

Next, the present-day Aoi procession has the mounted *kura-zukai* official carrying the all-important *gosaimon* imperial petition, protected in
a covering slung over his chest. At the rear of the procession comes the
palanquin *(onkoshi)* of the *saiō,* carried by eight male bearers and followed
by a retinue of twenty attendants. Traditionally, she would join the parade along Ichijō Avenue, starting not from the imperial palace but from
near her residence at Murasakino. It was one of the few times during the
year that she would spend the night at Kamigamo, returning the next day
in a smaller but still well-attended procession. Among the participants in
today's Aoi Festival procession through the streets of Kyoto, those holding actual rank in the imperial household, the palace, at Kamigamo or
Shimogamo shrines are few (if any); the majority are proxies or substi-
tutes for the real thing, which in the case of the *saiō* has not been seen in
Kyoto since 1204. The participants are selected primarily from student
applicants from Kyoto and Doshisha universities and from the families of
imperial palace staff members. Owing to the length of the procession, the
sultry heat of mid-May, and the heavy costumes worn, some degree of
stamina is required to reach the end of the day.

SHATŌ NO GI

For both shrines, the next part of the festival, the *shatō no gi,* is by far the
most important. Even if inclement weather forces cancellation of the parade (a joint, because controversial, decision of the three supervising organizations), this simple rite must be held with great solemnity at the
ceremonial center of each shrine.[15] Nothing less than national stability
and peace is at stake, or so it was seen during the days when heavy
rains and flooding could destroy the economic base of an agricultural society and thus threaten its rulers.[16] Nevertheless, the *gosaimon* petition to
Kamigamo Shrine is the only time the emperor petitions a *kami* outside
the imperial hierarchy for peace within the realm *(tenka kokka).*

To prepare for the arrival of the *gosaimon* petition and the imperial
messenger, the shrines have opened their doors. They have decorated their
sanctuaries with *aoi* and *katsura,* presented elaborate food offerings,[17] and
delivered their own *norito* prayers. They have also set up tent canopies
where nearly four hundred folding chairs await paying visitors (at 2,500
yen per seat, which also includes a bag containing a red bean and rice
lunch, a bottle of sake, candies, the shrine's newsletter, a set of postcards,
a brochure on the Aoi Festival, and a paper listing the groups involved

with the festival). At Shimogamo, the procession stops at the second torii, and imperial military escorts proceed to guard both sides of the main gate. At Kamigamo, while the procession also stops at the second torii, the closest anyone with official imperial connections comes is to the middle of the Mitarashi-gawa stream, nearly twenty-five meters from the main gate.

The degree of access permitted to centers of sacred power is often used as a spatial means of asserting the political autonomy of these sites. At Kamigamo, where the *chokushi* is kept at such distance, the shrine's cautious relationship to imperial authority is reflected in the positionings of the *shatō no gi*. At both shrines, the *chokushi* must remove his ceremonial sword before undergoing purifications administered by one of the priests within a partitioned-off enclosure. Although shielded from public view, he performs a sequence of purifications identical to those enacted by the Kamo priests on April 3, May 12, June 30, and so on, with the only variation being the use of an *ogushi* wand as the closing step. Next, he receives the *gosaimon* from its bearer and proceeds to the Hashidono. After three bows that take him from a standing position to one in which his forehead almost touches the floor, he opens the scarlet paper, a color reserved only for the Kamo shrines (just as blue is for Ise and yellow for all others), and delivers the petition without issuing a sound from his moving lips.

Just as distance is one of the shrine's ritual strategies, the inaudible petition symbolically announces two possible imperial strategies (according to interpretations by the Kamigamo priests): first, that the petition is meant exclusively for the *kami* and so should not be audible to human ears, and, second, that the *kami*'s ability to "hear" the *gosaimon* indicates an intimate connection between the emperor and Wake Ikazuchi. The petitioning completed, the head and associate head priests accompany the offerings of silk and *gosaimon* to the inner sanctuary. The *gosaimon* will remain in the sanctuary for an entire year, after which time it goes into the shrine's storehouse. The head priest then returns to relay the *kami*'s reply to the *chokushi* as well as to present him with a fresh, spiritually charged *aoi* flower *(shin-roku-no-aoi)*. The flower is placed on a small table between the priest and the messenger and receives *kashiwade* veneration by the head priest. The imperial messenger answers with his own *kashiwade* in the part of the ritual called *"awase-kashiwade,"* then formally receives the *aoi* from the head priest. After the priest intones a short prayer to the messenger (called *kaeshi-norito,* or "return *norito*"), they bow to each other and the *chokushi* departs.

Next, cued by the announcer, all eyes turn to the *saiō-dai*, who has been quietly sitting in a temporary pavilion on the other side of the court-yard facing the Hosodono hall. However, because she is not officially "imperial," she cannot ascend without the head priest (who is busy doing other things). Thus, for her part in the *shatō no gi*, she stands (after a great effort to keep her flowing robes in place), takes one tiny step forward, and performs a single elegant bow, flanked on either side by an attendant. Without turning, she backs up to her place and returns to a *seiza* sitting position.

Although the next step is not mentioned as a part of the formal historical structure of the festival, it is nevertheless integral to its contemporary practice. Moving with as much dignity as they can before the eyes of hundreds of onlookers, the VIPs of the festival come forth to perform *kashiwade* before the Hashidono. I simply list them in the order they appeared in 1992 and make no surmises concerning constitutional restrictions on state sponsorship of religious activities (see Nelson 1999): (1) imperial palace official in charge of the festival *(kunaichō-Kyōto jimusho-chō)*, (2) representative/messenger from the Central Association of Shrines (Jinja Honchō Kenpei-shi) in Tokyo bringing *gohei* as offering, (3) Head of the Kyoto prefecture Shinto shrine association *(Kyōto-fu jinja-chō chō)*, (4) Kamigamo official in charge of the festival *(tōsha no sekinin-yakuin)*, (5) chief of the "Organization for the Procession" *(aoi matsuri gyōretsu kyōsan-kai kaichō)*, (6) director of Kamo clan families *(tōsha shake dōzoku-kai riji-chō)*, (7) representative for all shrines in Japan *(zenkoku jinja daihyō)*, (8) head of the Commission to Preserve Cultural and Historical Properties *(zaidan hōjin dentō bunka hozon kyōkai riji-chō)*, (9) proxy for the Kyoto prefectural office *(Kyōto fu chi-ji dairi)*, (10) proxy for the Kyoto mayor's office *(Kyōto shichō dairi)*, (11) Head of the Kyoto Chamber of Commerce *(Kyōto shōko kaigi-shi)*, (12) Head of the Kyoto City Office of Tourism *(Kyōto-shi Kankō Kyōkai kaichō)*, (13) Head of the Tourism Office's fund-raising wing *(Kyōto-shi Kankō Shigen hogo zaidan)*, (14) president of Kokugakuin University, (15) president of Kogakkan University, (16) women in charge of the *saiō-dai*.

At this point in the present-day festival, the weather again plays a major factor. If it is a fine day, musicians *(beijū)* in the retinue of the messenger ascend to the Hashidono to sing a song in praise to the *kami (suruga uta)*, followed by a military escort parading two horses (whose light and dark colors represent *in-yō* balances) in a west-to-east circumambulation that requires three cycles to complete. Finally, the same attendants return to the Hashidono for a dance known as the *"azuma asobi."* The word *"azuma,"* implying "east," evokes the story of a legendary leader named Takeru-no-mikoto, whose eastern-born wife sacrificed herself during a rough water crossing. By doing so, she calmed a wrathful deity and thus saved her husband and his regime. Presumably, the *azuma asobi* is meant to serve a similar purpose with the thunder *kami* Wake Ikazuchi.

HASHIRI-UMA NO GI

The last part of the Aoi Festival again depends on the weather. When performed, it evokes a resonance with the opening stages of the elaborate festival held ten days earlier, the *keiba-shinji,* and offers closure by returning the rite to Kamo clan origins. The *hashiri-uma no gi* sees a return of horse running, with fourteen horses running in pairs from the first to the second torii. Those viewing this last phase of the festival may feel that it is for their own or the ritual participants' entertainment after a hard day's service to the *kami,* but the *hashiri-uma no gi* is said to be solely for the enjoyment of Wake Ikazuchi. A final horse-running event without public participation takes place near the site used for the *miare-sai.* A single horse (preferably white) runs at full speed along a path from north to south, after which the assembled priests and Kamo elders prostrate themselves in a low bow on the grass. Only after this final run will the doors to the sanctuary be closed and the ritual be ended formally with the removal of the food offerings and solemn closing bows.

MAY 17, 10:00 A.M.
Kencha-sai (Ritual for Offering Tea)

After one day of rest, the *kencha-sai* brings some of Kyoto's most respected families to the shrine to offer tribute through tea. The heads of one of Kyoto's two principal tea schools, the Ura senke and the Omote senke, perform this ritual on alternating years. Although they are uncertain of the event's history, the priests guess that it started before the Edo period, when the art of tea became an expression of refinement and sensibility as well as a gesture of gratitude or appreciation toward an honored guest (J. Anderson 1991). Since this ritual is conducted before the inner sanctuary of the shrine, the honored guest in this case is the deity himself. Many of the head master's students are permitted to attend, taking seats within the covered hall facing the Honden. The ritual itself is performed in this same area. Unlike most shrine events, the *kencha-sai* does not begin with opening words of supplication in front of the Honden, nor is there any calling of the deity to be present. The Honden doors are already open, waiting to receive offerings. Thus, the ritual begins with the placing of two large boxes containing sweets before the Gonden and the Honden.

After the head priest delivers the *norito* (and it is conveyed to the Gonden, where it rests on a small table to the side of the doors), the preparation of the tea commences. The master wears a white gauze mask over his face lest his breath contaminate the purity of the offering to be presented to the *kami*. As soon as the tea is poured into an unglazed ceramic cup, *gagaku* music begins from the far courtyard. The cup is transported up the steps to the Honden, where the associate head priest takes it behind the heavy silk fabric shielding the entrance. The entire process is repeated for the Gonden, although here, as is the case with other offerings, the tea is left outside the closed doors. When the ritual is completed, the participants assemble in the outer courtyard for a *naorai* consisting of tea and sweets.

JUNE 10, 10:00 A.M.

Otaue-sai (Ritual for Rice Planting)

Most shrines in the Kyoto area perform the *otaue-sai* in early June. Even though agriculture has taken a back seat to commerce and small industry, these rituals continue for the farming that does persist as well as to ensure abundance, nurturance, and plenty in all livelihoods. Unlike the standard *otaue-sai,* which usually has men and women in colorful farming attire and sedge hats actually planting rice in a consecrated field (as at Fushimi Inari in southern Kyoto or at Ise), the Kamigamo planting occurs in a different style altogether. The ritual begins with a procession and purification at the Tsuchinoya, then proceeds before the Honden, where, amidst the other offerings, carefully wrapped rice seedlings are consecrated. The head priest's *norito* references the earlier rite of divination for determining the proper time to plant, the April 3 *toge-sai,* and petitions the *kami* to imbue the seedlings with his energy. His prayer also promises to repay this largess by stacking up offerings in the fall after the harvest comes in.

Walking slowly, again in procession, the group of priests moves to the Sawada-sha, where round *mochi* (rice cakes), melons, and sake, along with the standard water and salt, are presented to the *kami*. The head priest then takes a large *gohei* wand and waves it left, right, left before dropping

229

Afternoon light, Iwamoto-sha
subordinate shrine, Kamigamo
grounds.

to his knees upon a round straw mat and positioning the *gohei* upright in front of him. Though there is scarcely space to kneel, he then prostrates himself before the *gohei* and shrine, his forehead nearly touching the earth. When this excruciatingly labored action has been performed four times, he ascends the narrow steps to place the wand against the doors of the shrine.

The other priests, who have been kneeling on mats in a line before the shrine's inner sanctuary (Haiden), are now joined by the head priest. Each priest receives a piece of white paper with which to pick up a rice cake and then is served special sake from an unglazed dish. In three quick sips, it is consumed. They wash their hands beside a wooden bucket, as when preparing for a procession to the Honden, and line up once again. The consecrated seedlings are then distributed to all the priests, who walk behind the head priest to the bridge over Nara-no-ogawa. Standing with their backs to the shrine and facing downstream, they toss the seedlings over their right shoulders into the flowing stream below. In the past, the seedlings were then retrieved by representatives of the farming community affiliated with shrine lands and taken to the fields for planting. Today, however, the seedlings are symbolically washed downstream to fertilize, by their consecrated power, all the fields they pass along the way. The priests then return to the Hashidono pavilion, where they bow to the main shrine before going back to the shrine's office.

JUNE 16, 10:00 A.M.

Nikkukō taisai (Rite for the *Shinsen-kai,* or Group Giving Food Offerings)

The prodigious amount of fruit, vegetables, fish and other food offerings needed for rituals at Kamigamo is donated by members of the *shinsen-kai.* These people, living far and wide, give either money or actual foodstuffs needed for the presentation of *shinsen* or *osonaemono* offerings. Compared to other shrine events acknowledging specific constituencies, this group's procession is decidedly low-key; they assemble in the Chokushiden but do not purify their hands before the entrance to the Shamusho as is done in most cases. Instead, they are led to the public *temizusha* for cleansing their hands and mouths, then enter the inner courtyard not through the Tower Gate but via the seldom-used Eastern Gate. During the ritual itself, other variations from standard form are noticeable, such as leaving the doors of the Honden closed when presenting *osonaemono,* a very short *norito,* and the addition of *gagaku* music. In twenty minutes (compared to thirty for the monthly *tsukinami-sai* attended only by priests and staff) the ritual is over, and the group is led out the Middle Gate and back to the Chokushiden for a full reception.

JUNE 30, 8:00 P.M.
Nagoshi-barae (Great Purification of Summer)

Twice during the year, on June 30 and on December 31, the Great Purification ritual of the Nakatomi (later Fujiwara) is performed at shrines throughout Japan as well as within the imperial court. As recorded in the *Engi shiki,* this *norito* petitions the *kami* to dispel impurities for the entire land and all who dwell there, from the emperor to the lowest farmer or fisherman (see Bock 1970; Philippi 1959). Both Kamo shrines received considerable patronage from the Fujiwara during the Heian period, during which time the *nagaoshi-barae* became renowned as an elegant ritual of summer.

The summer purification, owing to its great import for the coming harvest, is more elaborate than the winter. Priests and participants alike first pass through a seven-foot-tall ring of sedge grass *(chinowa)* as a preliminary purification. In the stream below the Horibashi Bridge, six *takigi* iron baskets are set up to hang about a meter above the stream. Shortly before 8:00 P.M. these are lit, and they are in full flame by the time the priests begin their opening purification within the Tsuchinoya. The ritual then follows the same purification process as outlined in the April 3 *togesai:* after taking seats within the Hashidono facing downstream, the priests perform three sets of self-purifications *(ji-barae)* using hemp, paper cuttings, and salt from the small tables facing them.

Two senior priests then take places by the pavilion's railing and begin shuffling stacks of *hitogata* and automobile-shaped paper cutouts (both sent in by parishioners) into the stream as the priests behind them chant the Nakatomi *norito.* Two younger priests with long bamboo poles stand streamside to keep the cutouts from becoming caught on the bridge's railing or drifting onto the rocks below. Because so many individual pieces of paper must be sent into the stream, the prayer is repeated over and over until, like the defilements it aims to dispel, every last one of the paper cutouts is gone. The priests then file off the Hashidono, and the remaining fires are unceremoniously dumped into the stream. For the next thirty minutes, groundskeepers wade in the stream, trying to unclog bankside eddies of their paper defilements. Once the cutouts again enter the flow of the stream, they will be carried to the *kami* of the deep ocean, who will take these impurities into her keeping, but, blessed with forgetfulness, she eventually wanders off and loses them (Philippi 1959:49).

SEPTEMBER 9, 1:00 P.M.
Karasu-sumō (Crow Sumo)

The Crow Sumo ritual has been discussed at length in Chapter 4, but I will review it briefly here. Drawing on the myth of the three-legged crow (*yatagarasu*) that led the legendary Jimmu into the Yamato region, the Kamo people hold that one of their ancestors, Taketsunomi-no-mikoto, was responsible for this transformation and imperial success. Thus, the ritual includes many land-claiming and land-protecting magical formulas and charms framed by the myth, which also work toward protecting the upcoming harvest. Additionally, young boys perform sumo in front of the Hosodono pavilion as a way of entertaining the *kami*. Since 1991 the *saiō-dai* has participated in this autumn festival.

OCTOBER 1, 11:00 A.M.
Adogawa-kansha-sai (Ritual of Gratitude to the Village of Adogawa)

Adogawa village is located on the west side of Lake Biwa in Shiga prefecture and has, for many generations, supplied freshwater fish (*masu,* or trout; and *ayu,* or sweetfish) to be used for Kamigamo *shinsen* offerings. These are not the only fish used, as red snapper appears frequently. This *kansha-sai* (rite of gratitude) is the shrine's way of acknowledging the relationship and thanking the members for their contributions in front of the *kami.* The upper shrine ritual is somewhat abbreviated, since the doors of the Honden remain closed, but the offerings are bestowed with great care, and the *norito* acknowledges the group and their long-standing contribution in easy-to-understand language. By and large, the *naorai* reception is the highlight of the group's journey to the shrine, since they are given attention and respect (not to mention premium sake) within a sanctified reciprocal relationship.

OCTOBER 27, 10:00 A.M.
Sosen-sai (Rites for Kamo Ancestors)

Unlike the *mitama matsuri* of March 22, which venerates the ancestral *kami* for current and past priests, employees, and others affiliated with the shrine in one way or another, the *sosen-sai* is strictly for people of Kamo descent. That it comes about one week before the Kuga Shrine fall festi-

233

val signifies its alignment with Kamo clan politics rather than with equinoctal Buddhist rites for departed spirits. Because the fact of death pervades this ritual of commemoration, it is held in the Chokushiden meeting rooms of the administration building's southern wing. As in the March 22 service, the northern, Kōyama-facing *tokonoma* becomes the site for the altar. The ritual is conducted by the head and associate head priests, a senior priest, and a *gonnegi* and proceeds in the same fashion as the *mitama matsuri,* with two slight variations. First, the *norito* is read by the head priest while standing, rather than kneeling, in front of the altar. Since the ancestral spirits are specifically Kamo, the prayer mentions Kyoto's northern regions, the land and water domains of the Kamo people, the Kamo ancestral "mother," Tamayorihime, and "grandfather," Taketsunomi, as well as the sixteen Kamo lineages.

Although not all of these branch families have survived to the present day, representatives of the four major ones *(nao-no-ryū, yuki-no-ichi-ryū, sao-no-ryū,* and *suei-no-ichi-ryū)* come forth after the *norito* to offer the leafy branches of the *sakaki* tree *(tamagushi)* before the altar and perform the *kashiwade.* When the *tamagushi* presentations are completed, the offerings removed, and the curtain lowered to conceal the altar once again, the group remains in the room to hear a lecture. In 1991 the speaker was a Heian Historical Museum researcher on the subject of Kamo connections to ancient "ice storage chambers" and their significance to the imperial court of the sixth century.[18] Following the lengthy lecture (which put many people to sleep), a *naorai* lunch reception was held.

NOVEMBER 3, 10:00 A.M.
Kuga Jinja aki-matsuri (The Autumn Festival of Kuga Shrine)

Kuga Jinja is the second principal *massha* of Kamigamo (the other being Ōta Shrine; see April 10) and is located on the west side of the Kamo River in what is called the Ōmiya section of Kyoto. Apparently, large trees surrounded the shrine in the old days, leading to the name "Ōmiya-no-mori" (the forest of Ōmiya). The *kami* of Kuga Shrine is the first ancestor of the Kamo clan (its "parent deity," or *oyagami*), Taketsunomi-no-mikoto. The shrine's first mention appears in the Jōgan period's *Sandai-jitsu-roku* (859) ranking of shrines, but the date of its original founding is unknown as is the reason for its name "Kuga." However, one might surmise from the enshrinement of the Kamo clan's *oyagami* that the Ōmiya-no-mori area was one of their early settlements before moving farther north to the better-protected mountain region. From the Kamakura period, the shrine came to be known simply as *"ujigami-sha,"* indicating a general public acknowledgment of its *kami*'s founding role as a protecting agent *(mamorigami)* even as the imperially connected upper Kamo Shrine came to venerate a different hierarchy (mother and son, as well as service to the court). During the Edo period, when pilgrimages to Ise *(okage mairi)* were in vogue (see Davis 1991), Kuga Shrine found itself part of a pilgrimage route for main religious institutions in northern Kyoto (including Daitoku-ji, Kamigamo, Ōta Shrine, and Matsugasaki Daikokuten), even marking its status as "number five" along the route. This route is today known by very few. In the fifth year of Meiji (1872), the shrine's original name was restored. Its greatest elevation of status occurred at the same time Kamigamo was named a *kanpei taisha,* or "shrine receiving imperial offerings," during the drive to modernization and national unity in the late nineteenth century.

Kuga Shrine's autumn festival is as close as any affiliated institution of Kamigamo comes to meeting expectations about what a Shinto *matsuri* should be (see Gilday 1988 for a classic account). Kamigamo itself is unusual among shrines in Japan in that it does not permit its *goshintai* (sacred essence of the *kami*) to be paraded around neighborhoods, as is common for most festival occasions. At Kuga Shrine, households, businesses, and private individuals in surrounding neighborhoods contribute their time, energy, and money to stage this festival of gratitude and revitalization before the coming harshness of winter. There is a portable shrine *(mikoshi)* for gorgeously attired children to pull and two for adult males. The day's events begin with a midmorning short ritual at the main building, conducted only by the head priest of Kuga Shrine, whereby the *goshintai* is transferred to the two adult *mikoshi* as well as to the children's. Once these are properly fitted and secured to supporting beams, they are carried out of the shrine precincts with great cries of *wasshoi, wasshoi!* and past the vendors who line the street leading to the shrine. However, they soon come to rest on wheeled wagons *(daisha)* to continue their journey through the streets of north-central Kyoto.

Fifty students from Kyoto University are hired as part-time labor (at four thousand yen, or U.S. $38, for six to seven hours of work), but only a few help pull the *mikoshi*. Most carry banners, sacred objects, or merely walk in the procession, which includes sixty-two people in the children's group, fifty-three in the largest adults' *mikoshi* group, twenty-six in the second adult *mikoshi,* and sixty-eight in the attendants' group. Horses were used for VIPs in the recent past, but these have been replaced by an old red convertible Toyota in which ride the head priest (who resides at the shrine but is a full-time senior priest at Kamigamo) and the head of Kuga Jinja's parishioners' group. Once the roughly four kilometer route has been traveled, the *mikoshi* return to the shrine and have their sacred essences again transferred to the inner sanctuary.

NOVEMBER 3
Shichi-go-san (Seven-Five-Three Festival)

For the entire month of November the shrine becomes a vehicle to ensure safe passage through periods of physical and social transition in the lives of children. Although there is no formal ritual in the upper shrine in honor of children, November 3 is listed as the day for beginning *shichi-go-san mairi*. So as not to interfere with a busy wedding season in the upper shrine,[19] the lower sanctuary (Gokitōden) is the site for wave after wave of families who wish for some kind of ritual acknowledgment for periods of development in their children's lives. The phenomenon of *shichi-go-san mairi* (a shrine visitation in years when girls are aged three or seven and boys are aged five) grew out of customs associated with samurai families during the middle Edo period that acknowledged certain intervals of social development (Nakamaki 1990:152). At age three, for example, girls adopted a more refined way of wearing their hair *(kami-oki)*, and, at age seven, they could wear an *obi* for the first time in a style more akin to that worn by women. Boys likewise distinguished themselves socially at age five by wearing loose-fitting *hakama* pantaloons over a formal kimono (a fashion innovation begun in imperial China over two thousand years ago and still a part of the attire worn by Shinto priests). It was not until the Taishō period that the *shichi-go-san* began to gain popularity, in part owing to the construction of Meiji Shrine in 1920 as a kind of *ujigami-sha* for all of Japan. However, Nakamaki notes that a book published in 1958 mentions the holiday as gaining in popularity in the Kyoto-Osaka region, so it appears that this holiday is quite new.

Since fashion has always been an important part of the *shichi-go-san,* the contemporary observance of this month-long November holiday finds children brought to shrines in their very best clothes and photographed extensively against the backdrop of the institution; many participate in a short ceremony of purification and blessing as well. Shrines view this holiday as a prime opportunity for bringing children into the sphere of the *kami* (it is also financially rewarding) and so compete for public attention, placing advertisements in local newspapers or contracting printing com-

panies to post colored advertisements on telephone poles and public notice boards. Kamigamo takes a typically low-key approach, posting generic
advertisements here and there in north Kyoto showing a young boy and
girl dressed in *shichi-go-san* finery, with the name of the shrine written in
by hand at the bottom.

In the outer courtyard visitors find a sign directing them to purchase
three tickets for five thousand yen (U.S. $42): the first will permit them
to enter the Gokitōden sanctuary (just inside the Tower Gate courtyard)
and be purified and blessed by two priests in a ten-minute ritual. They
will then receive a bag containing candy, coloring and comic books, a
small amulet, and the shrine's autumn newsletter. The next ticket allows
them to be photographed by one of the priests; the photo will later be
printed on a calendar for the coming year. The final ticket gives the child
his or her choice of toys (arranged by gender-specific areas). While five
thousand yen may at first seem somewhat expensive for these services,
most other shrines charge four thousand yen for a quick wave of the wand
of purification and a bag containing candy, a small toy, and a comic or coloring book. Of the twenty-five people I interviewed, no one complained
about the price; in fact, most thought the innovations at Kamigamo were
creative and well worth the expense. Credit must go to the associate head
priest, Mr. Takeuchi, who implemented these practices in his second year
at Kamigamo and then refined them in 1991.

The stream of visitors contracting these services from the shrine increased slightly at the end of the month. By November 10, some 306 children had been photographed; by the thirteenth, the number was 437; 680
by the seventeenth; and 911 by the twenty-eighth. When the last photo
was taken and toy distributed on the final Sunday of the month, November 29, some 946 children had been through the shrine. The sale of tickets grossed at least 4,730,000 yen (U.S. $39,416), but then there were
expenses to pay for the toys and the production of the calendars. Because
of the considerable work involved in conducting a ten-minute ritual for
hundreds of families and their children, the month of November is one
the junior priests (who do the majority of the work) approach with certain misgivings.

The ritual conducted in the Gokitōden follows the most abbreviated
format possible and is conducted by two priests, with frequent rotations.
First, the *kitōsha-sannyū* calls the service into being with drum beats, after which a *harae* is performed for the participants and offerings on an
eastward-facing altar. "Goody bags" for the children are placed on either

side of the altar, whose most dominant sacred object is a mirror set in a carved wooden base. A brief *norito* is read that includes the names and addresses of the children, and asks for protection from illness, misfortune, the cold snows of winter, and the heat of summer, and finally requests happiness.

Next, the *kitōsha-sanpai* requests the participants to bow twice *(ni hai)*, clap twice *(ni byoshi),* and bow again *(ippai)* in the standard *kashiwade* format, with instructions given by a priest. Many parents and grandparents, anxious to teach propriety, take a hands-on approach and physically guide the children in bowing low enough or clapping loud enough. Next, the *misuzu no gi* finds the entire family bowing while one of the priests shakes a *suzu* bell wand over their heads, signifying blessings that "fall upon them like soft rain." When this activity is completed, the priests distribute the bags directly from the altar and pour small sips of *omiki* for the adults *(kitōsha naorai),* then instruct the families where to go to redeem their next ticket for the calendar photo. The sumptuous furnishings of the hall, the sounds of the drum, *suzu,* and *norito,* and the instant reward for the children for sitting patiently through the ritual appear to provide a meaningful and satisfying experience for the parents, grandparents, and even the children I spoke with.[20]

NOVEMBER 12, 1:00 P.M.

Sōji-sai (Cleaning Ritual), *Gyōkei-sai* (Upper Shrine Cleaning Ritual),
Kanmiso-kinshin-sai (Changing of the *Kami*'s Vestments)

The first of this three-part ritual event is the ritual to clean up the various principal as well as subordinate shrines in preparation for the *ainame-sai* the following week. Using a stiff brush, a whisk broom, white cloth, and paper as tools, the priests disperse to every shrine connected with Kamigamo (including Ōta and Kuga shrines) and clean up the area just in front of the shrine's doors, where offerings are presented. For the smaller shrines, the dried *aoi* and *katsura* leaves placed back in May during the Kamo-sai are removed and deposited on the tray holding the utensils. No prayers or *kashiwade* are done at this time.

At 2:30, a procession from the administration building, complete with porters carrying a large wooden box containing the change of sacred vestments for the *kami,* arrives at the Tsuchinoya pavilion for an opening purification. Senior priests then step up to the *hashidono,* where five positions are set up in the same manner as for the May 12 and June 30 *nagoshi-barae* summer purifications. The large offering container is carried across the stream over the Hori Bridge and placed near the rock called *"ganjō,"* the site where offerings are placed during the Kamo-sai. Essentially, the purification done for the *gyōkei-sai* is identical to the summer purification—with bits of hemp thrown into the stream, small *hitogata* rubbed on the body and also tossed into the stream, rice and paper squares thrown out onto the wooden floor in front of the priests' positions, and cloth and hemp bark shredded into eight pieces and dropped into the stream.

The priests then exit from the far side of the Hashidono and form a line that will soon head into the inner sanctuary. But before they depart, an additional *harae* is performed over the large wooden box by waving two stout sticks (to which *shide* streamers are attached) in a vertical manner. The procession then crosses the Tower Gate bridge while the two sticks and the impurities they have absorbed are thrown into the stream to be (figuratively) carried away to the sea.

At 3:00 P.M., the *sōji-sai* begins at the Honden, immediately followed by the *kanmiso-kinshin-sai*. For a description of these events, see May 12, but note that for the November 12 rite, the "summer" kimono will come out of the Honden and the "winter" set will be placed within.

NOVEMBER 13, 10:00 A.M.
Ainame-sai (First Fruits Festival)

The ritual of thanksgiving and harvest, sometimes termed "first fruits" in English, goes by a variety of names in Japanese. The Kamo variety is the *ainame-sai,* but it is called the *niiname-sai* in the imperial household and the *kanname-sai* at the Ise shrines. According to Murakami, the *niiname-sai* is the most fundamental of all rituals for maintaining imperial authority (1977; see also Ellwood 1973, 1978). In its earlier form, the harvest festival was primarily pragmatic, in the sense of serving as a guarantee for another crop in the coming year. Regardless of locale, the rite's purpose evolved during Yamato times to acknowledge the *kami*'s participation in helping the harvest come to fruition and thus sustain the lives of the people, the nation, and its steward, the emperor. Only twenty-one shrines of long-standing affiliation with the court are permitted by their special status to offer this first fruits ritual in service to the emperor (see Grapard 1988). Murakami also points out that, of the thirteen principal rituals practiced in the imperial court today, eleven are what he considers post-Meiji, with only the *niiname-sai* qualifying as truly ancient (p. 75).

As at the other main *taisai* rituals at Kamigamo (see April 3, May 12), the food offerings are extensive and varied, but they are distinguished in this case by early presentation of freshly harvested sheaves of rice that are wrapped and placed on a special tray. As at other *taisai,* a full musical contingent *(gagaku)* accompanies the offerings from the shrine's southwest wing. A curious addition to the first fruits *shinsen* at Kamigamo are the *okebutsu* offerings. November was considered to be a month without flowers, so, as an innovation using available materials, at Kamigamo pine branches and one sprig from the *sakaki* tree are wrapped around sticks. These are offered to the shrine's *kami* in the same way that other food offerings are, yet belong to the special class of food offerings called *"geijin shinsen,"* or "local offerings for the *kami.*"

NOVEMBER 20, 10:00 A.M.

Nakaragi Jinja aki-matsuri (Fall Festival at Nakaragi Shrine)

The shrine of Nakaragi-sha marks the southern boundary of an area once considered wholly within Kamigamo precincts. It is found today within the Kyoto Botanical Gardens along Kitayama-dōri. Until recently, the shrine was neglected and had fallen into disrepair, caused primarily by crows picking at the layered-bark roof until leaks developed. In 1991, thanks to the efforts of the associate head priest at Kamigamo, donations of money, supplies, and labor were compiled to repair the little shrine and commemorate its *kami* on the customary date of its fall festival.

The origins of this shrine date back to the Nara period, when an immigrant community's expertise in sericulture gained this area a high reputation (Sawada 1974). A *kami* from "Awa-no-kuni" (southern Shikoku), Ame-no-futo-tama-no-mikoto, was "invited" to protect the area and its industry at an unknown date. However, on January 26, 1018, the area became part of Kamigamo Shrine's landholdings, and Nakaragi-sha was incorporated as a subordinate shrine *(sessha).*

On November 20, surrounded by maple trees of stunning shades of crimson, representatives of the Botanical Gardens, construction companies, and the shrine's elders assemble at 10:00 A.M. for the ritual. Even though the actual building is quite small, food, fruit, and drink offerings are conveyed to a table set before it, a *norito* is intoned, and the participants are allowed to present *tamagushi* offerings. Afterwards at the *naorai* held under a tent canopy especially erected for this purpose, all briefly endure a cold wind for a few sips of *omiki* and a box lunch that everyone takes away without opening. According to the associate head priest, future plans for the Nakaragi-sha fall observance are to have a procession of women dressed as Edo period silk weavers make a procession to the shrine and there participate in a ritual similar to the one performed in 1991. The combination of costumes, fall scenery, and Shinto ritual (not to mention attractive young ladies) would be sure to attract a large crowd and thus promote the name and reputation of Kamigamo Shrine.

DECEMBER 31, 4:00 P.M.
Oharae (Great Purification)

The last ritual act of the year repeats the basic sequence of the June 30 summer purification, although without the hanging fires placed in the stream. But while the summer purification looks ahead to the fall harvest season, the winter *oharae*'s ritual efficacy is aimed, first, toward the impurities individuals may have suffered since June 30 and, second, toward an auspicious start to the coming year. Since the new year's *hatsumōde* (first shrine visitation) period is crucial to the shrine's financial affairs, the purification also addresses these concerns, although at an implicit level. A number of young men and women have been hired as part-time workers to sell amulets and talismans to the crush of visitors during the first five days of the new year. These individuals, many of whom will be working in the upper shrine's courtyard close to the Honden, are also assembled for this purification. (For more detail, see June 30.)

CONCLUSION

The last thing a conclusion should do is to presume to have the final word. While summarizing and restating may be important, I have often gained greater insight when challenged, provoked, and enticed into areas extending beyond the scope of the work at hand. Like a stone thrown into the bounded pool of water of a book's contents, a conclusion should ripple outward to touch, lap against, and perhaps even disturb the far shore. Although my focus throughout this study has been a single shrine in northern Kyoto, I hope to have shown how its religious idioms are part of a constantly shifting web of social, political, and economic networks that enable certain activities while restricting others. Similar to human agency, the posture, approach, or (returning to the book's subtitle) guise assumed by a shrine in meeting its responsibilities and challenges varies according to circumstance and audience. Despite a need to adapt constantly to changing social realities, I believe it is still accurate to say the raison d'être of shrine Shinto is to promote, through ritual activities referencing transcendent powers, a sense of continuity, stability, and the management of uncertainty.

However, because shrine Shinto rituals rarely follow codified doctrines, reflect explicit theological agendas, or rely on charismatic leaders, these ritual evocations remain open to a variety of interpretations according to the needs, expectations, or politics of those coming to a shrine. Shrine visitors are like visitors to an art gallery; a multiplicity of perspectives and meanings are not only possible but essential if the experience is to hold relevance for a viewer's life. As discussed with regard to the Crow Sumo event, what to the Kamo descendants is an affirmation of their founding myth is to others an entertaining venue that references the elegance of the court, the rich traditions of sumo, or perhaps an individual's sense of being Japanese. Another brief look at the shrine's interlacing relationships will help to orient a closing but by no means final understanding of its position within Japanese society.

Chapters 1 and 2 showed how the first of these networks begins with the shrine as a physical yet culturally constituted place. Kamigamo is a neighborhood institution around which a particular clan of people, the Kamo, have formed key concepts and practices about dealing with sacred mysteries and forces, have developed group identity and status around these practices, and have used them to muster political influence with the court or military government. They have guarded, maintained, and (when necessary) tried to alter the shrine not only to meet their own needs but to put up a protective front for withstanding the frequently violent changes in political leadership throughout Kyoto's long history. That they represent one of the very few clan-based lineages in Japan still exerting an influence on the affairs of a major shrine (after 1,500 years) indicates the overall success and persistence of their tactics. To many Kamo descendants of the late twentieth century, their continuing duty is nothing less than to protect their heritage as the shrine's founding clan by perpetuating their ritual expertise and authority in important events such as the miare-sai (because their clan's ujigami is summoned to the shrine's sacred mountain) and the running of the horses (where the kami is entertained through their expertise as horsemen). As seen in chapters 4 and 7, their assertion of authority and legitimacy is not always accepted by the shrine's non-Kamo priestly administration, which seeks to encourage a more broad-based participation by the general public in shrine affairs.

To these ends, the shrine's second network concerns the services it offers. As the large signs at the first and second torii entrances advertising yaku yoke indicate (roughly translated as the prevention of misfortunes at certain stages of a person's life), the shrine encourages a recognition of culturally shared anxieties about the uncertainties and misfortunes of life and the efficacy of its rituals to somehow ward off these ill effects. Anyone is welcome to contract the shrine's services, whether to counter personal or financial woes, to nurture individual or group harmony with others, to achieve success in a wide range of endeavors, and so on throughout the expanding realm of human social affairs. As Reader (1991) and others have shown, Japanese religion has also provided a "cultural warmth" that stands in contrast to anxieties generated by the tensions, problems, and disorder of urban as well as modern life in general. For many individuals, the good old days of fixed hierarchies, clear and understandable boundaries between purity and impurity, and a sense of cultural and communal belonging are only a ritual or a festival away.

As an extension of this second network, the shrine's third institutional persona provides an attractive (even seductive) opportunity for those seeking to enhance, legitimate, authenticate, or display social status. Like Ashkenazi (1993) and Bestor (1988), I have stressed repeatedly that shrine festivals are regarded by the general public less as religious observances than as community-enhancing events with considerable entertainment value. In this regard, Kamigamo often functions in much the same way as shrines throughout Japan, becoming a locus for maintaining and augmenting dense neighborhood or citywide connections through which social bonds are constantly negotiated. However, because of the shrine's historical status as an elite institution, it does not exactly fit the mold of *matsuri*-in-the-street-Shinto, which many studies seem to hold is found everywhere in Japan. Like other elite Shinto institutions, Kamigamo does not parade portable shrines, has no raucous festivals, and (judging from the attitudes of its priests) prides itself on a certain distance from the norm.

Thus, while many people, groups, and organizations seek affiliation with the shrine, the majority are generally treated with polite circumspection until tangible evidence is forthcoming that translates into support for the shrine's current projects, ritual events, or general administration. This aid might be money, political networking, or public relations work (a form of networking called *nemawashi*), but with reciprocity so deeply a part of Japanese culture, the shrine can afford to choose the individuals and groups to whom to grant, by the power of association alone, an affiliation that still carries weight in overlapping political, social, and business circles. Three thousand of Kyoto's leading citizens may indeed have gathered in 1992 to have a birthday party for Kamigamo's head priest, but why limit the possibilities?

Finally, the political relationships shrines engage will have profound influences on the viability of the institution within Japanese society. Whose advice they heed, whose projects they support, and whose money they accept as contributions in exchange for shrine affiliation will rest on the integrity of individual head priests and members of a shrine's board of re-

gents. To what degree individual shrines follow the political agendas issuing from the Central Association of Shrines in Tokyo is also of prime
concern. Chapter 5 described the considerable power exercised by the
Jinja Honchō in certifying priests and coordinating appointments. What
should attract more media and scholarly attention are the variously subtle,
highly creative, and sometimes audacious ways that legitimate concerns—
such as the environment, the internationalization of trade and social exchanges, or the intense reflexivity brought about by Japan's economically
based encounter with the larger world (to name but a few)—have become part of nationalistic agendas espoused through the Jinja Honchō
(Teeuwen 1996; Sugata 1988).

Take, for example, the Seikyō Kankei o Tadasu-kai (Group for Correct
Government), working under the auspices of the Shintō Seiji Renmei
(League Promoting Ties between Politics and Shinto) and the Jinja Honchō. This group's leaders attempt, through its monthly newsletters, to
"enlighten" *(keimō suru)* members of the national diet, national media organizations, lawyers, and local politicians about the need for what can
only be described as the return to a modern-day symbiosis of politics and
religion *(matsurigoto)*. The well-connected Shintō Seiji Renmei is also busy
with an agenda calling for (1) maintaining respect for the imperial household, (2) "correcting" the relationship between politics and religion
(by keeping track of court cases engaging these themes, as mentioned
in O'Brien 1996), (3) creating war memorials at shrines nationwide
as unofficial but symbolically powerful extensions of Yasukuni Shrine,
(4) changing the U.S.-imposed constitution, and (5) turning the Day of
National Founding *(kenkoku kinen-bi;* see Chapter 7, February 11) into an
official government-sponsored holiday, complete with ceremonies attended by politicians.

Instead of encouraging wider, more diplomatic understandings or promoting networks between Japan's religious and political leaders and those
of other countries, these and other groups work to blur the issues by in-
vesting them with nationalistic qualities and associations. Like a cook
who uses too much salt, the flavor of nationalism emerges no matter what
intellectual or social "entrée" the public is served from these organizations. Issues about the environment, for example, frequently appear in the
Jinja Honchō's weekly newspaper, the *Jinja shinpō,* where they become a
forum for promoting a spiritual unity of human beings, Shinto shrines,
and the natural world. By promoting the nation's shrines as guardians of
the environment (photos of old and noteworthy trees appear regularly),

the paper suggests they must work to enhance this relationship by educating their parishioners about the environment from a "Shinto" perspective. While environmental education and preservation is a noble and important goal, readers are told of their responsibility to future generations and the national good rather than that for the environment itself. Bolstered by important social critics such as Umehara Takeshi (1992), who writes that in the "horizontal mutualism" of Japan's ancient culture is a way out of (economic) modernism's "philosophy of death," a genuine concern about the environment is shaped to fit the mold of deference to a national polity.

When one is tracing an ideological endeavor from its source outward, writers like Gluck (1985) and Ooms (1985) have demonstrated, it appears to be everywhere. Most shrines with full-time priests subscribe to the *Jinja shinpō,* raising the easy assumption that policy could be or perhaps is being orchestrated. But, for an ideology to be considered "successful," it must be able to "establish silences that suppress generalizable interests that run counter to the particular interests being served" (Ooms 1985 : 29). The next decade will deliver a verdict on whether the political action groups affiliated with the national shrine leadership were able to achieve their objectives. But by looking more closely at the destinations (the shrines themselves) of these attempts to foster exclusivity and national consensus, one finds a cautious acceptance at best and often a real resistance to these totalizing themes and agendas.

During the early 1990s, when acrimonious charges flew back and forth among the United States, Europe, and Japan over trade-related issues, I watched to see whether the shrill promotion of national and cultural interests voiced by politicians and some conservative media organizations (such as the Yomiuri network) would enter shrine discourse. To my surprise, I found a genuine reluctance on the part of the shrine's head priest to espouse the rhetoric of the moment, even to the point of leaving himself (and, by extension, the other priests) open to criticism from parishioners (see Chapter 7, January 5). "I'm old enough to remember that this kind of road leads nowhere," he said. "People like me have to set an example for others who did not experience directly those years leading up to the war."

Thus, what appears as passivity by the shrines in not challenging overtly the agendas of the Jinja Honchō and other neoconservative organizations should not necessarily be construed as consensus for these policies. As Bell notes, the strategies of domination attempted through ritual (or, I would add, through institutions specializing in ritual) do not appropriate minds and bodies as much as "engage them in a set of tensions that involve both domination and resistance" (1992:215).

As the critical divide between Japan's moderate conservatives and the "unreconstructed old right" (Hall 1992:19) continues, it is up to broadminded priests within shrine Shinto, following the example of elders like head priest Abe, to assert their integrity as educated men and women and defend their institutions from being used as pawns in these games of power. Distracted by particularistic interests, local shrine Shinto has never found a socially active role for itself. Even though the Jinja Honchō benefited from a multimillion dollar windfall in their fund-raising for Ise Shrine's 1993 rebuilding, little if any of the surplus was channeled into social programs; rather it went into promoting shrine interests and activities and bolstering shrine organization.

The need for social activism in response to the rights of women, minorities, and even common citizens wandering in Japan's tangled economic jungle cries out for organized response from the country's religious institutions. As suggested first by Earhart (1970a), the environment could be the issue around which shrines organize and empower local communities. After all, the natural world is considered the realm most obviously identified with kami and their powers. Standing up to golf course developers, demanding more public parks and natural recreation areas, and serving as watchdogs for companies polluting the ecosystem could all be justified as sanctified concerns of a shrine. Likewise, since restoring vitality and thus empowering individuals to go about their lives is key to so many rituals, shrines could also engage in issues concerning the debilitating discriminatory practices directed at women as well as Korean, Chinese, or buraku minorities. Each of these possibilities deserves sustained critical analysis, and I raise them here only to provoke discussion.

The twenty-first century will provide new and vital opportunities for a redefinition and reinvention of what this tradition can mean to Japanese society. I hope to have shown in this study that the flexibility, creativity, intelligence, and resources for change and transformation to address contemporary needs are amply available in shrines like Kamigamo Jinja; whether the present and coming generation of priests will find the way to move in new and increasingly relevant directions will be well worth watching.

SYMBOLS, PAVILIONS, AND SIGNS AT KAMIGAMO SHRINE

Among the most noticeable symbols of Kamigamo Shrine are the "standing sand cones," or *tatesuna*. These symbolize not only the original sacred mountain, Kōyama, but also the generative power of yin and yang, male (left cone) and female (right), that Shinto regards as worthy of veneration. This special sand is used in purifying an area, and visitors may purchase some to take home for use in their gardens or elsewhere. One might also notice the different representations of the *aoi* or "hollyhock" crest found on rooftops, railings, amulets, and banners. It too has yin-yang connotations, and it serves as the primary symbol associated with Kamigamo Shrine.

Most of the pavilions at Kamigamo Shrine are registered as "important cultural assets" or "treasures" by the national government. The structure immediately behind the "standing sand cones" is the Hosodono, used once a year during the Crow Sumo Festival (see sign F below for a description of the *saiin* tradition). On one side is the small shrine Hashimoto-sha, whose *kami* is Soto-orihime, with powers to guard crossings and transitions, while to the south bridging the stream is the Hashidono, where the imperial messenger delivers his prayer during the Aoi Festival of May and where important purifications are performed, as on June 30. Finally and most frequently used, the Tsuchinoya is the main site of purification before a ritual, where wooden wands are waved over priests and participants, then broken and cast into the river to be carried away "to the bottom of the sea." As one enters the Rōmon, or Tower Gate, the building to the right is the Gokitōden, a hall used for rituals of dedication or purification that individuals, families, companies, and others have requested the shrine to perform. Continuing up the stone stairs to the Chūmon, or Middle Gate, area (open to the general public only at New Year's), one looks inside to see the Honden (Main Hall of Wake Ikazuchi) on the right and the Gonden (Secondary Hall of Taketsunomi-no-mikoto) on the left. Both are registered national treasures.

SIGNS

The following descriptions are literal translations of the signs one sees on the shrine grounds. By matching the letters below with those on the map of Kamigamo Shrine precincts, the location of a sign can be paired with its description. Where necessary, brief clarifications have been added in brackets.

A. NOTICE: Riding vehicles or horses, fishing and hunting birds, cutting bamboo or trees: these three things are prohibited [within] shrine grounds.

B. NOTICE: After this point is shrine property. Without permission, you can't disturb the beauty of the area or its scenery, or [do things that] impair the dignity of the place. In addition, the following activities are prohibited:

Putting up stalls for the purpose of selling

Handing out flyers, brochures, advertisements, or political or religious messages

Putting up posters or billboards

Public speeches

Bothering the worshipers

Parishioners' Group
Kamo Wake Ikazuchi Jinja

C. SPECIAL PRESERVATION FOR HISTORICAL PLACES: The red lines on the map indicate a specially designated area of historical significance to be preserved. Kyoto city is controlling and regulating the reconstruction and rebuilding of houses and buildings, the cutting of trees and bamboo, and changes to the original landscape in this area. When it is necessary, the city buys land to maintain this area's historical flavor and is thus making an effort to preserve this area. Please cooperate to keep the landscape of the old city.

Kyoto City Planning Department

D. GEHEIDEN: When top-ranking officials Hō-ō and Jō-kō came to the shrine, they rested and took meals at this pavilion. It is currently used for the *keiba shinji* [the festival of racehorses] and the Kamo Festival. This building was rebuilt in 1628 and is registered as an "important cultural treasure."

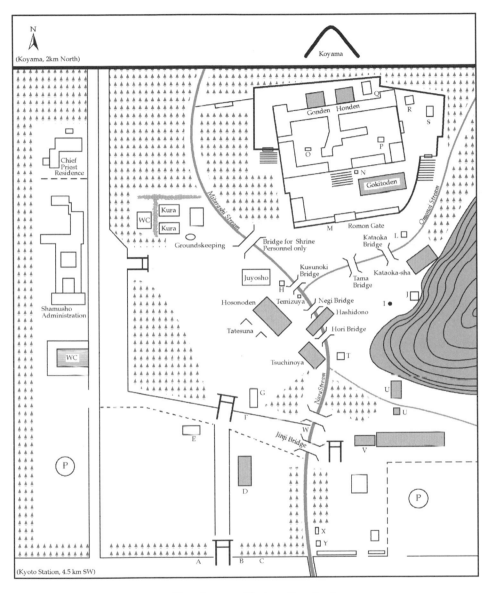

Kamigamo Shrine Precincts

E. SHINME-SHA: The shrine's white horse, thought to be a messenger and conveyance for the *kami,* is sheltered in this building on weekends and festival days, and is honored in its own ritual on January 7.

F. KAMIGAMO JINJA/KAMIGAMO SHRINE: The *kami* enshrined here is Wake Ikazuchi. The shrine worships this *kami* because of a mythological event in which Princess Tamayori was playing beside the little stream called Mitarashi and noticed a white-plumed arrow drifting by. She took it back to her palace and then put it under her pillow and eventually delivered a baby boy. Later on, this little boy, while worshiping, ascended into heaven via a hole he broke through the ceiling. The system of *saiin,* in which a daughter of the emperor is offered to the shrine to serve as a ritualist, started in 810. This is one of the oldest shrines in Kyoto. Farmers revered this *kami* because they believed it provided them a good harvest of the five essential staple crops: rice, barley, foxtail millet, millet, and beans. The shrine's founding myth and the virtues of the *kami* are found in a type of chant called "Kamo Yōkyoku," performed as a part of Nōh drama.

Kyoto Association for the Preservation of Historical Places

G. GAKUNOYA: [No description on sign. However, this building is used as a staging platform for a variety of events, such as the Crow Sumo or the Great Purification ritual. In 1994, the shrine began a September "moon-viewing" event consisting of a performance of *gagaku* music open to the general public.]

H. HASHIMOTO-SHA: Soto-orihime-no-kami, the deity of this shrine, is believed to protect bridges. [During the Heian period, this was a popular shrine for poets to visit.]

I. GANJŌ/PLACE OF THE SACRED ROCK: During the Kamo or Aoi Festival, the chief priest kneels before this sacred rock before receiving the *norito* [invocational prayer] from the imperial household messenger. This important gesture, which acknowledges a natural feature of the place thought to be sacred, shows the original form of Shinto.

J. SUWA-SHA: [No description available.]

K. KATAYAMA-MIKO JINJA is the most important of the secondary shrines at Kamigamo. It enshrines only one *kami,* Tamayorihime-no-mikoto. Named in an ancient book called the *Engi shiki* (ca. 927), this shrine is at least 1,100 years old. Princess Tamayori was of the highest rank in the Kamo clan. In addition to being the medium for the birth of Wake Ikazuchi [the principal *kami* of the main shrine], she also had power in the *saishi-ken,* a religious administrative organization of the time. Tradition holds that she was always beside Wake Ikazuchi and faithfully served him. Therefore, even today during a ritual at the main shrine, a priest first comes here and worships, as a way of reporting that the shrine is having a ritual honoring her son. Because she was also part of the *saiin* tradition in which early emperors gave one of their daughters to the shrine as a spirit medium, the imperial court continues to venerate Kamigamo Shrine, sending a messenger to pray here every year during the Aoi Festival. Katayama Shrine received special ranking on June 11, 1592, the eleventh year of the reign of Emperor Tenshō. There were once three huge earthen pots behind the shrine that contained water called *"yorube no mizu."* But during the Tenshō period, they were buried because of concern that this water could contract impurities and thus cause misfortunes. On the hillside above Katayama-sha is the shrine Suwa-sha, whose deities are Asuha-no-kami, Hahiki-no-kami, Ikui-no-kami, Sakai-no-kami, and Sunagai-no-kami. Asuha protects the land of Kamigamo, while Hahiki and the rest are more specific, ministering to the grounds and gardens themselves. Katayama Shrine is also called Kataoka-sha.

L. KAWAO-SHA: Mizuhanome-no-kami is enshrined here. Though the origin of this shrine is unknown, its name is mentioned in a book called *Kagen san-nen nenjū gyōji* written in the Kamakura period (1192–1333) and details the shrine's yearly ritual cycle. It says that this shrine has significance for New Year's celebrations. It seems likely that this shrine was here well before the Kamakura period. The *kami* of this shrine protects the stream called "Omonoi-gawa," which you see flowing behind you.

M. KAMOWAKE IKAZUCHI JINJA, commonly known as Kamigamo Jinja, has been called the most important shrine in Kyoto. The *kami* of thunder is enshrined here. The first principal virtue of this *kami* rests in its lightninglike power to wipe away misfortune and purify individuals born in unlucky years. This belief, called *"yaku yoke myōjin,"* is widespread throughout Japan. Its second principal virtue is found in its ability to protect against unlucky directions. This belief is based on the geomancy practiced in ancient times that held that north was a dangerous direction; thus Kyoto's northern regions needed the protection offered by this powerful *kami*.

Main Festivals of the Shrine

Kamo-sai (also called "Aoi Festival"): May 15
This festival began during the reign of Emperor Kinmei in the sixth century. Even today, the imperial family sends a messenger, who worships here on their behalf. The procession of this festival, which is eight hundred meters long and in which five hundred people participate, is like an elegant scroll painting. The Kamo Festival, popularly known as the Aoi, or Hollyhock, Festival, is one of the three biggest festivals in Kyoto.

Keiba shinji (The Ritual of the Racehorses): May 5
The horse race (in Japan) is said to originate from this shrine. This ritual became popular during the reign of Emperor Horikawa in the eleventh century

and has continued until today. It is designated by the City of Kyoto as an "intangible cultural property."

Nagoshi no harae (The Summer Purification Ritual): June 30
In this ritual held for the safety of one's household and life, one passes through a grass ring called *"chinowa"* and throws human effigies made of paper *(hitogata)* into the river both to rid oneself of impurities and to restore purity. This celebrated ritual is mentioned in the tanka poem called "Nara Stream" (Nara-no-ogawa), found in a collection of poems from the Kamakura period (1192–1333) called *Hyaku-nin isshu.*

Karasu-sumō (Crow Sumo): September 9
In this very unusual ritual, the priests imitate the voices of crows and their manner of jumping to the side, while children perform sumo for the entertainment of the *kami*. It has been designated by the city of Kyoto as an "intangible cultural property."

N. TANAO-SHA, whose *kami* are Kushiiwamado-no-ōkami and Toyoiwamado-no-ōkami, guards the entryway to buildings.

[Note: The internal shrines O through S are open to the public only at New Year's]

O. SUGIO-SHA: The *kami* here is Sugio-no-kami. The founding date is unknown but it is mentioned in the *Honchō seiki,* a book of the Heian period that says a huge Japanese cypress was blown down in this spot by a typhoon on October 27, 1153. An "important cultural treasure."

P. HAJIO-SHA: The *kami* of this shrine, Kamo-Tamayorihiko-no-mikoto, helps potters in making the vessels carrying sacred offerings [called *"shinsen"*] during shrine rituals. He is the son of Kamo-Taketsunomi-no-mikoto, who is, in turn, the grandfather of Wake Ikazuchi, the main deity of Kamigamo Shrine.

Q. WAKAMIYA JINJA: Although the founding date of this shrine is unknown, it is mentioned in the *Konjaku monogatari* and the *Eisho-ki,* both from the Kamakura period. During the Heian period, there was a popular belief in the powers of Wakamiya-no-kami.

R. YAMAO-SHA: The *kami* worshiped here is Ōyamatsumi-no-kami, brought from the shrine at Kibune. A book called the *Kyūshaki* mentions this shrine in the year 1268, but it was established before that.

S. SHINGŪ JINJA: The *kami* worshiped here is Takaokami-no-kami, believed to control excessive rain or sunshine. This *kami* was brought here from Kibune Shrine to the north and is documented in the book *Shamubuninki* as being established on August 25, 1049. Kibune Shrine was a subordinate shrine of Kamigamo Shrine until the Meiji Restoration. The *haiden* is an "important cultural treasure".

T. IWAMOTO-SHA: Uatsutsu-no-o-no-kami, Nakatsutsu-no-o-no-kami, and Sokotsutsu-no-o-no-kami are enshrined as three *kami* connected with purification. [This was another shrine that poets often visited during the Heian period.]

U. KAMO YAMAGUCHI JINJA: The *kami* enshrined here is Mitoshi-no-kami. No one knows when this shrine was originally founded, although it is mentioned in the tenth-century book *Engi shiki*. It also goes by the name Sawada Jinja, or Sawada-sha. This shrine's *kami* is in charge of protecting the farmland within the shrine's precincts.

V. NARA SHRINE: This shrine's *kami* is Naratoji-no-kami. The origin of this shrine is unknown, although it is listed in an early record of the history of the Sakyō part of Kyoto. The *kami* is in charge of meals, specifically breakfast and dinner, and also serves to protect the food offerings presented to the main *kami*. This building is registered as an "important cultural treasure."

W. NARA-NO-OGAWA (NARA STREAM)

> *Kaze soyogu, Nara-no-ogawa no yūgure wa,*
> *misogizo natsu no shirushi nari keru . . .*

"One knows it's early summer / when the priest performs a purification / in the Nara stream's faintly rustling breeze." This small river is the famous Nara Stream mentioned in the collection of poems from the Kamakura period (1192–1333) called *Ogura hyakunin isshu*. The poem, written by Fujiwara Ietaka, commemorates the Heian period practice of performing purifications called *"misogi"* at this stream in the early evening of midsummer.

X. YAMA-NO-MORI-SHA: The principal *kami* here is Susano-o-no-kami, followed by his wife, Inadahime no-mikoto, and Tagorihime-no-mikoto. These deities prevent epidemics.

Y. KAJITA-SHA: Seoritsuhime-no-kami is enshrined here. This was the place where, in the old days, people performed purifications before going to the main sanctuary. This *kami* is worshiped as the deity of the doorway.

KAMO-AFFILIATED SHRINES
IN JAPAN

As of September 1999, 562 shrines had joined an organization of Kamo-affiliated shrines. While some estimates place the total number of Kamo shrines around two thousand, this list, giving the number of shrines for each prefecture, from north to south, represents the first stage of organization building initiated by Kamigamo. Many of the shrines are not specifically "Kamo" but are thought to qualify because they have *raijin* thunder deities. Also of interest is the fact that several of these shrines (eighteen) have women listed as head priests. Many of the smaller shrines counted separately below share head priests with other shrines in the area.

Tokyo-to: 1	Kanagawa-ken: 7	Saitama-ken: 1
Gunma-ken: 13	Chiba-ken: 28	Ibaragi-ken: 22
Tochigi-ken: 82	Miyagi-ken: 17	Fukushima-ken: 30
Iwate-ken: 11	Aomori-ken: 15	Yamagata-ken: 10
Akita-ken: 5	Aichi-ken: 5	Shizuoka-ken: 15
Gifu-ken: 18	Nagano-ken: 5	Niigata-ken : 2
Fukui-ken: 18	Ishikawa-ken: 14	Toyama-ken: 22
Kyoto-fu: 17	Osaka-fu: 3	Nara-ken: 1
Hyōgo-ken: 41	Mie-ken: 5	Shiga-ken: 18
Wakayama-ken: 7	Tottori-ken: 22	Shimane-ken: 6
Okayama-ken: 10	Hiroshima-ken: 6	Yamaguchi-ken: 7
Tokushima-ken: 6	Kagawa-ken: 9	Ehime-ken: 9
Kōchi-ken: 9	Nagasaki-ken: 6	Fukuoka-ken: 16
Ōita-ken: 7	Saga-ken: 1	Kumamoto-ken: 2
Miyazaki-ken: 1	Hokkaido: 1	

NOTES

CHAPTER 1: OPENING ORIENTATIONS

1. The literature I will be citing throughout this study has served to inform and direct much of my thinking. Although I often mention a work in passing without delving into its specific content, this practice is not to be construed as a slight to its importance. Rather I often cite specific works as a springboard into topical areas of relevance for the issue under discussion.

2. I base this number on 82,000 questionnaires prepared for distribution by the Central Association of Shinto Shrines in late 1993 and on registered shrines listed in the Religious Juridical Persons Law *(Shūkyō hōjinhō)*. The number does not include the small roadside or unattended shrines one frequently sees in the countryside (see Bunkachō 1988: 58–59.) I have heard complaints against the semantic slippage of the English word "shrine" by a number of priests, most of whom would prefer the Japanese *"jinja"* to be used for a large institution to distinguish it from its Catholic, Sikh, or Islamic counterparts.

3. Only in a contemporary context is it accurate to think of Shinto ritual as separate from Buddhism and (to use a loaded word when talking about any Japanese institution) "unique" in itself. Although this separation began early in the Meiji period, it was finally realized at an institutional level after the end of World War II (see Fridell 1973; Sakurai 1992; Grapard 1984). In focusing on contemporary Shinto and the selected use of a wide repertoire of its practices specific to one shrine, I will not attempt to account systematically for rituals or symbols with Buddhist overtones and those within "the way of the *kami*"; nor will I reduce shrine Shinto to only

its political guise. Instead this study will present a sociocultural framework for understanding ritual events as they attempt to discipline and orient individuals to an operational ideology of continuity whereby priests and lay constituents select, invent, and maintain a highly reflexive sense of tradition, amenable to one's own sense of cultural identity.

4. Meiji Shrine in Tokyo was the most popular destination, with 3.44 million visitors. After that were two temples, Naritasan Shinshō-ji in Chiba (3.04 million) and Kawasaki Daishi in Kanagawa (3.01 million), followed by Sumiyoshi Taisha in Osaka (2.82 million) and Atsuta Jingū in Aichi (2.27 million visitors). These numbers come not from the institutions themselves but from metropolitan police departments in each area (*Yomiuri shinbun,* January 5, 1998). Not everyone who participates in these shrine visitations at New Year's is looking for a meaningful experience within a religious context. Nonetheless, these visitations remain significant enough that individuals are willing to endure crowds, cold, and financial expense in order to begin the new year in a manner that is socially sanctioned as efficacious. As one spike-haired, leather-jacketed motorcycle rider replied to my question of why he turned out at 2:00 A.M. on a freezing New Year's morning at Kamigamo Shrine, "Well, I did this as a kid with my parents and so it just feels right." The figure for New Year (or *hatsumōde*) visitations for the first five days of 1999 is 88,110,000, up 1.5 million from 1998 (*Yomiuri shinbun,* January 5, 1999).

5. The head priest of Kamigamo during the time of this study, Rev. Abe Makoto, recounted for me on several occasions an encounter he had in the 1930s with the dreaded military police *(kenpeitai)*. He was in charge of a shrine in Fukushima prefecture on the day the police came to examine the shrine's innermost sanctuary and catalog its *goshintai,* or sacred essence. Abe adamantly refused to allow them access and was willing to accept any punishment. Slapping his sword across the priest's desk, the head officer told him that he would pay dearly for his insubordination. However, when word got out of Abe's brave stance, even the senior military commander of the area commended him on his devotion to duty. No charges were brought nor was the *goshintai* ever subjected to cataloging. I will have more to say about these issues in the Conclusion.

6. Lebra's convincing article attributes this popularity to several factors (T. Lebra 1997). Among the most important was a policy instigated shortly after Akihito ascended the throne to "open the court." The new emperor and empress as well as their family were to become more visible, accessible, and interested in the general public through a process of naturalizing the barriers that had separated them. Crown prince Naruhito's romantic and highly public courtship and marriage to Masako was also significant in mustering highly favorable opinion polls about the family. Key to these changes is increased media exposure, something the imperial household can rely on as being generally favorable and sympathetic. Though there was a period of tabloid-inspired Empress Michiko bashing in the early 1990s, resulting in a psychogenic vocal disorder that removed her from the public eye for

nearly half a year, public sympathy (and right-wing pressure) was such that the mass media again voluntarily restrained itself from further disparagement of her style of managing the imperial family.

7. The forty-something suburban housewife who is the subject of Elisabeth Bumiller's book *The Secrets of Mariko* participates regularly in a kind of club that travels through the Tokyo area carrying portable shrines at festivals. About the experience of carrying the portable shrine *(mikoshi),* which is often rather rowdy and dangerous because of the participation of *yakuza* (Japanese mafia) in these events, she says: "I feel liberated. It feels like I'm going to a discotheque. I can relax. I can be myself" (Bumiller 1996:72).

8. Japan's Shinto priests first organized in 1898 in the Zenkoku Shinshoku-kai, changing their name in 1941 to the Dai Nihon Jingikai (Shinto Association of All Japan). The Jinja Honchō began almost immediately after the war to try and keep shrine lands intact (and protect them from individuals cutting down trees for economic gain [Creemers 1968:81]) after the Shinto Directive of 1945 threatened to dissolve large estates. Attested to by the spacious grounds of many shrines today, the endeavor was largely successful, thus securing a base of economic well-being at very little cost. According to Murakami (1970), the second major achievement came in 1952, when, thanks to an imperial ritual qualifying Akihito to succeed to the throne, the Jinja Honchō helped to capitalize on this positive atmosphere to revive the sullied reputations of shrines nationwide. A direct beneficiary was Kamigamo Shrine, whose historic and once hugely popular Aoi Festival was restarted in this year (see Chapter 7, May 15). In nearly every major political event challenging the constitutional separation of state and religion —from the governmental sponsorship of Akihito's marriage (1959), to the tumultuous 1960 U.S.-Japan Security Treaty protests, to the 1967 establishment of *kenkoku kinen-bi,* "the day of national founding" based on ancient rather than modern calendars, to the government-sponsored funeral of Emperor Hirohito (1989) or Akihito's imperial succession (1990)—the Jinja Honchō has been busily at work. The Jinja Honchō continues to promote shrine rituals as having significance for the nation as well as being the source of a broad-based public morality (see Teeuwen 1996).

CHAPTER 2: FREEDOM OF EXPRESSION:
THE VERY MODERN PRACTICE OF VISITING A SHINTO SHRINE

1. Rosalind Shaw (1992) has remarked that the term "syncretism" is in the process of being reclaimed by anthropological discourse, much the same way that "fetishism" was reclaimed by writers on postmodern topics. In its newly revised sense, syncretism refers to the composite, constructed, and contested nature of a religious tradition (and of tradition in general) rather than the oft-cited mechanistic merging of channels or tributaries of cultural influence into one dominant "stream."

2. Travel books, articles in newspaper travel-section inserts, and various narratives relating one's encounter with the Japanese are sources that provide accounts of the "religiosity of Japanese" based on superficial observations. Academic researchers may howl in protest, but there continues to be a real market for exoticizing Japanese religious and cultural practices (I would cite as an example Nicholas Kristoff's coverage in the *New York Times* between 1995 and 1998). In another cultural context, Pfaffenberger (1983) showed how the behavior of youthful, modern-day pilgrims in Sri Lanka, while appearing to be frivolous religious tourism from an academic perspective, was instead wholly consistent with culturally supplied symbols celebrating the relevance of the pilgrimage to modern life.

3. According to figures provided in 1992 by the Kyoto Tourist Association (Kyōto Kankō Kyōkai), the number of people making visits to the city in 1990 reached 38,620,000. Compared with the year 1963, in which about half this number (17,711,000) visited the city, the Tourist Association has become an active and important player in the financial health of both city and tourist sites. To use an official's own words, the Kankō Kyōkai is an organization subsidized by the city government to "protect and preserve the traditions of the city in a way that allows them to coexist with the economic realities of tourism." Despite the prolonged recession in Japan, 38,918,000 visitors came in 1997, the most recent year for which statistics are available. For more on the Tourist Association's involvement with "traditional" events, see my discussion of the Aoi Festival in Chapter 7.

4. Kamigamo's priests were fascinated by my observations of visitor movement and activity. They seemed aware that few visitors read the sign by the first torii, but when presented with percentages based on observations of over 112 visitors (where only 3 percent read the entire sign), they began discussing alternative locations as well as alternative ways of presenting the same information in a more accessible format.

5. While the meanings of signs in Japanese are impenetrable to the non-Japanese-reading foreign tourist, they may have an impact nonetheless. At Kamigamo as well as at numerous other shrines throughout Japan, the Hitatchi Corporation has donated signs signifying important cultural treasures. These markers are uniform in appearance, with neatly printed red and white characters against a brown background. However, at the bottom of the sign, immediately below the company's logo, its name appears in English in bright red letters. When I once inquired of a foreign visitor (on her way out of the shrine) whether she had any questions, she wanted only to know more about the relationship between Kamigamo and Hitatchi, Ltd. When I mentioned that to my knowledge there was no connection at all, she replied that since the Hitatchi-sponsored signs had the only English words in the entire shrine compound, she assumed an important relationship existed. She was nearly as surprised by my answer as I was by her question, although the greatest surprise was shown by the priests. No one who reads Japanese would have given the

slightest thought to the Hitatchi advertisement, so successfully have the conglomerates infiltrated every recess of Japanese social and, in this case, religious settings.

6. It was some time before I realized that I was one of the very few who followed the priests' prescribed course. I also realized that I was making an attempt to establish my credentials as someone "worthy" of studying Kamigamo Shrine by exhibiting the kind of standardized gestures the priests had themselves learned at the training universities of Kokugakuin and Kogakkan. After this realization, I stopped judging the variations of visitor activity as being incorrect or in some way deviant. I say with a mixture of embarrassment and pride that my hand-purification method at the *temizusha* basin received compliments from onlookers on more than one occasion ("My, you really know how to do it correctly! You say you learned it from a head priest? Well then, could you show me how to do it the same way?").

One way to think about this exchange is as reflecting a culturally valued pleasure of propriety gained by performing gestures thought appropriate to certain situations. And while the scene of a foreigner teaching Japanese a standardized hand-washing technique may appear to some as presumptuous, ludicrous, and perhaps downright silly (I sometimes share these views), there is an additional interpretation that should also be considered. Many Japanese feel themselves to be so distant from the traditions and practices of formal Shinto ritual behavior—it being as alien and exotic to them as is a foreigner in their midst—that they are willing and open to seek instruction from anyone apparently authorized to impart it. This fact in itself is interesting, but that they are disposed to learn perhaps reflects part of the ongoing reenchantment of tradition and the past so important to contemporary discourse on what it means to be Japanese.

7. Since the shrine's priests work in an administrative building away from the areas most frequented by visitors, the only person available for consultation (assuming a visitor was motivated to ask) would be the attendant at the amulet counter. At Kamigamo, this position is most often staffed by the shrine's female attendants *(miko)*, followed by the most junior priests, and finally by the employee from the upper *juyosho* close to the inner sanctuary.

8. Despite its flat approaches and walkways, Kamigamo Shrine is not accessible to the handicapped. On several occasions I have seen people in wheelchairs maneuver all the way to the Tower Gate's steps, where, able to go no farther, they gaze at the barrier before them the way a hiker might look at a chasm suddenly opened in the middle of a pleasant trail. I have seen shrine priests walk past these same individuals never once asking whether they would like to be carried into the shrine for a closer look. Because Kamigamo Shrine is a private corporation, it is doubtful whether Japan's few laws attempting to redress inadequate handicapped access would apply. In fact, the social stigma of handicapped individuals has in part been conditioned by religious discrimination directed against their infirmities. "Impurities" can be defined rather broadly to include people with atypical physical abilities,

just as these abilities or handicaps were thought, from the perspective of popular Buddhism's notions of karma, to be punishments for misdeeds in a past lifetime.

9. I have been told that the *kashiwade* (literally *kashiwa,* or "oak tree," and *te,* "hands") is significant because, like two leaves of the bisexual oak, the male and female hands come together in an act of worship.

10. Compare this tendency with William Christian's account of pilgrimage in Spain and with Catholicism in general, where a hierarchical stratification of a saint's rank and importance influences whether or not an individual will petition that saint for material benefits (1988 [1972]: 238).

11. I say this guardedly, since one can frequently find display racks for candles at shrines (particularly Inari shrines) throughout Japan. However, at major sites such as Kamigamo, Meiji, Ise, Izumo, and so forth, the lighting of candles is not a part of worshipers' activity before the central sanctuary. Most priests are nervous about devotional candles and the fire hazard they represent to buildings that are often classified as national treasures.

12. I believe that many of the general motivations bringing people to Kamigamo at night would also apply to other large shrines located within urban areas. An anecdote conveyed to me by a senior priest from Nagasaki's Suwa Shrine concerns a groundskeeper catching a young couple in flagrante delicto within the wooded grounds of Tokyo's Meiji Shrine. Escorting them to the exit, he roundly scolds them for engaging in such an act on the grounds of a sacred place, as well as insulting the spirit of Emperor Meiji. To which the young woman replies, "Meiji who?"

13. The vulnerability of shrines to acts of aggression became apparent in 1989 when the nation's attention was focused on the death of Emperor Hirohito and the retrospective this event provided on the tumultuous Showa years. Not surprisingly, because of the role shrine Shinto played before and during the war and the question of the former emperor's complicity in the war, several shrines were burned in nighttime terrorist attacks by the Chūkaku-ha, a radical student group, and the Kakudō-kyō, a radical workers' group. But, as subsequent attacks carried out during the enthronement proceedings of the Heisei emperor, Akihito, have proved, the quarrel of these radical groups is with the imperial institution and its continuing links to shrine Shinto. Eighteen firebombings at shrines nationwide occurred from the first year of Heisei (1990) to 1992, with one shrine completely burned and five badly damaged. Thirteen out of the eighteen attacks were claimed by the Chūkaku-ha. Additionally, during the *daijō-sai* ceremonies of 1992, nine attacks were made in and around Tokyo, leaving three shrines badly damaged.

Despite these dramatic means of protesting the links between shrine Shinto and the imperial household (even though most of these institutions did not enshrine deities of any special imperial distinction or status), every shrine that suffered damage has since been completely rebuilt. If anything, these attacks have served to solidify community support for the local shrine and its ritual occasions, and thus bolster rather than subvert many of the symbolic associations I have discussed elsewhere (Nelson 1992, 1993b).

CHAPTER 3: TOWARD AN IDEOLOGY OF SACRED PLACE

1. While I privilege the priestly explanation in this example, it is fair to say that the predominant cultural notion among Japanese is to see shrines as permanently housing the *kami*. This view is reflected in many folktales, movies, stories, and even cartoons, where shrines at night are especially unsettling and fearful in a way that Buddhist temples are not. No one seems to know just what might happen if one enters into the domain of the *kami* at night, but it is a place most Japanese generally avoid. Because Kamigamo has a spacious outer precinct at some distance from the inner sanctuaries, as seen in Chapter 2, people seem to feel less intimidated.

2. During his entire political career, François Mitterrand made a yearly "pilgrimage" to a rocky crag at Solutré in the Bourgogne region to commemorate his wartime escape from Germany and subsequent participation in resistance forces in the area. After he became president of France, flocks of journalists would accompany him as he climbed to the top and gazed wistfully out over the landscape. Due largely to their accounts, the visit took on the aura of a pilgrimage, with the rocky promontory evoking the "sacred" qualities of the nation: land, republic, family, history, and loyalty to all. The fact that the visit would occur during Pentecostal holidays added another layer of significance — that of the president offering predictions for the future of France (Abélès 1988).

3. A wonderful account of a demonstration held at Mount Rushmore by Oglala Sioux in the 1970s ("Sitting on Top of Teddy Roosevelt's Head") can be found in *Lame Deer: Seeker of Visions* by John (Fire) Lame Deer and John Erdoes. One "symbolic gesture" of an earlier demonstration involved making a human chain reaching out onto Roosevelt's head so that the brave soul at the end could relieve himself, thus expressing Indian grievances against the broken treaties and the tribal displacement and destruction that these giant statues represent.

4. Denis Cosgrove, drawing on the work of Scully, points out that the Greeks' siting of temples to the "young" god Apollo followed principles that might be thought of as a counterpoint to the generally accessible placement of Shinto shrines: wherever the most awesome characteristics of the old goddess of the earth were made manifest, wherever her symbols were most remote, tortuously approached, and largest in scale, there the temple was placed. But, asserting different spiritual agendas than Apollo's chthonic predecessors, the new temple was oriented in a way that complemented but also opposed the old forces (Cosgrove 1993:285).

5. The word "geomancy" is considered by some scholars to be a misnomer, referring to Arab forms of divination that spread into Europe and Africa in the first millennium. I will use the contemporary *"feng-shui"* as a convenience, although some

writers suggest other terms such as "topomancy" (Feuchtwang 1974), "telluric geomancy," or more new-age terms as "astro-biology" or "astro-ecology" (cited in Skinner 1982) in order to distinguish the location of lines of energy in a surrounding landscape from divinatory geomancy. Skinner points out two names used consistently in classical Chinese sources, the first being *ti li,* or "land patterns," and the second, from a Taoist source, *kan-yu,* or "cover and support." He also suggests that the term *"feng-shui"* is more accurately thought of as belonging to the "Form School," whereby actual topographical features are studied to determine the life force lines, in contrast to the "Compass School," which is concerned with a time axis and a complex set of relationships among sensitive directions as indicated by an elaborate twenty-four-point magnetic compass. This extraordinary instrument expanded observations of the physical landscape to reference thirty-eight circles of symbol sets including (to mention only a few) the trigrams and hexagrams of the *I ching,* the sexagenary cycle of stems and branches, the five elements, and astrological influences as well (Needham and Wang 1962:361; Meyer 1978:149). See also Bernard Faure 1987 for more on space and place in Chinese religious traditions and Yoon 1983 for a Korean perspective.

6. Such was their power in the Heian period that affairs of state or movements of the emperor could be brought to a halt if geomancers pronounced inauspicious influences afoot. The story is told of one poor emperor, who returning from a nighttime visit to one of his consorts, could not enter the palace because his timing coincided with that of a malevolent spirit. As a result of waiting in the cold night air, he caught cold and later died (Delmer Brown, personal communication).

7. The yang and thus protecting influence of 890-meter Atago-yama in the northwest would, according to a local architect knowledgeable about earth energies, be broken by the Hozukawa River, just north of Arashi-yama. I speculate that Atago-yama, even though higher than Hiei-zan (848 meters) would be considered a balancing rather than dominant element in the cosmology of the city. Its height and distinctive conical peak formation would render it yang, associated with the planet Mars and the element fire. Indeed, to this day one of Kyoto's fire festivals continues to be held at the base and summit of Atago-yama (see Casal 1967 for references on fire festivals in Japan). Hiei-zan on the other hand, with a rounded head and a long body, would correspond to Jupiter and the wood element. Between these two yang influences, and balancing their male properties, flow the Kamo, Takano, and Kiyotaki rivers, all yin and female influences.

8. See Matsunaga and Matsunaga 1974 (volume 1) for a detailed discussion concerning the social and political context for the establishment of Enryaku-ji and Tōji in the ninth century. Because of the problems posed by an increasingly powerful Buddhist clergy in Heijōkyō, the Heiankyō precincts were at first off limits to Buddhist institutions. Thus, while Tōji is outside the southern Rajōmon (Rashōmon) Gate proper, it nevertheless fortified the *urakimon* of the new capital. In any discus-

sion of medieval or early Shinto, it is vital to remember that Shinto was not a separate institution but syncretic with Buddhist institutions and ritual practices. Grapard, who has done so much to correct earlier stereotypes, mentions the importance in particular of the Shingon esoteric tradition, which provided a cosmology integrating the mind of the Buddha with natural landscapes. By elaborating the precept "form is emptiness, emptiness is form," a nationwide religious geography developed where the land "spoke in a natural language [that] people conceived of as a supernatural discourse" (Grapard 1994 : 383). Regions such as Yoshino, Kii, Shikoku, and Kunisaki were especially charged with religious significance. While recognizing the importance of Shingon, it is important to remember that esoteric knowledge was being carefully transmitted to the adept. When Buddhism did gain a broader cultural currency, it was layered on centuries of folk beliefs and practices that referenced both *kami* and malevolent spirits. Even today in Kyoto businesses or dwellings facing the north or northeast frequently have a tree planted in the inauspicious corner, a small charm under the eave of the roof, or salt piled in small cones. This last is frequently seen by the entries to houses and places of business, as salt is thought to purify and dispel evil influences.

9. Another Chinese precedent that was likely in play at this time is the pairing of lightning and thunder as instruments of divine retribution. The clearest example is Sugawara Michizane's deification into Tenjin, an angry and vengeful *onryō* spirit that sought revenge on the court officials who forced him into exile and early death in Kyushu. Hammond writes that while Chinese scholars disavowed the idea of a conscious heaven, popular attitudes prevailed to constitute a paradigm that encouraged "even the educated to see thunder as a tangible physical object and tempted many of them to believe that it struck the evil as punishment" (1994 : 499).

10. Today there are numerous bridges over the Kamo River, but as recently as the Meiji era the Misono-bashi area (some one hundred meters outside today's shrine boundary) was a site where rituals were enacted to benefit shrine, clan, and state interests downstream. Once within shrine precincts, the visitor crosses the Mitarashi-gawa over one of three bridges: Negibashi, Hōribashi, or Kusunokibashi. By crossing either of the first two, the visitor's route brings him or her to the Katayama Shrine and its splendid covered bridge over the serene Omonoi-gawa. Thus, one is cleansed a second time (or a third, if one stopped at the hand-cleansing basin) before entering the main gate to the inner courtyard.

11. The issue of "openness" became problematic during the rebuilding of Suwa Shrine in Nagasaki in the early 1980s (Nelson 1996b). The old buildings had been completely open to the environment and suffered accordingly from the high humidity of southern Japan. The rebuilding, instigated by a new head priest from the mountains of Nagano prefecture, not only encased the lower and middle halls of worship as well as the inner sanctuary (Haiden, Heiden, Honden) with glass and natural-wood paneling, the entire shrine was air-conditioned. Thus, during the steamy months of

summer, which reaches into September, parishioners and visitors (not to mention the priests in their multilayered robes) could worship in comfort. For priests who had grown attached to the old shrine's decrepit, close-to-nature ambience, the air-conditioning was an outrage. Yet many parishioners I talked with were more than pleased that the shrine went to such expense in consideration of their comfort.

12. One of the earliest works in English on this topic is Kishimoto 1958; see also Yamaguchi 1975. Other sources are Hori 1968, Grapard 1982, and Matsumae's "Early Kami Worship" (1993). Matsumae makes an important observation that not all Japanese *kami* were thought to descend from mountains. Exhibiting what he sees as a Southeast Asian link, some deities are believed to come from across the horizon of the sea.

13. This interpretation as well as those elsewhere in this discussion of the shrine's sexual symbolism are supported by a number of the priests. Other emblems central to Kamigamo's iconography that are said to convey sexual messages are the pairing of the *aoi* and *katsura*. As it was explained to me, the *katsura* is a tree characterized by its symmetrically forked branches. Thus, to place the *aoi* flower within a sprig of *katsura*, as is common during the Kamo Festival, is to symbolize sexual intercourse.

14. Kitamura notes there is confusion about the actual variety of this plant (1966, cited in McCullough and McCullough 1980:409). The *futaba-aoi* was used for decoration in the Kamo Festival and is characterized by a "creeping, ivylike plant with attractive pairs of heart-shaped leaves growing from rooted horizontal stems." It is, however, the *tachi-aoi* that appears on the shrine's amulets and is more accurately translated as "hollyhock" *(Althaea rosea)*, even though it was not used for decoration in the Kamo Festival. *Aoi* is translated as "heartvine" in the *Tale of Genji* (see Field 1987:48).

15. The *saiin* tradition will be discussed in chapters 4 and 7. An additional conveyor of sexual imagery is found at the Hosodono hall where, just behind the standing sand cones, the steps leading to the hall are demarcated by a *shimenawa*, or "sacred rope," marking the presence of a sacred area's border. But it is not just any *shimenawa*: whereas most have their ends tied around a pillar, post, or tree, this particular symbol has a long endpiece of some twenty centimeters that (thanks to a wire within) makes it stand erect. The priests I spoke with interpreted this symbol as a variation of the "lightning rod" tree once used to call the *kami* to the earth, but they did not contest the possibility that there was a strong sexual message as well, especially since the *shimenawa* is found at a pavilion constructed exclusively for a powerful female adept at divination. The *saiin* also enacted a role begun much earlier by Kamo female priestesses whereby during the *miare-sai* (see Chapter 7, May 12 entry) a consecrated woman *(areonna)* would go to a sacred site and receive the male *kami* as a "spirit husband." Anyone familiar with the rites of imperial succession knows that a similar event occurs for the new emperor, who receives a "spirit wife" within specially constructed halls.

16. When inquiring which amulet would be appropriate to provide protection during a trip to the United States, I was briefly and politely questioned before the attendant made a suggestion. If only flying, then the amulet carrying a picture of a jet would work; if I would only be in a car, then the all-purpose *kōtsū anzen,* or "transportation safety," seemed appropriate. However, because I would be doing both, as well as riding a bicycle and walking, the only possible choice was what the attendant called the "all-mighty" *(oru-maitii).* the amulet of the phallic *aoi.* I am happy to report that I had a very safe trip. This protective aspect can also be found at Nikkō, where the Tōshōgū mausoleum of Tokugawa Ieyasu is aligned with Nantai mountain long associated with phallic properties. Thus, it would appear Ieyasu's tomb architects were attempting to draw on this correspondence between the recently departed ruler and natural surroundings to protect and prolong the realm. I am grateful to Professor Delmer Brown for bringing this last point to my attention.

17. Isozaki points out how each of the twenty buildings at Katsura Imperial Palace represents a deep metaphor related to famous Japanese poetry (1992:20).

CHAPTER 4: KAMO MEMORIES AND HISTORIES

1. To designate this exchange as a "discourse" rather than using other possible terms (such as "controversy" or "dispute") permits a greater flexibility that can account for the possibility of "shifting, multiple, and competing" statements within a particular group rather than imputing to that group a unified stance vis-à-vis an opponent. To continue Abu-Lughod's remarks on "discourse" as an analytic term, it refuses the distinction between "ideas and practices or text and world" that other concepts too readily encourage (1991:148). By using "discourse," there is room to include in this discussion about Japan's struggle to legitimate traditions an occasional rocket attack (the minister of defense's house was hit three times in September 1992), an attempted assassination (six woefully misdirected bullets were fired at Kanemaru Shin, Japan's recent "shadow shogun"), and acts of arson (two shrines were torched during the official period of mourning for the previous emperor in 1989).

2. See Miyoshi Masao and H. D. Harootunian's *Postmodernism and Japan* (1989) and Yoshino Kosaku's *Cultural Nationalism in Contemporary Japan* (1992). I have also discussed these themes in Nelson 1992. An ongoing example is privileging the term for "regret" instead of "apology" in Japanese governmental statements about accepting responsibility for aggression (another taboo term) in the Pacific War.

3. This is my attempt to answer Ohnuki-Tierney's challenge that any study must address whether internal or external agents are involved in creating historical change (1990:18). Horner's excellent discussion (1992) stresses a contrast between an "invented tradition," which stresses what I see as an external or contextual nature of specific social and political situations, and "tradition as invention," which includes internal processual elements of selectivity and renewal. However,

to state the issue as a matter of categories and bifurcated contrasts imposes a rigidity that, as Ohnuki-Tierney says, works to "reinforce a false polarity that does not exist in practice" (p. 21).

4. This phrase comes from the government of Indira Gandhi during the nationwide state of emergency of 1976. As she attempted to quell opposition party moves to paralyze the nation through strikes and demonstrations, similarly poignant three-word messages ("adapt, adopt, improve") blanketed the country on billboards, eerily blinking television screens, and in the newspapers. That these slogans sound appropriate in the context of Japan and in discussions of social memory is not, I think, a matter of coincidence. Many of the same dynamics are at work whenever state agencies attempt selectively to order and orient popular opinion so as to identify state crises as national ones.

5. More than once, during my interviewing of the shrine's visitors, I heard the phrase *"mottai nai,"* or what a waste, when individuals responded to my question about the shrine's grounds. If they answered affirmatively my question about whether they had strolled through the shrine grounds, I asked for their reactions to the streams, groves, gardens, and grassy fields. "Very pretty," "peaceful," and "refreshing" were the usual replies, but there were also times when a visitor would reply "very pretty" and follow this immediately with an editorial comment on the prettiness—*mottai nai!* To many visitors, perhaps dreaming of what they would do with the chance to develop a shadowy grove of trees into a high-rise apartment building or remembering their own cramped living situation, the physical space a shrine controls is an expression of its power. I was also under this impression until the priests let me know that they too would love to "do something" with the "empty" spaces of the shrine but that severe restrictions and sanctions await even the formulation of plans by the Tokyo-based Jinja Honchō, the Kyoto Historical Society, and City Hall's Office for the Preservation of Historical Sites.

6. I am thinking here of Weber's discussion on religion and the problem of social evolution (1964 [1922]), Goody's work on Catholic hierarchies and institutions (1983), Appadurai's study of a south Indian temple (1981), and Gilsenan's portrayal of Islam (1982).

7. *"Dōzoku"* is composed of two characters, the first meaning "same" and the second "clan/family"; while my translation is not literal, it captures the intended political message of the term as it is employed by the group.

8. In an overt display of democratic politics, Inoue says that the Kamo priests have the "people" to thank for this privileged monopoly, not because they rallied to the priests' aid but because of their belief in the deities of the Kamo Shrine. Inoue implies that someone had to carry on the rituals and keep the shrine operating, and thus, as if by common rather than imperial consent, the eviscerated political organization of the Kamo simply transferred to the more specialized role of the priesthood (Inoue 1985 : 113). Inoue relegates to the shadows one of the basic ways that continuity was assured in the implementation of the Taihō codes of 701—namely, that the

title of *kuni no miyatsuko* replaced that of *agatanushi* and was granted to those heads of small tribal states that presided over important shrines located within their domains. The Yamato leaders were much too sensitive to potential problems in the provinces to permit "the people" any voice in state decisions. With an important and (even at that time) old shrine involved as well—with its extensive network of subsidiary shrines and powerful nature deities—the careful management of transferring power was all the more reason for the Yamato administration to be involved.

9. For additional information on the *ritsuryō* system and the momentous changes it brought about in the formation of the early state—especially its promulgation of an ideology that saw all individuals as obligated to worship the emperor—see Takeuchi 1958, Kiley 1973, and Miller 1980.

10. With habitations in Japan reaching back to at least thirty thousand years ago and possibly seventy to one hundred thousand years, this statement about the area's "original" inhabitants must be contextualized. Still, because "origins" are the issue, it is interesting that discoveries of Japanese archaeologists and physical anthropologists, such as Mori and Matsufuji (1988), not only push back the dates for the origins of human habitation of Japan—debunking the 30,000 B.C.E. date of early Jomon as too recent—but cite convincing evidence to substantiate this claim. A wooden artifact unearthed in 1981 has been dated by carbon-14 process to be roughly thirty thousand years old. Also, by surveying the work of scientists studying artifact stratification in the context of volcanic ash deposits from the three major eruptions of the last hundred thousand years (Aso: 70,000 B.C.E.; Aira: 22,000 B.C.E.; Kikai 6300 B.C.E.), they have ascertained that artifacts having stemmed points similar to those of Paleolithic Korean culture, points found in the Kanto Plain near Tokyo with origins in the Kozushima islands (which separated twenty thousand years ago), and fashioned stone tools (axes) dated by carbon 14 at 30,000 B.C.E. all demonstrate a Paleolithic culture with the ability to work wood and fashion boats (see Akazawa and Aikens 1986; also Pearson 1986).

Though the evidence could be considered circumstantial, it is important because it establishes the likelihood that interisland as well as continental contact reaches back at least to 30,000 B.C.E. and probably before. Mori and Matsufuji surmise that the first inhabitants settled in Japan when the archipelago was still attached to the continent anywhere from 200,000 to 120,000 B.C.E., with increasing settlements caused by peoples (and species) fleeing continental glaciation even after the land was separated by rising seas (1988:245). Pearson also states (1988) that regional and temporal variation in Paleolithic technology fifteen thousand years old is well documented, with a *kokeshi* doll-like human effigy, found in Oita prefecture, reaching back fifteen to twenty thousand years. With the northwestern tip of Hokkaido only 150 miles from the Siberian coast, with the islands of Iki and Tsushima providing stepping stones between the Korean and Kyushu coasts, and with warm currents from the South Seas passing close to the southeastern coast of Japan, scholars now surmise a steady flow of settlement and outside cultural influences all through

Japan's long prehistoric period. When placed within this context, the Kamo question hardly seems one of origins.

11. Ōwa, a folklorist, finds evidence of similar rituals in the former Harima area (currently southern Hyōgo prefecture), in the Osumi peninsula south of Miyazaki in southern Kyushu, and in the Tango peninsula of northeastern Kyushu. He conjectures that these are all mountain people's rites for enhancing communal solidarity and are the original form of the Kamo-sai (1986:19).

12. The Suma essay differs from the Fujiki chronology presented in the front of the book, which lists the date 780 as the beginning of the Kamo *agatanushi*. Fujiki mentions an occasion on which the title "Kamo Agatanushi" was bestowed on ten people as the first time the name appears in any text or document. However, Inoue also notes this early text and interprets it to account for people marrying in to the Kamo *agatanushi* who were thus given the name in a formal ceremony to mark their status and rights as clan members (1985:120). The importance of marriage politics and practices both into and out of the Kamo clan would be an important area of future study.

13. Inoue in his work on the *nijū ōken* system of administration and religion has no hesitation about restoring to women a prominent role in early shrine affairs, going so far as to compare the shrine's gender-assigned ritual functionaries to pre-Yamato kingdoms that were matriarchal in the structuring of their leadership (1985:110).

14. Even though the *saiin* were from the court, they were under the supervision of their Kamo handlers. In addition to numerous ritual preparations, there were taboo words that had to be regulated. For example, death was called "getting well," illness was "slumber," weeping was "shedding salt," blood was called "sweat," meat was "vegetables," and a tomb was a "clod of earth" (Bock 1970:10). Buddhism too was forbidden, even though the cult of Amida Buddha had won many devotees among the court. Emperor Saga had even provided funds for the construction of *jingūji* temples within both Kamigamo and Shimogamo precincts. Although periodically ordered to recite sutras on the *kami*'s behalf, the *Kamo engi* says, Buddhist priests were never permitted access to the kami (ibid.). Kamens (1990) has shown that the enforced taboos did not limit personal faith. The *saiin* used poetry regularly to express both their devotion as Buddhists and their frustrations concerning the prescriptions on their spiritual life. Not surprisingly perhaps, the Kamo shrines became during this period the patron deities of poetry. Specifically, the *sessha* subordinate shrines of Iwamoto and Hashimoto (see Appendix 1) were favored by aspiring and established poets. One Fujiwara Shunzei (1112–1204) prayed at Kamigamo each day for one thousand days in order that his descendants might inherit his success in *waka* as art and profession (Kamens 1990:7 n.).

15. Studies of ritual have advanced in recent years to the point that, depending on one's analytical purpose, a ritual can be interpreted, deconstructed, decoded, or "anthropologized" to the point that its original participants would hardly

recognize the end result. In presenting the Crow Sumo, I will try to let the logic of my informants structure the account rather than imposing theory or laboring to convert the event into neat and tidy analytical categories. Doing so restores autonomy and authority to the event in a way that both the priests and the parishioners' group intended for the audience on hand. There is a subtle kind of politics at work in any description because of the writer's authority in selecting, editing, and evoking other worlds and times, yet I will try to resist the paralyzing tendency to problematize each sentence, image, or association. Ethnography is unavoidably reflexive at heart, as "accounts and the setting they describe mutually elaborate and modify each other in a back-and-forth process" (G. Watson 1991:79). I will first swing forth to sketch out the event, then try in a moment to sally back and provide a reciprocity of perspectives, looking at the ritual's structure and overall "success" as a calculated performance, a rite of legitimation for the Kamo descendants, and a means of fostering communitywide participation and solidarity. I recognize, however, that the Heisenberg Principle is always at work, so that the "distance" my account travels to reach the reader necessarily renders it a construction rather than a portrayal of what actually occurred. For a background on the significance of sumo, see Cuyler 1979.

16. On using children in rituals, the priest of Kamo descent says:

"In the old days, the children had to be from farming families, but if we had that restriction today, there wouldn't be any kids at all! We used to put up a sign on notice boards at the local school, at the shrine, and at the ward office trying to recruit children to participate. I guess kids and their parents in the past thought it was rather embarrassing to put on a loincloth and participate in this event. We had a hard time getting enough kids. Of course, we could still do the ritual inside the shrine, which is its most important part, but if we didn't have enough kids for the sumo outside, it would really be a problem.

"So, six years ago we asked the sports club teacher whether he could help us out by asking boys in the sumo club, as well as in the baseball club—boys who have never worn anything but pants all their lives. But now that sumo is popular again—thanks to Takahanada and Wakahanada—we've seen a big difference in how kids participate. If you use adults, you get a clash of interests based on selfish concerns. Then, their energy and strength are manipulated to meet these interests. With children however, you don't have these complications. Also, after the match is over and someone wins and loses, you don't have these grudges that adults tend to have. Actually, without fail, adults would fight afterwards."

"Even Kamo adults?" I asked. "Especially Kamo adults!" was his answer.

17. Out of forty-two *shōen* estates in the entire nation in 1264, the Kamo shrines accounted for twenty-two of them (Suma, in Fujiki 1991:213). Among their holdings were estates in provinces such as Yamashiro (central Kyoto prefecture), Wakasa, Tamba (north Kyoto prefecture), Aki (Hiroshima prefecture), Iwami (Shimane prefecture), Mikawa (southern Aichi prefecture), Harima (southern Hyōgo

prefecture), Mimaska (eastern Okayama prefecture), and Izumo (eastern Tottori prefecture). A longer list can be found in note 8 to Chapter 7. Jeffrey Mass (1979) has translated legal documents from the Kamakura period showing conflicts that arose between *jitō* administrators newly appointed after the 1221 war and the *shōen* proprietors and cultivators. Several of these documents (Yamashiro, Izumo, Tamba, Wakasa, and Aki) involve Kamo estates. A somewhat chaotic listing of the holdings for Kamo Miōya Shrine (Shimogamo) has been assembled by Ponsonby-Fane and is said to cover twenty-five provinces (1933:55).

18. These points are from Ortner's (1990) discussion of cultural "schemas." Her use of this concept integrates structure and practice in a way that does not seem mechanical or functional. An individual can adopt temporarily and reenact a cultural schema (such as a code of hospitality, a custom of reciprocity, or the lesson of a folk story) that responds to a particular situation, but this situation should not be seen as a kind of determinism. Cultural schemas, she argues, help individuals to manipulate their culture even as they are constrained by a limited repertoire of meanings and appropriate contexts within which these meanings can find expression (p. 63).

CHAPTER 5: WARDEN + VIRTUOSO + SALARYMAN = PRIEST: THE ROLES OF RELIGIOUS SPECIALISTS IN INSTITUTIONAL PERSPECTIVE

1. An earlier version of the first part of this chapter appeared in Japanese in an edited tribute to the late Professor Yanagawa Keiichi (Nelson 1997b), a leader in the study of *matsuri*. As is customary to protect informants' identities, "Ishida Haruo" is a pseudonym.

2. By taking this approach, I risk upsetting traditionalists who hold that Shinto shrines are uniquely Japanese and have no parallels elsewhere in the world (Mayumi 1989). I also need to state my preference for using the word "priest" as opposed to the Japanese *kannushi*. The etymology for "priest" points to an Anglo-Saxon root, *prèost,* which is firmly within the Christian tradition (as are the other sources from Late Latin). However, English-language publications by the Jinja Honchō and Shinto scholars in general commonly use "priest" as an equivalent for *kannushi.* Although my use of the term is largely a matter of linguistic convenience, the word also summons (not inappropriately, I think) associations of solemnity, training, ritual expertise, hierarchy, and an occupational environment physically removed from the mainstream of secular corporate life.

3. This issue is raised in an ideological context by Hansen and Parrish in the Marcus volume (1983), as it concerns the hegemonic power of capitalist society. Some of their observations, while not specifically concerned with religious institutions, still bear on the discussion of elites. They point out that neither Marx nor Weber was successful in identifying in practice certain theoretical hypotheses concerning a politically coherent ruling class, for the former, and the embrace of legal

bureaucratic rationalism, for the latter. The authors argue that, in both cases, what is preferred in elite capitalist society are policies of rule that are factionalist rather than unified and practices of patronage, monocratism, and personalism instead of bureaucratic rationalism. Thus, they criticize earlier theorists' failure to see that "non-institutional forms of political organization can have enduring structural relevance to the organization of hegemonic power" (p. 260).

4. Several priests commute daily from as far away as Lake Biwa (ninety minutes by car), Yawata (sixty minutes by train and bus), and southern Yamashina (fifty minutes by car during rush hour).

5. See Gareth Morgan's *Images of Organization* (1986) for a complete listing of attributes of organizational power. I have freely modified and selected from these categories in assessing the power of Shinto priests.

6. I have already mentioned several of the many balancing acts priests must perform in their institutional roles. Researchers too have a tenuous equilibrium to maintain and, according to Talal Asad, all too easily become theologians if they assert the "primacy of meaning without regard for the discursive processes by which meanings are constructed" (1983: 246). For further comments, please see the Note on Fieldwork in Chapter 1.

7. Writers like Abe, because of their insider status within the national shrine network, have a vested interest in promoting the sacredness of the priesthood. Thus, his remarks concerning what priests are about must be seen as emic rather than etic assessments and must be accorded a validity that reflects his career and social position within shrine Shinto.

8. Bonuses would increase this total by perhaps one-fifth. However, because bonuses vary from company to company, I follow the Ministry of Labor's statistical tendency to not include them in the base figure (JETRO 1992: 120).

9. I saw firsthand the anguish of a coming graduate trying to win a sponsor at a shrine to assist him in his period of internship. He very much wanted to come to this particular shrine and had even enhanced his position by taking on a private research project (in addition to his regular university studies and examinations) concerning a family with shrine connections. Without a doubt, he knew far more about the shrine's history and its founders than did most of the priests, and yet time and again I saw him rebuffed through the stiff formality of perfunctory greetings and unacknowledged gifts. His case was all the more poignant because he did not come from a family with landholdings or high social status; instead, he had come to the priesthood after several years as a salaryman because of what he called a "spiritual awareness" *(seishin-teki no ishiki)* that had grown within him. One might assume that Japanese Buddhism, with its long tradition of providing refuge and sanctuary to a wide range of individuals from all social classes, would be more accommodating. However, I would caution against such a generalization. Again it is necessary to assess the particular temple to which the petition for an internship is made, the rank and status of its head priests, and its current economic or social situation.

10. Clark 1989, Cole 1979, Dore and Sako 1989, Friedman 1988, and Rohlen 1974 are only a few of the numerous works and ethnographies of Japanese workplaces. Kondo's 1990 book is the current paradigm for discussions of the workplace. The conclusions of the earlier studies run into difficulty when faced with workplaces (such as software developers, production studios for comics, or nightclubs and bars) whose employees change frequently.

11. It would be less than fair to omit the groundskeeper's voice from this discussion. A hard and diligent worker, he complains that the younger priests "know nothing about how to treat tools. If they get a phone call, they just drop their tool where they are standing and forget all about it." Like many people his age who find themselves working with people from a younger generation, he is quick to take examples (such as the tools) and find in them everything wrong with the current day and age. Generational differences in Japan are extreme, and the vehemence with which older people refer to the younger generation's comfort, lack of suffering, high expectations, *amae* or dependency, and so on is not to be dismissed. For other examinations of aspects of this topic, see Kumagai 1984, Nelson 1996b, P. Smith 1996, and Bumiller 1996.

12. The priests are quite sensitive about making public information on the shrine's budget and expenses, investments, average salary, and the like. However, the shrine's general operating fund can be estimated based on income received from the November children's holiday of "seven-five-three" *(shichi-go-san)* events. I was told this figure represented around 2.5 percent of the shrine's yearly income, which would create a budget of ¥189,200,000 or U.S. $1,718,180 (¥110 = $1).

13. It is instructive to look at an early version of the Matsushita Electric Company's Employee's Code (as cited in Pascal and Athos 1981) for its blending of secular and spiritual themes as well as its paternalistic linkage of the company to the nation. Representative of "Japan Incorporated" in the early 1980s, Matsushita's business principles were "To recognize our responsibilities as industrialists, to foster progress, to promote the general welfare of society, and to devote ourselves to the further development of world culture." More specifically, in regard to the employees of the company: "Progress and development can be realized only through the combined efforts and cooperation of each member of our Company. Each of us, therefore, shall keep this idea constantly in mind as we devote ourselves to the continuous improvement of our Company." Seven "spiritual" values are then reaffirmed to signal the moral universe within which the company and its employees operate: (1) national service through industry, (2) fairness, (3) harmony and cooperation, (4) struggle for betterment, (5) courtesy and humility, (6) adjustment and assimilation, and (7) gratitude.

By comparison, the shrine's code is far less programmatic, nationalistic, and paternalistic. Yet some of the same elements appear in both, a dimension of institutional life that conceals its contrived construction by positing an almost transcendental approach to its place in the world. The founder and president of the company, Matsushita Konosuke, was a frequent and generous benefactor of a number of shrines in south central Japan, including Ise and Tsubaki.

14. It would not be an overstatement to say that virtually every public policy, event, and appeal enacted since this incident has been sensitive to the need for controlling and, when possible, repairing the damage it caused to the reputation of Kamigamo Shrine. In a word, the everyday defensiveness of a Shinto shrine is multiplied when confronted by real and divisive controversies. And yet, it is in moments of controversy and crisis that a cultural order stands most revealed and is most revealing about the individuals that make it work. By relating this incident, I risk alienating certain members of the shrine's administrative and governing elite, yet because it was public knowledge during the time of its occurrence, and because other responsible members of the shrine spoke openly about it, I have no qualms about conveying its general outline. Kamigamo Shrine would not be in the advantageous social and political position it is in today without the dynamic of change this incident inadvertently initiated.

15. Ishida Takeshi (in Krauss et al. 1984: 17) has proposed a four-part schematic that compartmentalizes conflict according to terms first suggested by Doi. He focuses on the group vis-à-vis its own members *(uchi)* and outsiders *(soto),* and the arena in which the conflict is occurring, whether on the surface *(omote)* or backstage and informal *(ura).* For my purposes in thinking about shrine affairs, it is important to stress two difficulties that Ishida himself recognizes with this typology. First, it is all too easy to fall into the trap of cultural determinism by seeing these categories as unique to political culture. Second, posited as traits shared by all Japanese, they take on an ahistorical quality that does not account for the fast-changing nature of contemporary society. In the case of Kamigamo, the insider-outsider dichotomy breaks down because of individuals traversing areas supposed to be separate. Similarly, the *omote-ura* spatial metaphor works in some cases, such as the inner and outer shrine precincts, but again there are numerous examples of a nonspatial or conceptual nature— such as "on stage" rehearsals for important ritual events—that render the distinction fuzzy at best (see also Kato 1968).

16. People engaged in agriculture, as was the head *sōdai,* seem more inclined to convey initial disagreement through nonexpressive means. As Lebra comments, this silence is a complex mix of "compliance, endurance, grudge, and grievance" (Krauss et al. 1984: 44). Robert Smith's classic account (1978) of Kurusu villagers showing disagreement by silence regarding plans for a chicken processing factory to be built in their village is a prime example. My own experience based on a year's residence in a Kyushu farming village near Nagasaki also supports this view.

17. I am aware that much remains to be said about this incident. On what precise legal grounds was the case decided? What legal expenses did the shrine incur and how were these covered? To what extent was the Jinja Honchō involved in the

proceedings, both formally and behind the scenes? The list of questions is long and potentially informative about one of the ways conflict is resolved in Japan. However, because even mentioning this incident causes feelings of anger, betrayal, suspicion, and hostility on the part of some priests and defensive posturing to protect the shrine's image on the part of others, it will take some time (and the passing of several strong-willed individuals) before the incident can be examined in the kind of detail and depth required.

18. In the corporate world, after-hours drinking and eating *(tsukiai)* is as much a part of one's duties as is deskwork. In shrine affairs too, a similar tradition exists in the *naorai* postritual reception for those who participated. *Naorai* can be limited only to the priests in a particular ritual—as in the case of the monthly *tsukinami-sai*—when it is held in a narrow chamber near the Middle Gate. Or, as is the case at most shrines, the reception may begin formally, but it often progresses to general drunkenness and contentious camaraderie. On occasions when the group was large, I noticed that at least five priests (but not the authority figure of the head priest, who usually departed not long after his speech) would stay until the very end, serving beer and sake in liberal amounts and generally listening to opinions and complaints about shrine administration, community or city politics, or other topics that might intersect with shrine affairs.

CHAPTER 6: PERFORMING RITUAL

1. Statements highlighting one's particular discipline too often turn into theoretical ax grinding or, as Elizabeth Collins once commented, "slash-and-burn" scholarship that wastes others' work for the glory of one's own (personal communication). Here my intention is to highlight insights from the various approaches of anthropology to the world that have made a tremendous difference in my life and understanding. For example, before beginning my graduate studies, I observed a year's worth of rituals at a major Shinto shrine (Nelson 1996b). It was not until the very end of the year that I realized the shrine I was seeing was nothing at all like the shrine that was really there. For one thing, I was unaware of being used as a pawn between two warring factions of priests. Furthermore, many of the rituals I had been told were authentically ancient were, in fact, continually being tinkered with by the head priest to achieve greater dramatic effect. I felt like the narrator in Lawrence Durrell's *Alexandria Quartet* who finished and distributed to a trusted friend a confessional manuscript about his disastrous love affair in pre–World War II Alexandria, Egypt. In return, he received from his friend a book-length commentary *(Balthazaar)* that slowly yet irrevocably turned inside out his carefully constructed opinions, characters, and perceptions of events. Fortunately for me, anthropology came along to offer ways to think about what I had been through that made me feel less of a simpleton.

2. See Geertz' article on the Balinese funeral (1974) or Meyerhoff's classic article on an elderly man suddenly dying at his birthday party (1984) as examples of "real life" intruding upon ritual drama.

3. For a fuller discussion, one might start with Ishizaki's *Nihon no kamigami* (1992:251–319), Inoue Kiyoshi's *Nihon no rekishi* (1969), or the *Shintō jiten* entry (1994). An English-language attempt to trace the origins of the term *"kami"* (and find common ground with Christian concepts) is Keane 1980.

4. As discussed in Chapter 4, there is nothing particularly novel about such acts of appropriation. The Roman emperor Constantine, some twenty years after he reportedly converted to Christianity, continued to use the symbolism of Apollo on his coins and referred to himself as "sol invictus." David Wright (1992) argues that he did so not because of love for the symbolism, but because of the need to continue using iconography already familiar to the majority of his tax-paying subjects. For a highly spirited though contentious reading of Korean cultural contributions appropriated by Japanese social and political "architects," see Covell and Covell 1984.

5. Richard Pilgrim (1986) has suggested that Shinto worship—with its waiting for, receiving, and then attending to the temporary presence of *kami* within a place that is fundamentally void—has given Japanese culture one of its most striking qualities: the concept and expression of negative time and space *(ma)*. Pilgrim argues that negative space and time convey a metaphysical propensity for possession, manifestation, resignation, or acceptance—all appropriate as terms descriptive of the relationship of communities to their deities. From an anthropological perspective, the categories of sacred place in Shinto are not "substantive" (in the sense that waterfalls, mountains, trees, or clearings everywhere are ubiquitously sacred) but rather "situational," and can be thought of as conceptual "maps and labels that indicate as well as assert difference" (J. Smith 1987:104). As discussed in Chapter 3, with any ordering of the world or positioning of its topological attributes into symbolic constructs, researchers need to think of this process as having been negotiated by political and/or religious elites. Without this understanding, we all too easily become theologians if we assert the "primacy of meaning without regard for the discursive processes by which meanings are constructed" (Asad 1983:246).

6. From the Taihō reforms (701 C.E.) forward, imperial *kami*-worship began to incorporate Chinese-style words and processes (many of which were based in Taoist magical practices) administered by an immigrant priestly clan called the Kawachi no Fumi-be (Ueda 1979:56). Until this time, the Nakatomi had had a monopoly on supplying prayers of purification (one of which is still part of contemporary rituals; see Chapter 7, June 30) for the emperor and the state. But with the promotion of the Kawachi clan's style of purificatory incantations *(majinai no harae),* which drew on continental (as opposed to Yamato) vocabulary and sentence structures, a greater range and scope was hoped for. For reasons unknown, when the ruler Jitto died (702 C.E.), the Nakatomi were not permitted to perform their prayer, but the

Kawachi no Fumi-be priests were. Ueda believes that Taoist concepts of *tenno* (emperor), *shintō, kannagara* (way of the spirits), and even *kami* all found their way into both imperial and local forms of *kami*-worship, or what is now thought of as Shinto, around this time. Thus, it is not necessary (or even possible) to think of Shinto as uniquely Japanese (Kuroda 1981) or, as one encounters frequently in the literature (and as I have argued against in Nelson 1996b : 7), an "indigenous" religious system.

One final related point on this topic involves a rethinking of purificatory rites for the contemporary age. Ueda Kenji feels that the esoteric practices and language of *harae* are anachronistic and that its connection to Korean and Chinese sources renders it too much a product of syncretization (1991 : 104). He suggests that contemporary theologians avoid integrating the old Nakatomi *harae* purifications with other concerns such as modernizing rituals and festivals. Of course, he says, the classic purifications need some position in the new Shinto theology, but not a prominent one. Thus, while the veneration shown the old purification rituals is still considerable, leading scholars (with powerful institutional backing) are not beyond seeing them as impediments to be circumvented before their agendas of systematizing and streamlining shrine Shinto can proceed effectively.

7. *"Makoto"* is a term difficult to translate into a direct English equivalent but roughly embodies Western concepts of honesty, sincerity, and conscientiousness (Ross 1965 : 108). However, according to the numerous priests I spoke with, there is nothing complex about its practice: if an individual searches his or her heart while at the same time confronting outer situations, the basic balance and goodness of human beings will prevail. When it does not, the problem is not the fault of the individual but of the imposing external influences, making it necessary to restore one's "healthy" and "balanced" condition. This is accomplished via rituals that remind people of how things should be in the proper, archetypal pattern of social life. It is a neat and orderly arrangement: the result for Japanese religious and secular society is a flexible category of purity and impurity that absorbs extreme or rigid notions of good and bad, and depends as much on intention as on direct environmental and situational influences. The implications this arrangement poses for industrial or political policy-making are many and varied (see Nelson 1992). Indeed, this tendency has drawn sharp criticism from the West, as commentators (ranging from Robert Bellah in 1957, to Koschmann in 1978, to Karel van Wolferen in 1989) accuse the Japanese of being without transcendent principles that can order individual behavior or trade policies along lines of fairness, mutual good, or justice. An alternative reading of *makoto* is that of van Wolferen (1989 : 252), who sees it as a coercive practice whereby one's thinking and emotions are forced to comply with what is expected by the surrounding society or situation—"rearranging one's conscience to fit one's demeanor." Since an individual is always responding to what van Wolferen sees as "socio-political exigencies" and often advances or fails based on this outcome, *makoto* becomes but another strategy for ensuring one's survival in Japanese society by suppressing the self.

8. Several of the priests I talked to in Nagasaki expressed reservations about using the same wand of purification over and over, especially those who felt it to be a kind of magnet that drew out impurities. There was no consensus of opinion about exactly how it worked—whether as a magnet, a neutralizer, or a strong "wind" that dispersed these unseen defilements—but all agreed that to make a new one for each and every ritual would be extremely time-consuming although theoretically proper (Nelson 1996b: 117). It is likely, however, that earlier forms of ritual practice did use a new wand each time. It is also recorded that the codes of bodily cleanliness for priests were much stricter than they are today (see Herbert 1967) and required stream or sea purification before each ritual as well as acts of abstention. It must be remembered that, unlike the Buddhist clergy, there was no central organization controlling all ritual practices at all Shinto shrines, so wide latitudes of interpretation about purification were and still are common. Miyoshi Masao has remarked that within the purificatory practices of Shinto—in which "ritual bathing is meant to cleanse away not only the evil residuals of the past but the past itself"— can be found the "postmodern erasure of historicity" (1991: 15).

9. Further evidence could be found in areas of occupational status, certain linguistic forms and usages, and even the architectural design of living structures so as to clearly delineate what is pure and life-enhancing from what is thought to be, depending on the social context, defiled or dangerous. The Japanese house, for instance, with its raised living areas as a demarcation of inner and outer domains, clearly embodies broader cultural values about cleanliness (pure) and dirt (profane).

10. These offerings are distinguished between those that the *kami* will actually "consume" and those it will simply appreciate for aesthetic beauty. The essential quality of Japanese cuisine, with its attention to detail (such as food in harmony with the seasons, the shape of the dish, the coordination of colors, or having tastes resonate with each other), may all be said to derive from Shinto food offerings (Grapard 1983). See Chapter 7, note 17, for a listing of some important food offerings presented during the Aoi Festival.

11. This same emphasis on the correctness of reciting ritual prayers was carried to an extreme in the 1930s and 1940s as ceremonial readings of the Imperial Rescript on Education, one of the principal documents articulating Japan's wartime nationalism (see Gauntlett 1949), took on the quality of *norito*. School principals were required to read it while wearing formal clothing and white gloves, with the entire school body assembled. A mistake was cause for humiliation, censure, or, in some cases, even suicide (Delmer Brown, personal communication). Brown comments that logically, since *norito* reflect the concerns of a particular time and place, a history of Shinto should center on changes in the social concerns and wording of these prayers. However, after extended research at two major shrines, I have yet to be shown a single text. Trying diplomatically to refuse one of my many requests, a priest at Kamigamo said, "*Norito* is like the flame of a candle; once finished, there is nothing that can be studied, held in the hand, or pondered." While this in-

accessibility may be agonizing for religious historians, who rely so heavily on texts, a cultural anthropologist must accept it as a valid account of a religious reality and try to respect it. At the same time, this protective attitude regarding *norito* (and other aspects of shrine Shinto practice) needs to be placed within broader frames of reference about the maintenance of tradition and how institutional as well as individual power is perpetuated. Teeuwen reports that *norito* reverted to their prewar style of delivery and form following the implementation of new rules for rituals in 1971 (1996:184).

12. Despite the importance given to the language and power of words in the *norito,* it should be remembered that Shinto has no "holy" book, a vehicle that Weber saw as essential to a religion for transferring meaning, imparting stability, and providing the basis for proselytization. The sacred texts of the world's great religious traditions were, until recently, written in language inaccessible to the common person and valued more for what they were thought to contain than for what they actually said (Davis 1982:5). Lay parishioners in attendance at a Shinto ritual are usually unable to hear clearly what is said or to understand the majority of the archaic expressions and language, but they are well aware of the reason for the ritual in the first place. Thus, they can frame a *norito*'s spoken words with a certain degree of thematic coherence.

13. The offenses Susano-o committed are associated with the breach of orderly agricultural practices, such as skinning animals alive and breaking irrigation channels. Though these were probably the most important, he also committed social and cultural violations as well, one of the more graphic being the delight he took in flinging his own excrement around a ritual hall used for honoring the harvest's first fruits (see Philippi's *Kojiki* [1968: bk. 1, ch. 17]).

14. It is interesting that in the original text this dance was a case of spirit possession causing the dancing *kami* to "expose her breasts and push her skirt band down to her genitals" (Philippi 1968:84). A number of accounts from various peoples show that exhibitionism was used in religious rites not only to drive away undesirable influences, but also to amuse, entertain, and impart vitality to the divine powers (see Yusa 1994).

15. Not all shrines enact the *tamagushi* offerings and some will employ them for certain occasions but not for others. At Kamigamo, for example, the *tamagushi* is used only at services held at subordinate shrines located outside the inner precincts. There is still "audience participation," however, as all shrines, to my knowledge, allow worshipers to perform the *kashiwade* hand clapping either after the *miko* dance or, as at Kamigamo, immediately after the *norito.*

CHAPTER 7: KAMIGAMO'S YEARLY RITUAL CYCLE

1. Despite the large numbers of people participating in New Year's shrine visitations, nearly eighty-seven million in 1998, there are some who see this cultural

and social trend not as a retention of traditions but as a loss. When the Western calendar was adopted in Meiji 5 (1873), celebrations that had been focused on the seasonality, equinoxes, and solstices of the lunar calendar were thrown into disarray. Sonoda remarks that New Year's festivities (oshōgatsu) were originally centered on the family, with rituals conducted at home. Today, he says, this tradition has been "lost," and so people go to shrines instead to try and find that same "warm" feeling once created by family (1990:14). Many people will worship first at their neighborhood shrine, then go to a larger, more famous site the following day. In recent years, transportation corporations have been promoting picturesque shrines along routes they service in an attempt to capitalize on what Fujii Masao calls "a religiously floating population" (cited in Reader 1991:72).

2. Bugaku is considered one of the forms of gagaku, ceremonial court music. With origins in China, India, and Korea, the two main expressions of gagaku are tōgaku (originating in T'ang China, 618–907 C.E.) and komagaku from the Silla, Koguryo, and Paekche kingdoms of ancient Korea. Of the two main forms, komagaku has more pieces available for performance (Kodansha Illustrated Encyclopedia of Japan 1995:437).

3. To encourage greater participation, some city governments have given away trips to ski resorts or Tokyo Disneyland, or prizes covering the considerable costs of putting on and fitting a kimono. When the Tottori city government tried to move the seijin-shiki to August to circumvent the extravagance of paying for kimono and the like, the city's kimono retailers, kimono rental shops, beauty parlors, and photographers banded together and established a shin-seijin-shiki (new coming-of-age rite). From 1980 to 1991 two rival events were held in the city, but the persistence of the retailers gradually won them back their clientele, so that by 1991 85 percent came to the January seijin-shiki, forcing the city government to cancel the August ceremony.

4. Two weeks earlier in an experiment with internationalization, a number of foreign researchers and educators had been invited to the shrine to participate in a tsukinami-sai and have the opportunity to talk directly to the priests. One woman was astounded to learn that there are funeral rites in shrine Shinto and always have been, contrary to what she had been teaching for seven years! By and large, shrines today follow the guidelines proposed by the Jinja Honchō concerning funerary rites. Although there are similarities between the standard Shinto ritual, such as that performed for the tsukinami-sai, and the funeral ceremony, there are important differences. First, although a purification is performed at the beginning of the funeral rite for the ritual objects and participants (but, at the cemetery, there is no harae for the grave itself), it is seen as having little effect within the more encompassing atmosphere of death. Still, it must be performed. Next, the norito invocation is tailored to the needs of the family and the general situation, corresponding to the contextuality of all norito. However, at no point does the priest call either the spirit of the deceased or that of a particular kami to be present. Finally, tamagushi are offered by

both the priest and family members. In the graveside ritual I observed, a senior family member removed the *shide* paper attached to the *tamagushi* and affixed it to a floral wreath that remained on the grave.

After these formal rites are completed, once again local culture asserts a variety of ways to offset and nullify the effects of defilement. Most common is throwing salt over one's shoulder or making a small mound of salt outside the door to one's house and then stepping on it before entering. Several priests mentioned they also gargle with salty water at the earliest opportunity. Those familiar with stories in the *Kojiki* and the Nakatomi clan's *norito* of Great Purification in the *Engi shiki* can connect the contemporary use of salt to the purificatory powers of the ocean as set forth in the early myths.

Another interesting aspect of Shinto funerary rites was the location of cemeteries for priests and Kamo clan members. As at shrines elsewhere in Japan for over a thousand years, Kamigamo Shrine's cemetery was affiliated with a Buddhist temple (not on the shrine grounds). The location had to be one close to a river so the souls of individuals could travel to the ocean to be purified. Although priests say the gravesite did not come under the temple's spiritual jurisdiction, one can assume that until very recently there was little distinction in this or that grave, just as there was little distinction about whether the Buddhas or *kami* were involved in providing benefits to human beings. However, in the Taisho period, because of work on levees containing the Kamo River, part of the shrine's cemetery was moved to Saihō-ji on the flanks of Mount Funeyama and the other part to the Shōden-ji precincts (controlled by the Mori family, which also has strong Shinto ties). Here, one can look across the valley to the east and see the shrine as well as the river—an auspicious place for ancestors. And yet, unlike the Buddhist cemeteries, which were cared for by living relatives, the Kamigamo part of Saihō-ji's cemetery was, at the time of my visit, forlorn and unkept, with visitors and family members coming only at the equinoxes. My conclusion from the appearance of this cemetery was that, for those somewhat exceptional families considering themselves more or less exclusively Shinto, the veneration of ancestors takes place at one's home altar *(kamidana)* and not at the site of the grave itself. A rough sampling of ten Kamo families within the shrine's precincts confirmed my hypothesis and evoked a response that summed up the opinions of other individuals: "Why should I go to a place like that? The soul isn't there anyway, and, besides, I risk being attacked by all kinds of defilements, maybe even an evil spirit. Weren't you afraid?"

5. As I have mentioned elsewhere in this study, I am passing over particular details of the shrine's long history, such as the event in which six temples were expelled from shrine grounds before the Meiji separation of Shinto and Buddhism. It will most likely be discussed at length in the authorized history of Kamigamo Shrine to be published by the administration in the near future.

6. I will long remember this particular *naorai* because of several members of the audience, who had planned in advance to be ready to present their opinions to the

priests about how subsequent *mitama matsuri* might better be conducted. Of particular concern to them was the lack of reference to the emperor and Kamigamo's close connection to the imperial court, an association in which they had invested self-identity and through which they derived considerable emotional satisfaction. After several rounds of sake (and the departure of the head and associate head priests), two groups of four men each cornered two priests in different parts of the room to complain loudly and vehemently about this oversight. The priests did nothing to defend the thematic content of the ritual, but neither did they assign blame to the head or associate head priest; I watched for some time as they stoically endured tirades and accusations. When I asked them later how they felt about these "attacks," one said he basically agreed with their point of view, while the other said the men were just drunk and could not be taken seriously.

7. Dundes and Falassi (1976) provide a fascinating account of another symbolic complex associated with horses, also referencing power and fertility, in their study of the *palio* of Sienna, Italy.

8. The institutionalization of this event came during the early twelfth century, when twenty local areas (all of which were part of Kamigamo's *shōen* estate holdings) were designated as suppliers of horses for the event. These *shōen* are said to have been given to the shrine by Emperor Horikawa (1079–1107): (1) Mimasaka (north Okayama region), (2) Kaga (Kanazawa region), (3) Harima (Hyōgo), (4) Noto (Noto peninsula), (5) Awa (Tokushima region), (6) Mino (Aichi prefecture), (7) Ōmi (Shiga prefecture), (8) Wakasa (Fukui prefecture), (9) Awaji (Awaji island), (10) Izumo (Shimane prefecture), (11) Bizen (south Okayama), (12) Yamashiro (north Kyoto), (13) Tamba (north Kyoto), (14) Izumi (south Osaka area), (15) Suō (Yamaguchi area), (16) Io (Eihime prefecture), (17) Owari (Aichi prefecture), (18) Hōki (Shimane prefecture), (19) Mikawa (Aichi prefecture), (20) Bizen (eastern Okayama) (Kamo Wake Ikazuchi Jinja 1993).

9. This story has become part of the public perception of the running of the racehorses—promoted in a shrine pamphlet and told over loudspeakers in recent years. While interesting in itself, the subtext is twofold: the ritual commanded the presence of some of Japanese history's greatest luminaries, and even someone of Nobunaga's stature and notoriously vengeful character could not sway the Kamo people from their traditions.

10. Although I heard of no injuries incurred by the audience, in the early 1980s a senior Kamo priest from the shrine was kicked in the stomach during the *kanmuri-awase* (to be discussed in the text below) and taken away in an ambulance. He was operated on at once and made a partial recovery; however, other physical complications developed and, a year and a half later, the man unfortunately died.

11. I will not describe the exact route to the ritual site or its location except to say that it is not, as the priests repeatedly told me, at Kōyama. Although I made no prior agreement with the priests to withhold this information, I wish to assist in the preservation of this ritual that is endangered in a variety of ways. In 1992, two cam-

era crews (one from Tokyo TV and the other from the Jinja Honchō) were present in the courtyard to film the opening procession. Neither crew was permitted to accompany the procession, nor were they allowed access to the inner shrine. The director working under Jinja Honchō auspices was furious about being unable to film the placement of the newly charged *goshintai* within the shrine and the significance this held for the coming Aoi Festival. When he complained loudly (and rudely) to one of the priests that he would have to tell the Honchō about Kamigamo's noncooperation with the film project, the priest said simply that there was nothing he could do about it. No apologies were made for the exclusion of either of the film crews.

12. The *mikage-sai* of Shimogamo Jinja, held on the morning of May 12, intends the same result as Kamigamo's *miare-sai:* to fetch the fresh and rejuvenating numina of the *kami* (in this case Takenotsumi-no-mikoto and Tamayorihime) from the mountains and bring it to the shrine, the imperial court (via the shrine), and the community. Rather than the continuing secrecy of Kamigamo's *miare-sai,* the *mikage-sai* has apparently opted for the benefits of wide participation. Since Mikage mountain is some distance from Shimogamo, participants originally rode horses or walked to the site. Today, the priests come in private cars, while those in the general procession are bussed to within easy walking distance of the small mountainside shrine. After assembling below the lower torii, the priests lead a colorful array of men dressed in Edo period costumes, most of whom appear to be enjoying the outing. After reaching the shrine around midday, the priests go within the inner courtyard, which is then veiled from further public view by an orange and black cloth curtain. The other participants, shielded from sight by blue and white striped bunting, have box lunches and bottles of beer and sake waiting for them. Aided by a blustery wind that blew the inner compound's veiling curtains, I was able to see that the priests donned white gauze masks and white gloves as they approached the small Honden (to Tamayorihime) and Gonden (to Taketsunumi) to which the *kami* had been summoned. In the past, a horse played a key role in this ritual within the inner courtyard, but I am uncertain when its use was discontinued. The doors were opened carefully and, while everyone within the courtyard bowed low (the solemnity of the inner scene contrasts with the laughter and shouting of the other participants outside), the head priest of Shimogamo reached in and gently picked up a single *aoi* flower that he then shielded with his robes before placing it in a small wooden box. The container was covered with white silk and left on a pedestal before the Honden. The same procedure was repeated for the second sanctuary. Each box was again wrapped in white silk and handled by men dressed all in white, including face masks and gloves. By this time, the outside participants had assembled and prepared to follow the priests from the inner courtyard back down the hillside, with the box of the *goshintai* held slightly aloft. Just outside the lower torii, a *mikoshi* awaited, borne on the back of a flatbed truck rather than carried by bearers.

13. These offerings were called *"mitegura"* and usually consisted of food, drink, clothes, and utensils of everyday ritual or common use. At the Kamo-sai, however, the *mitegura* consists only of silk and material for clothes.

14. Ponsonby-Fane, the translator of the *Saimon,* is regarded by most scholars as an eccentric dilettante who squandered his family's wealth in Japan. Still, his long residence in Kyoto helped him gain access to many important documents. The Japanese government in the 1930s was concerned with justifying itself both at home and abroad, and Ponsonby-Fane played a role in this agenda that benefited himself and the government. Thus, while his translation of the *chokushi*'s prayer may not be entirely accurate from a scholarly point of view, it does give the reader a flavor of the imperial message to the deities and, I think, conveys its primary intention.

15. Decisions to cancel the procession to Kamigamo as well as other parts of the *shatō no gi* proceedings because of heavy rain in 1991 and 1992 led to considerable unhappiness on the part of Kamigamo's parishioners' group. When I inquired if there were reasons other than rain for the parade's cancellation, I learned from a priest that the decision involved the cost of dry cleaning the many costumes of the participants. Intervention by the tourist board during the 1970s forged an agreement whereby the procession could still be held on the sixteenth strictly for show. The Kamo descendants, however, felt the Aoi Festival is pointless without the final running of the horses (to be discussed in the text below). A Kamo elder angrily responded: "So what? We don't care if they cancel the procession. It is mostly just a bunch of college kids making extra money who yell *banzai* when the procession is cancelled and they don't have to walk any more. But the *hashiri uma no gi* must be held! That is what the *kami* demands. I'll worry the whole year that something bad is going to happen because we weren't permitted to do that part of the festival."

16. Since Japan has gradually shifted its priorities away from agriculture to become a leader in world manufacturing, the agricultural underpinnings of the Aoi Festival would appear, from a functional perspective, to be irrelevant to an urban society such as Kyoto. Yet the number of people who see the event (rising steadily each year from 37,000 in 1955 to 110,000 in 1991 and 145,000 in 1996), the traffic congestion it causes, and the amount of money involved in staging it attest to its importance as an event evoking over a thousand years of cultural history and cultural politics, not to mention its value as an entertaining public spectacle. I am grateful to Mr. Takahashi for these figures provided by the Kyoto police department to his staff at the Kyoto City Tourist Organization .

17. Preparation of the 160 different food offerings for the Kamo-sai takes a day and a night and is carried out with the aid of an early Meiji period text. The complexity and style of presentation deserves more than the cursory treatment I give here. The *shinsen* offerings are presented in two ways—the *geijin* and *naijin shinsen* (for the Kamo deities) are arranged on individual plates, and the *niwazumi shinsen* (for visiting *kami*) are placed in a large red-lacquered container that must be carried

by two bearers. (Below I use English equivalents, where I could find them, for some of the food offerings.)

(1) rice cakes *(mochi)* tied together with stalks of wild Indian rice (ten items), (2) carp, (3) pheasant, (4) red snapper (five), (5) white radishes (five), (6) lily bulbs *(yurine)* (five), (7) eggplant, (8) flying-fish (all semidried) (fifty), (9) dried seaweed (ten varieties), (10) siskin *(hiwada-no-saji),* (11) mackerel, (12) white rice, (13) onions (Kamigamo is supposedly the only shrine to use onions as *shinsen),* (14) *hiwada-no-chimaki,* (15) a wild rose, (16) sweetfish *(aiyu)* from Adogawa village on Lake Biwa, (17) offerings for the guardian lions/dogs before the Honden and the Gonden, (18) rice wine sake, called *okusuri* in this context. In the *niwazumi shinsen* lacquered container, stacked in five layers separated by pine boughs brought from Kōyama, are 120 kinds of offerings. Many replicate the *geijin shinsen* (with the exception of the onions and the pheasant), but there are also differences. For example, additional fish include salmon, dried cuttlefish, clams, horse-mackerel, bonito, *nushi,* saury pike, and so on, layer upon layer. Because of rain during the 1991 and 1992 festivals, the lid of this container was never removed during the *kensen* food offering in the preliminary ritual.

In response to a question about what is done with all this food, the priest in charge of its preparation said matter-of-factly that it is all buried. When the questioner persisted that surely it was not *all* buried, the priest said that what could be salvaged after two days of humid, warm weather was distributed among the priests and their families but that the raw foods were disposed of.

Formerly, the pottery conveying the offerings was also buried. Made exclusively for the shrine in the northern village of Kino (known for its long tradition of Korean-style pottery and thus another possible link between the shrine and Korean immigrants before its incorporation into the imperial system in 678), the last artisan making this unfired and unglazed ware has recently died, so the dishes are now washed and recycled. The impression of an oak leaf distinguishes some of these small vessels (called *haji*), while others bear the imprint of cloth where the potter's elbow was used to curve the plate properly. Some of the other offerings dishes without imprints have an oak leaf placed between the food and plate, recalling early ritual practices that used leaves in place of clay plates. For more on Shinto food offerings, see Iwai and Niwai 1981; *Shintō jiten* 1994:205.

18. The lecturer, Edani Hiroshi of the Heian Museum in Kyoto, presented a strong case for Kamo ties to the Korean peninsula based on technology of the fifth and sixth centuries used for ice production. He stated flatly that the Kamo people were in charge of making ice for the imperial household. They did this by digging chambers in the earth: large stone-lined pits *(himuro)* where ice could be stored through the hot summer months. Excavations have been carried out at sites such as Haibara (a main stop on the Kintetsu line), Keishu (near the site of the present-day Heian Museum), and near Kamigamo, with the scattered location of these sites revealing considerable Kamo settlement in areas other than northern Kyoto. This

technology has its origins in Korea, in such places as the castle site of Hangetsu and two sites east of Seoul along the Kanko (literally "east ice place") River. Edani also noted a model of a *himuro* ice pit that was found in imperial burial chambers in Korea. Although he did not specifically mention a direct link between the Korean-style *himuro* and those in Japan, the inference was clear that this transfer of technology did not happen by itself. Whether the skill was brought to Japan by Korean immigrants who later came to be known as Kamo is a matter of circumstantial evidence. Once the practice became established in Yamato-Japan, there was even a court department regulating *himuro* production, recounted in the *Engi shiki* as having occurred during the reign of Nintoku (313 C.E.).

19. The months of June, October, and November are currently promoted as "wedding seasons" in Japan. A huge industry has grown and profited immensely from this postwar phenomenon (see Edwards 1989; Goldstein-Gidoni 1997).

20. When I requested permission from the associate head priest to interview briefly some of the *shichi-go-san mairi* visitors for this study, he was curious about what I would ask them. I told him I was interested primarily in why they decided to make a visit to the shrine. "That's not the question to ask," he said, "because what they are doing is a matter of course *(atarimae)*. What you should ask them is why they came to Kamigamo for *shichi-go-san mairi*." And so I did, with these representative responses out of twenty-five interviews:

> Because there's a horse and the standing sand cones; it's a lovely site.
> My parents live nearby. It's convenient for parking. The scenery is beautiful.
> My husband came here when he was this age.
> The parking is convenient. It's a historical place.
> We're not doing *shichi-go-san mairi,* only taking photos for our New Year's cards.
> We live nearby. (eight responses)
> We only come twice a year, at New Year's and now.
> The parking lot is free, and since everything else about this holiday costs money, it's a nice break for a family like us!

SELECT CHARACTER GLOSSARY

agatanushi　県主

ainame-sai　相嘗祭

Amaterasu Ōmikami　天照大御神

aoi　葵

aoi-kaede　葵楓

aoi-zukuri　葵造り

areonna　阿礼女

areotoko　阿礼男

ashizoroe-shiki　足汰式

azuma asobi　東游

baba　馬場

bakufu　幕府

banbetsu　蕃別

be　部

beijū　陪従

bōsai-kankei-sha　防災関係者

bōsōzoku　暴走族

bugaku　舞楽

bunka no shōhinka　文化の商品化

butsumetsu　仏滅

chikai　誓い

chimaki　ちまき

chinkon　鎮魂

chinowa　茅ノ輪

chokkai　直階

choku-sai　勅祭

chokushi　勅使

Chokushiden　勅使殿

chōrei　朝礼

Chūkaku-ha　中核派

daihyō yakuin　代表役員

Daijōkan　太政官

daijō-sai　大嘗祭

dohyō　土俵

do-ikki　土一揆

dōzoku　同族

eboshi　烏帽子

ema　絵馬

enza　円座

feng-shui (Chinese)　風水

fumikesu　踏消す

furusato　ふるさと

futaba-aoi　双葉葵

gagaku　雅楽

ganjō　岩上

gasshō　合掌

Geheiden　外幣殿

gissha　牛車

gohei　御幣

(Go)kitōden　(御)祈祷殿

gomagi　護摩木

gongūji　権宮司

gonnegi　権禰宜

gonseikai　権正階

goriyaku　御利益

gosaimon　御祭文

goshintai　御神体

Gosho　御所

gyōretsu　行列

gūji　宮司

Haiden　拝殿

hairei　拝礼

hakama　袴

hakuba sōran shinji　白馬奏覧神事

hakudatsu suru　剥奪する

hamaya　破魔矢

harae, harai　祓

haraigushi　祓串

Hashidono　橋殿

hatsumōde　初詣

hatsu-u shinji　初卯神事

Heiankyō　平安京

Heiden　幣殿

Heijōkyō　平城京

hi　日

higatanori no gi　日形乗りの儀

himorogi　ひもろぎ (神籬)

himuro　氷室

hinoki　桧

hiōgi　桧扇

hitogata　人形

hōbei no gi　奉幣の儀

hokora　祠

Honden　本殿

Horibashi　祝橋

Hosodono　細殿

ie　家

ippai　一杯

issha no sōran　一社の騒乱

iwasaka　磐境

jichin-sai　地鎮祭

Jingū　神宮

jingūji　神宮寺

jinja　神社

Jinja Honchō　神社本庁

jizō　地蔵

jōe　浄衣

jōkai　浄階

jūni hitoe　十二単

jūyō bunka zai　重要文化財

juyosho　授与所

kadomatsu　門松

kagura　神楽

kaikei-ka　会計課

kakushu gokitō—jichinsai hoka
　　各種御祈祷—地鎮祭他

kami　神

kamidana　神棚

kamigakari　神懸, 神憑

Kamigamo Jinja　上賀茂神社

kami oroshi　神降ろし

Kamo Mioya Jinja　賀茂御祖神社

Kamo Wake Ikazuchi Jinja　賀茂別雷神社

kamutsumori　かむつ森

kanmuri　冠

kannagara　惟神

kannushi　神主

kanpai no gi　乾杯の儀

kanpei taisha　官幣大社

kansha-sai　感謝祭

karasu sumō　烏相撲

karōshi　過労死

kashiwa　柏

kashiwade　柏手

kasō　家相

Katayama Miko Jinja　片山御子神社

katsura　桂

kawai jinja　川合神社

kegare　穢れ

keiba　競馬

keidai-ka　境内課

keihitsu　警蹕

keizu　系図

kencha-sai　献茶祭

kenpeitai　憲兵隊

kenkoku kinen-bi　建国記念日

kensen　献饌

kessai　潔斎

ki　気

kiba minzoku　騎馬民族

Kibune Jinja　貴船神社

kimon　鬼門

kōbetsu　皇別

kodai būmu　古代ブーム

kōhai　後輩

Kojiki　古事記

kōken　後見

kokibashi　扱箸

Kōrei den　皇霊殿

koseki　戸籍

kōshin no gi　降神の儀

kotodama　言霊

kōtsū anzen　交通安全

Kōyama　神山

Kuga Jinja　久我神社

kugatachi　探湯

Kunaichō　宮内庁

kurabe-uma shinji　競馬神事

kurushii toki no kamidanomi　苦しい時の神頼み

kyōchi no gi　競馳の儀

Kyoto Kankō Kyōkai　京都観光協会

kyūchū no gi　宮中の儀

ma　間

makoto　真

majinai　呪

mamorigami　守り神

massha　末社

matsuri　祭

matsurigoto　祭事

Meiji Jingū　明治神宮

meikai　明階

miare-sai　御阿礼祭

mikage-sai　御蔭祭

miko　巫女

mikoshi　御輿

mimizuka　耳塚

misogi　禊

mitama matsuri　御魂まつり

mitanae shinji　御棚会神事

Mitarashi-gawa　御手洗川

mitegura　御幣

miya　宮

miyatsuko　造

mori　森

musha shinji　武射神事

myōjin　明神

nagoshi-barae　夏越祓

Nakaragi-sha　半木社

Nakamon　中門

Nakatomi　中臣

naorai　直会

Nara no ogawa　奈良の小川

negi　禰宜

nenbutsu　念仏

nenjū gyōji　年中行事

Nihongi / Nihon-shoki　日本紀 / 日本書紀

nihonjinron　日本人論

nijū ōken　二重王権

nikkukō taisai　日供講大祭

niiname-sai　新嘗祭

norijiri　乗尻

norito　祝詞

norito-sōjō　祝詞奏上

noroi　呪い

nyokan　女官

ofuda　お札

ogushi　御串

ohaka mairi　お墓参り

okibumi　置文

omairi　お参り

omamori　お守り

omigoromo　小忌衣

omiki　御神酒

omikuji　おみくじ

Omonoi-gawa　御物忌川

Omote senke　表千家

onkei　恩恵

onmyō (on'yō)　陰陽

onmyōdō (on'yōdo)　陰陽道

onnyōdai shubatsu no gi　陰陽代修祓の儀

onryō　怨霊

ōnusa　大幣

osōji-sai　御掃除祭

osonaemono　お供物

Ōta Jinja　大田神社

otaue-sai　御田植え祭

oyagami　祖神

oyo-yo / omikoshi　御輿

rachi　埒

reisai　例祭

riji-kai　理事会

ringi　稟議

Rōmon　楼門

rotō no gi　路頭の儀

saigi　祭儀

saiji-ka　祭事課

saiin　斎院

saiō　斎王

saisei itchi　祭政一致

saisen dorobō　賽銭泥棒

saishi　釵子

sahō　作法

sakaki　榊

sandō　参道

sanpai-sha　参拝者

sanyare-sai　さんやれ祭

sashi chigaeru　刺し違える

sashimuchi　指鞭

sato-kagura　里神楽

seijin-shiki　成人式

seikai　正階

seishin　精神

sekibō　石棒

sekinin yakuin　責任役員

senpai　先輩

senzo　先祖

sessha　摂社

setsubun　節分

shake　社家

shaku　笏

Shamusho　社務所

shatō no gi　社頭の儀

shichi-go-san　七五三

shimenawa　注連縄

Shimogamo Jinja　下鴨神社

shinbetsu　神別

shinboku　神木

shinji　神事

shinkan　神官

shinkō　信仰

shinnen kyōen-sai　新年竟宴祭

shinsen　神饌

shinshoku　神職

Shintō seiji renmei　神道政治連盟

shizen no shōhinka　自然の商品化

shōbu (competition)　勝負

shōbu (iris)　菖蒲

shōen　荘園

shōjō-sai　焼上祭

shomu-ka　庶務課

shōrei no gi　招霊の儀

shōshin no gi　昇神の儀

shubatsu　修祓

shugyō　修行

shukuhaku　宿泊

shukusai　祝祭

Shūkyō hōjinhō　宗教法人法

shunin　主任

sō　惣

sōdai　総代

sōhei　僧兵

sōran　騒乱

sosen-sai　祖先祭

souma no gi　走馬の儀

suruga uta　駿河歌

suzu　鈴

tachi-aoi　立葵

taian　大安

Taihō ritsuryō　大宝律令

taisai　大祭

Taketsunomi no mikoto　建角身命

Tamabashi　玉橋

tamagushi　玉串

tamajari　玉砂利

Tamayorihime　玉依姫

tantō　担当

tatari　たたり／祟り

tatefuda　立札

tatesuna　立砂

temizu no gi　手水の儀

temizusha　手水舎

tenka kokka　天下国家

tennō　天皇

tōban　当番

toge-sai　土解祭

tokonoma　床の間

tokusei ikki　徳政一揆

tone　刀禰

Tongū　頓宮

torii　鳥居

tōsha　当社

Tsuchinoya　土の舎

tsukigatanori no gi　月形乗の儀

tsukinami-sai　月次祭
uji　氏
ujigami　氏神
ujiko　氏子
ujiko sōdai kai　氏子総代会
ura-kimon　裏鬼門
Ura senke　裏千家
urayasu no mai　浦安の舞
ushi no toki mairi　丑の時参り

yaku yoke　厄除け
yakuza　やくざ
yamabushi　山伏
Yamato　大和
yatagarasu　八咫烏
yatoi　雇
yōdo-ka　用度課
yomigaeru　甦る
zendaimimon　前代未聞

WORKS CITED

Abe Masamichi. 1990. *Shinto ga yoku wakaru hon* (A book to understand Shinto well). Tokyo: PHP.

Abe, Takeshi. 1983. Heiankyō. In *The Kodansha Encyclopedia of Japan*. Tokyo: Kodansha Publishing.

Abélès, Marc. 1988. Modern Political Ritual: Ethnography of an Inauguration and a Pilgrimage by President Mitterrand. *Current Anthropology* 29 (3): 391–404.

Abu-Lughod, Lila. 1991. Writing against Culture. In *Recapturing Anthropology: Working in the Present,* ed. Richard Fox. Santa Fe: School of American Research Press.

Alles, Gregory D. 1988. Surface, Space and Intention: The Parthenon and the Kandāriya Mahadeva. *History of Religions* 27 (2): 1–36.

Akazawa, Takeru, and C. Melvin Aikens, eds. 1986. *Prehistoric Hunter-Gatherers in Japan: New Research Methods*. Tokyo: University of Tokyo Press.

Anderson, Benedict. 1983. *Imagined Communities: Reflections on the Origins and Spread of Nationalism*. London: Verso.

Anderson, Jennifer L. 1987. Japanese Tea Ritual: Religion in Practice. *Man* (n.s.), 22:475–498.

———. 1991. An Introduction to Japanese Tea Ritual. Albany: SUNY Press.

Aoki Tamotsu. 1990. *Nihon bunkaron no henyō* (Changes in theorizing Japanese culture). Tokyo: Chūōkōronsha.

Appadurai, Arjun. 1983. The Past as a Scarce Resource. *Man* (n.s.), 16:201–1219.

Asad, Talal. 1983. Anthropological Conceptions of Religion: Reflections on Geertz. *Man* (n.s.), 18:237–259.

Asahi shinbun. 1998. "Tatari" no o-torii, tsui ni itten (Despite a fear of reprisals, large shrine gateway to be relocated). December 12, p. 18.

Ashkenazi, Michael. 1990. Festival Management and the Corporate Analysis of Japanese Society. In *Unwrapping Japan,* ed. E. Ben-Ari and J. Hendry. Manchester: Manchester University Press.

———. 1993. *Matsuri.* Honolulu: University of Hawai'i Press.

Aston, W. G. 1921. *Shinto.* London: Constable.

———, trans. 1978 [1896]. *Nihongi: Chronicles of Japan from the Earliest Times to* A.D. 697. Tokyo: Charles E. Tuttle, reprint edition.

Baker, Alan R. H. 1992. On Ideology and Landscape. In *Ideology and Landscape in Historical Perspective,* ed. Alan Baker. Cambridge: Cambridge University Press.

Basso, Keith H. 1992. "Speaking with Names": Language and Landscape among the Western Apache. In *Rereading Cultural Anthropology,* ed. George Marcus. Durham, N.C.: Duke University Press.

Beer, Jennifer. 1995. Packaged Experiences: Japanese Tours in Southeast Asia. Ph.D. dissertation, Department of Anthropology, University of California, Berkeley.

Befu, Harumi. 1980. The Group Model of Japanese Society and an Alternative. *Rice University Studies* 66 (1): 169–187.

———. 1993. Symbols of Nationalism and Nihonjinron. In *Ideology and Practice,* ed. Roger Goodman. London: Routledge.

Behar, Ruth. 1986. *Santa Maria del Monte.* Princeton: Princeton University Press.

Bell, Catherine. 1992. *Ritual Theory, Ritual Practice.* Oxford: Oxford University Press.

———. 1997. *Ritual: Perspectives and Dimensions.* Oxford: Oxford University Press.

———. 1998. Performance. In *Critical Terms in Religious Studies,* ed. Mark Taylor. Chicago: University of Chicago Press.

Bellah, Robert N. 1957. *Tokugawa Religion: The Values of Pre-industrial Japan.* Glencoe, Ill.: Free Press.

———. 1970. *Beyond Belief.* New York: Harper and Row.

Bernier, Bernard. 1975. *Breaking the Cosmic Circle: Religion in a Japanese Village.* Cornell East Asia Papers 5. Ithaca, N.Y.: Cornell China-Japan Program.

Berry, Elizabeth. 1994. *The Culture of Civil War in Kyoto.* Berkeley: University of California Press.

Bestor, Theodore C. 1988. *Neighborhood Tokyo.* Stanford: Stanford University Press.

———. 1989. Lifestyles and Popular Culture in Urban Japan. In *Handbook of Japanese Popular Culture,* ed. Richard Powers and Hidetoshi Kato. New York: Greenwood Press.

Bix, Herbert P. 1986. *Peasant Protest in Japan, 1590–1884.* New Haven: Yale University Press.

Blake, William. 1971 [1804]. The Book of Milton.. In *The Complete Works of William Blake,* bk. 1, ed. Geoffrey Keynes, 29:5–12. Oxford: Oxford University Press.

Bloch, Maurice. 1974. Symbols, Song, Dance and Features of Articulation. *Archives européenes de sociologie* 15:55–81.

————. 1977. The Past and the Present in the Present. *Man* (n.s.), 12 : 278–92.

————. 1987. Political Implications of Religious Experience. In *Symbolic Textures,* ed. Goran Aijmer. Gothenburg Studies in Social Anthropology No. 10. Gothenburg: ACTA Unversitatis Gothoburgensis.

Bock, Felicia. 1970. *The Engi-shiki: Books 1–12 in Two Volumes.* Tokyo: Sophia University.

————. 1985. *Classical Learning and Taoist Practices in Early Japan.* Tempe: Arizona State University.

Bourdieu, Pierre. 1991. *Language and Symbolic Power.* Cambridge, Mass.: Harvard University Press.

Bownas, Geoffrey. 1963. *Japanese Rainmaking and Other Folk Practices.* London: Allen and Unwin.

Brandes, Stanley. 1988. *Power and Persuasion.* Philadelphia: University of Pennsylvania Press.

Brown, Delmer M. 1971. *Nationalism in Japan: An Introductory Historical Analysis.* Berkeley: University of California Press.

————. 1979. *The Future and the Past: A Translation and Study of the Gukansho, an Interpretive History of Japan Written in 1219.* Trans. Delmer Brown with Ichiro Ishida. Berkeley: University of California Press.

————. 1990. Lectures on Japanese Religion. Pacific School of Religion. Berkeley, Ca.

————. 1993. The Yamato Kingdom. In *The Cambridge History of Japan,* vol. 1, ed. Delmer Brown. Cambridge: Cambridge University Press.

————, ed. 1993. *The Cambridge History of Japan, Volume 1.* Cambridge: Cambridge University Press.

Brown, Delmer M., and James T. Araki, trans. 1964. *Studies in Shinto Thought.* Tokyo: Ministry of Education.

Brown, Delmer M., and Toshiya Torao. 1987. *Chronology of Japan.* Tokyo: Asuka Shobo.

Bumiller, Elisabeth. 1996. *The Secrets of Mariko: A Year in the Life of a Japanese Woman and Her Family.* New York: Random House

Bunkachō, ed. 1988. *Shūkyō nenkan* (A yearbook of religion). Tokyo: Gyōsei.

Bynum, Caroline W., S. Harrell, and P. Richman, eds. 1986. *Gender and Religion.* Boston: Beacon Press.

Calhoun, C. J. 1983. The Radicalism of Tradition. *American Journal of Sociology* 88 (5): 886–914.

Cannadine, David. 1983. The Context, Performance, and Meaning of Ritual: The British Monarchy and the "Invention of Tradition," c. 1820–1977. In *The Invention of Tradition,* ed. E. Hobsbawm and T. Ranger. Cambridge: Cambridge University Press.

Casal, U. A. 1967. *The Five Sacred Festivals of Ancient Japan: Their Symbolism and Historical Development.* Tokyo: Sophia University and Charles E. Tuttle.

Christian, William. 1988 [1972]. *Person and God in a Spanish Valley.* Princeton: Princeton University Press.

Clark, Rodney. 1989. *The Japanese Company.* New Haven: Yale University Press.

Clifford, James. 1988. *The Predicament of Culture.* Cambridge: Harvard Press.

Clifford, James, and George Marcus, eds. 1986. *Writing Culture: The Poetics and Politics of Ethnography.* Berkeley: University of California Press.

Cohen, Alvin P. 1978. Coercing the Rain Deities in Ancient China. *History of Religions* 17 (3/4): 244–265.

Cohen, Anthony P. 1986. Of Symbols and Boundaries, or, Does Ertie's Greatcoat Hold the Key? In *Symbolizing Boundaries: Identity and Diversity in British Cultures,* ed. A.Cohen. Manchester: Manchester University Press.

Cohen, Eric. 1992. Pilgrimage Centers: Concentric and Excentric. *Annals of Tourism Research* 19: 33–50.

Cohen, Percy. 1969. Theories of Myth. *Man* (n.s.), 3: 337–353.

Cohen, Ronald. 1978. Ethnicity: Problem and Focus in Anthropology. *Annual Review of Anthropology* 7: 379–401.

Cole, Robert. 1979. *Work, Mobility, and Participation: A Comparative Study of American and Japanese Industry.* Berkeley: University of California Press.

Comaroff, Jean. 1985. *Body of Power, Spirit of Resistance.* Chicago: University of Chicago Press.

Connerton, Paul. 1989. *How Societies Remember.* Cambridge: Cambridge University Press.

Cosgrove, Denis. 1986. The Geographical Study of Environmental Symbolism: Review and Prospect. Conference paper, twenty-fourth Congresso Italiano, Torino, Italy.

———. 1988. The Geometry of Landscape. In *The Iconography of Landscape,* ed. Denis Cosgrove and Stephen Daniels. Cambridge: Cambridge University Press.

———. 1993. Landscapes and Myths, Gods and Humans. In *Landscape: Politics and Perspectives,* ed. Barbara Bender. Oxford: Berg Publishing.

Covell, Jon C., and Alan Covell. 1984. *Japan's Hidden History: Korean Impact on Japanese Culture.* Elizabeth, N.J.: Hollym International.

Creemers, Wilhelmus H. M. 1976 [1968]. *Shrine Shinto after World War II.* Leiden: E. J. Brill.

Cuyler, Patricia L. 1979. *Sumo: From Rite to Sport.* New York and Tokyo: Weatherhill.

Czaja, Michael. 1974. *Gods of Myth and Stone: Phallicism in Japanese Folk Religion.* New York: Weatherhill.

Dale, Peter N. 1986. *The Myth of Japanese Uniqueness.* New York: St. Martin's Press.

Davis, J. 1982. Introduction. In *Religious Organization and Religious Experience,* ed. J. Davis. A.S.A. Monographs No. 21. London: Academic Press.

Davis, Winston. 1980. *Dōjō: Exorcism and Miracles in Modern Japan.* Stanford: Stanford University Press.

————. 1992. *Japanese Religion and Society: Paradigms of Structure and Change*. Albany, N.Y.: State University of New York Press.

Dean, Kenneth. 1993. *Taoist Ritual and Popular Cults of Southeast China*. Princeton: Princeton University Press.

De Vos, George A. 1973. *Socialization for Achievement*. Berkeley: University of California Press.

————. 1976. Introduction. In *Responses to Change*, ed. George De Vos. New York: D. Van Nostrand Company.

————. 1984. The Failure of Class Consciousness. In *The Incredibility of Western Prophets: the Japanese Religion of Family*. Amsterdam: Universiteit van Amsterdam.

————. 1992. *Social Cohesion and Alienation: Minorities in the United States and Japan*. Boulder: Westview Press.

De Vos, George A., and Takao Sofue. 1984. Religion and Family: Structural and Motivational Relationships. In *Religion and the Family in East Asia*, ed. George De Vos and Takao Sofue. Berkeley: University of California Press.

Dirks, Nicholas. 1994. Ritual as Resistance. In *Culture, History, Power: A Reader in Contemporary Social Theory*, ed. Dirks et al. Princeton: Princeton University Press.

Dirks, Nicholas, Geoff Eley, and Sherry Ortner. 1994. *Culture, History, Power: A Reader in Contemporary Social Theory*. Princeton: Princeton University Press.

Dissanayake, Wimal. 1996. Introduction/Agency and Cultural Understanding: Some Preliminary Remarks. In *Narratives of Agency: Self-Making in India, China, and Japan*, ed. W. Dissanayake. Minneapolis: University of Minnesota Press.

Dore, Ronald P. 1987. *Taking Japan Seriously: A Confucian Perspective on Leading Economic Issues*. Stanford: Stanford University Press.

Dore, Ronald, and M. Sako. 1989. *How the Japanese Learn to Work*. London: Routledge.

Douglas, Mary. 1986. *How Institutions Think*. Syracuse: New York University Press.

Dundes, Alan, and Alessandro Falassi. 1975. *La Terra in Piazza: An Interpretation of the Palio of Sienna*. Berkeley: University of California Press.

Durkheim, Emile. 1963. *Elementary Forms of the Religious Life*. Trans. Joseph Swain. London: Allen and Unwin.

Earhart, H. Byron. 1970a. The Ideal of Nature in Japanese Religion and Its Possible Significance for Environmental Concerns. *Contemporary Religions in Japan* 11 (1/2): 1–26.

————. 1970b. *A Religious Study of the Mount Haguro Sect of Shugendō: An Example of Japanese Mountain Religion*. Monumentica Nipponica. Tokyo: Sophia University.

————. 1984. *Religion in the Japanese Experience: Sources and Interpretations*. Belmont, Calif.: Wadsworth.

————. 1989. *Gedatsukai and Religion in Contemporary Japan: Returning to the Center*. Bloomington: Indiana University Press.

Edwards, Walter. 1989. *Modern Japan through Its Weddings.* Stanford: Stanford University Press.

Egami, Namio. 1964. The Formation of the People and the Origin of the State of Japan. *Memoirs of the Tōyō Bunkō* 23 : 35–70.

Ellwood, Robert S. 1973. *The Feast of Kingship: Accession Ceremonies in Ancient Japan.* Tokyo: Sophia University.

————. 1978. Harvest and Renewal at the Grand Shrine of Ise. In *Readings on Religion from Inside and Outside,* ed. Robert S. Ellwood. New Jersey: Prentice Hall.

Endō Masatake. 1993. Seijinshiki ga "shichi-go-san" ni natta: otona ni narenai wakamono (Coming-of-age ceremonies that have become like those for "seven-five-three": young people who won't become adults). *Aera,* January 12, 6–9.

Fardon, Richard. 1990. Introduction. In *Localizing Strategies: Regional Traditions of Ethnographic Writing,* ed. R. Fardon. Edinburgh: Scottish Academic Press.

Faure, Bernard. 1987. Space and Place in Chinese Religious Traditions. *History of Religions* 26 (4): 337–356.

Fentress, James, and Chris Wickham. 1992. *Social Memory.* Oxford: Basil Blackwell.

Fernandez, James W. 1985. *Persuasions and Performances: The Play of Tropes in Culture.* Bloomington: Indiana University Press.

Feuchtwang, Stephan. 1974. *An Anthropological Analysis of Chinese Geomancy.* Vientiane: Vithagna Press.

Field, Norma. 1987. *The Splendor of Longing in the Tale of Genji.* Princeton: Princeton University Press.

Firth, Raymond. 1973. *Symbols: Public and Private.* London: Allen and Unwin.

Fisher, Peter. 1987. Some Notes on Clergy and State in Japan. In *Contemporary European Writing on Japan: Scholarly Views from Eastern and Western Europe,* ed. Ian Nish. London: Paul Norbury.

Fortes, Meyer. 1987. *Religion, Morality, and the Person.* Ed. Jack Goody. Cambridge: Cambridge University Press.

Foucault, Michel. 1980. *Power/Knowledge: Selected Interviews and Other Writings, 1972–1977.* Trans. and ed. Colin Gordon. New York: Pantheon Books.

Foulk, T. Griffith. 1988. Zen in Modern Japan. In *Zen: Tradition and Transition,* ed. Kenneth Kraft. New York: Grove Press.

Fox, Richard. 1985. *Lions of the Punjab: Culture in the Making.* Berkeley: University of California Press.

————. 1990. Introduction. In *National Ideologies and the Production of National Cultures,* ed. R. Fox. Monograph Series 2. Washington, D.C.: American Anthropological Association.

————. 1991. *Recapturing Anthropology: Working in the Present.* Santa Fe: School of American Research Press.

Frager, Robert, and Thomas P. Rohlen. 1976. The Future of a Tradition: Japanese Spirit in the 1980's. In *Japan: The Paradox of Progress,* ed. L. Austin. New Haven: Yale University Press.

Fridell, Wilbur. 1973. *Japanese Shrine Mergers, 1906–12*. Tokyo: Sophia University.

———. 1985. Modern Japanese Nationalism: State Shinto, the Religion That Was "Not a Religion." In *Religion and Politics in the Modern World,* ed. Peter Merkl and Ninian Smart. New York: New York University Press.

Friedland, Roger, and Deirdre Boden. 1994. Introduction. In *NowHere: Space, Time, and Modernity,* ed. R. Friedland and D. Boden. Berkeley: University of California Press.

Friedman, David. 1988. *The Misunderstood Miracle: Industrial Development and Political Change in Japan.* Ithaca: Cornell University Press.

Fujii, Masao. 1983. Maintenance and Change in Japanese Traditional Funerals and Death-Related Behavior. *Japanese Journal of Religious Studies* 10 (1): 39–64.

Fujiki Masanao. 1992. *Kamo kannushi honnin-shi* (A history of Kamo priests). Kyoto: Zaidan Hōjin Kamo Agatanushi Dōzoku-kai.

Fujitani, Takashi. 1986. Japan's Modern National Ceremonies: A Historical Ethnography, 1868-1912. Ph.D. dissertation, University of California, Berkeley.

———. 1992. Electronic Pageantry and Japan's "Symbolic Emperor." *Journal of Asian Studies* 51 (4): 824–850.

Fukatsu, Masumi. 1987. A State Visit to Yasukuni Shrine. *Japan Quarterly* 34 : 18–24.

Fukunaga Mitsuji. 1982. *Dōkyō to Nihon bunka* (Taoism and Japanese culture). Kyoto: Jinmon Shoin.

Gadamer, Hans-Georg. 1975. *Truth and Method.* New York: Seabury Press.

Garon, Sheldon. 1986. State and Religion in Imperial Japan, 1912–1945. *Journal of Japanese Studies* 12 (2): 273–302.

Gauntlett, John Owen, trans. 1949. *Kokutai no Hongi: Cardinal Principles of the National Entity of Japan.* Ed. R. K. Hall. Cambridge, Mass.: Harvard University Press.

Geertz, Clifford. 1968. *Islam Observed: Religious Developments in Morocco and Indonesia.* New Haven: Yale University Press.

———. 1974. *The Interpretation of Culture.* New York: Basic Books.

———. 1988. *Works and Lives.* Stanford: Stanford University Press.

Gellner, Ernest. 1987. *Culture, Identity, and Politics.* Cambridge: Cambridge University Press.

Gerholm, Tomas. 1988. On Ritual: A Postmodernist View. *Ethnos* 53 (3/4): 191–203.

Gilday, Edmund T. 1988. The Pattern of Matsuri: Cosmic Schemes and Ritual Illusion in Japanese Festivals. Ph.D. dissertation, University of Chicago.

———. 1990. Power Plays in Japanese Festivals. *Journal of Ritual Studies* 4 (2): 263–295.

Gilsenan, Michael. 1982. *Recognizing Islam: An Anthropologist's Introduction.* London: Croom Helm.

Gluck, Carol. 1985. *Japan's Modern Myths: Ideology in the Late Meiji Period.* Princeton, N.J.: Princeton University Press.

Gluckman, Max. 1962. Introduction. In *Essays on the Ritual of Social Relations*, ed. Max Gluckman. Manchester: Manchester University Press.

Goffman, Erving. 1969. *Behavior in Public Places: Notes on the Social Organization of Gatherings.* London: Greenwood.

Goldstein-Gidoni, Ofra. 1997. *Packaged Japaneseness: Weddings, Business, and Brides.* Honolulu: University of Hawai'i Press.

Goodman, Lenn. 1972. *Ibn Tufayl's 'Hayy Ibn Yaqzân.* New York: Twayne Publishers.

Goody, Jack. 1961. Religion and Ritual: The Definitional Problem. *British Journal of Sociology* 15 : 142–163.

———. 1983. *The Development of the Family and Marriage in Europe.* Cambridge: Cambridge University Press.

Gorai Shigeru. 1994. *Nihonjin no shiseikan.* (Japanese views of death). Tokyo: Kadokawa Shoten.

Gorai Shigeru et al. 1980. *Kōza: Nihon no minzoku shūkyō* (Lectures on Japanese folk religions.) Tokyo: Kobundō.

Graburn, Nelson H. H. 1983. *To Pray, Pay, and Play: The Cultural Structure of Japanese Domestic Tourism.* Aix-en-Provence: Centre des Hautes Etudes Touristiques.

———. 1987. Material Symbols in Japanese Domestic Tourism. In *Mirror and Metaphor: Material and Social Constructions of Reality,* ed. D. Ingersoll and G. Bronitsky. Lanham, Md.: University Press of America.

———. 1995. The Past and Present in Japan: Nostalgia and Neo-traditionalism in Contemporary Japanese Domestic Tourism. In *Change in Tourism: People, Places, Processes,* ed. R. Butler and D. Pierce. London: Routledge.

Grapard, Allan. 1982. Flying Mountains and Walkers of Emptiness: Toward a Definition of Sacred Space in Japanese Religions. *History of Religions* 21 (3): 195–221.

———. 1983. Shinto. In *The Kodansha Encyclopedia of Japan.* Tokyo: Kodansha.

———. 1984. Japan's Ignored Cultural Revolution: The Separation of Shinto and Buddhist Divinities in Meiji [Shimbutsu Bunri] and a Case Study: Tōnomine. *History of Religions* 23 (3): 240–265.

———. 1988. Institution, Ritual and Ideology: The Twenty-two Shrine Temple Multiplexes of Heian Japan. *History of Religions* 27 (3): 246–269.

———. 1991. Women and Transgression in Japanese Myths. *Japanese Journal of Religious Studies* 18 (1): 1–18.

———. 1992. *Protocol of the Gods: A Study of the Kasuga Cult in Japanese History.* Berkeley: University of California Press.

———. 1994. Geosophia, Geognosis, and Geopiety: Orders of Significance in Japanese Representations of Space. In *NowHere: Space, Time, and Modernity,* ed. R. Friedland and D. Boden. Berkeley: University of California Press.

Groot, J. J. M. de. 1892–1910. *The Religious System of China.* 6 vols. Leiden: E. J. Brill.

Gutherie, Stewart. 1988. *A Japanese "New Religion": Risshō Kōsei-kai in a Mountain Hamlet.* Ann Arbor: Center for Japanese Studies.

Haga Shōji. 1981–1982. Meiji jingikansei no seiritsu to kokka saishi no saihen (The formation of the Meiji shrine system and the reorganization of state religious services). *Jinbun gakuhō* 49 : 33–46, 50 : 51–100.

Haley, John O. 1991. *Authority without Power: Law and the Japanese Paradox.* New York: Oxford University Press.

Hall, Ivan P. 1992. Samurai Legacies, American Illusions. *The National Interest,* summer, 14–25.

Hammond, Charles E. 1994. The Interpretation of Thunder. *Journal of Asian Studies* 53 (2): 487–503.

Handelman, Don. 1990. *Models and Mirrors: Towards an Anthropology of Public Events.* Cambridge: Cambridge University Press.

Handler, Richard. 1984. Review of *The Invention of Tradition. American Anthropologist* 86 : 1026.

Handler, Richard and Jocelyn Linnekin. 1984. Tradition, Genuine or Spurious. *Journal of American Folklore* 97 (385): 271–290.

Hardacre, Helen. 1986. *Kurozumikyō and the New Religions of Japan.* Princeton, N.J.: Princeton University Press.

———. 1989. *Shinto and the State: 1868–1988.* Princeton: Princeton University Press.

Harootunian, H. D. 1989. Visible Discourses / Invisible Ideologies. In *Postmodernism and Japan,* ed. M. Miyoshi and H. Harootunian. Durham, N.C.: Duke University Press.

Hastrup, Kirsten. 1996. *A Passage to Anthropology: Between Experience and Theory.* London: Routledge.

Hata, Ikuhiko. 1986. When Ideologues Rewrite History. *Japan Echo* 13 (4): 73–78.

Hayashiya Tatsusaburo, ed. 1991. *Shiryō Kyoto no rekishi* (A documented history of Kyoto). Vol. 1. Tokyo: Heibonsha.

Hecht, Richard D. 1994. The Construction and Management of Sacred Time and Space: Sabta Nur in the Church of the Holy Sepulcher. In *NowHere: Space, Time, and Modernity,* ed. R. Friedland and D. Boden. Berkeley: University of California Press.

Herbert, Jean. 1967. *Shinto; At the Fountainhead of Japan.* New York: Stein and Day.

Herzfeld, Michael. 1986. Of Definitions and Boundaries: The Status of Culture in the Culture of the State. In *Discourse and the Social Life of Meaning,* ed. P. Chock et al. Washington, D.C.: The Smithsonian Press.

Higo Kazuo. 1941. Kamo densetsu kō (Writings on the Kamo legend). In *Nihon shinwa no kenkyū.* Tokyo: Kawade Shobō.

Hiro, Sachiya, and Shichihei Yamamoto. 1986. Yasukuni Shrine and the Japanese Spirit World. *Japan Echo* 13 (2): 73–80.

Hishimura Isamu. 1987. *Nihon no shizen-gami* (Japanese nature *kami*). Tokyo: Arimine Shoten.

Hobsbawm, Eric, and Terrence Ranger, eds. 1983. *The Invention of Tradition*. New York: Cambridge University Press.

Holtom, D. C. 1963. *Modern Japan and Shinto Nationalism*. New York: Paragon Books.

Hori, Ichiro, ed. 1968. *Folk Religion in Japan: Continuity and Change*. Chicago: University of Chicago.

————. 1972. *Japanese Religion*. Tokyo: Kodansha International.

Horner, Alice. 1992. Conceptualizing Tradition. Ph.D. dissertation, University of California, Berkeley.

Hubert, H., and Marcel Mauss. 1981 [1898]. *Sacrifice: Its Nature and Function*. Trans. W. D. Halls. Chicago: University of Chicago Press.

Iisaka Yoshiaki. 1970. Sengoshi no okeru kokka to shūkyō (The state and religion in postwar Japan). *Sekai* 298:56–67.

Ikkai, Mariko. 1988. The "Senbetsu-Omiyage" Relationship: Traditional Reciprocity among Japanese Tourists. In *Anthropological Research on Contemporary Tourism: Student Papers from Berkeley*. Berkeley: Kroeber Anthropological Society.

Inoue Kiyoshi. 1969. *Nihon no rekishi* (History of Japan). Tokyo: Iwanami Shoten.

Inoue Mitsusada. 1985. Kamo agatanushi no kenkyū (Research on the Kamo *agatanushi*). In *Inoue Mitsusada chosaku-shū*, vol. 1. Tokyo: Iwanami Shoten.

Inoue, Mitsusada, and Delmer Brown. 1993. The Nara State. In *The Cambridge History of Japan*, vol. 1, ed. Delmer Brown. Cambridge: Cambridge University Press.

Inoue Nobutaka, ed. 1994. *Shinto jiten* (Dictionary of Shinto). Tokyo: Kobundō.

Inoue, Nobutaka, et al. 1979. A Festival with Anonymous Kami: The Kobe Matsuri. *Japanese Journal of Religious Studies* 6 (1–2): 163–185.

Institute for Japanese Culture and Classics. 1988. *Matsuri—Festival and Rite in Japanese Life*. Tokyo: Kokugakuin University.

Ishikawa Takashi. 1987. *Kokoro*. Tokyo: East Publications.

Ishimori Shūzō. 1991. Kankō geijutsu no seiritsu to tenkai (The formation and development of tourist art). In *Kankō to ongaku*, vol. 6 of *Minzoku ongaku sōsho*, ed. Ishimori Shūzō. Tokyo: Tokyo Shoseki.

Ishino, Hironobu. 1992. Rites and Rituals of the Kofun Period. *Japanese Journal of Religious Studies* 19 (2/3): 191–215.

Ishizaki Masaaki, ed. 1992. *Nihon no kamigami* (Japan's deities). Osaka: Taiyō Publications.

Isozaki, Arata. 1992. Escaping the Cycle of Eternal Recurrence. *New Perspectives Quarterly* 9 (2): 15–22.

Iwai Hiromi and Niwai Yūju. 1981. *Shinsen* (Shinto food offerings). Tokyo: Dōmeisha.

Iwata Keiji. 1975. Yoru: shūkyō izen (Night: Before religion). *Shokun* 7 (6): 94–110.

Jeremy, Michael, and M. E. Robinson. 1989. *Ceremony and Symbolism in the Japanese Home*. Honolulu: University of Hawai'i Press.

JETRO. 1997. *Nippon: Business Facts and Figures*. Tokyo: Jetro Publications.

Jinja Honchō. 1985. *Basic Terms of Shinto*. Revised Edition. Tokyo: Kokugakuin University and Institute for Japanese Culture and Classics.

————. 1992a. *Jinja Honchō kai-i kentei-shiken no annai* (Information on ranking examinations for qualifications). Jinja Honchō Publications.

————. 1992b. *Jinja katsudō ni taisuru zenkoku tōkei* (Statistics Concerning Activities at Nationwide Shrines). Jinja Honchō Publications.

Kageyama Haruki. 1972. *Shintaizan* (Divine mountains). Tokyo: Gakuseisha.

————. 1973. *The Arts of Shinto*. New York: Weatherhill and Shibundo.

Kamens, Edward. 1990. *The Buddhist Poetry of the Great Kamo Priestess: Daisaiin Senshi and Hosshin wakashū*. Michigan Monographs in Japanese Studies No. 5. Ann Arbor: University of Michigan Press.

Kamo Wake Ikazuchi Jinja. 1991. *Kamo-sai* (The Kamo Festival). Shrine publication.

————. 1993. *Kurabe-uma-shinji: kyū hyaku nen kinenbi* (Nine-hundred-year anniversary of the *kurabe-uma* festival). Shrine publication.

Kapferer, Bruce. 1984. The Ritual Process and the Problem of Reflexivity in Sinhalese Demon Exorcisms. In *Rite, Drama, Festival, Spectacle*, ed. J. MacAloon. Philadelphia: Institute for the Study of Human Issues.

————. 1988. Nationalism, Tradition, and Political Culture. In *Legends of People, Myths of State*. Washington, D.C.: Smithsonian Institution Press.

Kato, Genichi. 1973. *A Historical Study of the Religious Development of Shinto*. Tokyo: Japan Society for the Promotion of Science.

Kato Shinpei. 1988. *Nihonjin wa, doko kara kita ka?* (Where did the Japanese come from?). Tokyo: Iwanami Shinsho.

Katō Shūichi. 1968. *Nihon no uchi to soto* (Concepts of "inside" and "outside" in Japan). Tokyo: Bungei Shunjūsha.

Kawade, Kiyohiko. 1968. Saiinnai no seikatsu o shinobu (Looking back on the lifestyle of the saiin). *Shinto shi kenkyū* 16 (1): 26–46.

Keane, John J. 1980. A General Survey of the Word and Concept of Kami. *The Japan Missionary Bulletin*, August and September.

Keizai Kōhō Center. 1997. *An International Comparison*. Tokyo: Keidanren.

Kendall, Laurel. 1985. *Shamans, Housewives, and Other Restless Spirits*. Honolulu: University of Hawai'i Press.

Kertzer, David. 1988. *Ritual, Politics, and Power*. New Haven: Yale University Press.

Ketelaar, James. 1990. *Of Heretics and Martyrs in Meiji Japan*. Princeton: Princeton University Press.

Khanna, Madhu. 1991. Space, Time, and Nature in Indian Architecture. *Architecture and Design*, September/October, 51–63.

Kidder, J. Edward. 1975. *Early Buddhist Japan*. New York: Praeger.

————. 1993. The Earliest Societies in Japan. In *The Cambridge History of Japan*, vol. 1, ed. Delmer Brown. Cambridge: Cambridge University Press.

Kiley, Cornelius J. 1973. State and Dynasty in Archaic Yamato. *Journal of Asian Studies* 33 (1): 25–49.

Kishimoto, Hideo. 1958. The Role of Mountains in the Religious Life of the Japanese People. In *Proceedings of the Ninth International Congress for the History of Religions.* Tokyo: Tokyo University Press.

Kitagawa, Joseph. 1987. *On Understanding Japanese Religion.* Princeton: Princeton University Press.

————. 1988a. Introduction to "The Shinto World of the 1880s." *History of Religions* 27 (3): 321–325.

————. 1988b. Some Remarks on Shinto. *History of Religions* 27 (3): 227–245.

Klass, Morton. 1995. *Ordered Universes: Approaches to the Anthropology of Religion.* Boulder: Westview Press.

Kondo, Dorinne. 1990. *Crafting Selves: Power, Gender, and Discourses of Identity in a Japanese Workplace.* Chicago: University of Chicago Press.

Kondos, Vivienne. 1992. Politics of Ritual. *Australian Journal of Anthropology* 3 (3): 121–129.

Koschmann, J. Victor, ed. 1978. *Authority and the Individual in Japan: Citizen Protest in Historical Perspective.* Tokyo: University of Tokyo Press.

Krauss, Ellis S., Thomas P. Rohlen, and Patricia Steinhoff. 1984. *Conflict in Japan.* Honolulu: University of Hawai'i Press.

Kumagai, F. 1984. The Life Cycle of the Japanese Family. *Journal of Marriage and Family* 46 (1): 191–204.

Kurihara, Akira. 1990. The Emperor System as Japanese National Religion: The Emperor System Module in Everyday Consciousness. *Japanese Journal of Religious Studies* 17 (2/3): 315–340.

Kurita, Isamu. 1983. Revival of the Japanese Tradition. *Journal of Popular Culture* 17 (1): 130–134.

Kuroda, Toshio. 1981. Shinto in the History of Japanese Religion. *Journal of Japanese Studies* 7 (1): 1–21.

Kyōto-fu Bunka-zai Hogo Kikin (Foundation to Protect Cultural Treasures in Kyoto). 1980. *Kyōto no sha-ji* (Kyoto's shrines and temples). Kyōto: Kyōto-fu Bunka-zai Hogo Kikin.

La Fontaine, Jean. 1972. *Introduction to Interpretations of Ritual,* ed. J. La Fontaine. London: Tavistock.

————. 1987. *Initiation.* Middlesex: Penguin Books.

Lagerway, John. 1987. *Taoist Ritual in Chinese Society and History.* New York: Macmillan.

Lame Deer, John (Fire) and Richard Erdoes. 1972. *Lame Deer: Seeker of Visions.* New York: Pocket Books.

Lancaster, Lewis R. 1984. Buddhism and the Family in East Asia. In *Religion and the Family in East Asia,* ed. T. Sofue and G. De Vos. Berkeley: University of California Press.

Lancaster, Roger. 1988. *Thanks to God and the Revolution.* New York: Columbia University.

Leach, E. R. 1968a. *Encyclopedia of the Social Sciences,* vol. 13. New York: Macmillan.

————. 1968b. Introduction. In *Dialectic in Practical Religion,* ed. E. R. Leach. London: Cambridge University Press.

————. 1979. Ritualization in Man in Relation to Conceptual and Social Development. In *Reader in Comparative Religion,* ed. William Lessa and Evon Vogt. Fourth edition. New York: Harper and Row.

Lebra, Takie. 1993. *Above the Clouds: Status Culture of the Modern Japanese Nobility.* Berkeley: University of California Press.

————. 1997. Self and Other in Esteemed Status: The Changing Culture of the Japanese Royalty from Showa to Heisei. *Journal of Japanese Studies* 23 (2): 257–289.

Lebra, William P. 1966. *Okinawan Religion: Belief, Ritual, and Social Structure.* Honolulu: University Press of Hawai'i.

Ledyard, Gari. 1975. Galloping along with the Horseriders: Looking for the Founders of Japan. *Journal of Japanese Studies* 1 : 217–254.

LeVine, Steve. 1996. After Karl Marx, a 1,000-Year-Old Superman. *New York Times,* August 17, A4.

Lewis, David. 1993. Religious Rites in a Japanese Factory. In *Religion and Society in Modern Japan,* ed. M. Mullins, S. Shimazono, and P. Swanson. Berkeley: Asian Humanities Press.

Lewis, Gilbert. 1980. *Day of Shining Red. An Essay on Understanding Ritual.* Cambridge: Cambridge University Press.

Littleton, C. Scott. 1987. The Organization and Management of a Tokyo Shinto Shrine Festival. *Ethnology* 25 : 195–202.

Lokowandt, Ernst. 1981. *Zum Verhältnis von Staat und Shintō in Heutigen Japan.* Wiesbaden: Otto Harrassowitz.

MacAloon, John J., ed. 1984. *Rite, Drama, Festival, Spectacle: Rehearsals toward a Theory of Cultural Performance.* Philadelphia: Institute for the Study of Human Issues.

MacCannell, Dean. 1990. *The Tourist: A New Theory of the Leisure Class.* New York: Shocken Books. Originally published 1977.

Marcus, George, ed. 1983. *Elites: Ethnographic Issues.* Albuquerque: University of New Mexico Press.

Marcus, George, and Michael Fischer. 1986. *Anthropology as Cultural Critique.* Chicago: University of Chicago Press.

Mass, Jeffrey P. 1979. *The Development of Kamakura Rule, 1180–1250: A History with Documents.* Stanford: Stanford University Press.

———— 1990. The Kamakura Bakufu. In *The Cambridge History of Japan,* vol. 3, ed. Yamamura Kozo. Cambridge: Cambridge University Press.

Matsumae Takeshi. 1992. Kamo to Matsuo no raijin tachi (The thunder deities of Kamo and Matsuo). *Shinto taikei geppō* 106.

————. 1993. Early Kami Worship. In *The Cambridge History of Japan*, vol. 1, ed. Delmer Brown. Cambridge: Cambridge University Press.

Matsunaga, Daigan, and Alicia Matsunaga. 1974. *Foundation of Japanese Buddhism.* 2 vols. Los Angeles: Buddhist Books International.

Mayer, Adrian C. 1992. On the Gender of Shrines and the Daijōsai. *Japanese Journal of Religious Studies* 19 (1).

Mayumi Tsunedata. 1984. *Shintō no sekai* (The world of Shinto). Osaka: Tokishobō.

————. 1989. *Gendai shakai to jinja* (Contemporary society and shrines). Ise: Kōgakkan Daigaku.

McCullough, William, and Helen C. McCullough, trans. 1980. *A Tale of Flowering Fortunes: Annals of Japanese Aristocratic Life in the Heian Period.* 2 vols. Stanford: Stanford University Press.

McMullin, Neil. 1988. On Placating the Gods and Pacifying the Populace: The Case of the Gion Goryō Cult. *History of Religions* 27 (3): 270–293.

————. 1989. Historical and Historiographical Issues in the Study of Pre-Modern Japanese Religion. *Japanese Journal of Religious Studies* 16 (1): 3–40.

Meyer, Jeffrey. 1978. Feng-Shui of the Chinese City. *History of Religions* 8 (3):138–155.

————. 1991. *The Dragons of Tiananmen: Beijing as a Sacred City.* Columbia, S.C.: University of South Carolina Press.

Meyerhoff, Barbara. 1984. A Death in Due Time: Construction of Self and Culture in Ritual Drama. In *Rite, Drama, Festival, Spectacle: Rehearsals Toward a Theory of Cultural Performance,* ed. John MacAloon. Philadelphia: Institute for the Study of Human Issues.

Miller, Alan L. 1984. Ame no miso-ori me (The Heavenly Weaving Maiden): The Cosmic Weaver in Early Shinto Myth and Ritual. *History of Religions* 24 (1): 27–48.

————. 1991. The Garments of the Gods in Japanese Ritual. *Journal of Ritual Studies* 5 (2): 33–55.

Miller, Richard J. 1980. *Japan's First Bureaucracy: A Study of Eighth-Century Government.* Cornell University East Asia Papers 19. Ithaca, N.Y.

Misumi Haruo. 1979. *Matsuri to kamigami no sekai* (The world of festivals and *kami*). Tokyo: NHK Books.

Mitchell, W. J. T. 1986. *Iconology: Images, Text, Ideology.* Chicago: University of Chicago Press.

Miyata Noboru. 1970. *Kami no minzokushi* (Notes on *kami*). Tokyo: Iwanami Shoten.

————. 1987. Weather Watching and Emperorship. In *An Anthropological Profile of Japan,* ed. Masao Yamaguchi and Nobuhiro Nagashima. Supplement to *Current Anthropology* 28 (4): 13–18.

Miyoshi, Masao. 1979. *As We Saw Them: The First Japanese Embassy to the U.S., 1860.* Berkeley: University of California Press.

————. 1991. *Off Center.* Cambridge, Mass.: Harvard University Press.

Miyoshi, Masao, and H. D. Harootunian. 1989. Introduction. In *Postmodernism and Japan,* ed. M. Miyoshi and H. Harootunian. Durham, N.C.: Duke University Press.

Moeran, Brian. 1989. *Language and Popular Culture in Japan.* Manchester: Manchester University Press.

Moon, Okpyo. 1989. *From Paddy Field to Ski Slope: The Revitalisation of Tradition in Japanese Village Life.* Manchester: Manchester University Press.

Moore, Sally F., and Barbara G. Myerhoff. 1977. *Secular Ritual.* Assen/Amsterdam: Van Gorcum.

Morgan, Gareth. 1986. *Images of Organization.* Newbury Park, Calif.: Sage Publications.

Mori, Koichi, and Kazuto Matsufuji. 1988. Paleolithic Forest Dwellers Surmised. *Japan Quarterly* 35 (3): 243–247.

Morioka, Kiyomi. 1975. *Religion in Changing Japanese Society.* Tokyo: University of Tokyo Press.

———. 1977. The Appearance of Ancestor Worship in Modern Japan: The Years of Transition from the Meiji to the Taisho Periods. *Japanese Journal of Religious Studies* 4 (2/3): 183–212.

Morris, Brian. 1987. *Anthropological Studies of Religion.* Cambridge: Cambridge University Press.

Murakami Shigeyoshi. 1970. *Kokka Shintō* (State Shinto). Tokyo: Iwanami Shinsho.

———. 1977. *Tennō no saishi* (The emperor's religious rites). Tokyo: Iwanami Shinsho.

———. 1980. *Japanese Religion in the Modern Century.* Trans. H. Byron Earhart. Tokyo: University of Tokyo.

Muraoka, Tsunetsugu. 1964. *Studies in Shinto Thought.* Trans. Delmer M. Brown and James T. Araki. Tokyo: Ministry of Education.

Nagahara, Keiji. 1990. The Medieval Peasant. In *The Cambridge History of Japan,* vol. 3, ed. Yamamura Kozo. Cambridge: Cambridge University Press.

Nakamaki Hirochika. 1990. *Shūkyō ni nani ga okite iru ka?* (What's going on with religion?). Tokyo: Heibonsha.

Namihira, Emiko. 1987. Pollution in the Folk Belief System. In *An Anthropological Profile of Japan,* ed. Masao Yamaguchi and Nobuhiro Nagashima. Supplement to *Current Anthropology* 28 (4): 65–74.

Needham, Joseph, and Wang Ling. 1962. *Science and Civilisation in China,* vol. 2. Cambridge: Cambridge University Press.

Needham, Rodney. 1979. *Symbolic Classification.* The Goodyear Perspectives in Anthropology Series, ed. J. Fox. Santa Monica, Calif.: Goodyear Publishing.

Nelson, John K. 1987. Shintō to Amerika dōzoku minzoku no shinkō. (Parallels of Shinto with several Native American religious beliefs). *Mizugaki* 142:41–50.

———. 1991. Japan's Ideology of Modernization: A Guide to the Postwar Years. *Forum of Japan/U.S. Culture Center* 10:55–77.

————. 1992. Shinto Ritual: Managing Chaos in Contemporary Japan. *Ethnos* 57 (1/2): 77–104.

————. 1993a. Enduring Identities: The Guise of Shinto in Contemporary Japan. Ph.D. dissertation, University of California, Berkeley.

————. 1993b. Of Flowers and Phalli: Sexual Symbolism at Kamigamo Shrine. *Japanese Religions* 18 (1): 2–14.

————. 1994. Land Calming Rituals in Contemporary Japan. *Journal of Ritual Studies* 8 (2): 19–40.

————. 1996a. Freedom of Expression: The Very Modern Practice of Visiting a Shinto Shrine. *Japanese Journal of Religious Studies* 23 (1/2): 117–153.

————. 1996b. *A Year in the Life of a Shinto Shrine.* Seattle: University of Washington Press.

————. 1997a. Shinkan to jinja (Priests and shrines). In *Ajia no shūkyō to seishin bunka* (Asian religion and spiritual cultures), ed. Tamaru Noriyoshi and Tsuneya Wakimoto. Tokyo: Shinyōshu.

————. 1997b. Warden + Salaryman + Virtuoso = Priest: Paradigms within Japanese Shinto for Religious Specialists and Institutions. *Journal of Asian Studies* 56 (3): 678–707.

————. 1999. Shifting Paradigms of Religion and the State: Implications of the 1997 Supreme Court Decision for Social, Religious, and Political Change. *Modern Asian Studies* 33 (3).

NHK Hōsō Seiron-chōsa-sho. 1984. *Nihonjin no shūkyō-ishiki* (The religious consciousness of the Japanese). Tokyo: Nippon Hōsō Shuppankyōkai.

Nitschke, Gunter. 1989. Daijōsai and Shikinen Sengu. *Kyoto Journal,* Fall 1989/ Winter 1990.

Norbeck, Edward. 1970. *Religion and Society in Modern Japan.* Houston: Rice University.

————. 1977. A Sanction for Authority: Etiquette. In *The Anthropology of Power,* ed. Raymond Fogelson and Richard Adams. New York: Academic Press.

Norberg-Schulz, Christian. 1980. *Genus Loci: Toward a Phenomenology of Architecture.* New York: Rizzoli.

O'Brien, David. 1996. *To Dream of Dreams: Religious Freedom and Constitutional Politics in Postwar Japan.* Honolulu: University of Hawai'i Press.

Ohnuki-Tierney, Emiko. 1984. *Illness and Culture in Contemporary Japan.* Cambridge: Cambridge University Press.

————. 1987. *The Monkey as Mirror: Symbolic Transformations in Japanese History and Ritual.* Princeton, N.J.: Princeton University Press.

————, ed. 1990. *Culture through Time.* Stanford: Stanford University Press.

Omura, Eishō. 1988. Gendaijin to shūkyō (Modern people and religion). In *Gendaijin no shūkyō* (The religion of modern people), ed. E. Omura and S. Nishiyama. Tokyo: Yūhikaku.

Onaka, Toshirō. 1988. *A History of Nagata Shrine*. Trans. David Wicklund. Kyoto: Kawakita Publishing and Nagata Shrine.

Ono, Sokyo. 1984. *Shinto: The Kami Way*. Tokyo: Charles E. Tuttle.

Ono Susumu et al. 1974. *Kogo jiten* (A dictionary of old words). Tokyo: Iwanami Shoten.

Ooms, Herman. 1985. *Tokugawa Ideology: Early Constructs, 1570–1680*. Princeton, N.J.: Princeton University Press.

Ortner, Sherry B. 1989. Cultural Politics: Religious Activism and Ideological Transformation among 20th-Century Sherpas. *Dialectical Anthropology* 14: 197–211.

———. 1990. Patterns of History: Cultural Schemas in the Foundings of Sherpa Religious Institutions. In *Culture through Time*, ed. E. Ohnuki-Tierney. Stanford: Stanford University Press.

Otsuka Takematsu, ed. 1927. *Iwakura Tomomi kankei monjo*. Tokyo: Nihon Shiseki Kyōkai.

Ōwa Iwao. 1986. Kamogawa suikei to sono shūhen. In *Nihon no kamigami: jinja to seiichi*, vol. 5, ed. Tanigawa Keniichi. Tokyo: Hakusuisha.

Oxford English Dictionary (OED). 1989. Second edition. London: Oxford University Press.

———. 1993. Oxford: Clarendon Press.

Oyama, Kyōhei. 1990. Medieval shōen. In *The Cambridge History of Japan*, vol. 3, ed. Yamamura Kozo. Cambridge: Cambridge University Press.

Parkin, David. 1992. Ritual as Spatial Direction and Bodily Division. In *Understanding Rituals*, ed. Daniel de Coppett. London: Routledge.

Pascal, R., and A. Athos. 1981. *The Art of Japanese Management*. New York: Warner.

Pearson, Richard, ed. 1986. *Windows on the Japanese Past: Studies in Archaeology and Prehistory*. University of Michigan: Center for Japanese Studies.

Pfaffenberger, Bryan. 1983. Serious Pilgrims and Frivolous Tourists: The Chimera of Tourism in the Pilgrimages of Sri Lanka. *Annals of Tourism Research* 10: 57–74.

Philippi, Donald L. 1959. *Norito: A New Translation of the Ancient Japanese Ritual Prayers*. Tokyo: The Institute for Japanese Culture and Classics, Kokugakuin University.

———. 1968. *Kojiki*. Tokyo: University of Tokyo Press.

Pilgrim, Richard B. 1986. Intervals (Ma) in Space and Time: Foundations for a Religio-Aesthetic Paradigm in Japan. *History of Religions* 18: 255–277.

Plumb, J. H. 1970. *Death of the Past*. Boston: Houghton Mifflin.

Plutschow, Herbert. 1990. *Chaos and Cosmos: Ritual in Early and Medieval Japanese Literature*. Leiden: E. J. Brill.

Ponsonby-Fane, R. A. B. 1933. *Kamo Mioya Shrine*. London: Kegan Paul.

Pred, Allan. 1986. *Place, Practice and Structure*. Cambridge: Polity Press.

Pye, Michael. 1989. Shinto and the Typology of Religion. *Method and Theory in the Study of Religion* 1/2: 186–195.

Pyle, Kenneth B. 1969. *The New Generation in Meiji Japan: Problems of Cultural Identity, 1885–1895.* Stanford: Stanford University Press.

Rappaport, Roy A. 1980. Concluding Comments on Ritual and Reflexivity. *Semiotica* 30 (1/2): 181–193.

Reader, Ian. 1990. Returning to Respectability: A Religious Revival in Japan? *Japan Forum* 2 (1): 57–67.

———. 1991. *Religion in Contemporary Japan.* Honolulu: University of Hawai'i Press.

Redfield, Peter. 1996. Beneath a Modern Sky: Space Technology and Its Place on the Ground. *Science, Technology and Human Values* 21 (3).

Reinhart, A. Kevin. 1990. Impurity, No Danger. *History of Religions* 30 (1): 1–24.

Rinschede, Gisbert. 1992. Forms of Religious Tourism. *Annals of Tourism Research* 19:51–67.

Robertson, Jennifer. 1987. A Dialectic of Native and Newcomer: The Kodaira Citizens' Festival in Suburban Tokyo. *Anthropological Quarterly* 60 (3): 124–36.

———. 1988. Furusato Japan: The Culture and Politics of Nostalgia. *Politics, Culture, and Society* 1 (4): 494–518.

———. 1991. *Native and Newcomer: Making and Remaking a Japanese City.* Berkeley: University of California Press.

Rohlen, Thomas P. 1974. *For Harmony and Strength: Japanese White-Collar Organization in Anthropological Perspective.* Berkeley: University of California Press.

Rosebury, William. 1989. *Anthropologies and Histories.* New Brunswick: Rutgers Press.

Ross, William. 1965. *Shinto: The Way of Japan.* Boston: Beacon Press.

Ross-Bryant, Lynn. 1990. The Land in American Religious Experience. *Journal of the American Academy of Religion* 58 (3): 333–355.

Ruel, Malcolm. 1982. Christians as Believers. In *Religious Organization and Religious Experience,* ed. J. Davis. A.S.A. Monographs No. 21. London: Academic Press.

Sabean, David. 1984. *Power in the Blood.* Cambridge: Cambridge University Press.

Sadler, A. W. 1976. The Grammar of a Rite in Shinto. *Asian Folklore Studies* 35: 17–27.

Sahlins, Marshall. 1990. The Political Economy of Grandeur in Hawai'i from 1810 to 1830. In *Culture Through Time,* ed. E. Ohnuki-Tierney. Stanford: Stanford University Press.

Sakurai, Haruo. 1987. Tradition and Changes in Local Community Shrines. *Acta Asiatica* 51.

———. 1992. *Yomigaeru mura no kamigami* (Reviving village deities). Tokyo: Taimeidō.

Sakurai Katsunoshin, Nishikawa Masatami, and Sonoda Minoru. 1990. *Nihon Shintōron.* Tokyo: Gakuseisha.

Sansom, George. 1958. *A History of Japan to 1334.* Stanford: Stanford University Press.

Saso, Michel. 1978. *The Teachings of Taoist Master Chuang*. New Haven: Yale University Press.

Sawada Tomoji. 1973. *Kamo-sha saishin kō* (Writings on the deities of Kamo Shrine). Kyoto: Shintō Shigaku-kai.

Schipper, Kristofer. 1974. "The Written Memorial in Taoist Ceremonies." In *Religion and Ritual in Chinese Society*, ed. Arthur Wolf. Stanford: Stanford University Press.

———. 1982. *Le corps taoiste: Corps physique, corps social*. Paris: Fayard.

Schnell, Scott. 1999. *The Rousing Drum: Ritual Practice in a Japanese Community*. Honolulu: University of Hawai'i Press.

Seaman, Gary. 1986. Only Half-way to Godhead: The Chinese Geomancer as Alchemist and Cosmic Pivot. *Asian Folklore Studies* 45: 1–18.

Segawa Yoshinori. 1991. Umakai shūdan no kami matsuri (Cultic celebrations of horse-breeding groups). In *Kofun jidai no kenkyū* 3, ed. Ishino et al.

Seidensticker, Edward. 1982. *The Tale of Genji*. New York: Harmondsworth/Penguin.

Shaw, Rosalind. 1992. Problematizing Syncretism. Paper delivered at the American Anthropological Association annual conference, San Francisco, Calif.

Shibata Minoru. 1982. Miare shinji to Kamo matsuri (The Kamo Festival and the miare rite). In *Heiankyō no kamigami*, vol. 6. Tokyo: Shōgakka.

Shils, Edward. 1981. *Tradition*. Chicago: University of Chicago Press.

Shimode Sekiyo. 1980. Jingi shinkō to dōkyō to jukyō (Kami faith, Taoism, and Confucianism). In *Nihon no kodai shinkō* (Japan's ancient faith), vol. 1, ed. Ueda Masaaki. Tokyo: Gakuseisha.

Shinno Toshikazu. 1980. Seikatsu no naka no shūkyō (Religion within lifestyles). Tokyo: NHK Books.

Shintō daijiten (The great dictionary of Shinto). 1938. Vol. 1. Tokyo: Heibonsha.

Shintō jiten (Dictionary of Shinto). 1994. Ed. Inoue Nobutaka. Tokyo: Kobundō.

Shirayama Toshitarō. 1971. Kamo-sha to Kibune Jinja (Kamo and Kibune shrines). In *Shintō-shi kenkyū* 24 (5/6): 86–93.

Shimura Izuru, ed. 1967. *Kōjien*. Tokyo: Iwanami Shoten.

Silverblatt, Irene. 1988. Inca Imperial Dilemmas, Kinship, and History. *Comparative Studies in Society and History* 30: 83–102.

Skinner, Stephen. 1982. *The Living Earth Manual of Feng-shui*. London: Arkana Books.

Skorupski, John. 1976. *Symbol and Theory*. Cambridge: Cambridge University Press.

Smith, Jonathan Z. 1981. The Bare Facts of Ritual. *History of Religions* 20: 34–47.

———. 1987. *To Take Place*. Chicago: University of Chicago Press.

Smith, Patrick. 1997. *Japan: A Reinterpretation*. New York: Vintage Books.

Smith, Robert. 1978. *Kurusu*. Stanford: Stanford University Press.

———. 1983. *Japanese Society: Tradition, Self, and the Social Order*. Cambridge: Cambridge University Press.

————. 1984. Japanese Religious Attitudes from the Standpoint of the Comparative Study of Civilizations. In *Japanese Civilization in the Modern World: Cities and Urbanization,* ed. Tadao Umesao. Osaka: National Museum of Ethnology.

————. 1985. A Pattern of Japanese Society: Ie Society or Acknowledgement of Interdependence? *Journal of Japanese Studies* 11 (1): 29–45.

Smith, Valene. 1989. Introduction: The Quest in Guest. In *Hosts and Guests: The Anthropology of Tourism,* ed. Valene Smith. Philadelphia: University of Pennsylvania Press.

Smyers, Karen. 1999. *The Fox and the Jewel: A Study of Shared and Private Meanings in Japanese Inari Worship.* Honolulu: University of Hawai'i Press.

Sonoda, Koyu, and Delmer M. Brown. 1993. Early Buddha Worship. In *Cambridge History of Japan,* Vol. 1, ed. Delmer Brown. Cambridge: Cambridge University Press.

Sonoda, Minoru. 1975. The Traditional Festival in Urban Society. *Japanese Journal of Religious Studies* 2 : 103–136.

————. 1983. Secularity and Profanation in Japanese Religion. In *Cultural Identity and Modernization in Asian Countries.* Tokyo: Institute for Japanese Culture and Classics.

————. 1987. The Religious Situation in Japan in Relation to Shinto. *Acta Asiatica* 51 : 1–21.

————. 1988. Festival and Sacred Transgression. In *Matsuri: Festival and Rite in Japanese Life.* Tokyo: Institute for Japanese Culture and Classics.

————. 1990. *Matsuri no genshōgaku* (The phenomenology of *matsuri*). Tokyo: Kōbundō.

Sonoda Minoru, with Sakurai Katsunoshin and Nishikawa Masatami. 1990. *Nihon Shintō-ron.* Tokyo: Gakuseisha.

Steinmo, Sven, Kathleen Thelen, and Frank Longstreth, eds. 1992. *Structuring Politics: Historical Institutionalism in Comparative Analysis.* Cambridge: Cambridge University Press.

Strickmann, Michel. 1980. "History, Anthropology, and Chinese Religion." *Harvard Journal of Asiatic Studies* 40 : 201–248.

Sugata, Masaaki. 1988. Shinto Resurgence. *Japan Quarterly* 35 : 89–108.

Suzuki, Hiroyuki. 1993. Sense of Place: Expression in Modern Japanese Architecture. *The Japan Foundation Newsletter* 20 (4): 1–8.

Swanger, Eugene R. 1981. A Preliminary Examination of the *Omamori* Phenomenon. *Asian Folklore Studies* 40 : 237–252.

Swyngedouw, Jan. 1986. Religion in Contemporary Japanese Society. *The Japan Foundation Newsletter* 13 (4):3.

Tambiah, S. J. 1968. The Magic Power of Words. *Man* 3 : 174–208.

Takahashi Tōru. 1991. *Nihonshi o irodoru dōkyō no nazo* (Taoist riddles coloring Japanese history). Tokyo: Nihon Bungeisha.

Takaya Shigeo. 1984. *Ame no kami* (Rain deities). Tokyo: Iwasaki Bijutsu-sha.

Takayama, K. Peter. 1988. Revitalization Movement of Modern Japanese Civil Religion. *Sociological Analysis* 48 (4): 328–341.

———. 1990. Enshrinement and Persistency of Japanese Religion. *Journal of Church and State* 32 : 527–548.

Takeuchi Rizō. 1958. *Ritsuryōsei to kizoku seiken* (The *ritsuryō* system and the political power of the aristocracy). Tokyo: Iwanami Shoten.

Tanigawa Keniichi. 1985. *Onna no fudoki* (A local history of women). Tokyo: Kodansha.

Teeuwen, Mark. 1996. Jinja Honchō and Shrine Shintō Policy. *Japan Forum* 8 (2): 177–188.

Thomas, Julian. 1993. The Politics of Vision and the Archaeologies of Landscape. In *Landscape: Politics and Perspectives,* ed. Barbara Bender. Oxford: Berg.

Thompson, John. 1991. Introduction. In *Language and Symbolic Power,* ed. J. Thompson. Cambridge, Mass.: Harvard University Press.

Thompson, Kenneth. 1986. *Beliefs and Ideology.* London: Tavistock Publications.

Thompson, Richard H. 1989. *Theories of Ethnicity: A Critical Appraisal.* Westport, Conn.: Greenwood Press.

Thornton, Robert J. 1992. The Rhetoric of Ethnographic Holism. In *Rereading Cultural Anthropology,* ed. George Marcus. Durham, N.C.: Duke University Press.

Tokoro Isao. 1991. Kamo no kamigami to aoi matsuri (Kamo's *kami* and the Aoi Festival). In *Kamo Sai/Aoi Festival.* Kyoto: Kyoto Shoin.

Torigoe Kenzaburō. 1988. *Kamigami to tennō no aida* (Between many *kami* and the emperor). Tokyo: Asahi Shimbunsha.

Tsunoda, Ryusaku, and L. C. Goodrich, eds. 1951. History of the Kingdom of Wei (Wei Chi), c. AD 297. In *Japan in the Chinese Dynastic Histories.* Pasadena, Calif.: Perkins Asiatic Monograph 2.

Tuan, Yi-fu. 1977. *Space and Place: The Perspective of Experience.* Minneapolis: University of Minnesota Press.

Turner, Victor. 1969. *The Ritual Process.* Chicago: Aldine Publishing.

———. 1973a. The Center Out There: The Pilgrim's Goal. *History of Religions* 12 : 191–230.

———. 1973b. Symbols in African Ritual. *Science* 179 : 1100–1105.

Turner, Victor, and Edith Turner. 1978. *Image and Pilgrimage in Christian Culture.* New York: Columbia University Press.

Ueda, Kenji. 1972. Shinto. In *Japanese Religion,* ed. Ichiro Hori, trans. Yoshiya Abe and David Reid. Tokyo: Kodansha International.

———. 1979. Contemporary Social Change and Shinto Tradition. *Japanese Journal of Religious Studies* 6 (1/2): 303–327.

———. 1991. *Shintō Shingaku ronkō* (Writings on Shinto theology). Tokyo: Taimeidō.

Ueda Masaaki. 1979. *Dōkyō to kodai no tennōsei* (Ancient Taoism's emperor system). Tokyo: Tokuma Shoten.

Umehara, Takeshi. 1992. Ancient Japan Shows Postmodernism the Way. *New Perspectives Quarterly* 9 (1): 10–13.

Umesao Tadao. 1987. *Kyoto no seishin* (The spirit of Kyoto). Kyoto: Kadokawa Shoten.

Uno Masato. 1987. *Kigyō no jinja* (Shrines and business). Tokyo: Jinja Shimpō.

Upham, Frank. 1988. *Law and Social Change in Postwar Japan*. Cambridge: Harvard University Press.

Van Gennep, Arnold. 1965 [1908]. *The Rites of Passage*. London: Routledge.

van Wolferen, Karel. 1989. *The Enigma of Japanese Power*. New York: Knopf.

Wada Atsumu. 1986. Kodai no saishi to seiji (Ancient rituals and politics). In *Matsurigoto no tenkai* (The development of *matsurigoto*). Vol. 7 of the series Nihon no kodai (Ancient Japan), ed. Kishi Toshio. Tokyo: Chūōkōronsha.

Wada Sotsu. 1980. Fukuzoku to girei (Subjugation and rituals). In *Majinai to matsuri* (Magic and festivals), ed. Itō Mikiharu. Tokyo: Gakuseisha.

Wagatsuma, Hiroshi. 1982. Problems of Cultural Identity in Modern Japan. In *Ethnic Identity,* ed. G. De Vos and L. R. Ross. Chicago: University of Chicago Press.

Wakabayashi, Bob. 1986. *Anti-foreignism and Western Learning in Early-Modern Japan.* Cambridge, Mass.: Harvard University Press.

Waley, Arthur. n.d. *The Nō Plays of Japan.* New York: Grove Press.

Warner, Langdon. 1952. *The Enduring Art of Japan.* New York: Grove Press.

Watson, Graham. 1991. Rewriting Culture. In *Recapturing Anthropology: Working in the Present,* ed. Richard Fox. Santa Fe: School of American Research Press.

Watson, James L. 1985. Standardizing the Gods: The Promotion of T'ien Hou ("Empress of Heaven") along the South China Coast, 960–1960. In *Popular Culture in Late Imperial China,* ed. D. Johnson, A. Nathan, and E. Rawski. Berkeley: University of California Press.

Watsuji, Tetsurō. 1961. *Climate and Culture.* Trans. G. Bownas. Tokyo: Hokuseidō.

Weber, Max. 1964 [1922]. *The Sociology of Religion.* Boston: Beacon Press.

Weller, Robert P. 1994. *Resistance, Chaos and Control in China: Taiping Rebels, Taiwanese Ghosts and Tiananmen.* Seattle: University of Washington Press.

Wheatley, Paul, and Thomas See. 1978. *From Court to Capital.* Chicago: University of Chicago Press.

White, Hayden. 1973. *Metahistory: The Historical Imagination in Nineteenth-Century Europe.* Baltimore: Johns Hopkins University Press.

Willis, Paul. 1977. *Learning to Labour.* Westmead, U.K.: Saxon House.

Wolf, Eric. 1990. Facing Power: Old Insights, New Questions. *American Anthropologist* 93 : 14–19.

Woodard, William P. 1972. *The Allied Occupation of Japan, 1945–1952, and Japanese Religions.* Leiden: E. J. Brill.

Wright, David. 1992. Ceasar and Christ. Lecture in "World Civilizations," Department of Interdisciplinary Studies, University of California, Berkeley.

Wright, Patrick. 1985. *On Living in an Old Country.* London: Verso.

Yamaguchi Masao. 1975. Ko-fudoki ni okeru bunka to shizen (Brief description of culture versus nature in ancient topography). In *Bunka to ryogi-sei* (Culture and ambiguity), ed. Yamaguchi Masao. Tokyo: Iwanami Shoten.

———. 1977. Kingship, Theatricality and Marginal reality in Japan. In *Text and Context*, ed. R. K. Jain. Philadelphia: Institute for the Study of Human Issues.

———. 1987. Dual Structure of Emperorship. In *An Anthropological Profile of Japan*, ed. M. Yamaguchi and N. Nagashima. *Supplement of Current Anthropology* 28 (4): 7–18.

Yamaori Tetsuo. 1980. *Nihon shūkyō bunka no kōzō to sōkei* (The structure and basic model of Japanese religious culture). Tokyo: Tokyo Daigaku Shuppankai.

Yanagawa, Keiichi. 1988. The Sensation of *Matsuri*. In *Matsuri: Festival and Rite in Japanese Life*. Tokyo: Kokugakuin University.

Yanagita Kunio. 1946. *Nihon no matsuri* (Japan's festivals). Tokyo: Kobundō.

Yoon, Hong-key. 1983. Geomantic Relationship between Culture and Nature in Korea. *Asian Folklore and Social Life Monographs*, vol. 88, ed. Lou Tsu-K'uang. Taipei: Orient Cultural Service.

Yoshida, Teigo. 1981. The Stranger as God: The Place of the Outsider in Japanese Folk Religion. *Ethnology* 20 (2): 87–99.

———. 1984. Spirit Possession and Village Conflict. In *Conflict in Japan*, ed. Ellis S. Krauss et al. Honolulu: University of Hawai'i Press.

Yoshinari Isamu, ed. 1989. *Kojiki, Nihon shoki sōran* (A complete bibliography of the *Kojiki* and the *Nihon shoki*). Bessatsu rekishi dokuhon, jiten shiriizu, vol. 2. Tokyo.

Yoshino, Kosaku. 1992. *Cultural Nationalism in Contemporary Japan*. London: Routledge.

Yusa, Michiko. 1994. Women in Shinto: Images Remembered. In *Women and Religion*, ed. Arvind Sharma. Albany: SUNY Press.

Zuesse, Evan. 1979. *Ritual Cosmos*. Athens: Ohio University Press.

INDEX

ABOUT THE AUTHOR

John K. Nelson received his Ph.D. in cultural anthropology from the University of California, Berkeley. He is an assistant professor in the Department of Asian Studies at the University of Texas, Austin. The author of *A Year in the Life of a Shinto Shrine* (1996) and numerous articles, he has also produced two documentary films on the role of ritual, politics, and contemporary Shinto within Japanese society and culture.